Spain and its Literature
Essays in Memory of E. Allison Peers

Hispanic Studies TRAC
(Textual Research and Criticism)

Textual Research and Criticism (TRAC) publishes Spanish, Portuguese and Latin-American texts of literary, linguistic or historical interest not otherwise available in modern editions. The texts are accompanied by a substantial introductory monograph and full apparatus of critical footnotes. The series also publishes literary and critical studies. TRAC is firmly aimed at a scholarly readership.

Scholars are invited to apply to the Editors for further information and to submit a brief summary of their projected book. Contributions, which should not exceed 400 pages of typescript, will be assessed by eminent Hispanists in the appropriate areas.

Hispanic Studies TRAC
(Textual Research and Criticism)

Spain and its Literature
Essays in Memory of E. Allison Peers

edited, with an Introduction, by
Ann L. Mackenzie

LIVERPOOL UNIVERSITY PRESS
MODERN HUMANITIES RESEARCH ASSOCIATION

First published 1997 by
Liverpool University Press, PO Box 147, Liverpool, L69 3BX
Modern Humanities Research Association, London

British Library Cataloguing-in-Publication Data
A British Library CIP Record is available

ISBN Cased 085323-488-4
Paper 085323-660-7

The Editor records her profound indebtedness to the Modern Humanities Research Association, London, for a generous subvention which has made possible the publication of *Spain and its Literature: Essays in Memory of E. Allison Peers.*

Printed and bound in the European Community
by Antony Rowe, Chippenham, Wiltshire.

Edgar Allison Peers 1891-1952
Gilmour Professor of Spanish 1922-1952
University of Liverpool

CONTENTS

Introduction
ANN L. MACKENZIE 1

E. Allison Peers: A Centenary Reappraisal
GEOFFREY RIBBANS 19

E. Allison Peers: A Selective Bibliography
H. B. HALL† 35

Part I
From the Middle Ages to the Siglo de Oro

The Medieval Castilian Translation of Vegetius, *Epitoma de rei militaris*: An Introduction
P. E. RUSSELL 49

Two Letters of Devotional Advice to Nuns in the *Cancionero de Egerton* (Dutton LB3)
DOROTHY S. SEVERIN 65

Honey without God: Francisco de Osuna's Higher Memory
JOHN N. JONES 77

Judaeo-Islamic Traditions in Fray Luis de León: Wisdom, Unity and Light
AUDREY LUMSDEN-KOUVEL 89

The Mystical 'Dark Night' of San Juan de la Cruz as Interpreted in Poetic Summary
I. L. McCLELLAND 103

Further *Studies of the Spanish Mystics*: Allison Peers on Miguel de Molinos' *Spiritual Guide*
ANN L. MACKENZIE 109

Cervantes, Cardenio and Theobald
KENNETH MUIR† 141

Conceits and Connections: Three Golden-Age Sonnets at Work
IAN MACPHERSON 151

Part II
From the Dawn of Romanticism to the Twentieth Century

Sánchez's *Colección* and Percy's *Reliques*: The Editing of Medieval Poetry in the Dawn of Romanticism
ALAN DEYERMOND 171
Juan Antonio Pellicer and the Eighteenth-century Recovery of Early Spanish Literature
IAN MICHAEL 211
Luis Gutiérrez, Novelist and Impostor
MARTIN MURPHY 235
Rivas and Tragedy: The Cases of *El Duque de Aquitania* and *Malek-Adhel*
DONALD L. SHAW 253
More on *El moro expósito*
MARGARET A. REES 269
'The Bleeding Nun' and 'Our Lady of Paris'
J. E. VAREY 283
Bécquer, autor de *Doña Manuela*
JOAN ESTRUCH TOBELLA 303
'Hoy es siempre todavía': la plasticidad del ayer en los poemas de Antonio Machado
LUIS CAPARRÓS ESPERANTE 317
Alvaro Cunqueiro, Britain and Ireland
COLIN SMITH† 347
G/Z — A Missing Link in the Dis-affiliation of a Post-Romantic Expatriate in Revolt?
PATRICIA McDERMOTT... 361

Tabula in Memoriam 375

Introduction

> 'Not for a long time — perhaps not within memory — has Hispanism known as tragic a year as that now closing'. British Hispanism, never; for before these words, with which the last number of the *Bulletin* opened, had appeared in print the hand that wrote them too was still. With the death of Edgar Allison Peers on 21 December 1952 a record of a third of a century of brilliant and sustained devotion to the cause of Hispanic studies has closed, and with it a chapter in the history of these studies in Great Britain.

The 'Memorial Number' of the *Bulletin of Hispanic Studies* (XXX [1953], No. 117), dedicated to its illustrious founder-editor, began with these words, 'In Memoriam', written by William C. Atkinson, University of Glasgow. Forty years later, following upon the hundredth anniversary of Peers' birth, and the seventieth anniversary of the *Bulletin*, it seemed appropriate to celebrate again the influential career of this pioneering Hispanist, and to reassess his achievements as scholar, university teacher and educationist, through a series of special events and publications. Naturally, the University of Liverpool, where for thirty-two years, from 1920 until his death, Peers had pursued indefatigably his academic career, has been the source and centre of nearly all these activities in celebration. In 1991 the University approved funding to support the editing and publication of Peers' memoirs. Recently issued, after five years of research and preparation, as the first volume in the series **E. Allison Peers Publications**, *Redbrick University Revisited. The Autobiography of 'Bruce Truscot'*[1] not only sheds light on Peers' career as a Hispanist, but also on the opinions expressed in the books which in the 1940s he wrote pseudonymously about *Redbrick University*. These memoirs,

---

1 Edited, with introduction, commentary and notes, by Ann L. Mackenzie and Adrian R. Allan (Liverpool: Liverpool U. P., 1996), 520 pp.

contribute importantly to our knowledge of the early history of the 'Redbrick' University of Liverpool, but also are records with a broader significance — documenting the shifts in attitudes and conditions which influenced British universities during their critical period of development between the two world wars. In 1994 the editors of the Memoirs, Ann L. Mackenzie and Adrian R. Allan, together with Janice Carpenter, the Curator of the University's Art Collections, mounted at the University of Liverpool **Redbrick Revisited: The University of Liverpool 1920-1952** — to commemorate 'the career of E. Allison Peers, as "Bruce Truscot", author of *Redbrick University*'.[2] To coincide with this Exhibition, Geoffrey Ribbans, Brown University, Providence, one of Peers' successors as Gilmour Professor of Spanish and previous Editor of the *Bulletin of Hispanic Studies* (1963-1978), was invited to give the Fifth E. Allison Peers Lecture — which, appropriately, he did (10 June 1994) in the 'Redbrick' Victoria Building of the University of Liverpool. Professor Ribbans had already published in Spain (in *Serra d'Or*, September 1991), an article reflecting upon 'El centenari d'Edgar Allison Peers (1891-1952)', in which, especially in a section entitled 'Catalunya i la universitat', he observed Peers' noteworthy concern for Catalonia, and his contributions to informed understanding of its language, culture and history:

> Cal destacar especialment *Catalonia Infelix* (1937), perquè aquest llibre, juntament amb els estudis ja esmentats, indica ben clarament la veritable predilecció que sentia envers Catalunya i la llengua i la cultura catalanes, que va molt més enllà de l'ample concepte que abrigava de l'hispanisme.

He enlarged and developed his ideas and in particular his opinions of 'el llegat d'Allison Peers'[3] to produce the text of his lecture given at Liverpool — 'E. Allison Peers: A Centenary Reappraisal' — which, with a few revisions, is published in this Homage-Volume. In 1994 too there appeared a specially extended Monographic Number of the *Bulletin of Hispanic Studies* dedicated to Allison Peers. Funded by the Fundação

---

2 Brochure, so entitled, compiled by Adrian Allan and Ann L. Mackenzie (Liverpool: Univ. of Liverpool, 1994), 32 pp.

3 For this article see *Serra d'Or*, núm. 381 (setembre 1991), 25-26.

Gulbenkian, this Number, exclusively concerned with *Portugal: Its Culture, Influence and Civilization*, was produced to acknowledge gratefully Peers' commitment of personal energy and professional abilities throughout his career 'to expand the teaching of Portuguese in British institutions and to advance the study of Portugal and of its "Seaborne Empire" '.[4] Then in 1996, with subventions from the University of Glasgow and the Cañada Blanch Foundation, Paul Preston and Ann L. Mackenzie edited and produced a book of essays commemorating and assessing, sixty years on, *The Republic Besieged: Civil War in Spain 1936-1939*. The book was published 'In Memory of E. Allison Peers' in recognition of his contributions, through a series of influential histories, to the documentation of 'The Spanish Tragedy'. These histories established Peers in the late 1930s and early 1940s as the most trusted commentator on the Spanish Civil War — as,

> on this so controversial topic, the one dispassionate, reliable guide and mentor of the English-speaking world amidst a welter of confusing emotionalisms.[5]

Even nowadays, between fifty and sixty years after they were written, *The Spanish Tragedy 1930-1936* (1936), *The Spanish Dilemma* (1940), *Spain in Eclipse* (1943), revealing an extraordinary knowledge of contemporary Spain, represent some of the most enduring results of Peers' researches.[6]

The present volume is published in recognition of the major contribution which Peers made — through numerous books and articles — to the study and comprehension of literature in Spain. Of the twenty-one articles which make up this Homage-Volume, several are written by scholars who had been Peers' pupils or colleagues at the University of Liverpool: Ivy McClelland, Audrey Lumsden-Kouvel, Kenneth Muir, and the

4 See *Portugal: Its Culture, Influence and Civilization*, edited, with an Introduction, by Ann L. Mackenzie, *BHS*, LXXI, No. 1 (Liverpool: Liverpool U. P., 1994), 167 pp., at pp. 4-6.

5 See William C. Atkinson, 'In Memoriam', *Memorial Number, BHS*, XXX (1953), No. 117, 1-5, at p. 4.

6 See also *The Republic Besieged: Civil War in Spain 1936-1939*, ed. Paul Preston and Ann L. Mackenzie (Edinburgh: Edinburgh U. P., 1996), i-iv.

late Harold Hall who was to be one of Peers' successors, both in the Gilmour Chair and as the editor of the *Bulletin of Hispanic Studies*. A majority of the contributors are, in fact, members, past or present, of the Editorial Team or Editorial Board of the journal that Peers had founded and which, as Geoffrey Ribbans has observed, was 'perhaps his most lasting' achievement[7] — Alan Deyermond, Ann L. Mackenzie, Ian Macpherson, Patricia McDermott, Ian Michael, Geoffrey Ribbans, P. E. Russell, Dorothy S. Severin, Donald L. Shaw, Colin Smith, J. E. Varey ... Other contributors, from Britain, Spain and the United States, are specialists in Spanish subjects of research in which Peers is acknowledged to have been a pioneer and master: Margaret A. Rees, Joan Estruch Tobella, John N. Jones, Luis Caparrós Esperante and Martin Murphy. Essays from these twenty-one contributors could not possibly signify or represent all Peers' literary interests in Spain — the breadth and variety of which are clearly revealed in Harold Hall's 'Selective Bibliography' of Peers' publications, here reproduced. But several articles bring to mind his comparative studies of the literatures of France and England with those of Spain. And his ground-breaking cultivation, awe-inspiring in its extensive thoroughness, of two major fields of scholarship is remembered, developed or discussed, in a group of articles on the Spanish mystics and through a still larger collection of essays dealing with the origins, reality or aftermath of the Romantic Movement in Spain.

In **Part I** of ***Spain and its Literature***, leading the contributions **From the Middle Ages to the Siglo de Oro**, Peter Russell discusses 'The Medieval Castilian Translation of Vegetius, *Epitoma de rei militaris*', which to date has received comparatively little attention from scholars. The *Epitoma* was, 'in Latin and in translation, from the ninth century onwards, one of the most read and probably most influential of the Classical texts known of the Middle Ages' (51), and Russell produces evidence in plenty to convince us that it was as much

---

7 See Geoffrey W. Ribbans, 'Reality Plain or Fancy? Some Reflections on Galdós' Concept of Realism', *E. Allison Peers Lectures 1* (Liverpool: Liverpool U. P., 1986), 22 pp.; 'Preamble', 1-4, at p. 2.

read in the Peninsula as elsewhere. And military men were not the only students of the work, which provided writers of sermons and collectors of *sententiae* throughout Europe with a rich mine of *exempla* and aphorisms. Russell also identifies and discusses some of the problems encountered by medieval translators: difficulties created by the down-to-earth Latin of the original text, that was moreover rich in military terms of which many had no vernacular equivalents. There were, too, 'some problems about making Vegetius' account of Roman armies fit the facts, particularly the social facts, of medieval life' (53). Russell has also much of value to say about Fray Alonso de San Cristóbal, the translator, on the date of composition, and about the *glosas* which are a unique feature of this Castilian version. These glosses include, besides straightforward commentaries on the text, seven *glosas espirituales*, but Russell warns against interpreting Fray Alonso's translation as an *a lo divino* work — which is 'to miss the real purpose of the translation and the reason for its popularity' (60).

In contrast, the texts which concern Dorothy Severin are unquestionably written for religious purposes. These are 'Two Letters of Devotional Advice to Nuns in the *Cancionero de Egerton*'. Giving a foretaste of her forthcoming edition of this Songbook (Dutton LB3), Severin edits the letters, with original orthography, besides commenting concisely on their possible authors and recipients, their possible sources, and their 'semi-mystical' inclinations.

From these possibly 'semi-mystical' texts, and out of the Middle Ages, we move forward into the Golden Age and discussion of several essentially mystical works and authors — in four articles dealing with a major field of Peers' researches. Robert Sencourt commented in 1953:

> There have been other professors of Spanish as learned and more exact. None, however, can compare with him [Peers] ... for deepening and widening the knowledge of the two towering Carmelite mystics who are as much part of the literary history of Spain as they are sovereign over the realm of mystical theology.

And, as Sencourt was equally aware, Peers had not restricted his *Studies of the Spanish Mystics* to Santa Teresa de Jesús and San Juan de la Cruz: 'he had turned his gaze to the wide range of Spanish mystics, and among the lesser names he related one to another as no Spaniard had ever done'.[8] Appropriately, therefore, the articles here published concern different names and differing stages in the Golden-Age development of Spanish mysticism. In 'Honey without God: Francisco de Osuna's Higher Memory', John N. Jones continues and deepens the investigations of Peers into the works of 'the grandfather of Spanish Christian mysticism' (77). Osuna, a significant author, too little studied even now, exercised a profoundly formative influence on both Santa Teresa and San Juan de la Cruz. Interested in Peers' sensitive perception that Osuna is not a Quietist, Jones nevertheless disagrees with Peers, and with the majority of other critics, through believing that Recollection (*recogimiento*), of which Quiet is a part, is not for Osuna the highest state or stage of the mystical experience. Through an analysis of Osuna's *Tercer Abecedario Espiritual* Jones, demonstrating that his opinion is more firmly grounded than previously held views, establishes that Osuna posits a state beyond Quiet, that 'harmonizes the mind's relation to God with its relation to the world' (79): person, God and world are essentially connected, and the task of the contemplative is to perceive the connections. Thus, concludes Jones, 'the mysticism of, say, Santa Teresa de Ávila, whose God dwells among the pots and pans, is not a corrective to any Quietism on Osuna's part, but heir to a tradition Osuna synthesizes, enriches and helps convey' (88). 'Judaeo-Islamic Traditions in Fray Luis de León', as perceived especially in *De los nombres de Cristo*, preoccupy Audrey Lumsden-Kouvel. Thus she discusses his concepts, or themes, of wisdom, unity and light, taking account of the metaphysical framework of which they form part, and considers, as specific channels of Judaeo-Islamic influence upon his work, the *Fons vitae* of Solomon Ibn Gabirol and the *Dialoghi d'amore* of Leone Ebreo. Her article, closely argued and provocative of further thought and research on this topic, indicates that Luis de León owes much to 'a Judaeo-Arabic tradition transmitted through the *Fons vitae* and the *Dialoghi d'amore*, a tradition none the less powerful for being

---

8 Both quotations from Robert Sencourt are taken from his obituary 'Edgar Allison Peers: A Tribute', *The Tablet*, 10 January 1953.

unconfessed and perhaps unconsciously operative on his thought' (101). Ivy McClelland, moving with critical sureness of tread, illuminates 'The Mystical "Dark Night" of San Juan de la Cruz as Interpreted in Poetic Summary'. Analysing the poem's deliberately restrained intensity, and how it expresses 'the Mystical need to accommodate what is indescribable to what is humanly understandable' (106), she concludes that San Juan's artistic genius in 'Noche oscura' 'is most notably revealed in his ability to project an overall impression of Mystical atmosphere' (108). Commenting on Allison Peers' 'Further *Studies of the Spanish Mystics*', Ann L. Mackenzie introduces, edits and annotates his unfinished and hitherto unpublished essay on 'Miguel de Molinos' *Spiritual Guide*' — to which she adds, in conclusion, a catalogue of Peers' papers on the mystics, housed in the Sydney Jones Library, Liverpool University. Regrettably, Peers did not live to accomplish a fourth book of *Studies of the Spanish Mystics*, of which his observations on the *Guía espiritual* (1675) and the Quietist character of Molinos' mysticism should have formed part.

Despite Peers' predominant interests in the works of the mystics, he by no means neglected to study other more secular writers and manifestations of literature in the Golden Age of Spain — Lope de Vega, lyric poetry, Cervantes and the novel. Late articles, on Cervantes in England (1947, 1950), confirm also Peers' enduring concerns with English literature.[9] In fact, as Kenneth Muir reminds us, 'Allison Peers first made his name as an English scholar' (141). So in contributing an article on 'Cervantes, Cardenio and Theobald', Muir chooses a topic that is doubly appropriate. Muir discusses a play (performed 1612-13) in which Shakespeare is known to have collaborated with Fletcher and which is based on the story of Cardenio from *Don Quijote*, Part I. The original play is no longer extant, but Theobald's play, *Double Falshood*, is — or so its author claimed — an adaptation made from a manuscript of the original work. Observing that 'Fletcher certainly and Shakespeare probably could read Spanish' (143-44), Muir explains the attractions for both dramatists of the theme of forgiveness in the Cardenio

9 See, for example, 'Cervantes en Inglaterra', *Homenaje a Cervantes*, ed. Francisco Sánchez Castañer (Valencia: Mediterráneo, 1950), 410-27.

story, and comments also perceptively on the problems which dramatization of this 'deliberately confused narrative' (146) posed. Muir surmises, tentatively but persuasively, that Theobald's alterations to the now lost original drama, were 'mostly disastrous. Shakespeare's scenes were vandalized ...; but those of Fletcher, with whose style he was more sympathetic, were left relatively undamaged' (150). There follows, to complete the contributions dealing with the Siglo de Oro, an essay by Ian Macpherson which discusses 'Conceits and Connections: Three Golden-Age Sonnets at Work'. The three sonnets are Góngora's 'La dulce boca que a gustar convida', Quevedo's 'En crespa tempestad del oro undoso', and Sor Juana's 'Verde embeleso de la vida humana'. Macpherson is concerned 'with the way in which the linguistic, rhetorical and structural devices employed by these three very different poets operate in relation to each other, and with how they underpin and enhance the message of the poems in which they figure' (152-53). Macpherson's analysis of the 'underlying connections' which establish the structure of these sonnets, and of 'the tight-knit causal relationships between their imagery and range of illustration' deepens significantly our perception of 'their coherence, symmetry and structural perfection' (167).

The *Memorial Number* of the *Bulletin of Hispanic Studies* dedicated to Allison Peers in 1953 was, as William C. Atkinson commented in its opening article, 'for a variety of reasons — the pressure of life on the living, a wave of indisposition on both sides of the Atlantic — ... less fully representative than had been hoped'. Atkinson conceded that readers would

> miss in particular an appraisal of the historian of Spanish romanticism, in whose *magnum opus* is to be seen the culmination of twenty years of spadework that included the writing of four books and some forty articles as a preliminary clearing of the ground, while its footnotes bear witness to a whole school of graduate research in this field inspired by the author's example.[10]

Readers of this Homage-Volume, in contrast, will discover, occupying its entire Second Part, a full collection of articles

10 See Atkinson, 'In Memoriam', *Memorial Number*, *BHS*, 4.

relevant, in their different aspects, to the eighteenth-century beginnings, the nineteenth-century development or the twentieth-century aftermath of the Romantic Movement in Spain. Most of these articles, leading **From the Dawn of Romanticism to the Twentieth Century** — several of which refer to Peers' pioneering researches and influential opinions, whether in agreement or in disagreement — serve to demonstrate, more than fifty years later, the accuracy of a prediction made by Nicholson B. Adams in 1941, in a review of Peers' two-volume *History* of this subject: 'All future studies of any aspect of Spanish Romanticism will inevitably take Mr Peers' work as a point of departure'.[11]

The articles contributed by Alan Deyermond and Ian Michael without doubt would have been of particular interest and special value to Allison Peers, given his interpretation of Spanish Romanticism as 'Revival' and 'Revolt', and the thorough studies he conducted into 'the roots of Spanish romanticism in Spain's literature of the Middle Ages and Golden Age and the growing protests in the eighteenth century, in theory and in practice, against neo-classic restraints'.[12] In a substantial and penetrating study, Deyermond compares, contrasts and discusses 'Sánchez's *Colección* and Percy's *Reliques*: The Editing of Medieval Poetry in the Dawn of Romanticism'. Separating both men from the Enlightenment scholars of the previous generation, and making them forerunners in the coming of Romanticism, is the concern which they share 'for medieval poetry as poetry, not merely as historical evidence' (207). Reception of the *Reliques* and Sánchez's *Colección* was remarkably different. Percy's *Reliques* was an 'instant and resounding success', and had an influence, direct and indirect, that was at least as great on European Romantic literature as it was in England. In contrast, Sánchez's *Colección* initially aroused an interest so small that publication 'petered out' (190). Yet it was Sánchez who was the true innovator as an editor of medieval texts, not simply in Spain but in Europe as a whole. And whereas Percy's influence

---

11 See his review of E. Allison Peers, *A History of the Romantic Movement in Spain*, *HR*, IX (1941), 500-07, at p. 500.

12 *Ibid.*, 501.

was to wane before growing scholarly doubts about the *Reliques*, Sánchez's work, which was not finally superseded until nearly two centuries after the first volume of the *Colección* appeared, gained 'the respect of succeeding generations of scholars' (190). Deyermond observes only two or three significant features of Sánchez's work 'that set him apart from the best scholarship of our own day ... One is the suppression of some passages of the *Libro de Buen Amor* on moral grounds'. Another is 'the low frequency of explanatory and critical notes'. In other respects 'he is a modern scholar, trying to do, with limited resources, what the best scholars try to do today' (206). Investigating a related field, Ian Michael records, with supporting documentation not previously published in its original form, the noteworthy activities of librarians attached to the Royal Public Library (later, the Biblioteca Nacional) in Madrid during the second half of the eighteenth century. They were responsible for the rediscovery of manuscripts of Spanish literature written before the fifteenth century, and for 'a revival of scholarship and learning which led to numerous important publications' (211). Michael considers especially the work of 'Juan Antonio Pellicer and the Eighteenth-century Recovery of Early Spanish Literature'. Pellicer and his colleagues were determined to make available for public use, through published collections, 'all Spanish writings of previous ages' (213). Michael observes in these librarians 'a Romantic view *avant la lettre* of the "primitiveness" of medieval literature', combined, however, with a strongly nationalistic conviction that Spain's early literature was 'just as important as that of France, England or Germany, and it was their task to bring it to light' (214).

An early nineteenth-century novel in epistolary form occupies the critical attention of Martin Murphy, who also reconstructs the picaresque career of its author, 'Luis Gutiérrez, Novelist and Impostor'. Murphy has consulted sources in the Archivo Histórico Nacional in Madrid and the Archivo Municipal, Seville, as also documents in the Foreign Office, in the Canning Archives and belonging to the Hispanic Society of America. His investigations confirm that the greatest work of fiction by this author of *Cornelia Bororquia*, and former Trinitarian friar, was 'the one he played out in real life in

London, Lisbon and Seville' (251), where he was executed in 1809 as a French spy. The work of 'a gifted writer in whom idealism coexisted with disingenuousness' (239), *Cornelia Bororquia* is, in Murphy's informed opinion, a '*roman à thèse* of the Enlightenment, intended to illustrate the evils of religious intolerance and drawing its inspiration from Rousseau and Samuel Richardson' (237). Frequently reissued, the novel circulated in differently adapted, expanded and popularized forms. A work notably influenced by Gutiérrez is *Vargas*, Blanco White's anonymously published novel. Murphy suggests that Blanco could have known *Cornelia Bororquia* in its original form, as well as through the expanded adaptation by Diego Correa, *La Judit Española*, conceding, nevertheless, that Blanco 'is more akin to Correa than to Gutiérrez in the violence of his tone and language' (244).

In two articles which follow Donald Shaw and Margaret A. Rees are each in turn differently concerned with the same writer of the Romantic age — the favourite subject of two major books by Allison Peers: *Rivas and Romanticism in Spain* and *Ángel de Saavedra, Duque de Rivas. A Critical Study.*[13] Shaw continues investigations, undertaken in other important essays, into Rivas' evolution as a dramatist and 'Rivas and Tragedy', considering especially, in this essay, 'The Cases of *El Duque de Aquitania* and *Malek-Adhel*'. Shaw finds the principal reason why *Malek-Adhel* is a much better play than *El Duque de Aquitania* through a profoundly reasoned analysis and comparison of both dramas as tragedies. In *El Duque de Aquitania*, which, Shaw believes, is 'not a tragedy at all' (255), Rivas reverts to the idea he had begun to reject in *Aliatar* of 'an ultimately harmonious Providential universe', 'of a fatherly world according to design, attempting, without success, to contradict *Aliatar* and to halt the process of insight which was leading him towards *Don Álvaro*' (258). In contrast to *El Duque de Aquitania*, and all Rivas' earlier plays, *Malek-Adhel* 'for the first time contains a really tragic conflict and generates a sense of genuine pathos' (258-59); 'for the first time in his theatre we find in *Malek-Adhel* a clash of equally justified forces

---

13 Both were published in 1923. See below, Hall, 'E. Allison Peers: A Selective Bibilography', 35-45.

accompanied by prominent elements of tragic irony. Rivas had at last set his foot on the path that would lead to *Don Álvaro*' (267). Agreeing with Peers that Rivas failed to become leader of the Spanish Romantics because he 'alternated reactionary works so exasperatingly with progressive [ones]' (259), Shaw, nevertheless, concludes that '*El Duque de Aquitania* and *Malek Adhel* illustrate in the work of the same author the polarization of outlook which was to characterize the Spanish Romantic movement as a whole. Rivas' ambivalence is more visible than that of some of his more progressive minded contemporaries' (267). Margaret A. Rees engages in a profound analysis of a different kind of work by Rivas, adding to previous studies and critically opposed opinions 'More on *El moro expósito*'. Much more, indeed, is offered, and much that is new, on imagery, descriptions, characters, supernatural elements, themes and motifs. As regards haunted atmosphere and 'blood-quaffing ghosts', Rees finds in *El moro* 'the same world of supernatural terror as Lewis' *The Monk* (1796) ... Rivas is superb in his ability to create spine-chilling atmospheres' (279). On the more human plane, Rees discovers in the 'expósito' a 'blood brother of Hernani as well as of Don Álvaro. Perhaps at roughly the same time that Hugo was creating his mysterious outlaw to champion the French Romantic theatre, Rivas in Malta was conjuring up the image of his own hero' (279). Equally interesting is Rees' opinion that, as far as descriptive themes and techniques are concerned, 'in 1829 Rivas in *El moro* and Hugo in *Les Orientales* were writing in parallel rather than as master and disciple' (278). Rees observes many Romantic traits present from the opening of *El moro*, among which are the three main characteristics of Romanticism identified by Donald Shaw: 'a negative view of life, love as the only real existential prop, and regular reference to adverse fate'. In particular, the idea of fate 'forms the very spine of this work from start to finish' (282). Rees' article reveals that 'despite *El moro*'s long gestation and its exposure to the French literary world in the later stages, it is a unified whole', and, despite the superficiality of the character-portrayal, and some other arguable shortcomings, it is 'the eminently readable work of a master story-teller' (282).

Another contributor who shares with Allison Peers interests in French Romanticism generally,[14] and in Hugo particularly, is John Varey. In ' "The Bleeding Nun" and "Our Lady of Paris" ', Varey discusses the probable influence on a key episode of Hugo's *Notre-Dame de Paris* of *La Nonne sanglante*. This dramatic vignette was regularly part of the repertoire in performances of the phantasmagoria put on by Robertson (who had perfected the phantasmagoria by developing the 'magic lantern') and his imitators, through many countries in Europe from the end of the eighteenth century through to the 1830s. One of these countries was Spain, and it is even possible that, as a child, Hugo had seen the phantasmagoria, including 'The Bleeding Nun' episode, performed in Madrid while he was there, with his family, in 1811-12. Varey believes — and through the force of both argument and evidence persuades us to share his opinion — that the famous episode in *Notre-Dame de Paris* in which Esmeralda appears ghost-like before the priest, 'growing larger than life as she advances in the moonlight, is a reflection of the scene of *La Nonne sanglante* adapted to Hugo's purpose' (301). Varey accepts that a source of both the episode and the scene is to be found in Lewis' *The Monk*, but does not believe that Hugo and Robertson are separately interpreting that common source. Several elements of Hugo's description recall *La Nonne sanglante* as phantasmagorically depicted by Robertson: the tolling of the bell, the extinction of the lamp, the unnatural moonlight ... Hugo, 'as he penned the description of the appearance of Esmeralda before the priest, viewed the original bleeding nun through the lens of Robertson's theatrical recreation' (294). Varey concludes, convincingly, that 'Robertson's performances are an indication of the importance of popular entertainment as a link between the neo-Gothic and the Romantic, and in Spain the phantasmagoria, certainly from 1806 ..., introduced Spanish audiences to themes and motifs which were to become typical of Romantic writers writing some three decades later' (301).

To complete this Homage-Volume, the articles which follow, dealing with post-Romantic and modern works and authors,

---

14 See especially, M. B. Finch and E. Allison Peers, *The Origins of French Romanticism* (London: Constable, 1920).

carry us on through the later nineteenth century and up to the Present Time. Joan Estruch Tobella discusses 'Bécquer, autor de *Doña Manuela*', a politico-satirical newspaper directed against the 'Unión Liberal', the only number of which appeared in Madrid in September 1865. Conducting an 'análisis intrínseco', Estruch collects sufficient evidence, despite the poet's own denials, to attribute to Bécquer at least authorship of the 'Editorial' of *Doña Manuela* and probably also editorial responsibility for the entire publication. The newspaper, especially its editorial — 'una pieza magistral de la sátira política' which is here reproduced and annotated — reveals much of artistic, personal and biographical importance about the poet: 'primero, que Bécquer participó activamente en la agitada vida política de su tiempo y que, por tanto, es ilusoria su tradicional imagen de poeta angelical, alejado de la prosaica realidad social; segundo, que Bécquer, hasta cuando escribía libelos políticos, era un gran escritor, puesto que seguía utilizando su personal estilo, el mismo que hallamos en lo mejor de su obra' (315). Luis Caparrós Esperante discusses ' "Hoy es siempre todavía": la plasticidad del ayer en los poemas de Antonio Machado'. The subject of Peers' Taylorian Lecture, delivered in 1939, Antonio Machado had been, as Peers reveals in his correspondence with Manuel Machado, 'predilecto poeta mío desde el día en que hace treinta años leí por primera vez unas "Soledades" suyas'.[15] Caparrós treats an often previously considered theme, yet succeeds admirably in exploring the significances of Machado's poetry as 'palabra esencial en el tiempo'. Caparrós' principal objective 'es hacer evidentes algunos procedimientos de simbolización con un claro valor constructivo, esto es, algunos recursos literarios que le sirven a Antonio Machado para construir poemas ... más que sobre el tiempo, poemas saturados de temporalidad' (317). Perceiving poetry as 'la única vía para salvar lo esencial del pasado, para vencer los rígidos condicionantes de la existencia, que es tiempo en orden inflexible, sucesión inalterable, flecha lanzada al futuro' (318), Caparrós demonstrates 'la coherencia, casi diría,

15 Letter to Manuel Machado, dated 11 June 1939, the text of which is reproduced in Pablo González Alonso, *Cartas a los Machado* (Sevilla: Diputación Provincial de Sevilla, 1981), 157-58.

el sistema — recurrente, organizado, previsible — con que Antonio Machado temporaliza sus poemas', and he demonstrates this 'en su desarrollo lógico ... desde el último al primer libro' of Machado's poetry (318). In 'Alvaro Cunqueiro, Britain and Ireland' Colin Smith confirms that 'while Cunqueiro's sensibility was formed in the languages, people and landscapes of his native Galicia, his fund of information and of literary inspiration knew no frontiers' (347). Among the English and Anglo-Irish writers of special importance in Cunqueiro's formation was Edward John Plunkett, Lord Dunsany, whose early work, *A Dreamer's Tales* was read by Cunqueiro in Spanish translation, as *Cuentos de un soñador*. This was the book which Cunqueiro himself perceived as a key influence on his youthful imagination and interest in depicting worlds of fantasy: 'un libro decisivo en la dirección que tomaría mi obra literaria' (349). The other writer who had a decisive and permanent influence upon the Galician's imagination, thoroughly explored in this article, was Shakespeare. Smith, while acknowledging the numerous references to and evocations of Shakespearian characters and scenes in Cunqueiro's work, is particularly concerned with an altogether different category of artistic debt: Cunqueiro's 'radical rewriting', in 1958, of 'a universally known and canonical text' (355-56), to create his prose drama *O incerto señor Don Hamlet, príncipe de Dinamarca*. For Cunqueiro something in *Hamlet* was not quite right, and after lengthy meditation there came to him the 'revelación' which was to provide the essence of his *Don Hamlet*: the revelation that the usurper, not the dead king, was 'o verdadeiro pai de Hamlet'. As Smith comments, 'this entry of overtly Oedipal myth and psychology into the play transforms the basis of the Shakespearian original into something completely new' (357). Finally, Patricia McDermott proposes 'G/Z — A Missing Link in the Dis-affiliation of a Post-Romantic Expatriate in Revolt?'. In her view, and she argues convincingly, Goytisolo's *Reivindicación del conde don Julián* gave many of his fellow dissidents, enduring a spiritual internal exile through the last years of Franco's dictatorship, 'a fix on their own hallucinatory reality, a heightening of awareness from the expanded vision of the hallucination of external exile; just as Zorrilla's *Granada* was a shot in the arm for Catholic

Traditionalists in an age of revolution in Europe'. While appreciating that Peers could not have foreseen, in 1940, 'how far the spirit of Romantic Revolt would go in the "shock of the new" administered by *Reivindicación del conde don Julián*', McDermott reminds us that Peers had judged the failure of the Romantic movement in Spain to be 'of small importance by comparison with its success as a permeating influence' (372). In this his judgement has been proved correct. 'The spirit of Romanticism survived its out-dated rhetoric and continued to link the post-Modernist to a polemical literary past, in the process of textual (dis)affiliation in the brief but brilliant renaissance of prose fiction provoked by reaction to the continuing repression of Franco's Spain in the last decade of the dictatorship' (372).

In his 'Preamble' to the first E. Allison Peers Lecture delivered at the University of Liverpool in 1985, Geoffrey Ribbans summed up Peers' contribution to Hispanism and scholarship as follows:

> In the area of personal scholarship, Peers devoted himself to his research with an iron discipline and an unyielding timetable, setting out to produce at least a book a year over a period of nearly three decades. The volume and range of his studies are quite remarkable and ranged from the Catalan mystical philosopher Ramon Llull, through the Golden Age to contemporary Spain, with many pauses in between, and occasional excursions into Portugal and Latin America. Much of this was spade-work on almost virgin ground and it is difficult to appreciate today how much Peers did to create an awareness of Hispanic culture, as well as making important specific contributions to areas like Catalan literature, the sixteenth-century mystics and the Romantic writers. Much of this basic research, notably the data provided in his monumental *History of the Romantic Movement in Spain*, retains its scholarly and documentary value.[16]

The respect which scholars still have for Allison Peers is perceived not only in the references to his writings in the

16 See Ribbans, 'Reality Plain or Fancy? Some Reflections on Galdós' Concept of Realism', 2.

articles of this *Festschrift*, but in the numerous subscribers to the *Tabula in Memoriam*. That respect is not least evident in the fact that the Modern Humanities Research Association — an organization which Peers founded in 1918, and of which he was the first Secretary, and an early President[17] — has cooperated with Liverpool University Press in the publication of *Spain and its Literature: Essays in Memory of E. Allison Peers.*

17 My thanks are due to David A. Wells, Honorary Secretary, Modern Humanities Research Association, for making available photocopies of the minutes of the first meetings of the Association, in Peers' unmistakably tiny handwriting. Peers, President of the MHRA, 1931-32, delivered his Presidential Address on a characteristic subject: 'The Study of Spanish Romanticism' (published in *MHRA. Annual Bulletin of the Modern Humanities Research Association* [December 1932], No. 11, 1-16).

E. Allison Peers: A Centenary Reappraisal[1]

GEOFFREY RIBBANS

Brown University

I never knew Allison Peers personally. At the time of his death in December 1952, I was already in my first university post at Queen's University, Belfast, and I remember my Head of Department, Professor Ignacio González-Llubera, commenting on the news. Peers' name and reputation were of course highly familiar, if controversial, to any young Hispanist; the surprise, shared throughout the academic world, was to learn that he was the 'Bruce Truscot' who had written about 'Redbrick University' during and after the war, works which I and my contemporaries had read avidly before and during our university studies. When I myself arrived in Liverpool as Gilmour Professor in 1963, many traces of Peers' legacy remained, though perhaps not quite as many as might have been expected.

As a Hispanist Peers was one of what we may call the second phase of modern academic specialists in the subject. The members of the first group of university teachers — such worthy figures as Arteaga at Oxford and Penzol at Leeds — left little permanent impact. The scholars whose formation dates from before the First World War who are most remembered today were not closely associated with university teaching of the

1 I am very conscious of the tentative and personal nature of this reappraisal, lacking as it does access to all possible sources and a thorough research effort; I hope, however, that it will help focus on some of the issues of early British Hispanism and encourage further investigation.

subject: Sir Henry Thomas, keeper of printed books at the British Museum, was primarily a meticulous bibliographer, and Henry Chaytor, a clergyman and classicist who rose to the position of Master of St Catharine's College, Cambridge, was a specialist in Romance Languages who not infrequently made discriminating contributions to Hispanic subjects. The most important of the early specialists was James Fitzmaurice-Kelly. He was an independent scholar and Fellow of the British Academy, who for most of his life had no university affiliation, but who had published extensively, including a famous History of Spanish Literature, a landmark in its time, and widely used in Spain in its Spanish translation.

A significant change occurred as universities began at last to take modern languages seriously. The University of Liverpool, which had received its independent charter five years before, gave the lead by establishing (1908), thanks to an endowment by Captain George Gilmour, the first modern Chair of Spanish. After intense competition[2] Fitzmaurice-Kelly was appointed in 1909 at the age of fifty-one. In 1916 he transferred to the newly established Cervantes Chair of Spanish at King's College, London. He died in 1923; as Peers himself added rather pointedly, 'For thirteen years Fitzmaurice-Kelly was the only Professor of Spanish in the country'. Peers himself, of course, was the second. He had been serving as lecturer in charge of the department for two years, and, after much bitter dispute, he was appointed in 1922, at the age of thirty-one, to the Gilmour

2 Peers' own account may be somewhat prejudiced: 'there was no Spanish Chair in the country until Captain Gilmour endowed one at Liverpool in 1908, and even then the greatest difficulty was found in securing a holder with any pretensions to scholarship. ... There were dozens of candidates, nearly all of the wrong kind. ... In the end it was decided to invite James Fitzmaurice-Kelly, an independent scholar well known in several countries for his *Life of Cervantes* and his *History of Spanish Literature*, but without university training or academic experience' (*Spanish Now* [Liverpool: Institute of Hispanic Studies, 2nd ed., 1945], 83). Among the one hundred and sixty candidates were Fernando de Arteaga, Milton Buchanan, Camille Pitollet, Martin Hume and Tomás Navarro Tomás, all short-listed; Julio Cejador and Ramón Pérez de Ayala are also known to have shown interest (Liverpool University archives; courtesy of the archivist, Adrian Allan)

MINISTERIO DE INSTRUCCION PUBLICA
JUNTA PARA AMPLIACION DE ESTUDIOS

PENSIONES EN EL EXTRANJERO
PATRONATO DE ESTUDIANTES
CENTRO DE ESTUDIOS HISTORICOS
ESCUELA DE HISTORIA EN ROMA
INSTITUTO NACIONAL DE CIENCIAS
INVESTIGACIONES PALEONTOLOGICAS
INSTITUTO-ESCUELA DE 2a ENSEÑANZA
ENSEÑANZA DEL ESPAÑOL EN EL EXTRANJERO
RESIDENCIAS DE ESTUDIANTES

10 de Mayo de 1922

Mr. A. Bruce Boswell.

Muy señor mío :

Recibo su segunda carta del 6 del corriente, (habiéndose extraviado la primera), y me apresuro a contestarle acerca de la pregunta relativa al Sr. Peers, candidato a la cátedra de Español de la Faculty of Arts de la Universidad de Liverpool.

Conozco algunos de los trabajos publicados por el Sr. Peers, los cuales demuestran que el autor ha estudiado detalladamente el movimiento romántico en España. Las cuidadosas investigaciones del Sr. Peers en los periodos de esa época, no solo de Madrid sino hasta en los menos conocidos de provincias, sus estudios en las bibliotecas provinciales y particulares, sobre todo en Barcelona y Cádiz, han sido fructuosos, pues aclaran y rectifican muchos puntos hasta ahora confusos o inexactos de este periodo de la Literatura Española.

En el libro de Lecturas fonéticas, demuestra el Sr. Peers un conocimiento suficiente de la lengua española, proporcionando de este modo un instrumento útil para la enseñanza de este idioma, en un aspecto que carece casi por completo de bibliografía y de elementos utilizables. Me remito a la autorizada opinión del Sr. Navarro Tomás, expuesta en la REVISTA DE FILOLOGIA ESPAÑOLA, tomo VII, pag. 392, que elogia las buenas cualidades de las obras del Sr. Peers.

Me es muy grato manifestarle esto, y ofrecerme de usted atentamente

R Menéndez Pidal

'... a long letter from Menéndez Pidal, undoubtedly the greatest living Spanish scholar, in the linguistic and literary field' (Peers, *Redbrick University Revisited*, ch. 6, 157-59), was written (10 May 1922) to the Dean of the Faculty of Arts in support of Peers' election to the Gilmour Chair of Spanish.

Reproduced in facsimile, by courtesy of the Archives, University of Liverpool.

Chair.[3] Fitzmaurice-Kelly, previously a member of the so-called 'New Testament' movement, fiercely opposed Peers' appointment. Ann Mackenzie and Adrian Allan have thrown light on the exact grounds for this opposition from Peers' own autobiographical writing.[4] I limit myself to indicating the intriguing generational gap: the age of patrician independent scholars imbued with fastidious erudition but with little concern for teaching was giving way to that of professional academics; and Peers was seen, understandably perhaps but hardly justly, as a brash example of the latter, with the qualities of a schoolmaster and a publicist.

Edgar Allison Peers was born in 1891 at Leighton Buzzard. He was a Scholar and Prizeman at Christ College, Cambridge, where he took First Class Honours with distinction in Medieval and Modern Languages in 1912. No doubt inevitably, he appears to have specialized more in French and German than in Spanish at this stage. As he himself declared, 'Brought up, as I was, in the "French-with-German" tradition, I accepted the assumption ... that French was the only modern language which an educated man needed to know and developed a prejudice in favour of French which it took years to uproot'.[5] He also had an enduring interest in English literature; his first book, the result of the award of the Harness Prize of 1913 (one of several prizes he won), was entitled *Elizabethan Drama and its Mad Folk* (1914). He taught English Literature during a visiting appointment at Madrid, and he later gave it to be understood that Bruce Truscot's speciality was English Literature. Despite his substantial academic honours, employment prospects in

---

3 Thomas Kelly, in his *For Advancement of Learning: The University of Liverpool, 1881-1981* (Liverpool: Liverpool U. P., 1981), notes that 'The appointment was opposed by the New Testament group, and was made only after stormy debates in Faculty, Senate and Council. Faculty recommended, by fourteen votes to thirteen, merely a three-year extension of Peers' existing appointment as Lecturer-in-charge, but this decision was overruled by Senate, and Council eventually accepted Senate's recommendation for appointment to a chair' (220).

4 E. Allison Peers, *Redbrick University Revisited. The Autobiography of 'Bruce Truscot'*, edited, with introduction, commentary and notes, by Ann L. Mackenzie and Adrian R. Allan (Liverpool: Liverpool U. P., 1996).

5 See *Spanish Now*, vii.

universities were evidently not good. Peers therefore proceeded to take a Teachers' Diploma and to embark on a career in secondary teaching, first, for several years, at Mill Hill and Felsted Schools (1913-1919) and then, in 1919, at Wellington College. Up to the time of his appointment at Liverpool he had not apparently shown any particular dedication to Spanish; he declares in *Spanish Now* that he had taught six languages at one stage or other. In 1918 and 1920 he published two studies on French literature, on Vigny and Romanticism respectively. Some Hispanic articles commence in 1920, but his first books — an edition of the poetry of Manuel de Cabanyes, a translation of Llull's *Llibre de l'amic i l'amat* and *Rivas and Romanticism in Spain* — did not appear until 1923, after he had obtained the professorship. From then on his distinctive works on Ramon Llull, the mystics and the Romantics begin to appear in rapid succession.[6]

What I have termed the second generation of Hispanists consisted of a group of gifted men born towards the end of the nineteenth century; they represented the first consolidation of the subject as a university study. Its key members, apart from Peers himself, were Professors González-Llubera (Belfast), William Entwistle (Glasgow and then Oxford) and — slightly younger, a pupil of Llubera's — William Atkinson (Glasgow); also worthy of mention are L. B. Walton (Edinburgh) and J. W. Rees (Manchester) — the latter more influential as a teacher and promoter of scholarship than as an active researcher himself. Two other scholars, the prolific Aubrey Bell, and J. B. Trend, appointed to the Cambridge chair in 1933, continued the rather more amateur tradition in a *belles lettres* style.

Of all his contemporaries Peers was by far the most enterprising, dynamic and assertive concerning his subject. He embarked on an indefatigable campaign in favour of the teaching of Spanish and Hispanic culture in schools and universities. Even before he was appointed to the Gilmour Chair he had founded an enduring Summer School, with courses in Liverpool and Santander. He was extremely

6 A bibliography of his Hispanic publications by H. B. Hall, which appeared in the *Memorial Number*: *BHS*, XXX (1953), No. 117, 12-20, is reprinted in this volume.

conscious, as a result of his pedagogic background, of the need for close liaison with schools and spared no effort to encourage the teaching of Spanish in secondary schools, with the result that Liverpool and Merseyside had at the time of his death an overwhelmingly higher proportion of examination candidates in Spanish than anywhere else in the country, a tendency which has endured until very recently. He and his pupils brought out numerous publications — vocabularies, elementary grammars, editions, bibliographies — to foster Spanish teaching. He tirelessly gave lectures and organized courses and conferences for teachers. His efforts were consolidated by the foundation in 1934 of an Institute of Hispanic Studies, with branches throughout the country, and continued with undiminished vigour until his death. As W. C. Atkinson says forthrightly in his obituary notice:

> The subject has now both found and established itself.
>
> A variety of causes has worked to this end, but the prime mover in the creation of the new climate of opinion was one man, E. Allison Peers.[7]

He did not neglect national organizations either; he was the founder and first secretary (1918-29) at Cambridge of a highly significant new organization, the Modern Humanities Research Association, which came to publish the *Modern Language Review*, and was later the Association's President (1931-32). During the war, he took a leading part in the foundation of the Hispanic Council, and was its Educational Director from 1943 to 1946. He gave such prestigious lectures as the Rede Lecture at Cambridge, the Taylorian Lecture at Oxford and the Centennial Lecture at New York University. Highly respected abroad, he held eminent visiting posts in Spain (Madrid and Barcelona) and in the United States. But some honours eluded him: he must have been disappointed, for example, not to have been invited to accept one of the distinguished chairs at Oxford, Cambridge or London when they became vacant.

As an individual Allison Peers aroused much controversy. Many people found him imperious, cold and calculating, and excessively concerned with his own subject and his role in it. He

---

7 *Memorial Number*, *BHS*, XXX (1953), No. 117, 2.

had the reputation of being mean; a rather too prominent concern in *Redbrick University* is with salaries and pensions. He was undoubtedly an extremely methodical man, who measured his time with care. It is said that he would allocate a brief period of time — typically, ten minutes — for consultation with a student or junior colleague and strictly adhere to it. Sir James Mountford[8] tells the story that he would attend a Senate meeting for a short time, then go away to do some work and come back in an hour or so's time to see if they were still deliberating. The evidence of Bruce Truscot fits this pattern. He emphasizes that research is even more important than teaching and that administrative duties should be thought of as secondary to both; he is scathingly critical of idle professors who have abandoned research and publication, something nobody could possibly say of Peers.

What was it that caused a rift between Peers and other emerging Hispanists in the later 1930s and 1940s, sufficient to delay the founding of a British Association of Hispanists until after his death? Dislike of his activities as a publicist and his capacity for self-advertisement was without doubt a factor, but more academic reasons were also present. In his thirty-year tenure of the Gilmour chair Peers developed an incredible rhythm of production, scarcely satisfied with less than a book-length publication a year; his bibliography includes in fact more than fifty books, some of them multi-volumed. At a time when there was a need not only for much basic research but for accurate dissemination of information, including many desirable translations, his multifarious publications served a very useful function. It has to be admitted, however, that his brand of scholarship was extensive and diffuse rather than intensive and precise. To the virtues of his extraordinarily wide reading, clear exposition and factual accuracy he added the defect of prolix discursive description, to the detriment of selection and analysis. In my view (and here no doubt my own prejudices come to the surface) his criticism betrays a late-Romantic outlook typical of the Edwardian era against which the best minds of the coming generation were already reacting; perhaps his nearest counterpart in English Literature was Sir

8 'Bruce Truscot', *Memorial Number*, *BHS*, XXX (1953), No. 117, 10-11.

Herbert Grierson. The more philologically based, less obtrusive, traditional scholarship of his contemporaries Entwistle and Llubera did not suffer from this limitation. He was even less attuned to the New Criticism of close reading fostered by T. S. Eliot and I. V. Richards, which propounded an ideal of complexity and subtlety related to classical models; one of its classic texts, Empson's *Seven Types of Ambiguity*, was light years away from Peers' approach. Nor was Peers' attitude consonant with another influential critical direction: the moral earnestness espoused by F. R. Leavis and his school. The criteria evinced by his *Spain: A Companion to Spanish Studies* (1929; many re-editions) and his *Critical Anthology of Spanish Verse* (1948) are largely anachronistic. It was not surprising therefore that those Hispanists, with E. M. Wilson and A. A. Parker in the forefront, who brought New Criticism into Hispanic Studies found little to commend in Peers' neo-Romantic assumptions. In the area of research, too, different preferences prevailed: Romanticism and the Middle Ages for Peers, the Baroque for the newer generation. Peers found himself, probably without realizing it, somewhat outside the mainstream of the best criticism of his time. As a consequence, although he produced many estimable individual scholars — I. L. McClelland, Reginald Brown, Audrey Lumsden, Norman Lamb, Jack Metford, H. B. Hall, to name the best-known — they do not form a coherent school, and the most distinguished, like Ivy McClelland (the deserving recipient of a special Homage Number: *BHS,* LXVIII, January 1991), have tended to pull away from excessive dependence on his example. A special mention should be made of Harold Hall, Peers' staunch if unobtrusive assistant and trusted counsellor for many years, a mainstay of the *Bulletin* and, for a tragically short time (1978-81), Editor of the journal and holder of the Gilmour Chair.[9]

A rather uncritical concept of Romanticism, I suggest, lies at the heart of Peers' approach. He makes a series of dubious assumptions that flow on one from another: that Romanticism is an inherent quality, and is good; that Spain is essentially Romantic; that consequently the great figures of the Golden Age are Romantic; that the Romantic movement was a movement of

9 See my Memoir, *BHS*, LVIII (1981), 345-47.

revival as well as of revolt; and that Romantic values permeate all Spanish literature. Malcolm Read[10] has perceptively drawn attention to his and Bell's concern with travel; more than the conscious ideological trait Read sees in this tendency, I suspect its attraction may be a *costumbrista* throwback. In what may be Peers' most lasting scholarly work — his two-volume *History of the Romantic Movement in Spain* (Cambridge University Press, 1940; Spanish translation in Gredos) — these defects are to some extent outweighed by the extensive documentary material included. Another major area of study is Spanish mysticism. As well as having a pragmatic cast of mind and a deep sensuality, he held strong religious convictions (he was a devout high Anglican and lay preacher) which predisposed him towards the mystical. I do not feel competent to assess his qualities as a critic or commentator in this field, but his many frequently quoted studies, editions and translations of St Teresa and St John of the Cross,[11] as well as other devotional literature extending outside Spain (*Behind that Wall*, 1947), open up areas of literary experience which were previously inaccessible.

Part of the positive side of Peers' style of scholarship is that he automatically embraces a very diversified view of Hispanic studies, in contrast, for example, to my almost exclusively Castilian courses in London. He fostered an extremely broad-based programme by establishing a 'School of Hispanic Studies' rather than a simple department, and making the curious addition to his professorial title of 'Honorary Lecturer in

---

10 'Travelling South: Ideology and Hispanism', *Journal of Hispanic Philology*, XV (1991), 193-207, at 198-200. Read's article forms part of a recent very critical attitude towards the whole development of British Hispanism; see also his 'Writing in the Institution: The Politics of British Hispanism,' *JHP*, XV (1991), 140-48. While I welcome such a reassessment, it seems to me that Read's censures are too all-embracing and that greater differentiation needs to be applied to the various strands which constitute Hispanic scholarship.

11 Among the more important are: *Spanish Mysticism* (1924); *Studies of the Spanish Mystics*, 2 vols (1927-1930); *The Complete Works of St John of the Cross*, 3 vols (1934-1935); *The Complete Works of St Teresa*, 3 vols (1945); *The Poems of St John of the Cross* (1947); *The Letters of Saint Teresa*, 2 vols (1951); *A Handbook to the Life and Times of St Teresa and St John of the Cross* (1954).

Portuguese and Catalan'. To attain this goal, he negotiated with the Instituto de Alta Cultura for an eminent Portuguese *leitor* (for many years Luis Rebelo and later Fermín Crespo) and secured from Barcelona a most distinguished series of Catalan lectors, starting with Ferran Soldevila before the Spanish War and continuing after it with scholars of the calibre of Joan Triadú, Jordi Carbonell and Joaquim Molas: a tradition which continued under his successors until Joan-Lluís Marfany consolidated a continuous Catalan presence in Liverpool. Peers was not alone in having a panoramic view of Hispanism: Llubera in Belfast, Atkinson in Glasgow, Frank Pierce in Sheffield, Edward Sarmiento in Newcastle all contributed effectively to some part of this wider vision, but Peers' example was the most far-reaching. I have no doubt (and here I can claim to speak from personal experience) that it was largely as a result of Peers' earlier enterprise that Liverpool was chosen as one of the Parry Centres to develop interdisciplinary Latin-American studies, an undertaking which has given such rewarding results.

One enduring characteristic is Allison Peers' personal attachment to Catalonia. From the beginning of his career he showed an intense interest in Catalan literature. To his beloved Ramon Llull he devoted half a dozen books, many of them translations which permit access to one of the most endearing figures of the Middle Ages. He wrote extensively on the *Renaixença*, the Catalan literary revival of the nineteenth century, and on more modern writers like Verdaguer and Maragall.[12] On the political plane, he witnessed the proclamation of the 'Catalan State within a Federal Republic' in Barcelona in 1931 and was much moved by the experience; and he did not hesitate to refer to it as the 'liberation' of Catalonia. In one of his essays he declares that 'Without any sort of doubt, as it seems to me, he was the greatest figure of the Second Spanish Republic';[13] the 'he' was not Azaña, or any other figure of the central government, but the man who made the Barcelona 1931 proclamation: Francesc Macià, 'l'avi', the first

12 See the essays contained in *St John of the Cross and Other Lectures and Addresses* (London: Faber & Faber, 1946).

13 See *St. John of the Cross* ..., 190.

president of the Catalan autonomous government, the Generalitat. The doyen of Catalan scholarship, Jordi Rubió i Balaguer, had every justification in proclaiming him, in the Memorial number of the *Bulletin of Hispanic Studies*, as 'Amic de Catalunya, en els bons temps i també en els dolents'.[14] In the light of this, Sir James Mountford's playful suggestion that he was in the pay of the Generalitat is hardly surprising. A complementary quality was his extraordinary knowledge of contemporary Spain. This manifested itself throughout his career by his penchant for travel books and articles, but even more remarkable was his acquaintanceship with contemporary history.

Before I refer to this aspect, however, we must turn to his major achievement: the establishment, in December 1923, of a journal entitled the *Bulletin of Spanish Studies*. The idea derived from the Summer School, for Peers wanted to construct a means of maintaining and enhancing the interest and knowledge imparted in these courses. It was an entirely private venture and by its very nature extremely precarious in its finances; appeals for subscriptions and donations were frequent and urgent. It is curious to note that until 1931, when the financial situation stabilized, no editor is listed; only then do we learn that 'in future a signed editorial article, in which the familiar plural of past volumes will be discarded, is to introduce each issue'.[15]

As the subtitle, 'A Record and Review of their Progress' implies, the *Bulletin* set out initially to provide regular and up-to-date information about Spanish activities and publications in Britain and abroad. Much of the material was written by Peers himself. Indeed, such was his fecundity that he felt impelled to invent a whole series of apochryphal figures — Erik Crofts, F. K. Lloyd, N. Young, Trevor C. Smith, Mary Crowther — so as not to appear to occupy excessive space in issue after issue of the *Bulletin of Spanish Studies*; the first occurs even in the first number. On at least one occasion he even stooped to the practice of using a pseudonym to praise his own work.

Among the regular features were news-letters from Spanish

14 See *Memorial Number*, *BHS*, XXX (1953), No. 117, 9-10.

15 See *BSS*, VIII (January 1931), No. 29, 1.

and Portuguese cities — first Madrid, then Lisbon and Barcelona and occasionally from other cities as well. Later considerable coverage of Latin America was added. The first 'Carta desde Madrid' in the first issue refers to Primo de Rivera's *coup d'état*, and in due course the dictator's fall, the proclamation of the Second Republic[16] and particularly the outbreak of the Civil War were fully reported. From April 1930 a new feature, 'Spain Week by Week', began to appear and continued throughout and beyond the Civil War. In this way Peers provided an up-to-the moment and systematic account of the tragic events in Spain and printed documents of considerable historical interest. These pages provided the essential material for his books on modern Spanish history, *The Spanish Tragedy 1930-1936: Dictatorship, Republic, Chaos* (1936), *Catalonia Infelix* (1937), *The Spanish Dilemma* (1940) and *Spain in Eclipse* (1943). They are a valuable source of purely political history, of great documentary, and at times eyewitness, value, although they show little penetration into underlying causes, especially social and economic ones, and tend to treat Spanish politics by the rules of British parliamentary democracy. Peers' Civil War archives now form part of the Special Collections lodged in the Sidney Jones Library at Liverpool, and, along with the Blanco White papers, add substantially to the Hispanic resources of the University.[17]

The strength of the journal was now such that it was able to survive unscathed both the Spanish upheaval and the constraints of the Second World War. By the time it celebrated its quarter-century in 1948 it had increased in size from an initial forty pages per issue to sixty-eight pages per issue, and was now publishing more substantial and more scholarly articles, including several commemorative numbers, and more extensive reviews. In the hundredth number Peers made a reaffirmation of his editorial policy:

---

16 The anonymous Madrid correspondent was not alone in being caught out, when he declared in January 1931 that there was no danger of a Republic being proclaimed.

17 See Derek Lomax's Bibliography of *The Peers [Civil War] Collection in Liverpool University Library*, published in *Iberian Studies*, II (1973), No. 1, 40-51.

> There were those who wanted to turn it into a 'learned review', which it has never been, and I hope never will be ... There were others who wanted to make it a chatty magazine of little educational value, and still more who would have had it cater exclusively for teachers. Between these extremes it has tried to steer a steady course. It is addressed, not to the academic specialist as such, nor to the pedagogue as such, but to the educated man or woman of broad interests who is conversant with the Spanish language and seeks information on all that concerns Spanish life and culture.[18]

In the following issue two important changes, both important for the future, were made. First, the name was changed to *Bulletin of Hispanic Studies*, to reflect the growing interest in Latin America and Portugal.[19] Second, an editorial board of eight scholars was set up. Such innovations eased the way towards a new dispensation when Peers died four years later. The journal which had reflected Peers' own brand of scholarship and proselytizing and was largely composed by him or his associates and pupils had by this time come to seem rather parochial. It was ready to take on a new function. Thanks to Albert Sloman's active and scholarly leadership, the *Bulletin of Hispanic Studies* became what Peers had hoped it would never be: a 'learned review'. We should see this as an understandable, natural and indeed inevitable development, for what was now required was a review of the highest academic standards to provide for the increasing and varied Hispanic scholars being produced by a number of British universities. This development could not have been accomplished if a journal had not already been in place, with an established position, an administrative structure and a core of loyal subscribers: in this way Peers' efforts enabled others to lead Hispanism in new and very different directions.

---

18 'Twenty-five Years', *BHS*, XXV (1948), No. 3, 200. For further details see the account I gave as Editor of the *Bulletin*'s history in the special Supplement to Volume L (December, 1973), including full indices, published to mark its fiftieth anniversary.

19 Peers had in fact hoped to establish a separate *Bulletin of Portuguese Studies,* but owing to financial restraints was obliged simply to open out the existing publication.

Peers' major contribution to Hispanic Studies is beyond doubt. Without him the discipline would have been less prepared for the difficulties of the Second World War, less capable of seizing, as it did so eagerly, the opportunities of the post-war expansion and even of withstanding the onslaughts of the destructive policies inaugurated by the Thatcher government. In his creation of an image of *Redbrick University*, striving for academic and social prestige against the composite ancient university tradition of Oxbridge, he contributed substantially to a new confidence in institutions like Liverpool University which we have since come to take for granted. In hindsight, its imposing Victoria Tower can be seen as the quintessential Redbrick University. He fought strenuously against outside interference, conceived of at that time as coming from local authorities and lay members of Council, but his arguments carry equal weight against the much more powerful menace of imperious demands from the central government or managerial administration. If his concern with some eight regional universities has been largely superseded, given the proliferation, in the post-war expansion, of 'plate-glass' universities, technical universities (the ex-CATs) and former polytechnics, his affirmations of the priority of research, the necessity of adequate funding, the importance of student residences and the dignity of scholarship are by no means irrelevant.

The valuable example he offered of the range Hispanic Studies should encompass has had salutary effects on the discipline as a whole. Moreover, British scholars would do well, it seems to me, to adopt something of his proselytizing zeal in support of the subject and the humanities, to recognize the need for good public relations and in particular to offer friendly encouragement and support to hard-pressed school-teachers.

I would rate Peers' permanent legacy for Hispanic Studies in Britain under three headings. The first, and most important in my view, is the *Bulletin of Hispanic Studies*, with its international reputation largely deriving from its continued vigour and rigorous academic standards. Today it is just as much of an achievement, and just as difficult a task, to have an article accepted for the *BHS* as it ever was. At a time when, in the United States in particular, publication in first-class refereed journals is imperative such acceptance is often a key to academic success.

The other debts specifically concern Liverpool. Second among Peers' legacies I would stress the extremely broad-based programme of study which is still in place, backed up by outstanding library resources. And third, a fine Institute of Latin-American Studies with diverse interdisciplinary strengths working in co-operation with Hispanic Studies, among other disciplines. Neither of these would be in existence in its present form, and neither, I suspect, would be so effective, without the energy and foresight of the remarkable man whose memory we commemorate here. The University of Liverpool is fortunate to be able to perpetuate his name.[20]

20 'E. Allison Peers: A Centenary Reappraisal' was the Fifth E. Allison Peers Lecture, delivered on 10 June 1994, in the Jack Leggate Theatre of the Victoria Building, University of Liverpool. It coincided with an exhibition in the University's Art Gallery mounted by Ann L. Mackenzie, Adrian Allan and Janice Carpenter 'to celebrate the career of E. Allison Peers, as "Bruce Truscot", author of *Redbrick University*'.

E. Allison Peers
A Selective Bibliography*

H. B. HALL†

University of Liverpool

This is a list of the more important of Professor Peers' contributions in the Hispanic field. It omits:

(a) most items of under five pages
(b) all reviews of books
(c) all plain texts and school editions
(d) grammar, translation and composition courses
(e) the regular items 'Spain Week by Week', 'Latin America', and the chronicle of the Spanish Civil War, which appeared in this journal
(f) works concerned with English and French studies
(g) general pedagogical studies
(h) the 'Bruce Truscot' books**

---

* This Bibliography, chronologically ordered, first appeared in the 'Memorial Number' of the *Bulletin of Hispanic Studies* (XXX [1953], No. 117, 12-20). In reprinting it here, the Editor has added or completed references to those major publications which were still forthcoming when Peers died. She has included his essay on Miguel de Molinos, published for the first time in this Volume. She has also listed his recently published Autobiography, since it contains, in the memoirs of both Peers and 'Bruce Truscot', material important to the history of British Hispanism. (AM)

** For a Bibliography of the 'Bruce Truscot' publications see Peers, *Redbrick University Revisited*, *ed. cit.*, 495.

Abbreviations used:

BBMP, Boletín de la Biblioteca Menéndez y Pelayo
BH, Bulletin Hispanique
BHS, Bulletin of Hispanic Studies
BSS, Bulletin of Spanish Studies
CR, Contemporary Review
DR, Dublin Review
HR, Hispanic Review
JIHS, Journal of the Institute of Hispanic Studies
ML, Modern Languages
MLN, Modern Language Notes
MLR, Modern Language Review
MP, Modern Philology
NC, The Nineteenth Century
PQ, Philological Quarterly
RFE, Revista de Filología Española
RH, Revue Hispanique
SP, Studies in Philology
UR, Universities Review

1 *A Phonetic Spanish Reader.* Extracts from great writers, selected and transcribed (into the script of the International Phonetic Association) (Manchester: Manchester U. P., 1920), xii + 111 pp.
2 'Some Provincial Periodicals in Spain during the Romantic Movement', *MLR*, XV (1920), 374-91.
3 'Some Spanish Conceptions of Romanticism', *MLR*, XVI (1921), 281-96.
4 'Sidelights on Byronism in Spain', *RH*, L (1921), 359-66.
5 'A Survey of the Influence of Sir Walter Scott in Spain' (with Philip H. Churchman), *RH*, LV (1922), 227-310.
6 'Periodical Contributions of Sevilla to Romanticism', *BH*, XXIV (1922), 198-202.
7 'The *Moro expósito* and Spanish Romanticism', *SP*, XIX (1922), 308-16.
8 'The Fortunes of Lamartine in Spain', *MLN*, XXXVII (1922), 458-65.

9 *Rivas and Romanticism in Spain* (Liverpool: Liverpool U. P., 1923), xi + 132 pp.

10 *The Poems of Manuel de Cabanyes*, edited with critical introduction, notes, and bibliography (Manchester: Manchester U. P., 1923), vii + 152 pp.

11 'The "Pessimism" of Manuel de Cabanyes', *MP*, XXI (1923), 49-52.

12 *The Book of the Lover and the Beloved*, translated from the Catalan of Ramon Lull, with an introductory essay (London: SPCK, 1923), viii + 106 pp. [2nd, revised, edition, 1945].

13 'Ángel de Saavedra, Duque de Rivas. A Critical Study', *RH*, LVIII (1923), 1-600.

14 'Later Spanish Conceptions of Romanticism', *MLR*, XVIII (1923), 37-50.

15 'Literary Pilgrimages in Spain', *BSS*, I (1923-24), 11-15, 48-56.

16 *Spanish Mysticism: A Preliminary Survey* (London: Methuen, 1924), xi + 277 pp.

17 'La influencia de Chateaubriand en España', *RFE*, XI (1924), 351-82.

18 'The Literary Activities of the Spanish *emigrados* in England (1814-1834)', *MLR*, XIX (1924), 315-24, 445-58.

19 'El Romanticismo en España. Caracteres especiales de su desenvolvimiento en algunas provincias', *BBMP*, VI (1924), 67-83, 157-73, 211-23, 302-20.

20 'Minor English Influences on Spanish Romanticism', *RH*, LXII (1924), 440-58.

21 'A Precursor of St Teresa: Francisco de Osuna', *BSS*, II (1924), 3-12.

22 'Some Observations on *El desengaño en un sueño*', *Homenaje ofrecido a Menéndez Pidal: miscelánea de estudios lingüísticos, literarios e históricos* (Madrid, 1925) I, 583-87.

23 'Lullian Studies', *BSS*, II (1924-25), 73-80, 119-26; III (1925-26), 3-9, 121-28, 159-65.

24 *The Art of Contemplation*, translated from the Catalan of Ramon Lull, with an introductory essay (London: SPCK, 1925), 117 pp.

25 *Thoughts of Blessed Ramon Lull for Every Day* (London: Burns, Oates & Washbourne, 1925), vi + 108 pp.
26 'The Influence of Ossian in Spain', *PQ*, IV (1925), 121-38.
27 'El Romanticismo en España: bibliografía', *BBMP*, VII (1925), 250-69.
28 *Blanquerna: A Thirteenth-century Romance*, translated from the Catalan of Ramon Lull, with an introductory essay (London: Jarrolds, 1926), 536 pp.
29 *The Tree of Love*, translated from the Catalan of Ramon Lull, with an introductory essay (London: SPCK, 1926), viii + 128 pp.
30 *Royal Seville* (New York/London: Harper, 1926), viii + 132 pp.
31 'Studies in the Influence of Sir Walter Scott in Spain', *RH*, LXVIII (1926), 1-160.
32 'The Influence of Young and Gray in Spain', *MLR*, XXI (1926), 404-18.
33 'Milton in Spain', *SP*, XXIII (1926), 169-83.
34 'San Pedro de Alcántara', *BSS*, III (1926), 60-68.
35 *Studies of the Spanish Mystics*, Vol. I (London: Sheldon Press, 1927), xvii + 471 pp. [2nd, revised, edition, London: SPCK, 1951, xviii + 388 pp.].
36 *Santander* (London/New York: Knopf, 1927), xi + 144 pp.
37 *A Life of Ramon Lull.* Written by an unknown hand about 1311, and now first translated from the Catalan with notes and an appendix (the Catalan and Latin versions) (London: Burns, Oates & Washbourne, 1927), vii + 86 pp.
38 *The Book of the Beasts*, translated from the Catalan of Ramon Lull (London: Burns, Oates & Washbourne, 1927), ix + 90 pp.
39 'A Forgotten Franciscan Mystic, Bernardino de Laredo', *DR*, (1927), No. 362, 33-50.
40 'The Nature of Spanish Romanticism', *MHRA*, I (1927), 26-32.
41 'The Real Blasco Ibáñez', *CR* (1928), 599-604.
42 'Spanish Studies in England, 1920-1927', *ML*, IX (1928), 175-80.
43 'Fra Josef of Montserrat', *DR* (1928), No. 366, 36-54.

44 'Ramon Lull and the World of To-day', *Hispania* (USA), XI (1928), 459-67.
45 'Some Pictures from Granada', *BSS*, V (1928), 2-15.
46 *Ramon Lull: A Biography* (London: Sheldon Press, 1929), xviii + 452 pp.
47 *Granada* (London/New York: Knopf, 1929), 115 pp.
48 *A Book of Exercises for the Spiritual Life*, translated from the Spanish of García de Cisneros (Barcelona: Monastery of Montserrat, 1929), 335 pp.
49 *The Teaching of Spanish in Evening Schools and Part-Time Day Schools*, Board of Education Pamphlet No. 76 (London, 1929).
50 *Spain: A Companion to Spanish Studies* (ed. and contrib.) (London: Methuen, 1929), x + 302 pp. [4th, revised, edition, 1948].
51 *Studies of the Spanish Mystics*, Vol. II (London: Sheldon Press, 1930), xiv + 478 pp.
52 *Spain: A Companion to Spanish Travel* (London: Harrap, 1930), xx + 264 pp.
53 *The Book of St. James* (New York: Macmillan, 1931).
54 'The Liberation of Catalonia', *CR* (June 1931).
55 *María Fernanda*, by H. Pérez de la Ossa (translated) (London: Eyre & Spottiswoode, 1931), 242 pp.
56 'Spanish Romanticism. Some Notes and Documents', *BSS*, VIII (1931), 18-24, 144-49, 197-205.
57 *St. John of the Cross* (The Rede Lecture, 1932) (Cambridge: Cambridge U. P., 1932), 76 pp.
58 *The Pyrenees* (London: Harrap, 1932), 270 pp.
59 *Songs of the Lover and the Beloved* (translated) (London: SPCK, 1932), 37 pp.
60 'The Influence of Manzoni in Spain', *A Miscellany of Studies in Romance Languages and Literature* (Cambridge: Heffer, 1932), 370-84.
61 'The Vogue of Victor Hugo in Spain' (with Adelaide Parker), *MLR*, XXVII (1932), 36-57.
62 'The Spanish Universities' (with María V. de Lara), *UR*, V (October 1932), No. 1, 41-44.
63 'The Study of Spanish Romanticism', *MHRA*, XI (1932), 1-16.
64 'The Vogue of Alfieri in Spain', *HR*, I (1933),122-40.

65 'The Catalan Statute and the Cortes', *BSS*, IX (1932), 199-208; X (1933), 16-28.
66 'The Term "Romanticism" in Spain', *RH*, LXXXI (1933), 2e partie, 411-18.
67 'La universalidad de Ramon Lull', *BSS*, X (1933), 127-35.
68 'The Influence of Victor Hugo on Spanish Poetry and Prose Fiction' (with Adelaide Parker), *MLR*, XXVIII (1933), 50-61.
69 'The Influence of Victor Hugo on Spanish Drama' (with Adelaide Parker), *MLR*, XXVIII (1933), 205-16.
70 *Les poesies de Manuel de Cabanyes* (Catalan translation by G. Galcerán of Introduction to No. 10) (Barcelona: Oliva de Vilanova, 1933), 76 pp.
71 'Manuel de Cabanyes and the Catalan Renaissance', *BSS*, X (1933), 203-07.
72 *The Complete Works of St John of the Cross* (translated and edited) (London: Burns, Oates & Washbourne, 1934-35), 3 vols. I, lxxvii + 486 pp.; II, ix + 470 pp.; III, viii + 470 pp. [3rd, revised, edition, 1953].
73 *The Romantics of Spain* (translated from the Spanish of E. Piñeyro, with Bibliography) (Liverpool: Liverpool Institute of Hispanic Studies, 1934), x + 256 pp.
74 'Catalonia and the Sixth of October', *CR* (December 1934), 671-76.
75 'Crisis in Spain', *NC* (November 1934), 505-12.
76 'La universalitat de Ramon Llull', *Paraula Cristiana* (October 1934), 340-50.
77 'Inaugural Address: Institute of Hispanic Studies', *BSS*, XI (1934), 186-200.
78 'Ramon Llull, Doctor Il·luminat', *Bon Pastor* (Barcelona), IX (1935), 38-43.
79 *San Sebastián and the Basque Country* (under the pseudonym 'Trevor C. Smith') (Liverpool: Liverpool Institute of Hispanic Studies, 1935), 96 pp.
80 'Lope de Vega: prólogo al tercer centenario de su muerte', *BSS*, XII (1935), 174-85.
81 'Two More Years of the Spanish Republic', *Studies* (December 1935), 543-57.

82 'The Vogue of Alexandre Dumas *père* in Spain', *Homenatge a Antoni Rubió i Lluch* (Barcelona, 1936), I, 553-78.
83 'The Lope de Vega Tercentenary in Retrospect', *BSS*, XIII (1936), 27-36.
84 'The Spanish Elections', *CR* (April 1936), 409-13.
85 'Spanish and the World of Business', *JIHS*, II (1936), 26-35.
86 *The Spanish Tragedy 1930-1936: Dictatorship, Republic, Chaos* (London: Methuen, 1936), xvi + 248 pp. [6th, revised, edition, 1937].
87 'The Basques and the Spanish Civil War', *Studies* (1936), 529-44.
88 'The Catalonians in Gallipoli and Greece', *Year Book of the Hellenic Travellers' Club* (1937), 101-06.
89 'Catalonia and the Spanish Civil War', *Studies* (1937), 1-25.
90 'General Franco's New Spain', *DR* (1937), 221-31.
91 *Catalonia Infelix* (London: Methuen, 1937), xxiv + 326 pp.
92 'Catalonia in Arms', *CR* (1937), 530-37.
93 'Catalonian Chronicle', *CR* (1937), 410-15.
94 'Behind the Lines in Barcelona and Valencia', *Studies*, XXVI (1937), 553-67.
95 *A Handbook to the Study and Teaching of Spanish* (ed. and contrib.) (London: Methuen, 1938), xvi + 344 pp.
96 *Our Debt to Spain* (London: Burns, Oates & Washbourne, 1938), xiv + 146 pp.
97 *The Church in Spain, 1737-1937* (London: Burns, Oates & Washbourne, 1938), iv + 41 pp.
98 'Two Hundred Years of Spanish Church History', *Thought* (1938), 269-82.
99 'Bakunin and Spanish Anarchism', *Studies*, XXVII (1938), 136-41.
100 'Spanish Studies: Their Permanent and Unchanging Value', *JIHS*, IV (1938), 22-30.
101 'Contemporary Spanish Poets: Pedro Salinas', *BSS*, XV (1938), 202-06.
102 'The Spanish Civil War in 1938 and the Future', *Studies*, XXVIII (1939), 571-82.

103 'Majorca', *JIHS*, V (1939), 21-37.
104 'The Construction of the New Spanish State', *DR* (1939), 247-56.
105 'Spain Revisited and Some Reflections', *Studies*, XXIX (1939), 606-18.
106 *Spain, the Church and the Orders* (London: Eyre & Spottiswoode, 1939), xii + 220 pp.
107 *Liverpool Studies in Spanish Literature*, First Series (ed.) (Liverpool: Institute of Hispanic Studies, 1940), xii + 274 pp.
108 *A History of the Romantic Movement in Spain* (Cambridge: Cambridge U. P., 1940), 2 vols. I, xxiii + 349 pp.; II, xii + 470 pp.
109 'Reconstruction in Spain', *Studies*, XXX (1940), 210-20.
110 'Spain, 1926-1939', *Encyclopaedia Britannica* (new ed.) (London, 1940).
111 'Les Études Hispaniques en Grande Bretagne', *Occident* (Paris), I (1940), 81-86.
112 *Antonio Machado* (The Taylorian Lecture, 1939) (Oxford: Clarendon Press, 1940), 42 pp.
113 *The Spanish Dilemma* (London: Methuen, 1940), xii + 130 pp.
114 'General Franco and the Axis', *The Fortnightly* (1941), 321-30.
115 'The Reign of Alfonso XIII', *BSS*, XVIII (1941), 105-14.
116 'Light-Imagery in *El estudiante de Salamanca*', *HR*, IX (1941), 199-209.
117 'Mysticism in the Poetry of Fray Luis de León', *BSS*, XIX (1942), 25-40.
118 'The San Juan de la Cruz Quatercentenary', *BSS,* XIX (1942), 121-25, 178-86; XX (1943), 105-10.
119 'Notes on the Historical Problem of Castilian Mysticism', *HR*, X (1942), 18-33.
120 'The Ideas and Sentiments of Núñez de Arce's *Gritos del combate*', *HR*, XI (1943), 1-16.
121 *Spain in Eclipse* (London: Methuen, 1943), xii + 276 pp.
122 *Spirit of Flame* (London: SCM Press, 1943), 164 pp.
123 *Spanish—Now* (London: Methuen, 1944), x + 114 pp.
124 'Ángel Ganivet', *BSS*, XXI (1944), 199-208.

125 'Aspects of the Art of García Lorca', *BSS*, XXI (1944), 17-22.

126 'Mysticism in the Religious Verse of the Golden Age', *BSS*, XXI (1944), 133-45, 217-23; XXII (1945), 38-43.

127 'How Can We Introduce Spanish?', *BSS*, XXII (1945), 113-28.

128 'Francesc Macià', *BSS*, XXII (1945), 76-86.

129 *Mother of Carmel* (London: SCM Press, 1945), 164 pp.

130 *'New' Tongues: Modern Language Teaching of the Future* (London: Pitman, 1945), 164 pp.

131 *The Complete Works of St Teresa* (translated and edited) (London: Sheed & Ward, 1945), 3 vols. I, lviii + 316 pp.; II, xxviii + 420 pp.; III, xxiv + 388 pp.

132 *Fool of Love: The Life of Ramon Lull* (London: SCM Press, 1946), 128 pp.

133 *St John of the Cross and Other Lectures and Addresses* (London: Faber & Faber, 1946), 232 pp.

134 *Liverpool Studies in Spanish Literature*, Second Series (ed.) (Liverpool: Institute of Hispanic Studies, 1946), viii + 212 pp.

135 *Gabriela Mistral* (Liverpool: Institute of Hispanic Studies, 1946), 16 pp.

136 'Spain Revisited', *The Fortnightly* (1946), 348-52.

137 'St Teresa, Foundress', *BSS*, XXIII (1946), 248-60.

138 *The Poems of St John of the Cross* (English and Spanish text) (London: Burns, Oates & Washbourne, 1947), xii + 81 pp.

139 *Behind that Wall* (London: SCM Press, 1947), 126 pp.

140 *El misticismo español* (Spanish version of No. 16) (Madrid/Buenos Aires: Espasa-Calpe, 1947), 216 pp.

141 'Cervantes and England', *DR* (January, April, 1947).

142 'Problems of Translation', *Britain Today* (August/September, 1947).

143 'Cervantes in England', *BSS*, XXIV (1947), 226-38.

144 *A Critical Anthology of Spanish Verse* (Liverpool: Liverpool U. P., 1948), l + 742 pp.

145 *Madre del Carmelo* (Spanish version of No. 129) (Madrid: CSIC, 1948), 266 pp.

146 'Twenty-five Years', *BSS*, XXV (1948), 199-206.

147 'The "Viaje de Estudios" in Spain', *BHS*, XXVI (1949), 210-24.

148 *A Short History of the Romantic Movement in Spain* (Liverpool: Institute of Hispanic Studies, 1949), x + 230 pp.

149 Articles on: Spain since 1500, Portugal since 1500, Spanish Civil War, Franco, Pombal, Salazar, Alfonso XIII, Basque Provinces, Catalonia, Galicia (and 82 shorter articles), in *Chambers' Encyclopaedia*, new ed. (London, 1950).

150 *San Juan de la Cruz, espíritu de llama* (Spanish version of No. 122) (Madrid: CSIC, 1950), 260 pp.

151 'The Religious Verse of Pedro Espinosa', *Estudios de filología e historia literaria* [*Boletín del Instituto Caro y Cuervo*, V (1949)] (Bogotá, 1950), 293-300.

152 'Aportación de los hispanistas extranjeros al estudio de Cervantes', *Actas de la Asamblea Cervantina de la Lengua Española* (Madrid: *Revista de Filología Española* [1948], 1950), 151-88.

153 'Cervantes en Inglaterra', *Homenaje a Cervantes*, ed. Francisco Sánchez Castañer (Valencia: Mediterráneo, 1950), 410-27.

154 'The World of Saint Teresa's Letters', *Studies* (1950), 289-302.

155 'Mysticism in the Poetry of Lope de Vega', *Estudios dedicados a Menéndez Pidal* (Madrid: CSIC/ Patronato Menéndez y Pelayo/Instituto Miguel de Cervantes, 1950), I, 349-58.

156 *The Mystics of Spain* (London: Allen & Unwin, 1951), 192 pp.

157 'Majorca Revisited', *The Fortnightly* (1951), 385-90.

158 *The Ascent of Mount Sion*, by Bernardino de Laredo (translated and edited) (London: Faber & Faber, 1951), 275 pp.

159 *The Letters of Saint Teresa* (translated) (London: Burns, Oates & Washbourne, 1951), 2 vols, xxiv + 1006 pp.

160 'A Newly Discovered Teresan Autograph', *MLR*, XLVI (1951), 447-51.

161 'The Mother of Carmel in Her Letters', *Cross and Crown*, III (1951), 392-403.

162 'The Source and the Technique of San Juan de la Cruz's Poem *Un pastorcico*', *HR*, XX (1952), 248-53.

163 'The First English Professor of Spanish: Antonio Alcalá Galiano', *Estudios Hispánicos: Homenaje a Archer M. Huntington* (Wellesley, Mass.: Wellesley College, 1952), 491-97.

164 'St Teresa as a Writer', *Studies*, XLI (1952), 43-54.

165 'La Santa andariega', *Clavileño*, III (1952), No. 14, 5-10.

166 'Some Women Mystics of the Seventeenth Century', *BHS*, XXIX (1952), 193-201.

167 *St Teresa of Jesus and Other Essays and Addresses* London: Faber & Faber, 1953), 315 pp.

168 'The Alleged Debts of San Juan de la Cruz to Boscán and Garcilaso de la Vega (I)', *HR*, XXI (1953), 1-19 ('to be continued').

169 *A Handbook to the Life and Times of St Teresa and St John of the Cross* (London: Burns Oates & Washbourne, 1954), vii + 277 pp.

170 *Historia del movimiento romántico español* [Spanish version of No. 108] (Madrid: Gredos, 1954), 2 vols. I, 550 pp; II, 708 pp.

171 *Studies of the Spanish Mystics*, Vol. III, ed. I. L. McClelland (London: SPCK, 1960), xxiv + 338 pp.

172 *Redbrick University Revisited: The Autobiography of 'Bruce Truscot'*, edited, with introduction, commentary and notes, by Ann L. Mackenzie and Adrian R. Allan (Liverpool: Liverpool U. P., 1996), 520 pp.

173 'Miguel de Molinos' *Spiritual Guide*', *Spain and its Literature. Essays in Memory of E. Allison Peers*, ed. Ann L. Mackenzie (Liverpool: Liverpool U. P./London: MHRA, 1997), 109-40, at 115-37.

Spain and its Literature

Part I

From the Middle Ages to the Siglo de Oro

The Medieval Castilian Translation of Vegetius, *Epitoma de rei militaris*: An Introduction

P. E. RUSSELL

Oxford

The medieval Castilian translation of Vegetius' textbook on military organization and science seems, despite the considerable number of MSS which survive, to have received surprisingly little attention from scholars. This is partly, no doubt, because it has been judged, despite the central role of war in medieval culture and society, to be merely a translation of a Latin technical work on a par with, say, the translation of Palladius' agricultural manual and therefore of little interest to students of medieval literature and thought. One may suspect, too, that Scudieri Ruggieri's conclusion, in 1958, that the main purpose of the translation is to offer a version of Vegetius *a lo divino*[1] has not served to make scholars rush to study it.

Seven manuscripts of the Castilian translation (*De la cavallería e del arte de las batallas*) are known to me, all copied in the fifteenth century. They are:

(i) Biblioteca de Palacio (BPM), II-569, fols 1r-129r. From the Gondomar Library. Full description in *Catálogo de los Mss de la Biblioteca de Palacio*, ed. María Luisa

1 Jole Scudieri Ruggieri, 'Un Vegezio a lo divino', *CN*, XXIII (1953), 207-15.

López-Vidriero (in the press).[2] (Referred to as BPM 569 in the present study.)

(ii) Biblioteca Menéndez y Pelayo, Santander, MS 94 (previously MS 351). (MP 94)

(iii) Biblioteca del Escorial, P.I.23. From the Conde-Duque's library. (E1)

(iv) Biblioteca del Escorial, &.II.18. May have belonged to Isabel la Católica (Zarco Cuevas, *Catálogo de los manuscritos españoles*, I, 276). (E2)

(v) Bibliothèque Nationale, Paris, Fonds espagnol 211; No. 101 in Alfred Morel-Fatio, *Catalogue des manuscrits espagnoles ...*, Bibliothèque Nationale, Département des Manuscrits (Paris: Imprimerie Nationale, 1892). (BN Paris 1)[3]

(vi) Bibliothèque Nationale, Paris, MS 102 in Morel-Fatio, *Catalogue.* According to Morel-Fatio, this MS (not seen) omits all the translator's glosses. (BN Paris 2)

(vii) Biblioteca Nacional, Madrid, MS 10445, fols 151r-153v. A small fragment included in a manuscript from the Osuna library containing the translator's dedication and prologue and the opening passages of the translation — see Mario Schiff, *La Bibliothèque du Marquis de Santillane*, BEHE (Paris, 1905; repr. Amsterdam: Gérard Th. Van Heusden, 1970), 68, 75-76.

A point which needs to be made right away is that in fact, despite what the translator promises at some length in his prologue, the chapter-by-chapter glosses in which he there

2 I am grateful to the Patrimonio Nacional for allowing me personal access to this MS and for permission to reproduce it, to the Directora of the Biblioteca de Palacio for permitting me to see a copy of the entry in her new catalogue now at press and to Professor Ian Michael for securing for me a photocopy of BPM MS 569 and for checking a number of queries about the MS for me in the same Library. In the present article, unless otherwise stated, textual quotations from the Palacio MS are referred to by the abbreviation BPM 569.

3 I am grateful to Dr Nicholas Kronk for his kind help in securing a microfilm of this MS for me.

announced his intention to interpret the *Epitoma* in terms of Christian allegory or moral doctrine play a much less prominent role than he suggests. They were apparently sometimes dropped altogether by copyists.[4] When they are present they only appear sporadically in the various manuscripts and, especially after Libro I, are often not present at all for long stretches. The other type of gloss mentioned in the translator's prologue takes the form of his own personal exegesis and commentary on the chapter he has just translated. Such glosses are supplied much more consistently though by no means regularly. The marginal comments and the underlinings in other hands that are characteristic, for example of BPM 569, leave little room for doubt that it was Vegetius' own text in translation that people wanted to read.

Since any discussion of the Castilian translator's work necessarily presupposes some knowledge of the salient facts about the Latin text it will be appropriate before proceeding further to recall briefly the essential features of the latter and to suggest why it came to be, in Latin and in translation, from the ninth century onwards, one of the most read and probably most influential of the Classical texts known of the Middle Ages.[5]

The late-Roman emperor to whom the *Epitoma* is directed by Vegetius was most probably Theodosius I (AD 379-395). It is a substantial work. Its four books mainly deal with (i) the selection and training of recruits, (ii) the organization of the Roman army's legions, (iii) administration and tactics, (iv) siege warfare and naval warfare. As its name suggests, the *Epitoma*

4 See Alfred Morel-Fatio, *Catalogue des manuscrits espagnols et des manuscrits portugais*, Bibliothèque Nationale, Départment des Manuscrits (Paris: Imprimerie Nationale, 1892), No. 102, 35 (not seen).

5 Thanks to the recently published work of Dr N. P. Milner (*Vegetius: Epitome of Military Science*, trans. with notes and introduction by N. P. Milner, Translated Texts for Historians 16 [Liverpool: Liverpool U. P., 1993]), English-speaking students of Vegetius now have at their disposal an annotated translation of Vegetius into English together with an up-to-date introduction which sets out succinctly the various problems his work presents. For the Latin text of the *Epitoma* I use the text of C. Lang (Flavi Vegeti Renati, *Epitoma rei militaris*, recensvit Carolvs Lang [Stuttgart: Teubner, 1885; reprint, 1967]).

is not an original work by Vegetius; it is a scissors-and-paste job in which the named and unnamed military treatises (mostly now lost) of several well-known Roman writers belonging to widely different periods of Roman history have been put together, with the result that the work does not describe the Roman army as it was in Vegetius' time (the fourth century AD) or exactly as it was at any one time. As Dr Milner has shown,[6] the *Epitoma* was written with a political purpose, that of showing the emperor how, by returning to earlier ways and particularly by cutting down on late-Roman reliance on cavalry and on non-ethnic troops generally, the imperial army, once more centred round its traditional legions made up of Roman citizens, could, Vegetius believed, recover its ancient superiority over the barbarians. Vegetius *qua* epitomizer was not, though, entirely passive. He intervened in the work from time to time by manipulating his sources to justify the political points he had in mind or to introduce opinions of his own. He himself was not a soldier but a high-ranking imperial civil servant. There are some grounds for thinking that he may possibly have been born in or had connections with Roman Hispania.[7] Vegetius' authority in the Middle Ages may have gained from the fact that, as well as being a Classical writer he was also a Christian one as he makes clear in II, 5 where, describing the oath taken by recruits to the legion, he writes '*Iurant autem per Deum et Christum et sanctum Spiritum et per maiestatem imperatoris, quae secundum Deum generi humano diligenda est et colenda*',[8] which the translator renders:

> juran por Dios e por Jhesu Christo [BPM 569, fol. 43v] su fijo e por el Espíritu Santo e por la magestad del Emperador que guardarán la fed e farán fed e lealtad e estarán por el bien común del ynperio e de la tierra e del señorío de Roma.

One other work attributed to Vegetius, the *Mulomedecina* — a veterinary treatise on horses and cattle — survives and was also known, studied and translated in the Middle Ages, sometimes along with the *Epitoma*.

As is well-known to students of medieval warfare the

6 *Op. cit.*, xviii.

7 Milner, *op. cit.*, xxii-xxiii.

8 See Lang, *op. cit.*, 40.

Epitoma, throughout the European Middle Ages and into the sixteenth century, was, together with Frontinus' *Strategemata* (first century AD), the main instructional guide on the art of war available to princes and generals. Manuscripts of the *Epitoma* in Latin therefore abound in European libraries, including those of the Iberian Peninsula. Scholars have sometimes expressed surprise that the Middle Ages, at any rate in the Latin West, never produced a proper art of war of its own that took account of the way various aspects of medieval military affairs had moved since Roman times. One reason for this was that medieval Europeans did not see any cause for abandoning Vegetius. One remembers in this connection the well-known lines of Chrétien de Troyes at the beginning of his twelfth-century romance *Cligés*, where he unhesitatingly identifies contemporary chivalry with Greek and Roman military habits, claiming that the *chevalierie* of the ancients, along with their learning, had been inherited by the Frenchmen of his day. In any case much of the organizational and tactical precepts and advice contained in the *Epitoma* did indeed remain basically sound for the Middle Ages (and later). Thus when Vegetius wrote about the use of mobile towers in sieges (Liber IV) he was dealing with a weapon very much used by medieval armies and when, in the fourteenth century, tension-catapults (*carroballista*) began to be substituted by cannon, what Vegetius had to say about the handling and functioning of the catapults (II, 25) was still largely valid for cannon.

Nevertheless there were, as the work of the medieval translators shows, some problems about making Vegetius' account of Roman armies fit the facts, particularly the social facts, of medieval life. One of the most difficult of these was that, for Vegetius, the mainstay and most prestigious figure in a Roman army was the unmounted legionary recruited from the peasantry or from among artisans employed on physically demanding trades. Somehow this feature had to be reconciled with the fact that the élite of a late-medieval army was formed by the mounted knights with the rank of noble. There were, of course, also serious language problems for the translators arising out of the fact that the *Epitoma*, because of its subject matter, was not written in the kind of Latin that usually came their way. Here a clerical translator might enjoy a special advantage, as the commentaries of the priestly translator of the *Epitoma* show that he did, arising from his familiarity with the descriptions of military affairs in the Vulgate. Except in the prologues to each book of the *Epitoma*, where some influence of rhetoric is apparent, the manual is written in a down-to-earth Latin in which Vegetius continuously enters into the minutest details of military organization, engineering, weapons and tactics that requires the use of a vocabulary of Latin military terms for which the medieval vernaculars often had no synonyms and which current Latin dictionaries did not mention, forcing the translator to omit whole passages, to fall back on paraphrases or simply to resort to guesswork.

There is plenty of evidence that Vegetius' book was as much studied in the Iberian Peninsula as it was elsewhere. Alfonso the Wise, in Partida II, when discussing how knights should be selected, refers his readers as a matter of course to the authority of 'un sabio que habie nombre Vegecio que fabló de la orden de caballería' (tit. xxi, ley ii), thus inevitably giving the impression that Vegetius was an ancient authority on chivalry as this was understood in Alfonso's time. But the Castilian king, arising out of this reference, soon finds himself obliged to make some attempt to explain why Vegetius' precepts (*Epitoma*, I, chapter vii) about the categories of person specially suited for recruitment as legionaries into the Roman army were not workable in a Spanish context. He writes *à propos* of this question, following Vegetius:

> antiguamente para facer caballeros escogien de los venadores de monte, que son homes que sufren grande lacería, et carpinteros, et ferreros et pedreros, porque usan mucho á ferir et son fuertes de manos: et otrosi de los carniceros por razon que usan matar las cosas vivas et esparcer la sangre dellas ...[9]

This was clearly difficult to reconcile with Alfonso's introductory declaration (ley i) that 'caballería fue llamada antiguamente la compaña de los nobles homes'. He solved the problem by asserting that, as time went on, it had been found that recruits from the social classes mentioned by Vegetius lacked the necessary *vergüenza* needed to provide that extra

9 Alfonso el Sabio, *Las siete partidas*, Real Academia de la Historia II (Madrid: Imprenta Real, 1807), 198.

spur to make them able to defeat a strong enemy. In consequence, he concludes, 'tovieron por bien los sabidores destas cosas que catasen homes para esto que hobiesen naturalmente en sí vergüenza'.[10]

Another thirteenth-century Castilian book which is full of quotations from Vegetius and is cited in his commentaries by our translator is Fray Gil de Zamora's *De preconiis Hispanie* (*c.*1282) which, when it discusses military organization and tactics, is really little more than an anthology of excerpts from the *Epitoma.* The authority of Vegecio in fourteenth-century Spain is attested in Don Juan Manuel's *Libro del caballero y del escudero* (1326) where the Caballero Anciano says to the Escudero 'si vos quisiéredes saber todo esto que me preguntastes de la cavallería conplidamente, leed un libro que fizo un sabio que dizen Vejeçio, et y lo fallaredes todo' (cap. XIX).[11] The lack of a Castilian translation was soon to be partly remedied. Aegidius of Colonna's *De regimine principum*, the standard text-book for the instruction of princes, was translated in the 1340s for the benefit of the future Pedro I by a friar, Juan García de Castrojeriz.[12] The Castilian translator frequently recommends the prince to study 'el libro que fizo Vegeçio de la cavallería'. In Libro III he is in the habit of citing the *Epitoma* at length when he sets about explaining what every ruler must know about the art of war on land or at sea. So much of the essential Vegetius is contained in this version of Aegidius of Colonna's work that its existence may have made it seem

---

10 Alfonso el Sabio, *Las siete partidas*, 198. The problem of the status of a *cavallero* in ancient times preoccupied mid-fifteenth-century proto-humanists. In 1444 Santillana asked Alonso de Cartagena for his views. The latter replied at length the same year, giving his opinion that to translate *miles* as 'caballero' as was usual 'le trahemos de gran tiempo equivocado' since in Latin it could refer to any combatant, whether he fought on foot or on horseback. He recommended the use of the term 'combatiente' as the equivalent of *miles*, reserving the word 'caballero' for someone knighted by the king 'u otro que armarlo pueda' (Marqués de Santillana, *Questión* in *Prosistas castellanos del siglo XV*, I, ed. Mario Penna [Madrid: BAE, 1959], 235-45).

11 *Obras de Don Juan Manuel*, ed de José Mª Castro y Calvo y Martín de Riquer, Clásicos Hispánicos I (Barcelona: CSIC, 1955), 15.

12 I have used the Seville incunable edition (Seville: Meinardo Ungut e Stanislao Polono compañeros, 20 octubre 1494).

unnecessary for any potential translator to undertake the daunting task of translating the entire text of Vegetius into Castilian.

As far as translations into the vernacular went the Iberian Peninsula was well behind France and Italy. There were several medieval French translations.[13] The most successful was that of Jean de Meun, author of the second part of the *Roman de la rose*, who translated Vegetius into French in 1284 (*L'Art de chevalerie*).[14]

It is said that it was Meun's version which was translated into Catalan by En Jaume Castellà with the title *Vegeci del mester darmes e de la art de cavalleria*, but a cursory examination of the two texts casts doubt on this claim. The Catalan translation survives in a single early fifteenth-century MS now in private hands in Spain.[15] It was not used by Fray Alonso de San Cristóbal. There is also a thirteenth-century Italian translation by Bono Giamboni, *Delle cose e arti della cavalleria*. This, which seeks to keep more closely to the Latin text than do the French translations, has nevertheless been criticized like them for its erroneous readings and its omissions[16] — a feature in fact common to most medieval translators whose main concern was usually to get the gist of the Classical text into the vernacular as rapidly as possible.

---

13 See Paul Meyer, 'Les Anciens Traductions français de Vegèce et en particulier Jean de Vignai', *Romania*, XXV (1896), 401-43 and J. A. Wiseman, '*L'Epitome rei militaris* de Vegèce et sa fortune au Moyen Age', *Medium Aevum*, LXXXV (1979), 13-31.

14 Jean de Meun, *L'Art de chevalerie, traduction de 'De re militari' de Végèce*, publié avec une étude sur cette traduction et sur *Li Abrejance de l'ordre de chevalerie de Juan Priorat* par Ulysse Robert, SATF (Paris: Librarie de Firmin Didot et Cie, 1897) is still useful but has been superseded by *Li abregemenz noble honme Vegesce Flave René dez establissemenz apartenanz a chevalerie, traduction par Jean de Meun ...*, ed. Leena Lofstedt, *Annales Academiae Scientiarum Fennicae* (Helsinki, 1977).

15 I am grateful to Professor Brian Tate for having drawn my attention to the existence of this unique MS from the Phillipps collection which surfaced in 1972 and is now in the library of Don Bartolomé March.

16 *Di Vegezio Flavio, dell'arte della guerra, libri iv, volgarizzamento di Bono Giamboni*, ed. Francesco Fontani (Florence, 1815). See Cesare Segre, 'Jean de Meun e Bono Giamboni tradutori de Vegezio', *AAST*, LXXXVII (1952-53), 119-53.

The problem of the identification of the Castilian translator and that of the date of his translation are closely connected. The identity of the translator is beyond doubt since he discloses it in the opening dedication to the king in BPM 569,

> yo Frey Alfonso de San Christóval, maestro en theolegía, vuestro servidor e vuestro devoto orador, beso umillmente vuestros pies e vuestras manos e me encomiendo en la vuestra alta merçed commo de mi señor natural. Señor, por quanto fue la vuestra merçed de me mandar romançar en nuestro lenguaje el libro e la obra que fizo Vegeçio de la cavallería e del arte de las batallas ...[17]

The explicit to *EI* makes it clear that the translator belonged to the Dominican Order ('Este libro romanço fray Alfonso de Sant Cristóval maestro en tolosía de la orden de los pedricadores', fol. 94r). The translator was then one Fray Alonso de San Cristóbal, a Dominican who held the degree of master in theology and the post of royal orator. The king of Castile who requested the translation is identified in the dedication as 'Don Enrique'. Amador de los Ríos described the translator as a Dominican 'celebrado en la corte de don Juan II, cual predicador excelente' and declared that the monarch to whom the work is dedicated is Henry IV.[18] If we accept Henry IV as the likely dedicatee then the full chancery-style listing of the places over which the kings of Castile ruled with which the translator's dedication opens supplies a probable *terminus post quem* and *terminus ante quem* for the translation. In 1463 Henry IV, who had succeeded to the throne in 1454, managed to capture Gibraltar from the Moors, an event which was hailed as a famous victory. His chancery lost no time in adding this toponym after Algeciras to the list of the king's dominions. Fray Alonso de San Cristóbal's dedication does not mention Gibraltar.

In fact, however, there are good grounds for supposing that the dedicatee was not Henry IV but Henry III (1390-1406). Dominican records show that a Fray Alonso de San Cristóbal, like the translator of Vegetius a *magistrum in theologia*, was assigned to the Dominican house in Salamanca — then the

17 BPM 569, fol 1r.

18 José Amador de los Ríos, *Historia crítica de la literatura española*, VI (Madrid, 1865), 325.

most prestigious of the Dominican houses in Castile — as *lector principalis* in theology by the chapter-general held in Zaragoza in 1391-92.[19] The same records suggest that he had moved from this post (to the court?) by 1396. The exact coincidences of name, religious order, qualifications and status between this Dominican theologian and the translator of Vegetius are striking. The latter reveals himself in his commentaries on the text of Vegetius and in his *glosas espirituales* to be learned in theology and to have a penchant for writing in a style employed by preachers addressing an educated congregation. It may be added that Fray Alonso was, as we would expect, a reasonably competent Latinist. He was also well-read generally, particularly in philosophy and history though his references to pagan Latin authors, however, show no sign that he was in the slightest way responsive to the burgeoning protohumanism of the time of John II and Henry IV.[20] The fact that Fray Alonso was approached by the king to undertake the translation of Vegetius also lends some weight to the tradition that he had joined the court after leaving his post at Salamanca. While dating by language is a notoriously dangerous enterprise it may safely be said that there is nothing about the language of the translation that is inconsistent with a text dating from the late fourteenth or very early fifteenth century. The translator's

19 *'In conventu Salmantino ponimus lectorem principalem fr. Alfonsum de sancto Christophoro, magistrum in theologia'* (*Monumenta ord. FF. praed. historica*), VIII (Romae, 1900), 53. In the 1396 chapter general at Clairmont another *lector principalis* was assigned to the Salamancan convent (65). Ruggiero Scudieri rejected perhaps rather too hastily the possibility that the person referred to might be the translator of Vegetius on the grounds that 'por motivi cronologici non possiamo identificarlo con l'omonimo domenicano' (207, n.2). At Avignon in 1386, one Fray Gonzalo de San Cristóbal had been assigned *ad legendum bibliam* at Salamanca (20); in 1388 he was promoted *ad legendam sentencias ibidem* (35). I have so far found no other references to Fray Alonso in Dominican documents. San Cristóbal is a place near Medina del Campo. It seems unlikely, in the light of the foregoing, though not entirely impossible, that there can have been another Dominican theologian and teacher at San Esteban in Salamanca also known as Alonso de San Cristóbal after the one referred to in this note.

20 His stereotyped way of referring to Classical authors ('el sabio Omero', 'el sabio que llaman Iuvenal', 'Tulio el romano' etc.) has a distinctly medieval ring about it.

commentaries on individual chapters of Vegetius' book contain occasional historical and other references which I hoped might show definitively whether the translation must have been made after 1406, but I have not come across any evidence in the commentaries that helps in this way. Nevertheless, it seems clear enough that the Alonso de San Cristóbal referred to in the Dominican records cited above must be regarded, unless new and conclusive contrary evidence becomes available, as the probable translator of Vegetius into Castilian. If he flourished in the 1390s he could well, as Amador de los Ríos claims, have also been prominent at the court of John II (1406-54) in that king's earlier years.

Another point that requires clearing up is the question of the *glosas* which are a unique feature of the Castilian translation. In most manuscripts Fray Alonso makes much in his dedication of his intention not only to supply one set of glosses in the form of a straight commentary chapter by chapter on what Vegetius has to say, but also to supply another set following the first in which he will interpret Vegetius' text in terms of Christian allegory to help his readers learn how to fight 'contra los henemigos espirituales'. He remarks,

> (BPM 569, fol. 1r) Otrosý considerando que en el fecho de la cavallería e de las peleas non solamente fabló Vegeçio, mas otros muchos sabidores dixeron muchas cosas en esta razón que conc[ue]rdan con lo que dixo (fol. lv) Vegeçio, por ende ... pensé de partir esta obra en tres partes. en la primera parte fablaré e diré lo que dixo Vegeçio en sus libros [romançándolo] lo más claramente que yo pudiere. La segunda parte será bien commo glosa puesta en la [margen] del libro,[21] que es de dichos de los sabidores que concuerdan con lo que dixo Vegeçio e declaran sus dichos en algunos logares. La tercera parte será puesta ayuso, que fablará spiritualmente trayendo los dichos de Vegeçio a las vezes a las vertudes e a las vezes a los pecados e a las costunbres desta vida en que vevimos ...

After each of the early chapters of Libro I Fray Alonso does

21 The commentary glosses do not appear in the margins of any MS I have seen as, according to the translator, they were to do in the autograph MS. They are always positioned in the text, usually under the heading 'Glosa', after the translated chapter and before the *glosas espirituales* on the occasions when these are also present.

indeed insert secondary glosses that make a sustained if rather forced attempt at Christian allegorization. But by the time he had written seven such glosses he seems to have realized that, when committing himself to interpreting allegorically each of the one hundred and twenty-five chapters of the *Epitoma*, he had set himself a task to which Vegetius' manual usually simply did not lend itself. Thereafter the *glosas espirituales* only appear very sporadically. On the other hand, the glosses in the form of straightforward commentaries on the text fared much better. They usually but not always follow each chapter in Libro I, as promised, though they start to be omitted towards its end and also only appear fairly irregularly in the remaining three books. The marginal comments by readers in other hands in BPM 509 as well as the underlinings in other manuscripts make it clear that what readers were interested in was Vegetius' book, not in Alfonso de San Cristóbal's allegorizing or moralizing. It will be seen therefore that, apart from the fact that it is in no sense a *contrafactum* of the original Latin text, to describe the Castilian translation as an *a lo divino* work, or even as a work in which the sporadic attempts to draw Christian conclusions from Vegetius' manual are significant, is to miss the real purpose of the translation and the reason for its popularity.

Vegetius himself, in his dedication to the emperor, had remarked of his treatise that to compose it 'neither linguistic elegance nor intellectual acumen was needed, but painstaking and faithful labour',[22] a passage which his translator renders, perhaps with some personal fellow-feeling, as 'presentar vos he esta obrezilla en la qual non es mucho neçesaria agudeça de engenio nin sotileza, mas es neçesaria travajo con ardideza fiel'.[23] Obviously much hard work has indeed gone into the business of trying to understand the often difficult military terminology used in the Latin and of seeking vernacular equivalents for it. The same cannot be said of the style in which the results of the translator's efforts are presented. Neither *agudeza de ingenio* nor *sutileza* are indeed visible there. As is the case with many medieval translations from Latin into the

22 Milner, *op. cit.*, 2.

23 Castilian translation from BPM, 569, fol 5r.

vernacular, Fray Alonso's praiseworthy efforts to master as best he can the basic meaning of the original text are not accompanied by any interest in presenting his material in a form which makes any serious attempt at achieving a modicum of stylistic ease. The base linguistic and syntactical registers used by Fray Alonso are very narrow so that the translation seems thin, wooden and repetitious. It is very noticeable that Fray Alonso is a much better writer in his commentaries and *glosas*. These are written in a much more relaxed, more individual and more popularist style which, particularly in the case of the *glosas espirituales*, reminds us that the translator was a professional preacher and sermon writer who had been appointed an official orator at court. His translation thus illustrates once again the correctness of a point made by Jean Rychner concerning thirteenth- and fourteenth-century translations from Latin into French: the haste with which medieval translators usually do their work means that they give a misleading impression of what the literary language of the period was capable of achieving when used by writers of original prose.[24] Pervading the whole of *De la cavallería e del arte de las batallas* is a sense that its monkish translator is doggedly carrying out as an academic exercise a task set him by the king which has taken him into an alien, soldier's world of which he has no direct experience and can therefore bring no personally acquired insights to help him to grasp the unspoken assumptions, military and political, that lie behind Vegetius' manual.

Judging by the number of manuscripts which survive, these characteristics of Fray Alonso's work were no hindrance to its popularity among military men with no Latin. Indeed Vegetius simplified in the way described may have been useful to them in a way that a stricter translation could not have been. But there is ample evidence that military men were not the only medieval readers of Vegetius in Latin or in translation. The *Epitoma rei militaris* furnished, all over Europe, a source of *exempla* for

---

24 See Peter Russell, *Traducciones y traductores en la Península Ibérica (1400-1550)*, Universidad Autónoma de Barcelona: Escuela Universitaria de Traductores e Intérpretes (Bellaterra: Universidad Autónoma de Barcelona, 1985), 22.

writers of sermons[25] and, more surprisingly, was a source of aphorisms for inclusion in collections of *sententiae*.[26] Nor should it be forgotten that, when they read Vegetius, either in Latin or in the original, Castilian military men and friars could not avoid acquiring on the way a good deal of real information about what the Roman world was like as, for example, when they learned that the despised rural levies (*peones*) of their own time had in those days provided the recruits who became the famous legionaries, thanks to whom Roman armies had conquered the known world. The General Rules for War with which Liber III of the *Epitoma* ends also contain, with their emphasis on caution, planning, discipline and a careful assessment of the odds before risking battle, material which must have surprised the Castilian knights who read or heard about them. They, imbued with the ideology of chivalry in a rather simplistic form, were well-known in the fourteenth century for their conviction that not discipline but brio was the supreme military virtue.

For all the popularity of Vegetius and of Fray Alonso de San Cristóbal's translation in fifteenth-century Castile, no printer of *incunabula* seems to have printed it. This was certainly not due to any diminishment of interest in Vegetius' manual in Latin after the invention of printing. The *Epitoma* was much printed in Europe generally all through the sixteenth century. Perhaps, with the development of humanistic scholarship in Spain, the friar's translation had come to be seen as too crude and too defective both textually and linguistically to merit publication. Or perhaps printers, like some later scholars, were misled by Fray Alonso's dedication into supposing that what he

---

25 G. R. Owst, *Literature and Pulpit in Medieval England* (Oxford: Basil Blackwell, 1966; ed. repr.), notes of John of Bromyard's *Summa praedicantium* that, among other Classical authors, he cites Vegetius 'whose *De militari* is much in vogue with our preachers ...' (181). For further evidence about the interest of the friars in Vegetius see Beryl Smalley, *English Friars and Antiquity in the Fourteenth Century* (Oxford: Blackwell, 1960), *passim*. In Catalonia the famous fifteenth-century court preacher Felip de Malla includes Vegetius among the other Classical *autoritates* he cites.

26 BN Madrid, MS 9522 is a vademecum of *sententiae* on ethics, rhetoric, politics, economics and so on. One of its sections, regrettably incomplete, is headed 'Notabilia Vegecii'.

offered was Vegetius converted into a work of Christian doctrine. No Spanish translation appeared in print in Spain until 1764, when the *Instituciones militares de Fl. Vegecio Reanto*, newly translated by Jaime D. Viana, was published in Madrid.[27]

27 Since this article went to press I have been able to establish that the Catalan MS referred to in note 15 is to be found in the library of the Fundación March Servera in Palma de Mallorca (MS 103/V3/3). I am grateful to the Librarian, Dr Fernando Lorenzo Pérez Martínez, for sending me a partial photocopy of this MS. I also understand that there is (not seen) an unpublished doctoral thesis by María Teresa Callejas Berdones, *Edición crítica y traducción del 'Epitoma rei militaris' de Vegetius, Libros I y II, a la luz de los manuscritos españoles y de los más antiguos testimonios europeos* (Universidad Complutense de Madrid, 1982). I owe both these pieces of additional information to Professor Ian Michael's kind help.

Two Letters of Devotional Advice to Nuns in the *Cancionero de Egerton* (Dutton LB3)

DOROTHY S. SEVERIN

University of Liverpool

Like many of the so-called *cancioneros* of the late fifteenth century, the Egerton *cancionero* (BL Egerton 939) has the character of a miscellany of prose and poetry. Two personal letters of consolation link it to the aristocratic De Foix family, who were closely related to Ferdinand the Catholic Monarch.[1] Two other personal letters in this collection are written to devout nuns, and it is possible that both letters are written by the same 'buen rreligioso' to the same nun.

The first of these, at fols. 33r-36r, is written by someone who protests that he is not himself devout enough to write to a devout person ('caresco de deuçion para escreuir a personas devotas'), and writes only at her insistence. This commonplace comes directly from the pseudo-St Bernard epistle to his sister, which was printed in Spanish by the early sixteenth century.[2] The writer then launches himself into a homily which first

1 See my edition of this *cancionero*, forthcoming in *Two Spanish Songbooks: The 'Cancionero Capitular de la Colombina' (SV2) and the 'Cancionero de Egerton' (LB3)*, Hispanic Studies TRAC (Textual Research and Criticism) 11 (Liverpool: Liverpool U. P.). For this version I have modernized punctuation and accentuation.

2 *Sermones de Sant Bernardo traduzido de la letra en lengua castellana por el protonotario maestre Rodrigo de Santa Ella, arcediano de Reyna, escritos a una religiosa su hermana del modo de bien biuir* (Logroño: Miguel de Eguía, 1529).

considers the theme of temptation and then glosses the theme 'la mi anima es rregalada quando el mi amado me habla'. The intense contemplation of the love of God through personal prayer to that divine love occupies the central part of the letter, which concludes with a series of quotations on the topic of love from the Church Fathers: Bernard, Jerome, Ambrose, Augustine and Anselm. The writer was using, at least partially, an index of quotations by Thomas Hibernicus under the title *Amor*. A survey of early Spanish translations also gives some clues to possible sources from popular works by these Saints (some of them supposititious). The letter ends with a fervent prayer for the nun to Christ, identified by His virtues, asking when the soul will be united with Him in eternal glory. The nature of this letter is in keeping with the personal, semi-mystical devotion which was common in the late fifteenth century in orders like the Hieronymites. The writer's protestations of his lack of devotional credentials do not accord with his extensive devotional knowledge, although one must suspect that he might not have been in religious orders despite his expertise. The high standard of writing suggests a professional writer at the very least.

The second letter (36v-39v) states in the rubric explicitly that it is by 'vn buen rreligioso', although rubrics are notoriously untrustworthy. This is specifically an answer to a letter by a devout nun ('vuestra deuota letra escripta en la santa semana de pasión rresçebí en el santo ochauario de la rresureçión'). This is a contemplation of the way of the Cross and the Passion, again written in a style very current in Spain in the late fifteenth century, although the passages of description are not particularly graphic or gruesome in their contemplation of the Passion. In fact, the contemplation of the Passion is recommended in fairly lofty terms: 'que non se alcança el fruto desto árbol disfrutando en las escuelas, rreboluiendo los libros, afeytando las palabras, edificando grandes edifiçios para orar, fingiendo grandes aparejos de ornamentos y rretrates pintados para contemplar, avnque todo esto sea bueno en sus tienpos'. The good thief in particular captures the attention of the writer, as do the Virgin and Saint John.

Towards the end of this letter the writer takes up the same

theme as the writer of the first letter; he writes at the insistence of the nun: 'Mandásteme & desmandásteme que todavía vos escriviese & avnque me escusé que non sabía cosa que para vos fuese que pudiese ditar *de nuevo*, no açebtastes mi escusa, e por tanto tomé la péñola en la mano, & non me occurió mejor tema para fablar con esa vuestra devota ánima que de la hecha de vuestra carta, & la rreçebta quando yo la rreçebí, ca la fezistes en la día que leyán en la Semana Santa la pasión de Vuestro Esposo, & yo la rresçebí en su santa rresureçión' (my italics). It would seem that he is writing to her *again*, a positive sign that we are dealing with the writer of the first epistle. This also casts doubt on the rubric that claims the writer is a 'buen rreligioso', as the first writer seems to refute this claim. He calls her 'mi fija señora' and 'señora hija hermana bendita' at two points in the letter, but this could be a religious formula instead of literally meaning that she is his daughter or relative. However, Enrique de Villena and Isabel de Villena are one possibility; while Alonso de Cartagena (or indeed other writer members of the Santa María clan) and Teresa de Cartagena, or even Gómez Manrique and his sister also spring to mind as possibilities. When speaking of the good thief the writer refers to chronic illness: 'Grande gozo es a los dolientes de yncurables dolençias quando se hablan con aquellos que se curaron de aquellas o peores'. Teresa was, of course, deaf.

The texts of the two letters are as follows:

[ID2762]LB3-16(33r-36r)(Prose)

Deuota hermana, porque algunas vezes con grande instançia me aués rrogado que vos escriuiese vna carta, acordé de vos escreuir aquesta avnque con alguna pena, porque non tengo en costunbre de escreuir a mugeres, e porque caresco de deuoçión para escreuir a personas deuotas. E si la carta no fuere tal, súplalo vuestra caridat y perdone mi pobre dezir.[3] Como Nuestro Señor Dios aya hecho al onbre para la gloria, quiere que aquí sea esaminado por diuersas tentaçiones,

3 'Amada hermana en Jesuchristo: mucho tiempo ha que me rogaste que te escriuiese algunas santas amonestaciones, pero sabiendo que esta escrito que es soberuia querer el hombre enseñar a mejor que si, halleme indigno para hazer tal obra. E a esta causa lo he algun tiempo dilatado', pseudo-Bernard, *Sermones*, fol. V recto.

o segund que el onbre ha rrresçebido de Dios Nuestro Señor mayores dones espirituales, o lo entiende fazer mayor en paraýso, tanto le examina aquí por mayores tribulaçiones segund que los santos doctores ponen, porque cada vno con muy grand estudio se deue aparejar a estar aperçibido todos tienpos si saluar se quiere. Que al tienpo que veen venir la tentaçión, que luego la contrasten, e luego con esfuerço la echen, así como hazen aquellos que son electos a gloria por dar honor a Dios en su vitoria, con todo su estudio & esfuerço contrastan al enemigo. El Señor que vee su santa entençión, enbíales & crésçeles las tentaçiones por que ganen, e en esto se conosçen los miserables que desechan esta batalla tan prouechosa & se dexan todos vençer & caer en los pecados acostunbrados, & non se abstienen por temor ni por amor de Dios, nin por vergüença de la gente, ni por su vejez. Es tal la ley diuinal & costunbre de Nuestro Señor que tanto quanto más vee la persona virtuosa & victoriosa en las tentaçiones, tanto consiente que más sea conbatida & por más fuertes tentaçiones & [fol. 33v] por más demonios. Hermana, deues pensar cómo Nuestro Señor Ihesu Christo fue tentado,[4] pero las sus tentaçiones non fueron de pecados carnales, ca bien conosçié el diablo la su alta santidat & a las personas altas que vee lleneramente enseñorear la carne, non las tienta de pecados carnales, ca vee que de balde se trabajaría; mas tiéntales de pecados spirituales ascondidos, sotiles & cubiertos so espeçie de bien, así como es presunçión o estimaçión de sí mesmo & blasfemia ascondida, estimando Dios ser, a ellos obliga y non les hazer lo que deue & que non se deue aver, así con ellos como con los otros, destas & otras muchas tentaçiones son tentadas las personas que aquí se esfuerçan seruir al muy alto Dios Señor Nuestro Ihesu Christo y de llegarse a Él. Pero para huyr destas sotiles tentaçiones, conuiene que vos abraçés con la terçera virtud teologal que es caridad & amor de Dios grande. Aquésta vos fará así ardiente que otra cosa non podáys pensar nin hablar nin obrar sinón aquello en que cabe la honrra & loor de nuestro señor Dios. Deues sienpre pensar todos los tienpos que deues hazer dezir & obrar aquello que es a Nuestro Señor Dios plaziente, & esquiuar, todo lo que a Él es desplaziente, y cómo lo podríades altamente contenplar, & sienpre en todas las cosas buscad a Dios y a todas las criaturas que a vos se llegaren preguntad cómo vos podrés llegar a Dios, y cómo le podrés mucho amar, y cómo vos podrés del enbriagar, y dígala la vuestra ánima — O dulçura de amor, o amor de dulçura, cómate el mi coraçón y las entrañas de la mi ánima sean [fol. 34r] llenas del tu vino. Deuota hermana, si açertáys a gustar deste vino y vos enborracháys bien dél, sin dubda saliréys con grande amor

4 The temptation in the wilderness, Matthew 4, 1-11, Mark 1, 12-13, Luke 4, 1-13.

de Nuestro Señor por las calles y plaças así como loca, diziendo — Yo peno, yo desfallesco por amor de mi Criador y Saluador Ihesu Christo. O marauillosa y ynstimable virtud de amor, a Dios abaxa a la tierra, alça el ánima a la gloria, y a Dios y al ánima en vno ata con engrudo de amor, a Dios haze onbre y al onbre haze Dios, a lo tenporal haze perdurable, mata lo mortal, y lo mortal haze ynmortal, y a lo baxo haze alto, al enemigo haze amigo, al sieruo haze hijo, y lo abobinable haze glorioso, y la cosa fria haze ençender de fuego, la cosa obscura házela clara, la cosa dura házela rregalada. Deuota hermana, pensando con grande amor en el Señor que estas cosas haze y quánd dulçemente vos habla por la sagrada escritura, puede dezir la vuestra ánima — La mi ánima es rregalada quando el mi amado me habla.[5] O palabra marauillosa, o palabra muy deleytable, yo muy vil sierua Tuya, Señor Dios mío, que avn non soy digna de ser llamada alguna criatura ni de serlo como soy atada a Ti con tanto atamiento de caridat, por tal que a la Tu palabra sea hecha rregalada por amor. O ardor de amor que las cosas de dentro del alma derramadas en Dios, porque la mi ánima era a las cosas amadas y lo de dentro della era muy aconpañado, agora por ardor de amor se rregala, agora sale fuera de sí y en Dios de todo en todo se derrama, el lugar propio desanpara y en Dios corre, es absor-[fol. 34v]bida de Dios y es oluidada de sí mesma. O amor, qué Te daré, que me heziste, Señor, biuo. Yo ya non biuo, mas biue en mí Ihesu Christo mi Señor, virtud tuya que no se puede contar. O amor, quel lodo transfiguras en Dios, pues así es, qué cosa es más poderosa que Tú, qué cosa es mas dulçe que Tú. Con deseo Te rruego, qué cosa ay mas alegre que Tú, qué cosa ay más noble que Tú. Yo Te rruego, buen amor, que pones en el çielo la cosa terrenal, que me rrespondas a esto. Menbrándome de Ti, desfallesco, y fázesme ser ayuntado al Tu muy amado. Pues así es, dezid — O ánima mía, ama a Dios Padre por amor singular, que tan noblemente de ninguna cosa te formó, a Dios Fijo, que tan ynstimable te formó muriendo por ti, a Dios Spíritu Santo, que tan misericordiosamente y dulçemente muchas vezes confortándote te guardó de pecado. Pues así es, ama a Dios Padre fuertemente, por tal que por ningund amor peligroso seáys vençida, amad a Dios Hijo sabiamente, por tal que por ningund otro amor engañosamente seáys atraýda, amad a Dios Spíritu Santo dulçemente, por tal que por ningund otro amor seáys veninosamente enfeçionada. O en otra manera, segund dize Sant Bernaldo — O ánima christiana, aprende de Nuestro Señor Ihesu Christo en qué manera deuas amar a ese mesmo Christo. Amalde dulçemente, fuertemente prudentemente. Dulçemente por tal que por el amor del todo amor vos sea hecho vil, Él solo vos deue ser hecho miel en la boca, dulçura en la oreja, alegría en

5 Song of Songs, 5,6 — 'My soul failed me when he spoke'.

el coraçón. Prudentemente por tal que el vuestro amor en el sol y non en otro ninguno [fol. 35r] continuamente se ardesca fuertemente, por tal que la vuestra flaqueza todas las cosas duras y ásperas por Dios gozosamente las sufráys y digáys — El mi trabajo apenas es de vna ora, y si más es, non lo siento por el amor.[6] Gerónimo así — El christiano cada día vaya por amor en Ihesu Christo, porque todas cosas sufra por Él fasta que venga a Él. Amemos sienpre a Ihesu Christo y queramos sienpre llegarnos a los sus abraços y ligeramente serán vistas todas las cosas ligeras.[7] Anbrosio — O ánima, trata sienpre en la tu voluntad quánd dulçemente te amó Ihesu Christo en la encarnaçión, quánd prudentemente en la conversaçión, quánd fuertemente en la pasión. Ningunt amor ay mayor, ninguna caridat ay más linpia, ningunt amor ay más fuerte. El ynoçente es muerto por ti, ninguna cosa hallando en ti que amase. Dize Sant Agostín — Quando amo a mi Dios, non amo la semejança o la hermosura del tienpo o el rresplandor de la luz, porque estas cosas son amigables a los ojos, non las dulçes molodías [*sic*], non los enguentos que suaue & mucho huelen, non la mana y las mieles, non los mienbros de la carne conuenibles a los abraços, non amo aquestas cosas quando amo a Dios, mas amo vna luz, una boz, vn olor, vn manjar, vn abraço del omne de dentro, adonde el lugar del ánima rresplandeçe aquella cosa que non toma lugar, adonde suena aquella cosa que non toma tienpo, adonde bien huele aquello que non derrama el soplo, adonde sabe aquello que la hartura non mengua, adonde se allega [fol. 35v] aquello que la conpañía non aparta.[8] O hermana, verdaderamente el fruto de la

6 This is quoted by Thomas Hibernicus, *Flores* (Placentia, 1483) under *amor*: 'Dilexit nos deus dulciter sapienter fortiter. Dulciter nempe carne induit dixerim, quia carnem induit, sapienter quia culpam cauit. Fortiter quia mortem sustinuit. Disce ergo christiane a Christo quem admodum diligas Christum. Disce amare dulciter ne illecti, prudenter ne decepti, fortiter ne compressi deficiamus. Bernardus super cantica, sermone XX. My thanks to Professor J. E. Cross for suggesting Thomas Hibernicus as a possible source.

7 *Cf. Epistolas de S. Hieronymo*, trans. Juan de Molina (Valencia: Juan Joffre, 1520), Book IV, epistle I, dedicated to the Virgen Eustochio, daughter of Saint Paula, especially stanza eleven, which is addressed to Eustochio and all Christians 'para que facilmente sepan los tormentos y trabajos desta vida por graues que sean pues vengan por ell amor de dios ...', at clxii *verso*.

8 This is in fact Rabanus Maurus, very loosely translated, and found again under *amor* in Thomas Hibernicus, 'Amor diuinus est ignis, lux, mel, vinum sol. Ignis in meditatione purificas mentem a sordibus. Lux est in oratione, mentem irradians claritate virtutum. Mel est in gratiarum actione, mentem dulcoran dulcedine de uinorum beneficiorum. Vinum est in contenplatione. Mente inebrians suaui iocunda delectatione. Sol est i eterna

caridat es grande, mas es oculto. En verdat, en las aduersidades sufre, en las prosperidades es tenplada, en las pasiones dubdosas es fuerte, en las buenas obras es alegre, en las tentaçiones muy segura, en ospedar es muy liberal, entre los verdaderos hermanos es muy bienauenturada, entre los falsos es muy paçiente, es segura entre las cosas malas, entre las aborresçibles es benífica, entre las yras es plazentera, entre las açechanças es ynoçente, entre las maldades geme, en la verdad rrespira. Sant Bernaldo dize — Amor, de ti nasçe la estremidad de las costunbres, la pureza de los talantes, la sotileza de los entendimientos, la santidad de los deseos, la claridad de las obras, la preñés de las virtudes, la dignidat de los merescimientos, el alteza de los gualardones. Bernaldo — O ánima, quant dulçe es el manjar de la caridad, el qual aliuia a los cansados, haze fuerte a los flacos, alegre a los tristes, y el yugo de la verdat haze suaue y carga dél ligera.[9] Dize más Sant Bernaldo — Yo confieso non sentí la carga del día y del calor, mas traygo la carga suaue y ligera. Digo en verdat, la mi (obra a+)penas es de vna ora, y si más es, non la siento por el amor. Qué más. O hermana, tanta es la fuerça del amor que es nesçesario que seáys quales aquello que amáys y al qual por talante vos ayuntáes en la semejança d'Él y en alguna manera en Él seáys trasformada por compañía de amor, así como el fierro es trasformado en el fuego. Dize Sant Agostín — Bienauenturado es aquel [fol. 36r] que te ama y al enemigo por ti y al amigo en ti. Pues así es, toda criatura vos sea fecha vil por tal que sólo el Vuestro Criador vos sea hecho dulçe en el coraçón.[10] Sant Enselmo dize — O caridat, que sienpre ardes y nunca te apagas. Dios mío, ençiéndeme, dame aquello que mandas, manda aquello que quieres. Y Sant Agostín dize — O omne, amemos sienpre a Ihesu Christo, y queramos sienpre allegarnos a los sus abraços. Y cada cosa difíçile será vista ser ligera. Deuota hermana, para alçar más el afecto al amor diuinal, dezid así — O muy amado Señor Ihesu Christo, o muy manso, o muy piadoso, o muy conpaçiente, o muy dulçe, o muy deseable, o muy exçelente, o muy esperable, o muy fiel, o muy glorioso, o muy graçioso, o muy alegre, o muy caritatiuo, o muy largo, o muy liberal, o muy noble, o muy poderoso, o muy tenperable, o muy claro, o

---

beatitudine. Mentem clarificans serenissimo lumine & suauissimo calore mente exhilarans ineffabili beatitudine gaudio & perenni iubilatoione. Rabanus in quondam sermone'.

9 The source seems rather to be Matthew II, 28-30.

10 This is Augustine according to Thomas Hibernicus, again under *amor*, 'Augustinus li confessionum: "Beatus qui amat te & amicum in te inimicum propter te. Solus ille carum amittit cui omnes in illo cari sunt qui non amittitur. Te nemo amittit nisi qui dimittit & quo itur nisi a te placato ad te iratum'.

muy placable, o muy manso, o muy derecho, o muy rrecreador, o muy suficiente, o muy linpio, o muy seguro, o muy tolerable, o muy prouechoso, o muy verdadero, o Ihesu Christo, Padre y Señor Nuestro, quándo me abraçaré contigo, quándo Te veré, quándo me holgaré contigo en la Tu gloria para sienpre sin fin. Deuota hermana, plega al eterno Dios que en tal manera auremos al nuestro amado buen Ihesu que quando vos hablare sea verificado en vos lo que arriba es dicho — La mi ánima es rregalada quando el mi amado me habla.

[fol. 36v]

[ID2763]LB3-17(36v-41v)(Prose),

Carta que enbió vn buen rreligioso a vna deuota hermana.

Señora esposa de mi Señor, cuya gracia sienpre en vuestro coraçón perseuere, vuestra deuota letra escripta en la santa semana de pasión rresçebí en el santo ochauario de la rresureçión. Estas son dos gloriosas memorias de vuestro esposo que deuen ser muy prestas en vuestra contenplaçión. Paresçen muy distantes & son muy vezinas, porque la vna es puerta para la otra. Ca non puede alguno gozar el gozo de la Santa rresureçión si primero non siente el grand trabajo de la pasión. Si fue forçado padesçer Nuestro Señor para entrar en su propia Gloria, como dize Sant Lucas,[11] quanto más a nos para entrar en la gloria agena, que ni es nuestra por herençia, ni por conpra. Grande presunçión sin dubda & locura es la nuestra tenernos en tanto que aquello que Nuestro Señor & todos los apóstoles, mártires, confesores & vírgines alcançaron con tan diuersos trabajos, pensemos nos aver, haziendo nuestras voluntades. Non lo digo porque nuestros méritos sean bastantes para alcançar tan soberano bien sin el mérito de la pasión suya, mas por esperança de aquélla sin méritos propios en los que han hedad llámase presunçión o locura, mas non esperança. Y a esta contenpla-[fol. 37r]çión, deuota señora, mucho dispone & aderesça la virginidat que escogistes, porque los vírgines sobre todos tienen cruçificada su carne, & por tanto sienten más aýna la pasión y el amor del cruçifixo. Ca quien beue ante que aya sed, o quandoquier que le aquexa luego beue, non sabe por çierto lo que sufre quien la detiene por fuerte que la tenga en tienpo del estío. Por tanto creed que cruçificar la carne non aprouecha sinón para creçer en el amor del cruçifixo. Aquél es el cubil en que auedes de rreposar con vuestro esposo, sola con solo, cruçificada con cruçificado. Aquél es el libro de la vida en que en pocas fojas deprenderedes la mayor çiençia del mundo.

---

11 Luke 24, 46-47.

Como Nuestro Señor mostró, todo el estudio de los omnes ser loco en buscar el estado, nonbradía, honor & fama, deleytes, hazienda, pues el rrrey de los rreyes desnudo & escarnesçido con fiel & vinagre fizo las carnestoliendas desta miserable vida. De la tal liçión auedes de mirar dos cosas para conosçer quáles somos en la maliçia & quién es Nuestro Señor en bondat. Nuestra grande maliçia & dolençia paresçe en la grandeza de la medeçina, ca por çierto grande es la llaga que tal física rrequiere, grande [fol. 37v] es la culpa que por muerte de corderos ni sacrifiçio de bezerros ni por muerte de todos los omnes que a ella fueron condepnados non pudo ser curada sinón por muerte del mesmo físico que muriendo por los enfermos los sanó, açotado por ellos los libró, pagando por ellos los absoluió. Non pudo ser mayor bondat & caridat en el físico ni mayor dolençia en los enfermos. Por esta consideraçión sobiredes muy ligera al amor de Nuestro Señor. Tanta caridat mirando & marauillando, desçenderedes más aýna a considerar nuestra enfermedat & propia miseria que es todo el solar de la vmilldat. O qué escalera tan alta, tan presta, tan segura para sobir sin miedo a mirar & marauillar, a deleytar, espaçiar el spíritu & ensanchar el coraçón, esperar, confiar, deleytarle, contentarle para non desear otra cosa. O qué letuario cordial, o qué panar de miel gostar aquella hiel que beuió, aquel vinagre que tomó. Éstos son los abraços de vuestro esposo, éstos son los besos, los deleytes del matrimonio. Non es todo cruz lo que se [fol. 38r] gosta de la cruz, que quiere dezir que non es todo tormento lo que de aquel tormento con deuoçión se piensa. Por esto cantamos dulçe arbol, dulçes clauos, dulçe peso sin pesar, lleno de todo plazer. Piensa, deuota virgen, que non se alcança el fruto deste árbol disputando en las escuelas, rreboluiendo los libros, afeytando las palabras, edificando grandes edifiçios para orar, faziendo grandes aparejos de ornamentos & rretretes pintados para contenplar, avnque todo esto sea bueno en sus tienpos. Pero más aýna se goza mirando, marauillando, callando, apartándose de lo público, del bolliçio & del negosçio seglar, sinón quanto la obidiençia manda & la caridat rrequiere. O señora, qué grande bien vos fizo Dios a las mugeres en la santa contenplaçión tan apartada, tan secreta, tan quieta, tan deleytosa, & sabes por qué, que non tenedes tantos colores para vos apartar destos abraços como los omnes que nos sacan a enseñar, a pedricar, a castigar, a gouernar & avn a guerrear en las órdenes de la caualleria corporal. Buenos abtos son, mas rrequieren varones perfectos que non se derramen, que non se estraguen, [fol. 38v] adobando a los otros que tales se estén en la plaça como en la cámara, así fuertes contra los soberuios que queden blandos a los vmildes, ansí discurran andando por el mundo & con el mundo que estén quietos en su spíritu como si estouiesen ençerrados, que vean & non cobdiçien, que oyan contra sí mesmos & non lo sientan como non deuen. Quien será éste, & alabarlo emos, varón digno de tanta alabança. Non sé quién por tal se tiene muy presentuoso, o muy santo apóstol o su semejante. Ninguna destas ocasiones de apartamiento de la contenplaçión tenedes vosotras, ca el broslar & el filar non es abto que quiere mucha conpaña para salir de la sonbra deste árbol de la vera cruz del jardín de tal arboleda, de tal verdura donde oyredes cantar aquel dulçe rruyseñor, como demanda por nos en quanto omne perdón al Padre segunt la diuinidat, como encomienda aquella bendita Madre & Virgen al virgen Sant Juan,[12] como rresponde al santo ladrón tan copiosamente, tan piadosamente, tan prestamente. Non le puso el libramiento del paraýso muy alexos como a los patriarcas, non ascondido en figuras como a los profetas, non le respondió a la demanda [fol. 39r] como a los apóstolos fijos del Zebedeo que non sabían lo que se demandauan, mas a ocho palabras de demanda otras ocho por cuenta fallarás de rrepuesta & non más. O qué demanda, o qué rrepuesta. — Acuérdate, Señor, de mí quando vinieres en el tu reyno. — Çiertamente te digo ,oy serás comigo en el paraýso.[13] Piense aquí la deuota ánima que nuestras oraçiones non alcançan lo que quieren por muchas palabras sinón por grande fe & grande deuoçión, grande amor. Quantos salmos fizo Dauid, quantas petiçiones los profetas, & nunca tal rrepuesta ouieron fasta — Oy en el paraýso. Non ay cras ni ayer, todo es oy. Porque aquella breue oraçión salió de la mayor fee que jamás omne pecador en esta vida touo en su coraçón & mostró en su confisión por la boca. O fee sin conparaçión, llamar rrey aquel que veýa consigo aconpañado en el tormento, demandándole misericordia quando viniese en el su rreyno, castigar al otro peruerso ladrón que estaua blasfemando & confesar tan abiertamente su vida mala y la pena que padesçía ser justa. O santo ladrón — dónde aprendiste tan grand çiençia, conosçiste tan grand sabiduría? Los sabios [fol. 39v] de la ley estauan escarnesçiendo, procurando su muerte, & tú le confiesas rrey. O omne sin ley que nunca letra leýste nin sopiste al sinón furtar, — dónde hurtaste tan grande fee, arrebataste tan aýna tanta deuoçión, tomaste ante que todos la posesión del paraýso? Por aquella mesma fee que touiste te rrogamos, por aquella confisión que feziste te llamamos, pues ya veniste de la cruz al rreyno que demandaste por tu oraçión, ayamos parte en la gloria donde entraste, amén. Direýs agora vos, mi fija señora, que me he derramado mucho por esta arboleda. Perdónadme, que encontrando con el santo ladrón non me pude pasar sin hablarle, sin encomendarme a él, sin gozarme con él. Grande gozo es a los dolientes de yncurables dolençias quando se hablan con aquellos que se curaron de aquéllas o

12 John 19, 25-27.

13 The Good Thief, Luke 23, 39-43.

peores. Con quánto plazer les suelen preguntar por el físico donde mora, o quién es, o cómo fueron curados, qué les costó, si fueron las melezinas muy amargas, si ouo menester fierros, fuego, o si es cosa que se puede sofrir & soportar de tales rremedios. Deseo fablar con este ladrón tan bendito por saber bien cómo fue tan aýna curado, tan graçiosa & ligeramente librado. Ca a la verdat, aquel [fol. 40r] santo día non veo santo alguno a quien me ose llegar a hablar de mis culpas, a descobrir mis llagas sinón a él. Que busque a Sant Pedro, el saçerdote mayor está ocupado en llorar su pecado porque tres vezes negó a su Maestro & Señor. Con rrazón me rresponderá — Déxame llorar mi culpa, & consiguiendo el perdón que demando rrogaré por ti. Que quiera estar con Sant Juan, va huyendo & non ay quien lo alcançen desnudo, que le podré dezir de mis culpas a quien non quiere esperar. Quise con el fablar açerca del árbol de la santa cruz. Vilo estar ocupado en tomar su posesión de aquella santa encomienda que le dieron de Nuestra Señora, ca él mesmo dize que luego la tomó en suya, quiere dezir en su Señora, para la seruir & guardar. Pero pare yo mientes lo que tomaua Sant Juan, porque desque ouiese espaçio para hablar & dsemandar merçed a tan exçelente Señora, hallé buen entrada por su rruego deste tan amigo & secretario, mas aquella ora non era conueniente para demandar misericordia a la Madre de misericordia penetrada del cuchillo de la muerte de tan exçelente Fijo tan sin misericordia & con tanta crueldat muerto delante sus ojos. Así que mirando a toda (la+) familia de Nuestro Señor en este santo día, non fallo persona que tan bien ni tan espaçiosamente fable en plaça con Él nin por Él sinón sólo con el ladrón, después que començó Nuestro Señor [fol. 40v] Rrey la batalla de la pasión. Dad vno que vna buena sola palabra dixiese a Él o rrepondiese por Él, entrad con Él en casa de Anás, en casa de Cayfás, & en casa de Pilatos. Aconpañaldo fasta la cruz & escuchad bien lo que dizen, & veredes si ay oreja católica que tal cosa pueda oýr sin espanto, sin rreteñirle los oýdos. Con todo esto ouo alguno que dixiese — Mal dicho es esto que dezides contra este ynoçente, contra tan santo varón, sinón solo el ladrón santo. Pilatus dixo algunas palabras en su escusa, pero luego las rreuocó el mezquino con sus manos. Non touo coraçón para rresistir a la maliçia. Ca con grande miedo luego consintió en ella & fizo todo lo que ellos demandaron. Miro yo al bendito ladrón de espaçio fablar con el Rrey, rrresponder por el vn solo escudero suyo, vn solo diçípulo, vn solo priuado, vn solo canonizado por la boca de Nuestro Señor en esta vida. A quién me puedo llegar mejor aquel día que rruegue por mi salud sinón al que es çierto de la suya después de tan grande dolençia. Por tanto pensad que antes que partiese desta vida el santo ladrón quise estar con Él & encomendarme a Él, & avn agora non acabaría de hablar d'Él sinón porque el Rrey quiere partir. Açércase ya la ora de la nona. Beuido ha para caminar vinagre sobre çinco mill açotes. Veredes si bastan para vn beuer & para emendar [fol. 41r] nuestro mal biuir contra la maliçia humanal. Ya peresçe el testimonio çelestial. El sol se escuresçe, la cortina del tenplo se rronpe & peresçe, rrónpense las piedras, ábrense las sepolturas, rresuçitan algunos muertos. El sol escuresçe a los ynfieles para amanesçera los católicos. Rrónpese la cortina del tenplo por que perescan los secretos de las escrituras & figuras antiguas.Rrónpense las piedras para rronper nuestros duros coraçones a contriçión & a conpasión de la cruel pasión de Nuestro Rredenptor. Ábrense los munimentos para abrir todas nuestras culpas por pura confisión. Rresuçitan al terçero día los finados con Nuestro Señor para que dexada la vida vieja rresuçitemos en vida nueua todos conformes a Él. E así el bueno & dulçe Señor entre tantos testimonios de su santidat & de la otra parte escarnios dela maliçia humanal, clamando, orando, llorando, rrecomendada aquella preçiosísima ánima & ofreçida en preçio & en pago, conplido de nuestra rredençión, ynclinando la cabeça, espiró sospirando más por nuestros pecados que por sus dolores. Señora hija hermana bendita, en esta spiraçión rrespiremos de todas nuestras angustias, sospiremos por nuestras culpas, aspiremos a seguir sus vías, esperemos sus yndulgençias de todas nuestras dolençias. Mandástesme & demandástesme que todavía vos escriuiese & avnque me escusé que non [fol. 41v] sabía cosa que para vos fuese que pudiese ditar de nueuo, non açebtastes mi escusa, e por tanto tomé la péñola en la mano, & non me ocurrió mejor tema para fablar con esa vuestra deuota ánima que de la hecha de vuestra carta, & la rreçebta quando yo la rresçebí, ca la fezistes en el día que leýan en la Semana Santa la pasión de Vuestro Esposo, & yo la rresçebí en su santa rresureçión. De lo que pensaua comigo hablando en mi spíritu quise comunicar con el vuestro, así como si ya fuésemos destos sacos mortales despojados por muerte, e porque el pensar de Nuestro Señor con algund amor para despertar la deuoçión non rrequiere forma escolástica para que vaya polido de palabras, distinto en orden de capítulos, actorizado por glosas & dichos de doctores. Ca el pensamiento del amor non cura que vaya en orden, lo que quiere dezir sinón solamente abrirse como puede, como el que tiene grande dolor non está esperando de abrir al físico sus angustias en rrimos o en oraçión rretórica sinón a bozes o comoquier que puede. Así non cure de tener la péñola sinón dexarla correr como hiziese mas áyna correr las lágrimas & desleýr & domar la dureza deste coraçión de fierro, & así me fue fablando con vos fasta ver la partida de Nuestro Señor, que fue la hecha desta vuestra carta & la desecha de la carta obligatoria que nuestro enemigo tenía sobre nos, la qual non se pudo quitar.

Honey without God: Francisco de Osuna's Higher Memory

JOHN N. JONES

Yale University

The works of Francisco de Osuna (1492?-1540?), the grandfather of Spanish Christian mysticism, were enormously popular in sixteenth-century Western Europe. His Castilian and Latin works underwent dozens of editions, influencing Juan de la Cruz and Juan de Ávila, among others. Santa Teresa de Ávila identifies Osuna's *Tercer Abecedario Espiritual* as formative for her early spiritual development. From the beginning, in the earliest studies of his thought, Osuna has been interpreted in light of Quietism, that is, the view that in order to achieve union with God one must ultimately reject thought about the objects of the world.[1] Eduard Boehmer discusses Osuna in relation to the *beata* Francisca Hernández and the Spanish *alumbrados*.[2] Henry Charles Lea, influenced

1 For the sake of this study, I will limit the discussion of Quietism to the question 'What is the status of objects of sense regarding the mystical union with God?' Quietism can be defined in a number of other ways, however. As we shall see, Osuna's use of 'Quiet' includes both a renunciation of the world and a gesture beyond renunciation. But even this broader conception of Quiet falls short of the reconciliation between sense objects and mind that Osuna's higher memory makes possible.

2 Eduard Boehmer, *Franzisca Hernández und Frai Franzisco Ortiz: Anfänge reformatischer Bewegungen in Spanien unter Kaiser Karl V* (Leipzig: H. Haessel, 1865), 233-310, 'Anhang: Franzisco de Osuna'. Fidèle De Ros (*Un maître de Sainte Thérèse, le Père François d'Osuna, sa vie, son oeuvre, sa doctrine spirituelle*, in *Études de Théologie Historique* [Paris: G. Beauchesne,

by Boehmer's work and supposing that mystics of all religious traditions tend toward Quietism, writes that Osuna himself is a Quietist.[3] E. Allison Peers, on the other hand, the first scholar to translate into English any portion of Osuna's work,[4] implies that Osuna's affirmations of the beauty of creation and creation's role in contemplation are not Quietistic in tone, noting that Osuna claims to reject Quietism. None the less, Peers, along with the vast majority of scholars, accepts the idea that the state of Quiet occupies the highest level in Osuna's mysticism. This raises the question: if every passage of his central mystical text, *Tercer Abecedario Espiritual*, merely prepares the way for the 'no pensar nada' of *Tercer Abecedario Espiritual*, treatise 21, why is it that, as Peers maintains, Osuna is not a Quietist?

It is possible to vindicate Peers' insight. Osuna is not a Quietist because, quite simply, Quiet does not occupy the highest level in his mystical theology. Osuna explicitly states this in *Tercer Abecedario Espiritual*, though with so little fanfare that the reader may easily overlook the claim and its significance: the 'memoria más alta' announced in the eleventh treatise of his *Tercer Abecedario Espiritual* is higher than the state of Quiet.[5] In this essay, I very briefly discuss why, for Osuna, the mind must abandon thoughts about the objects of

---

1936], ix), cites C. A. Wilkens as well ('Zur Geschichte der spanischen Mystik, Teresa de Jesus', *Zeitschrift für Wissenschaftliche Theologie*, V [1862], 111-180).

3 Henry Charles Lea, *Chapters from the Religious History of Spain connected with the Inquisition* (Philadelphia: Lea Brothers and Company, 1890), 223. Lea also addresses Quietism as antinomianism.

4 Peers, *Studies of the Spanish Mystics*, vol. I (henceforth, *Studies* I) (London: Sheldon Press, 1927), 118 *ff*. In a footnote, Peers dismisses Lea's claim that Osuna is 'virtually' a Quietist, saying 'it is clear that [Lea] entirely misreads Osuna, and can hardly have studied him with any care'. This judgement is a bit severe. The difficulty in interpreting Osuna stems as much from Osuna's labyrinthine style as from any carelessness on the reader's part.

5 *Tercer Abecedario Espiritual* will be the only work of Osuna's cited in this essay. De Ros (*op. cit.*, xii-xiii) understandably regrets that most commentators discuss only this work and, rarely, the *Fourth Alphabet*. The problem I address here, however, is not unfamiliarity with all of Osuna's texts, but an incomplete reading of one text.

the world.[6] I then call attention to Osuna's higher memory. By understanding that Osuna posits a state beyond Quiet, and that in Osuna's opinion this state harmonizes the mind's relation to God with its relation to the world, one can more adequately interpret both the work's climax — the well-known twenty-first treatise — and its prologue. In other words, this higher memory, which forms part of the very structure of Osuna's theology, is integrated into *Tercer Abecedario Espiritual* from beginning to end.[7]

I The mind lets go of objects

Perhaps the most frequently-repeated claim about Osuna's theology is that he considers *recogimiento* (recollection) to be the highest stage of the mystical life. *Recoger* conveys both senses of 'to recollect': to remember a fact or an image and to gather objects together again. Osuna's discussion of the senses and memory draws heavily from Augustine of Hippo's *De Trinitate*. Augustine asks what it could mean to say that humans are created in the image of God.[8] He discusses the mind's operations regarding objects of sense, whether directly

---

6 The details of how Osuna advises one to let go of the objects of the senses are discussed by de Ros. In this study, I do not address the differences among the sorts of persons Osuna counsels and the kinds of renunciation appropriate to each. For instance, being 'deaf and blind and dumb' does not occur at the same stage as 'thinking nothing'. Yet both stages are similar with respect to the marginalization of the phenomenal world. However many methods Osuna may have for letting go of the world, *no* such method represents the highest stage of mystical ascent in Osuna's system.

7 Laura Calvert argues convincingly that the apparently random connections Osuna makes among various symbols in fact conform to consistent patterns. She begins this task in the introduction to her *Ideas and Style in the Spiritual Alphabets of Francis of Osuna* (unpublished doctoral dissertation, Ohio State Univ., 1966), especially 7-27. Her later writings on Osuna carry out the task (see *Francisco de Osuna and the Spirit of the Letter* [Chapel Hill, NC: Univ. of North Carolina, 1973]). As De Ros (*op. cit.*, 428) has noted, Osuna does not offer an explicit outline of his theology. So this essay strives to continue Calvert's project in another realm, showing Osuna's consistent use of the concept of higher memory.

8 That is, in the image of the Trinity in the individual soul. Previous writers do not emphasize the Trinitarian nature of the image (Origen) or locate the image in corporate humanity (Gregory of Nyssa).

perceived or remembered, then other operations (or modes) that do not pertain to the senses. Although memory, will, and understanding operate together, only one, memory, predominates. The point at which the modes are united through memory is the point of contact between mind and God. To gather together one's scattered thoughts is to remember God's presence in the soul. As we shall see, Osuna employs similar language.

In the title of treatise 3 of *Tercer Abecedario Espiritual*, Osuna 'muestra cómo se ha de haver el anima con Dios, diciendo: ciego y sordo y mudo deves ser y manso siempre'.[9] If one is filled with impressions from the senses, one will not be able to approach God, since God cannot be known by the senses. Interpreting Paul's ascent to the third heaven in Acts 9, Osuna writes:

> ... y no solamente estava ciego de la ceguedad corporal, que no hace al caso presente, mas también estava ciego de la ceguedad espiritual de que hablamos por la otra figurada, lo cual paresce, pues que él dice que no sabía si entonces estava en el cuerpo ó fuera del cuerpo. Y también digo que su ánima estava entonces ciega, porque en tal manera fué suspensa, que las potencias inferiores, esto es, los sentidos exteriores é interiores, y así mesmo la razón, no pudieron salir en sus operaciones; mas cesaron por entonces de sus actos é obras, siendo las operaciones destas potencias del todo quitadas entretanto que duró aquel su arrebatamiento ...[10]

Sense information operates in two ways. A person can perceive an object directly or can have a memory of what the object was like, for instance, its shape or colour. Osuna follows Augustine in distinguishing between the two senses, exterior and interior, and in subordinating both as inferior to other mental processes. The functioning of both, moreover, is interrupted in a rapture such as Paul's.

---

9 *Tercer Abecedario Español.* In Nueva Biblioteca de Autores Españoles, vol. 16, *Escritores místicos españoles* I, ed. Miguel Mir (Madrid: Casa Editorial Bailly-Baillière, 1911), 348. All Spanish quotations are from this volume. Except where otherwise noted, all English translations are from Mary E. Giles' lucid translation *Third Spiritual Alphabet* (New York/ Ramsey/Toronto: Paulist Press, 1981).

10 Mir, *ed. cit.*, 350.

Elsewhere, Osuna will make clear that he does not place a high value on all raptures.[11] He mentions rapture only in order to call attention to the existence of a mental state in which the mind's activity is not directed toward sense data. In cases such as Paul's, moreover, this state is not a sign of mental dysfunction but a moment of divine import, a heavenly ascent. As a result, Osuna claims, it is possible for the mind to let go of any thought of objects of the senses.

Osuna will devote much of *Tercer Abecedario Espiritual* to the question of abandonment of the objects of sense. Since this aspect of his thought has already been recognized and studied well,[12] let us proceed to a less understood topic. What follows abandonment?

II The mind regathers the objects

The eleventh treatise of *Tercer Abecedario Espiritual* 'nos amonesta que traigamos a Dios en nuestra memoria'.[13] In the second chapter, 'de cómo devemos traer ocupada nuestra memoria',[14] Osuna, praising memory, argues that objects have a permanent existence, living eternally as ideas in God's memory:

> [A]llí mejor que en dechado están las ideas de todas las cosas y las razones seminales de todo lo posible; en tal manera que, aunque la cosa muera en sí mesmo, no muere en la memoria de Dios; mas siempre están en ella todas las cosas registradas é muy conoscidas según son, para que allí como en perfecto libro de la vida lean los ángeles lo que Dios quiere que sepan. En aquel solo libro se halla esciencia de los individuos, porque allí son inmortales, participando de la inmortalidad que sólo Dios tiene; al cual y por el cual y en el cual todas las cosas biven.[15]

---

11 Osuna's prologue, in Mir, *ed. cit.*, 320-23, esp. p. 321. Strictly speaking, Osuna recognizes two kinds of raptures, experienced by two kinds of mystics. But the line between the two raptures is not firm, and their difference is not important to the present essay.

12 Much of de Ros' book is devoted to this topic.

13 Mir, *ed. cit.*, 440, title.

14 *Ibid.*, 441.

15 *Ibid.*, 442.

Osuna has already advised one to be 'deaf and blind and dumb': 'desembaraza el corazón y vacia todo lo criado'.[16] Yet this passage suggests that the same objects of creation removed from thought in order to achieve union with God are eternally present in God's memory.[17] In fact, when discussing the image of God that each person is, Osuna writes:

> No seas, pues, tú, o hombre que eres imagen de Dios, tan olvidadizo que parezcas imagen contrahecha é muy al revés de aquello que representa; porque si en Dios todas las cosas biven y en ti todas las todas mueren, seréis muy contrarios.[18]

The question for the reader is: how can the one seeking union with God be both blind to and in memory of the objects of the world? Osuna gives two answers. First, objects can remind one of God if what is valuable in them is credited to God. Osuna explains:

> ... [A]sí que con el pan más te mantiene Dios que el pan, y con el vino te da Dios más fuerza que no él, y con la miel te da Dios más dulcedumbre que no ella, porque la miel sin Dios no sería dulce y Dios sin ella lo es ... é tú no miras en ello aunque cuasi cada vez que beves el buen vino de tu tinaja te acuerdas de la viña ó majuelo que lo lleva, sin el cual no solamente el vino no tuviera ser, mas aun no tiene ser ni sabor ni color ni olor sin Dios, que cada momento le da ser y lo conserva y le da las operaciones consiguientes y que le pertenece.[19]

Osuna is referring to God as cause. Without God, nothing could be what it is or do what it does; for instance, honey would not be sweet. Being blind to the objects of the world does not mean ignoring their existence, but rather using them in a different way. Reasoning about objects will not lead one away from God if in the very act of thinking about each object one relates it to God's sustaining activity. Properly understood, creation can point away from itself to God.

Second, Osuna continues, beyond all the kinds of

---

16 *Ibid.*, 348; 355, title of treatise four.

17 On the basis of neoplatonic passages such as this, I conclude that Osuna, despite his frequent references to Jean Gerson, remains virtually untouched by nominalism.

18 Mir, *ed. cit.*, 442.

19 *Ibid.*, 444.

remembering or recollection he has been discussing lies 'otra memoria más alta':[20]

> La perfecta memoria de Dios que yo aquí querría amonestar es un ejercicio de más importancia y más alto que no el que hemos dicho; y conviene mucho á los que siguen el recogimiento, porque lo presupone; é para que sea perfecta esta memoria de Dios es menester que caiga sobre el recogimiento, la cual lo perfecciona y le da más biveza.[21]

Even perfect recollection is a death, Osuna writes, because the exterior senses are not used, but the higher memory of God is a 'resurrección espiritual':

> ... [C]a esta memoria de Dios hace que obren todas las cosas interiores y exteriores del hombre, dándoles una operación sencilla que se compadece con el recogimiento; la cual no es sino una representación de Dios en su desnudo ser.[22]

This is remarkable language. 'Higher' and 'loftier' show that in the hierarchy of stages this one is above recollection. The metaphor of death, for recollection, and the metaphor of resurrection, for higher memory, show emphatically that recollection is not the highest state in the unitive life.[23]

---

20 *Ibid.*, 444, title of chapter 3.

21 *Ibid.* The phrase 'que caiga sobre el recogimiento' is remarkable. One might expect Osuna to have continued the metaphor of ascent for this memory beyond recollection. But 'caer' clarifies the work that this memory is supposed to do. If the enraptured ascend to heaven, those whose mental faculties are harmonized fall (or 'tumble') back to earth and the objects of the senses.

22 Mir, *ed. cit.*, 444.

23 In a list of Osuna's metaphors for the spiritual life, Hans-Jürgen Prien correctly includes 'resurrection', but incorrectly suggests that Osuna applies the metaphor to recollection itself (*Francisco de Ossuna: Mystik und Rechtfertigung. Ein Beitrag zur Erforschung der spanischen Theologie und Frömmigkeit in der ersten Hälfte des sechzehnten Jahrhunderts* [Hamburg: Hamburg Univ., 1967], 60).

In *Studies* I, 109, Peers makes passing mention of this higher memory. He implies that it is hard to reconcile the operation of memory with a Quietude in which the mind's faculties cease their operation. Since he is convinced that the Prayer of Quiet must be the pinnacle of Osuna's theology, however, he shifts higher memory to a stage, which he calls active exercise, preceding Quiet. Yet this demotion is quite the opposite of what Osuna

How does this higher memory function? Osuna describes it at length:

> Esta memoria de Dios que hemos de tener no es sensitiva, quiero decir que más obra en este negocio la memoria intelectiva que no la sensitiva; porque la sensitiva tiene en sí la representación de la cosa sin derramarse á condiciones que particularizan la cosa, sino en universal y generalmente. Por una manera alta se acuerda de Dios que un ser no limitado, una bondad no medible, un principio que no se comienza, un fin que no se acaba, un henchimiento que nada deja vacio, una fuerza invencible, un saber que nada ignora; en tal manera, que cuando nos acordásemos de Dios y le pusiésemos algún nombre, luego hemos de generalizar el tal nombre quitándole todo lo que pueda sonar limitación ó imperfección, asi como si le dijéramos ser piélago hemos de añadir sin suelo ni ribera, y si lo llamásemos maestro hemos de añadir universal, que no puede errar; si lo llamáremos majestad hemos de añadir que no puede ser disminuída, y desta manera siempre obrará la memoria intelectiva sin que cese el recogimiento á un solo bien.[24]

Previously, as we saw, Osuna discussed and diminished the importance of the direct perception of objects and the memory of such perception. The intellectual memory here discussed, however, does not displace the sensitive memory but enables it to function without separating one from God. The sentence 'intellectual memory operates here rather than sensitive memory' could be somewhat misleading in this regard. The former need not always operate *independently* of the latter; its manner of operation is merely different.

For the purpose of this study, it is not necessary to analyse in detail what this manner of operation is.[25] It suffices to notice

---

proposes. Quiet is not the 'reward and crown' of higher memory (101): higher memory perfects and moves beyond Quiet.

Laura Calvert ('The Exercise of Recollection According to Osuna', *Journal of Religious Studies*, XV [1989], Nos. 1-2, 65) mentions this higher memory, but does not investigate its relation to recollection.

24 Mir, *ed. cit.*, 444-45.

25 A fuller understanding of this passage might require a study of the translations of and influential commentaries on the pseudo-Dionysian corpus available to Osuna. The passage appears to employ both the specific names of God in and the abstractive theological method of *The Divine Names*. Calvert has also suggested a link between the passage and Aquinas' thought (*Ideas*,

that Osuna describes a way to move beyond Quiet, beyond the opposition between world and God. One kind of memory of God revivifies the perception of and memory of the world.

Although Osuna does not mention this principle of integration repeatedly, he applies it consistently throughout his work. Indeed, this higher memory helps one interpret both the climax and beginning of Osuna's *Tercer Abecedario Espiritual* more adequately. For instance, in the title of treatise 21 of *Tercer Abecedario Espiritual*, the most widely read treatise in Osuna's writings, Osuna advises one: 'intimamente asosiega y acalla tu entendimiento'.[26] The language of quiet, calm and silence predominate in this passage. At first glance, the title could seem to imply that Osuna's God is found only when the world is left behind. Osuna guards against this misreading in two ways. First, he indicates that, unlike an earlier stage of Quiet, the highest of the three stages of Quiet is not purely empty, a mere rejection of thought about the things of the world. The soul 'se ve[e] tan endiosada y unida á su molde [de Dios] ...'. That is, the mind is not thinking about any 'thing' because it is thinking about the God who is beyond finitude, beyond all things.[27] Second, even this highest kind of Quiet is a preparation for a more complete union with God:

> [E]ste no pensar nada es más que suena ... [E]ste no pensar nada de que hablamos, por bajo que sea, es un disponerse el hombre desasiéndose y desembarazándose para bolar con el corazón á sólo Dios que nos lo demanda libre y muy entero.[28]

So *no pensar nada*, one of the most famous phrases in Spanish mysticism, is not mere emptiness, nor does it represent the end of the mystical life. This kind of thinking-nothing is a preliminary to detachment, a preparation for being made whole.[29] Once this wholeness is achieved, it is no longer

---

85).

26 Mir, *ed. cit.*, 558.

27 Calvert ('The Exercise of Recollection according to Osuna', 55) has characterized this as thinking about the Infinite.

28 Mir, *ed. cit.*, 567.

29 Osuna's example for this third stage of Quiet makes this point clearly. He refers to a man who, sitting in church listening to a sermon, was so completely caught up in God that he understood nothing of the sermon's

necessary to distance oneself from the objects of the world, since they no longer interfere with the remembering of God.

This higher memory clarifies the meaning of the prologue as well. There, Osuna, apparently criticizing *dejados* (those advocating mental abandon), who unknowingly veer away from recollection and 'se apartaron de las otras sendillas algo deleitosas',[30] argues that objects of sense, such as the humanity of Christ, are ultimately not impediments to recollection:

> De manera que imperfección nuestra es tener necesidad de nos apartar de los sanctos pensamientos de cosas criadas, para nos levantar á sólo Dios más enteramente.[31]

Although detachment is necessary, it is only temporary. Osuna continues:

> Es empero de notar que aquesta imperfección ó falta que ponemos en los varones muy allegados á Dios es mejor que nuestra común perfección, porque no se dice ser imperfección sino en respecto de otro estado más perfecto ...[32]

In other words, ultimately there will be a place for creation, though to arrive at such a place one must temporarily pass through abandonment. Osuna proceeds to emphasize how abandonment is not the final destination in the contemplative life. In anticipation of his claim, mentioned above, that the sensitive nature and intellectual nature can function together,

---

content. This is quite different from the higher memory, in which the mind can harmonize an awareness of the objects of the senses even as it is focused on God.

Regarding Osuna's clarification of the various senses of Quiet in recollection, it is worth noting that Osuna himself does not endorse the phrase 'no pensar nada' as a good description of the stages of Quiet in recollection; it is a criticism waged against recollection by the uninformed and undevout (Mir, *ed. cit.*, 566).

30 Mir, *ed. cit.*, 320.

31 *Ibid.* Giles (*op. cit.*, 39) translates '... our imperfection is to think we must detach ourselves from holy thoughts about creation in order to rise more completely to God alone'. This translation, however, might leave the mistaken impression that no detachment is necessary at any point in the mystical life. I would render the passage as 'it is our imperfection to have to detach ourselves ...'.

32 Mir, *ed. cit.*, 320-21.

he writes:

> En el cielo no havrá privación de sentidos ni arrobamientos; é aun agora [in this earthly life] hay muchas personas muy allegadas á Dios que no los tienen; y la causa desto es porque en los sanctos cada cosa ejercita lo que le conviene, sin estorvarse una á otra ni disminuir su fuerza ... la gracia no desordena ni destruye la naturaleza, antes la perfecciona en sus operaciones, como la medicina sanando al hombre enfermo.[33]

The division between nature and grace is not a problem for Osuna. The things of this world belong to God and assist people in their ascent to God:

> [A]sí lo corporal fué criado para que ayudase á lo espiritual, en especial á nuestra ánima, que de otra manera no puede comenzar á elevarse á las cosas invisibles de Dios.[34]

One's understanding of the world must be altered.[35] Yet this alteration is just the beginning, and what happens thereafter is material for Osuna's later *Alphabets* — for instance, the *Fourth Alphabet*, which discusses the various ways in which love binds one to others.[36]

Conclusion

Recollection, of which Quiet is a part, is for Osuna not the highest stage of the unitive life.[37] By speaking of a memory

---

33 *Ibid.*, 321.

34 Mir, *ed. cit.*, 321.

35 Peers (*Studies* I, 88) sees this clearly: 'It is true [for Osuna] that for the weakness of our [human] nature we have perforce at times to cast out from our minds all created things. But this is the fault of ourselves, and not theirs'. Recognizing this probably plays a large part in Peers' conclusion that Osuna is not a Quietist.

36 When discussing the importance of the figure of the virgin for Osuna, Calvert characterizes 'the experience of *recogimiento* [as] that of "conceiving" Christ mentally ...' (*Ideas*, 205). This suggests a link between Osuna and mystics such as Eckhart, who writes of the birth of Christ in the soul. For Eckhart, and especially for Jan van Ruusbroeck, the mystical life is an alternation between detachment from the world and reappropriation of the world.

37 As Peers indicates (esp. 99 *ff*) and as de Ros and Calvert agree,

higher than recollection, a memory capable of reappropriating the world, Osuna relativizes Quietism as one stage among others in the mystical life. Osuna's ability to integrate mystical union and engagement with the things of the world is of some importance for understanding later Spanish mysticism. For Osuna, affirmation of the intrinsic worth of objects in the world is not an empty gesture, an afterthought appended to a system that fundamentally marginalizes or distrusts the world. In Osuna's system, world, God, and person are inherently linked. The task of the contemplative is simply to realize how this can be so. As a result, the mysticism of, say, Santa Teresa de Ávila, whose God dwells among the pots and pans, is not a corrective to any Quietism on Osuna's part, but heir to a tradition Osuna synthesizes, enriches and helps convey.

Why does Osuna write so effusively about Quiet, if not himself a Quietist? Like his Christian predecessors, Osuna regards detachment from the things of the world as a necessary stage in contemplation. Accordingly, the teachings of Francisca Hernández and others associated with *dejamiento* cannot be dismissed summarily. Osuna shares their belief that God cannot be grasped when the mind is occupied with the things of the world. Yet, Osuna adds, the problem lies not with things but with the disordered mind. As God heals the mind, the mind learns that the world and God belong together. If honey without God is not sweet, neither is God without honey.

Osuna uses 'recollection' in both a general and specific way. So one might wish to argue that the 'higher memory' is itself part of recollection, broadly conceived. Be that as it may, treatise eleven must be taken seriously. For Osuna, Quiet is not the pinnacle of the mystical life, even if that is true of recollection.

Judaeo-Islamic Traditions in Fray Luis de León: Wisdom, Unity and Light

AUDREY LUMSDEN-KOUVEL

University of Illinois at Chicago

The question to be discussed here is the way in which the writings of Fray Luis de León may reveal patterns of thought rooted in the centuries-old Judaeo-Islamic tradition.[1] The concepts, or themes, to be considered are those of wisdom, unity, and light, within the metaphysical framework which they form part of, and the specific channels, the treatise of the Spanish philosopher-poet, Solomon Ibn Gabirol (*c*.1021-1051?) known as the *Fons vitae*, with some reference to his poetry, and the *Dialoghi d'amore* of Leone Ebreo (*c*.1460-?).

Ibn Gabirol, who lived during what has been called the 'late blooming of Muslim Hispania's Indian Summer',[2] is a product of the dominant influence exercised by Islam on the emerging of a Jewish theology, based on philosophic principles, the notion of which was, as Bernard Lewis has asserted, 'alien to the Jews of Biblical and Talmudic times' (80). Though Ibn Gabirol wrote poetry in Hebrew, his philosophical work was written in Arabic, and reveals his deep knowledge of Islamic Aristotelianism and Neoplatonism. The *Fons vitae* is a Latin translation of the original Arabic, now lost, prepared for Raimundo, Archbishop of

---

1 Bernard Lewis, *The Jews of Islam* (Princeton: Princeton U. P., 1984), 67-106.

2 Stanley G. Payne, *A History of Spain and Portugal* (Madison: Wisconsin U. P., 1973), 2 vols; I, 30.

Toledo in the twelfth century.[3] It constitutes the first of three projected treatises and is cast in the form of a dialogue between a master and his pupil. It is hardly surprising that Ibn Gabirol's work should have been assimilated to the Christian canon, since there is no overt indication of Hebrew doctrine nor even a reference to the Talmud. No Arabic or Jewish philosopher is mentioned; only Plato is named (three times). The Scholastics accepted the work as belonging to the Arabic philosophic tradition, and the author of the *Fons vitae*, disguised as Avicebron, was separated from the famous Hebrew poet, Ibn Gabirol, a separation that continued until the mid-nineteenth century.[4]

The unifying theme of the work is the wisdom which is the fount of life named in the title and which is the primary attribute of God in the *Royal Crown*, Ibn Gabirol's great religious poem, written in Hebrew: 'Thou art wise. And wisdom is the fount of life and from Thee it welleth'.[5] Essential to a comprehension of Ibn Gabirol's thought and its connection to that of Luis de León, is this concept of wisdom, which is rooted both in Proverbs 8 and in the cabalistic Hokhmah, the primordial emanation of God,[6] as well as being strongly influenced by Arabic philosophical views of the 'Universal Intelligence'.[7]

Central to Hebrew theology, as it was to Ibn Gabirol, and also to Luis de León, is the essential unity of God, expressed in Deut. 6.4: 'The Lord our God is One God'. Speaking both as believer and poet, Ibn Gabirol sets forth the relation of the One God to his creation in a Hebrew poem:

---

3 *Avencebrolis Fons Vitae,* edited by Clemens Bäumker, (Münster: Aschendorff, 1892). All references are to this text.

4 For background on the identification of Ibn Gabirol with Avicebron, see S. Munk, *Mélanges de philosophie juive et arabe* (Paris: Frank, 1859), 151-73 and Ermenegildo Bertola, *Salomon Ibn Gabirol* (Padua: CEDAM, 1953), 25-28.

5 *Selected Religious Poems of Solomon Ibn Gabirol*, trans. Israel Zangwill (Philadelphia: Jewish Publication Society of America, 1923), 87. All further references to the *Royal Crown* are to this edition.

6 Gershom G. Scholem, *Major Trends in Jewish Mysticism*, 1946 (New York: Schocken, 1960), 212-13.

7 See Bertola, *op. cit.*, 61-68.

All that is created, above and below,
Witness, declare, all as one:
'The Lord is One, and his name One'.[8]

But the poet presents the transition from the Unity of God to the multiplicity of Creation in this poem as effected by means of the thirty-two paths — the ten stages of the Cabbalistic Sefiroth and the twenty-two letters of the Hebrew alphabet — exactly as set forth in the first paragraph of the *Sefer Yetsirah* ('Book of Creation').[9] In combination, these constitute the thirty-two secret paths of wisdom through which God has created all that exists.[10] In this sense, the act of creation is seen as analogous to verbal utterance rather than to building or making:

> similitudo creationis est locutio, scilicet cum prolatione verbi, quando loquitur per illud, habet esse materia, quae sustinet formam verbi manifestam et formam eius occultam scilicet intellectum quem significat; et existentia eorum simul. (336, 21-24)

> (The comparison of creation is to speech, that is to say, with the utterance of a word, when it is spoken for that purpose, it has a material essence, which sustains the manifest form of the word and also its hidden intellectual form, that is to say, the meaning which it signifies; and the simultaneous existence of these.)

Thus, the Creator, acting through the power of His first attribute of wisdom (Hokhmah), gives rise to a unified Intelligence which by stages produces multiple creations which are in microcosm a reflection of the Divine unity.

In the introductory section of the *Nombres de Cristo* of Luis de León, in which he expounds his theory of names, we may see that the name is for him the intellectual substance into which is subsumed the physical presence of all created things:

> El nombre, si avemos de dezirlo en pocas palabras, es una palabra breve, que se sustituye por aquello de quien se dice y se toma por ello mismo. O nombre es aquello mismo que se nombra, no en el

---

8 *The Jewish Poets of Spain (900-1250)*, trans. David Goldstein (London: Penguin, 1982), 95.

9 The earliest extant text in Hebrew which embodies a theoretical approach to the problems of cosmology and cosmogony (see Scholem, *Major Trends in Jewish Mysticism*, 76-78).

10 Scholem, *op. cit.*, 75-76.

> ser real y verdadero que ello tiene, sino en el ser que le da nuestra boca y entendimiento.[11]

For Luis de León the 'nombre' fulfils the same function as the 'locutio' of Ibn Gabirol. As he repeats in 'Fazes de Dios', the original world is equated with the Word: 'Y después del mundo original, que es el Verbo ...' (202).

The sixteenth-century Spanish theologian, then, like the eleventh-century Judaic philosopher, embraces the theory of the 'word', or the 'name', which expresses the intellectual essence of the thing, and provides a way of reconciling unity with multiplicity without falling into either Neoplatonic emanationism or pantheism. For, as Luis de León explains in the passages following the previous quotation, the unity of God is thereby replicated in the unity of this intellectual comprehension which is shared by man. The concept of the microcosm is developed with a philosophical depth far exceeding the usual commonplaces of the Renaissance:

> Porque se ha de entender que la perfectión [*sic*] de todas las cosas, y señaladamente de aquellas que son capaces de entendimiento y razón, consiste en que cada una dellas tenga en sí a todas las otras, y en que, siendo una, sea todas cuanto le fuere posible; porque en esto se avezina a Dios, que en sí lo contiene todo. (155)

The concept of unity is expanded to represent the ultimate goal of all created things: 'consiste, pues, la perfeción de las cosas en que cada uno de nosotros sea un mundo perfecto' (155). This perfect microcosm contains everything and is contained by everything, all partaking of the same essence ('ser'). In this way, 'aquesta máchina del universo' is held together in an enchaining embrace, and the multitude of its differences is reduced to unity. In words which underline the paradoxical nature of that unity in multiplicity which he is trying to express, the purpose is:

> para que por esta manera, estando todos en mí y yo en todas los otros, ... se reduzga a unidad la muchedumbre de sus differencias ... y para que, estendiéndose y como desplegándose delante de los

---

11 *De los nombres de Cristo*, ed. Cristóbal Cuevas (Madrid: Cátedra, 1982), 155. All further references to the *Nombres* are to this edition.

ojos la variedad y diversidad, vença y reyne y ponga su silla la unidad sobre todo. (155-56)

There remains to explore the connection between wisdom and unity, and here again the concepts of Ibn Gabirol seem to throw light on the underlying thought of Luis de León. In the hierarchy of creation envisioned by the Jewish philosopher in the *Fons vitae*, the Prime Essence, inaccessible and unknowable by nature, is followed by the first creation *ab extra,* that is, Intellect, or Universal Intelligence, of which, as we have seen, human intelligence is the microcosm. Human intellect is the highest part of man, as Universal Intelligence is the highest and most perfect created being.[12] The search for wisdom is the activity of this highest part of man and the goal of his existence on earth, according to the *Fons vitae*. Man must strive after knowledge to achieve happiness: 'ut multum studeat ad illam, quia propter hoc consequetur felicitatem' (4). It is clear from this passage that by knowledge more than a merely rational inquiry is meant. Knowledge is followed by action (*opus*, *operatio*), which frees the soul from all that holds it back from its true nature, to which it must return: 'through knowledge', says the Master, 'the soul is joined to the higher world. For knowledge leads to action (*opus*) and action separates the soul from its adversaries which hurt it, and brings it back to its own true nature and substance. Knowledge and activity together free the soul entirely from the captivity of nature and purify it from its shadows and darkness, so that the soul returns to its most high abode' (4-5). The potential of the soul is in knowledge of itself, and its actuality is in the perfection of this knowledge; contrarily, imperfection is ignorance, and hence man's life must be a progression from ignorance to knowledge, from potential to actuality (5). Knowledge has three parts, or areas: knowledge of Matter and Form, knowledge of the Divine Will (*voluntas*), and knowledge of the Prime Essence. Matter and Form constitute the universe of the created, the Prime Essence is the Cause and between them is the mediating Divine Will (10). But, since it is impossible to know directly the true being of the Prime Essence, which is superior to all things and infinite (6), it

12 On the gnoseology of Ibn Gabirol, see Bertola, *Salomon Ibn Gabirol*, chap. X, 153-65.

may be known only indirectly from what is generated from it. Beyond even the lofty mysteries (*alta secreta*) of the knowledge of the operations of the Divine Will in Matter and Form, which is where the incomplete *Fons vitae* ends, lies a third kind of knowledge, the knowledge of the Creative Will *beyond* Matter and Form and unmixed with them. And so, at the close of the treatise, the Master tells his Pupil that he will be able to ascend to the knowledge of this highest power (*virtus altissima*)

> per suspensione animi in virtute secundum quod est permixta materiae et formae, et per elevatione tui per hanc virtutem gradatim usque quo pervenias ad principium eius et originem. (338)
>
> (only through suspension of the soul with regard to the areas of admixed Matter and Form, and by raising yourself by degrees through this power until you reach to its origin and beginning.)

This approximation to the Divine, it should be noted, is not a mystical union which fuses the human soul with God: it is clear throughout that Ibn Gabirol preserves the notion of a transcendent Deity who remains apart from his creation. But that knowledge which the human soul must pursue as its aim and which purifies it from corporeal things makes it free to issue into spheres of pure spirituality (257-58) until it reaches the sphere of Universal Intelligence. This highest point of human knowledge is intuitive knowledge, which includes all things. The union of the human intellect with the Universal Intelligence produces that essential knowledge of everything which is the ideal of all men, and which, as Bertola points out, derives from Ibn Gabirol's roots in Judaic and Islamic traditions blended with philosophic rationalism.[13]

The *Fons vitae* had begun by asking the question of man's purpose in life; the answer comes at the end: 'iam pervenit ad ultimum finem et fit spiritualis, divinus, dilectabilis' (322). This delight (*dilectatio*) enjoyed by the wise man is a combination of knowledge and the happiness which comes from the understanding of the unity of creation.

In a Christian dress, this is what Luis de León is saying as he opens his *Nombres*, that this apprehension of the unity of all

---

13 Bertola, *Salomon Ibn Gabirol*, 164-65.

is the divine in man; 'porque en esto se avecina a Dios, que en sí lo contiene todo'. It is exactly as Ibn Gabirol had argued, 'el fin y como el blanco adonde embían sus desseos todas las criaturas', the desire, or urge, of all things, 'el pío general de todas las cosas', in Fray Luis' vivid popularism (155).

Just as Ibn Gabirol pointed out how man progresses from ignorance to knowledge 'by attaching his soul to the higher world so that like may return to like' (4) and must start by knowing himself, and then attain knowledge of all things, so in the ode 'A Francisco Salinas' Fray Luis pictures the soul 'como se conoce, / en suerte y pensamientos se mejora'.[14] This view of knowledge raises to a higher plane the ode, 'Cuando será que pueda ...' (22-24), often misconstrued as a kind of cosmic travelogue exemplifying Renaissance curiosity regarding the natural world. In this poem, Luis de León is concerned with the total comprehension of all things simultaneously from a point beyond our earth, where he may contemplate 'la verdad pura sin velo'.

The 'Noche serena' ode likewise should be compared with Ibn Gabirol's *Royal Crown*, in which the poet reviews the cosmos as a series of concentric spheres encircling the earth. Beyond the circles of the planets and the fixed stars is the ninth, which moves the heavens from east to west, and the tenth, the sphere of Intelligence, where the cohorts of angels and ministers watch the movements of the Lord God, who himself is unapproachable:

> For beyond the sphere of Intelligence hast thou
> established the throne of Thy Glory;
> There standeth the splendour of Thy veiled
> habitation,
> And the mystery and the foundation.
> Thus far reacheth Intelligence, but cometh
> here to a standstill,
> For higher still hast Thou mounted, and
> ascended Thy mighty throne,
> 'And no man may go up with Thee.' (102)

The three concluding stanzas of the 'Noche serena' offer a

14 *The Original Poems*, ed. Edward Sarmiento (Manchester: Manchester U. P., 1953), 10. All further references to the *Poesías* are to this edition.

similar ecstatic view of what is beyond the spheres:

aquí asentado
en rico y alto asiento
está el amor sagrado
de glorias y deleites rodeado. (20)

The connection becomes even clearer in a passage from Fray Luis' Latin commentary on Psalm XXVI, first pointed out by P. José Llobera in his 1931 edition of the *Poesías originales*:

> For absolute and complete happiness is contained in two things: in the contemplation of God and in the knowledge of the temple of God, that is to say, of his universe, which in its unity is the most majestic and the greatest temple. For this knowledge of the nature of things is added like a finishing touch to that vision and contemplation of God, in which all happiness consists. Therefore are the blessed made aware of these parts and matters of nature in that heavenly future life and take supreme pleasure in this knowledge. For what other more pleasing spectacle may be displayed to pure and well-disposed souls than this, which God will reveal to them from the highest and most radiant point of the heavens ...[15] (author's translation)

The metaphysical framework of the *Fons vitae* derives from the emanational scheme of Neoplatonism, but with an important distinction, already alluded to. The unknowable First Essence operates by the action of Will to bring into being Universal Form and Matter, which are the highest order of created things. In a series of graphic images, Ibn Gabirol compares the Divine Will to the writer; Form, to the writing; and Matter, to the tablet or sheet written upon (326). The Divine Will, joining together Form and Matter, is the 'virtus spiritualis' infused into all Matter and is likened to the sun's power of diffusing light, while Form is the light, and Matter the air (327). Finally, to exemplify the creative act of will, the Master offers the image of a spring, flowing without interruption, motionlessly and timelessly ('sicut exitus aquae emanantis a sua origine ... est sine intermissione et sine quiete ... sine motu et sine tempore' [330]). Although Ibn Gabirol's theory of *voluntas* is perhaps the most difficult area of his

---

15 In *Psalm* xxvi, *Opera* (Salamanca: Colegio Episcopal de Calatrava, 1891-1895), vol. I, 137-38.

philosophical scheme,[16] it is clear that this is the essential element in passing from the unity of the Creator to the multiplicity of Creation: Will is Divine action as Wisdom is the Divine mind.

A final comparison illustrates the close connection between the thought of Ibn Gabirol and Luis de León:

> The imprinting however of Form on Matter when it reaches it by the Creative Will is like the resulting form in a mirror which comes to it from a person looking into it. Hence according to this example, Matter receives Form from the Creative Will as a mirror receives a form from a person looking into it, while however the mirror does not receive the essence of the person from whom it receives the form. (330-31)

Just as Ibn Gabirol makes clear the transcendence of the unknowable Prime Essence, so Fray Luis establishes the unity of God and his separation from his creatures. Immediately after insisting upon the ultimate desire of man, as of all creatures, to approach the unity of God, he uses the very same example of the mirrors as does his predecessor to illustrate how the multiplicity of things is reproduced in man's understanding ('en nuestro entendimiento') and yet remains a reflection of a transcendental unity:

> De lo qual puede ser como exemplo lo que en el espejo acontece. Que si juntamos muchos espejos y los ponemos delante los ojos, la imagen del rostro, que es uno, reluze una misma y en un mismo tiempo en cada uno dellos, y de ellos todas aquellas imágenes, sin confundirse, se tornan juntamente a los ojos, y de los ojos al alma de aquel que en los espejos se mira. (156-57)[17]

Although Leone Ebreo is not among the authors mentioned by Luis de León, he stands in the line of the Judaeo-Islamic tradition we have been speaking of and shows his familiarity with Arabic philosophic concepts, which he reviews together

---

16 Bertola, *Salomon Ibn Gabirol*, 104-05.

17 The image of the mirror reflecting the beholder derives ultimately from Plotinus, but it should be noted that in Ibn Gabirol and Fray Luis de León the reflection is carefully distinguished from that which it reflects: 'the mirror does not receive the essence of the person from whom it receives the form', in the words of Ibn Gabirol (330).

with theories of Plato and Aristotle in his *Dialoghi d'amore*.[18] Ebreo makes reference to Ibn Gabirol, however, whom he knows as belonging to Judaism, since he speaks of 'our [teacher] Albenzubron ... in his book, *De Fonte Vitae*', and central to the development of his theory of love is the interrelationship of wisdom and unity we have noted in Ibn Gabirol: 'for as God is one with the most perfect simplicity of unity, that which derives from Him must needs be one with entire unity' (191). In a section in Dialogue I, 'On Love and Desire', he presents an argument remarkably similar to that of Fray Luis in the introductory 'De los nombres en general'. Happiness, he says, 'consists in knowledge of one thing only, ... comprising in itself all the objects in the Universe' (44). This happiness is obtained 'in the single apprehension of active intellect', and the interlocutor Philo, when questioned by his companion Sophia as to the nature of this intellect, offers a finely tuned explanation, owing much to various Arabic views on the Active Intellect, which, in 'copulation', as he puts it, with the human intellect, is able to effect a joint vision of all reality:

> I will only say that those who meditate most on God, affirm — and I agree — that the Active Intellect, which gives light to our power of understanding, is God Most High; and hence they are convinced that happiness lies in the cognition of the Divine Intellect, which contains in Itself all things before, and more perfectly than, any created intellect ... To Him all things tend, as to their most perfect end; in Him they subsist without multiplication or division, in utter simplicity and unity. He is true happiness ... Whoever could see with His sight, would see all in perfect unity ... And as the human and angelic intellect contemplates, according to its capacity and virtue, all things united in highest perfection, so it partakes of His happiness, and becomes and remains happy, conformably with the quality of its being. (45-46)

This concept of an interlocking universe in which all elements are bound by a cosmic attraction ('el pío general de las cosas' of Fray Luis) is sometimes seen by Leone Ebreo from the point of view of each element as 'a way or a ladder leading up to the ultimate and highest perfection' (444). This is the analogy

18 *The Philosophy of Love (Dialoghi d'amore)*, trans. F. Friederberg-Seeley and Jean H. Barnes, ed. Cecil Roth (London: Soncini Press, 1937). All further references are to this edition.

which underlies the structure of many of the odes of Luis de León which portray the soul's ascent, from the body's first quickening, through the senses (the hearing of music, the viewing of the starry sky),[19] through the spheres of the rational soul up to the limits where knowing becomes contemplation and the threshold to that unhindered enjoyment of truth-in-light — the union with the Divine Intellect when the impeding layers of matter have been stripped away. But the final representation of the total structure of the cosmos adopted by Leone Hebreo more exactly renders the complexity of the two-fold dynamic of the soul, which, receiving from above its power, must then ascend to rejoin its source. The Intellect, deriving from the Will of the Supreme Creator, in Ibn Gabirol's terms, returns to him as a circle, which descends from its highest point in one hemisphere and then ascends up the other and so back to its starting point. Leone Ebreo clearly spells out the Arabic origin of this image which illustrates how 'the hierarchy of created beings descends not only to the last sphere of the moon, but even to First Matter, the least of all things; and thence it turns again with the inclination, love and desire of this First Matter to approximate to Divine Perfection' (335). Philo explains to his interlocutor Sophia:

> In this way the Arabs make the universe to be a circle, the beginning of which is God; and from Him a continuous chain of being descends to first matter, which is the most removed from the Divinity, and there the circle turns and ascends through the various degrees of being until it reaches the point of origin, to wit, divine beauty, with which the human intellect is finally united. (335)

In the concluding pages of the *Dialoghi d'amore*, Leone Ebreo, in the person of Philo, sketches out the whole circle of the cosmos, first in order of descent, from the angelic nature in

---

19 A contemporary Hebrew poet, Samuel Ha-Nagid (993-1056), has a poem with a remarkably similar opening to Fray Luis' 'Noche serena'

> I look up to the sky and the stars,
> And down to the earth and the things that creep there,
> And I consider in my heart how their creation
> Was planned with wisdom in every detail.
>
> (*The Jewish Poets of Spain*, *ed. cit.*, 57)

its degrees, which corresponds to the tenth sphere of Intelligence of the *Royal Crown*, with its 'radiance of souls' and 'high angels' 'established under the throne of Thy glory' (100-01, 102) — which is the unmoving sphere evoked by Fray Luis at the conclusion of the ode 'A Felipe Ruiz':

> Veré sin movimiento
> en la más alta esfera las moradas
> del gozo y del contento,
> de oro y de luz labradas,
> de espíritus dichosos habitadas. (24)

With the use of the sphere as an explanatory key to the structure of the cosmos, we reach the heart of the syncretic symbolism transmitted via Arabic channels from its origins in the Aristotelian cosmology to the Judaic tradition, where it blended with the wheels of Jewish mysticism. Leone Hebreo indicates his familiarity with these currents: 'The Greeks counted eight spheres, the Arabians nine, and the ancient Hebrews and some modern thinkers ten' (334). Although Luis de León nowhere specifically indicates his debt to any of these sources, it seems clear that he was drawing on this tradition.

The importance of light in these images should be noted. In calling attention to the role of light in the revival of Neoplatonism in the Middle Ages, Vicente Cantarino has pointed out the distinctions made in the *Fons vitae* between *Lux*, the origin and inaccessible source of light, *lumen emanans*, or light as the Creative Will (*voluntas*), and *lumen emanatum*, which is the light irradiated through the cosmos.[20] This 'trinity' of light finds an equivalence in passages of the *Nombres de Cristo* where Luis de León compares the Christian Trinity to the light of the sun (521-23). God is the source of light which cannot be viewed (*Lux*), and proceeding from him is the ray, which is the Son (*lumen emanans*). At the same time, the 'sol immenso y claríssimo' apostrophized by Marcelo, is seen as an ever-flowing spring — the 'fuente de vida' earlier mentioned (511). This image of the ceaseless activity flowing from the source of light, also used as an image for the *voluntas* by Ibn Gabirol, is here boldly applied to Christ, the second Person of

---

20 Vicente Cantarino, 'Ibn Gabirol's Metaphysic of Light', *Studia Islamica*, XXVI (1967), 49.

the Trinity:

> Y como el sol produze siempre su rayo, que no produxo ayer y cessó oy de produzirlo, sino siempre le produze y, con produzirle siempre, no le produze por partes, sino siempre y continuamente sale dél entero y perfecto, assí Dios siempre, desde toda su eternidad, engendró y engendra y engendrará a su hijo y siempre enteramente. (522-23)

For Luis de León, speaking through Marcelo, the Son of God is the power of God operating on the universe, and, like Ibn Gabirol's *voluntas*, is the direct agent of Creation. In the concluding section of the *Nombres*, Fray Luis makes a final identification of the themes we have been concerned with — light and wisdom — with the Son of God, the 'más alta cosa que procede de Dios': 'Y assí es luz nascida de luz, y fuente de todas las luzes, y sabiduría de sabiduría nascida, y manantial de todo el saber ...' (622).

In this conclusion, we may perhaps see that Luis de León owes much to a Judaeo-Arabic tradition transmitted through the *Fons vitae* and the *Dialoghi d'amore*, a tradition none the less powerful for being unconfessed and perhaps unconsciously operative on his thought.

The Mystical 'Dark Night' of San Juan de la Cruz as Interpreted in Poetic Summary

I. L. McCLELLAND

University of Glasgow

To a literary analyst, such as San Juan de la Cruz, literary artistry is a means rather than an end. For literary poets of spiritual imagination, though not classifiable as Mystics, artistry can fleetingly move on a spiritual level. Such poets, on a lower spiritual level than that of the dedicated Mystics, can be at a greater literary advantage. Since a practical Mystic's interest lies not merely in a passing or incidental awareness of spiritual realities, but in the development of that awareness, he is exposed to difficulties of rationalist expression. Many spiritually minded literary writers, especially poets, have effectively referred to momentary awareness of Divine realities. 'And I have felt a presence', says Wordsworth, recalling his visit to the area of Tintern Abbey, '... that disturbs me with the joy of elevated thought, a sense sublime ...'. Others speak of various forms of spiritual influence and inspiration. But the dedicated Mystic needs to analyse, for reasons of his own spiritual understanding, and spiritual development, the complex aspects of the whole of the Mystic Way: that is, the human means of cooperating intelligently with Divine directives.

The short poem beginning 'En una noche escura' (*sic*) interprets the period of 'dark night' in the Mystic Way as a stage between the trained activity of definable prayer and meditation, and the passage to a more advanced stage of vibrant inactivity, or contemplation. This is developed in

Mystical meaning by the poet in his two prose treatises on the poem: *Subida del Monte Carmelo* and *Noche escura del alma.*[1] Their difference from each other in tone and atmosphere is significant. For these treatises represent different, though related aspects and stages of experience. Significantly, too, it seems, neither treatise passes in commentary beyond the opening verses of the poem's eight stanzas. Whether manuscripts concerned with the remaining stanzas have been lost or not completed by the author is not known.[2] But it would seem not unlikely that the writer might have had difficulty in deciding how to describe the indescribable Mystic suggestions in later verses which represent a spiritual movement from Mystical darkness towards Mystical illumination. The *Subida del Monte Carmelo* is written in terms of the relationship between 'God' and the 'Soul' (named especially in these words) with the deeply spiritual objectivity of a Carmelite Director, and with constant reference to biblical writers. Notably, the treatise stresses the spiritual means of distinguishing between the rights and wrongs of natural human thought and behaviour. And once the soul in the dark night of faith and with its 'casa' — its state of moral thought and behaviour — is in moral order ('casa sosegada') then that soul can proceed to the stage of spiritual meditation, the first stage of the Mystic Way. Comments on the poem's first two stanzas with reference to the soul's self-controlled movement in dark faith towards spiritual development, include practical warnings. It is urged to avoid superstition, for example, relating to sensual images or apparent visions, and to sense-impressions in general. It is warned against undue dependence on the blessing of joy experienced temporarily in prayer; on personal preferences concerning the stylistic form of Church services, or the quality of Church music etc. In fact, this treatise displays Juan de la Cruz's gift for disciplined critical analysis.

The tone and atmosphere of the second treatise, which

---

1 See the translated edition in E. Allison Peers, *The Complete Works of St John of the Cross* (London: Burns, Oates & Washbourne, 1934), vol. I. All references are to this edition. My quotations from the original poem are from *The Oxford Book of Spanish Verse* (Oxford: Clarendon Press, 1925).

2 *Ed. cit.*, liii *ff.*

provides an alternative interpretation of the same stanzas, seems more vitally personal and less objectively academic. No longer is the writer instructing beginners in techniques of meditation, but drawing them towards The Mystical Way of contemplation, as travelled fervently by himself. Now the tone and argument express an ever deepening understanding of the need to seek spiritual illumination by the 'dark' process of abandoning mental and sensual self-awareness. The tone and argument are suggestive of the writer's present and continuing experience. Related, however, to his treatise for beginners are his characteristic references at every stage of his argument to biblical or other religious authorities; his general use of the names 'soul' and 'God' regarding spiritual relationships — as distinct from the names 'Lover' and 'Beloved' in the poem (terms used variously, by various writers, to denote *either* God *or* the soul); and his detailed and emphatic warnings against the influence on the Mystic Way of sensual and imaginative instincts deriving still from the background of human nature. Among important points made in this treatise is one which emphasizes the purity of Divine Union in the high stage of contemplation, and the consequent need for the soul's complete purgation.[3] Another stresses the inability of the soul in a pure state of contemplation to describe that state. Whereby one is reminded of the Middle English, anonymous *Cloud of Unknowing* where the soul, in the darkness of contemplative adoration, is advised to reduce its thought exclusively to the word 'God'.[4] 'Cloud' was a word used in similar circumstances by Juan de la Cruz[5] and quoted by him from Lamentations.[6] In accordance with his treatise for beginners, Juan de la Cruz continues to display in the treatise on the Dark Night for contemplatives, such characteristics as his reference at every stage of his argument to Scriptural or other religious authorities; his general reference, concerning holy relationships, to the names 'soul' and 'God' and his detailed and emphatic

3 *Ed. cit.*, 400.

4 See *The Cloud of Unkowning* translated into modern English by Clifton Wolters (Harmondsworth: Penguin, 1961), 98 *ff.*

5 *Ed. cit.*, 418.

6 See Lamentations 3, 44.

warning against the intrusion of sensual and imaginative suggestion. This treatise breaks off in its extant form with a brief entry into the poem's third stanza, beginning 'En la noche dichosa', which indicates that material and mental darkness can be spiritually illuminating.

The tone of the short poem is of deliberately restrained intensity. It expresses the Mystical need to accommodate what is indescribable to what is humanly understandable. The names 'Lover' and 'Beloved' had of course been used traditionally in religious references to a relationship between 'God' and the 'Soul', and expressed metaphorically an indescribably Divine parallel to a describable human ideal of affection. Not only is it the obvious Song of Songs which inspires the poet, and to which he refers.[7] This terminological tradition continues during the Middle Ages in such notable examples as Ramon Lull's 'Book of the Lover and the Beloved' — *Libre de Amich e Amat* — and, well after the lifetime of San Juan de la Cruz, and in areas outside Spain, the biblical terminology of 'Lover' and 'Beloved' continues to be echoed; as, for instance, in the Wesleyan hymn 'Jesu Lover of my soul — Let me to Thy bosom fly'. It must be remembered then, that Juan de la Cruz's terminology, in respect of Mystical love, belongs to an international and traditional context. For his own part Juan de la Cruz had an artistic nature. In poetry he presented his ideas dressed in pictorial imagery. At the climax of the poem, in the last stanza in which the Lover-soul, after passing through illuminative darkness, rests with the Beloved in peaceful embrace ('Quedéme y olvidéme, / el rostro recliné sobre el Amado') the emotional atmosphere is broadly reminiscent of the writer's prose comparison of a converted soul's rest in God, with the peace of a child asleep in its mother's arms. 'It must be known, then,' says Juan de la Cruz, 'that the soul, after it has been definitely converted to the service of God is, as a rule, spiritually nurtured and caressed by God, even as is the tender child by its loving mother, who

---

7 See the English translation by E. Allison Peers, *The Book of the Lover and the Beloved* (London: Society for the Promotion of Christian Knowledge, 1928; reprinted from the edition of 1923).

warms it with the heat of her bosom'.[8] Though, in the poem it is the Divine Beloved who, to signify acceptance of the Lover-soul's high moral and spiritual standards, is ready to accompany that soul, in holy peace, by resting in her arms.

The atmosphere of spiritual intensity in this poem is achieved with the help of the writer's sensitive choice of words. Evidently he had a musical ear. When the Lover-soul, now in control of its 'ansias', and departing from worldly temptations ('estando ya mi casa sosegada'), moves into spiritual darkness, the rhyme-endings are of deep and soft vowels and smooth consonants: '... es*cura*, '... inflam*ada*', '... vent*ura*', 'not*ada*', '*soseg*ada'.

Midway through the poem, when the Lover-soul becomes aware that spiritual darkness can be illuminative, the sharper rhyme-sounds suggest higher and stronger awareness: 'Oh noche, que *guiaste*, / ... / oh noche, que *juntaste* / Amado con amada, / ...'. Later stanzas return to the soft endings suggestive of peace. The specially strong sounds of the final stanza ('Qued*é*me y olvid*é*me, / el rostro reclin*é* sobre el Amado, / ces*ó* todo, y d*ejéme*') help to accentuate the realistic force of the meaning of spiritual commitment.

Certainly from the standpoint of artistry San Juan de la Cruz's originality in his poem lies more in its atmospheric sound-effects and in the dramatic general movement, through scenic darkness to illuminative solution, than in its imagery largely borrowed from tradition, and especially from the Song of Songs. The idealistic lilies, so frequently mentioned in the Song of Songs, are used in the poet's final lines: 'Cesó todo, y dejéme, / dejando mi cuidado / entre las azucenas olvidado'. Even more notably, some seemingly sensual details, expressing intimacy, in lines preceding the final stanza, — the Beloved's touch on the Lover's neck, controlling influences of the senses — are based directly, or indirectly, on physical references in the Song of Songs. Mention of the Beloved's hair appears also to be inspired by similar references in the Song of Songs to the Beloved's physical appearance. Undoubtedly the sensual details would have been explained on a different, that is a purely spiritual level, in the last, or unfinished prose

8 See the *Treatise on the Dark Night, ed. cit.*, 350-51.

commentary, with special reference to the line concerning the Divine touch: 'y todos mis sentidos suspendía' — meaning the removal of the soul from the life of sense.

Altogether, San Juan de la Cruz's artistic genius in this poem is most notably revealed in his ability to project an overall impression of Mystical atmosphere.

Further *Studies of the Spanish Mystics*: Allison Peers on Miguel de Molinos' *Spiritual Guide*

ANN L. MACKENZIE
University of Glasgow

I

Introduction

> Nobody has done so much as Professor Allison Peers to awaken the interest of the English-reading public in the lives and writings of the great Spanish mystics, and he has addressed himself with equal relevance to the expert scholar and the intelligent amateur. On the popular level his two small books *Spirit of Flame* and *Mother of Carmel* could hardly be bettered as introductions to the teaching of the two giants of Spanish mysticism, St John of the Cross and St Teresa of Jesus ... At the other extreme we have his translations of P. Silverio de Santa Teresa's critical editions of the works of the same two great Carmelite saints, his biography of Ramon Lull, and the two volumes (to which we learn a third is to be added) of *Studies of the Spanish Mystics*. Nor does this exhaust the list of Professor Peers' contributions to the subject to which he has devoted his life.[1]

E. L. Mascall's observations — made in his review of Peers' revised edition (1951) of *Studies of the Spanish Mystics*, Volume I (1927) — serve opportunely to remind us of the depth and extent of Peers' scholarly commitment to researches into Spanish mysticism throughout his career. Within two years of his appointment to the Gilmour Chair of Spanish at Liverpool,

---

1 E. L. Mascall, Review of *Studies of the Spanish Mystics*, I (2nd edition, revised, 1951), *BHS*, XXIX (1952), No. 113, 64-65, at p. 64.

Peers had already published his first books in this field: his translation, with introductory essay, of Ramon Lull, *The Book of the Lover and the Beloved*, in 1923; and *Spanish Mysticism: A Preliminary Survey*, in 1924. From then on he continued steadily with his researches and continued likewise to increase his numerous publications on mysticism in Spain until his death in 1952. That very year his article on 'Some Women Mystics of the Seventeenth Century' was published. Several more studies were to appear posthumously: *St Teresa of Jesus and Other Essays and Addresses* in 1953, *A Handbook to the Life and Times of St Teresa and St John of the Cross* in 1954, and, most importantly, *Studies of the Spanish Mystics*, Volume III — which, edited anonymously by Ivy McClelland, was published thirty years after Volume II, in 1960.[2]

This third book, therefore, became the final volume of 'sus magníficos *Studies*', which, in a way, does not seem inappropriate. For the *Studies* make up a work perceived to have, intrinsically, 'un triple carácter, porque es histórica, expositiva y crítica al mismo tiempo'.[3] Nevertheless, it had once been Peers' intention to write at least four, and perhaps even more than four, volumes of *Studies of the Spanish Mystics*. Decades previously, in the Preface to *Spanish Mysticism: A Preliminary Survey*, he had referred to the 'vastness' of his subject, 'which would require many volumes to do it justice'.[4] And in the Preface which he wrote to *Studies of the Spanish Mystics*, Volume II, published in 1930, Peers revealed that, in addition to the primary sources researched for this second volume, he had already examined 'masses of completely forgotten mystical work in out-of-the-way Spanish libraries' which could 'not yet be utilized',[5] but which, clearly, he expected to provide him with material for subsequent books.

2 For full details of all publications mentioned see above, H. B. Hall, 'E. Allison Peers: A Selective Bibliography', 35-45.

3 See Fr Crisógono de J. S., C. D., Review of *Studies of the Spanish Mystics*, II (1930), *BHS*, VIII (1931), No. 30, 118-20, at p. 118.

4 See *Spanish Mysticism: A Preliminary Survey* (London: Methuen, 1924), vii.

5 See *Studies of the Spanish Mystics*, II (London: Sheldon Press, 1930), viii.

Momentous events in Spain and Europe — the Spanish Civil War followed by the Second World War — prevented until 1947, as Peers himself explains, his further essential researches into Spanish libraries. Completion of Volume III of the *Studies* — in which was finally utilized much, but by no means all, of the material on 'the lesser mystics' gathered in the 1920s — was to be delayed, in consequence, for many years.[6]

In the Preface to Volume III, which he composed only a few months before his death, Peers referred to the book as 'this third and final volume of the *Studies*'.[7] Clearly he had come to realize that the projected further studies, for which already he had examined sources and made notes, were destined never to be realized. Among these ambitious projects left uncompleted was: *Studies of the Spanish Mystics*, Volume IV.

We know the subject on which Peers would have concentrated his attention had he lived to accomplish a fourth book of *Studies of the Spanish Mystics.* As early as 1929, when he wrote the Preface to Volume II of the *Studies*, he had wished to trace 'the history of both the essential and the secondary tenets of the Spanish quietists down to the point where they converge in Falconi, and concluding ... with a study of Molinos'. Originally, it had been Peers' intention that such a history would form part of Volume II. 'It soon became clear [to him], however, that this process would require so much space as to increase the size of this [second] volume [on the Spanish mystics] to an impracticable extent, and also that it would destroy the proportion between the various elements and aspects of the entire subject.' As a result, Peers decided, as he tells us himself, 'to devote another book at some time in the future to the sources and manifestations of Spanish quietism'.[8]

Peers does not omit to tell us more precisely what he had in mind to accomplish in this further book of the *Studies* — which was:

---

6 See Peers' Preface to *Studies of the Spanish Mystics*, III, ed. I. L. McClelland (London: SPCK, 1960), vii.

7 *Studies of the Spanish Mystics*, III, vii.

8 For these observations cited, see Preface, *Studies of the Spanish Mystics*, II, viii. The Preface is dated 23 December 1929; the book, as we have seen, appeared the following year.

> to outline in the necessary detail the rise of quietism in Spain; to estimate the extent — never yet, I believe, seriously and fully discussed — to which it had its roots in Spanish orthodoxy; to consider critically, not only the prohibited *Letters* of Falconi, but also the curious *Straight Road* and *Brief Compendium*, which I think I am the first to rescue from the oblivion of the monastic library;[9] and finally to study Molinos, as he should be studied, in close relation to his contemporaries in Spain and elsewhere.[10]

How much progress he had managed to make with this work can be assessed, with reasonable accuracy, through scrutiny of Peers' surviving **Papers on the Spanish Mystics**, which are lodged, in considerable numbers, in the Sydney Jones Library of Liverpool University. A significant proportion of these **Collected Papers** — of which a catalogue is published below, for the benefit of other researchers — relate to the projected Fourth Volume of *Studies of the Spanish Mystics*. There are, in envelopes and packets, large quantities of detailed notes and drafted commentaries in manuscript concerned with Quietism and individual Quietists. There are, additionally, in eleven packets of 'Peers papers unpublished', 'Notes on Sta Teresa, S.J.X., and other mystics' — material that had been intended, we may assume, to form the basis of Peers' projected account of the growth of Quietism in Spain, from 'its roots in Spanish orthodoxy'. Particularly remarkable is the mass of papers that Peers had already compiled for his planned study of the controversial work and doctrine of Miguel de Molinos.

Among Peers' papers on Molinos there is preserved the draft, in manuscript, of an essay, or chapter, on Molinos' *Guía*

---

9 The final chapter XII of *Studies of the Spanish Mystics*, II is concerned with Juan Falconi. But Peers, as he himself says, reviews the works of Falconi 'without attempting a formal synthesis of his doctrines, or tracing them back, in any detail, to such Spanish writers as may have inspired them'. Peers also refrains from discussing, in Volume II, the statement that Falconi is 'generally regarded as the father of quietism', but indicates that he will undertake 'a future consideration of this difficult and complicated theme' (350). Later in this same chapter on Falconi, Peers declares that 'a full examination of the *Straight Road* and a criticism of its principles belong to a future volume' (386) — surely yet another allusion to his projected Volume IV of the *Studies*.

10 *Studies of the Spanish Mystics*, II, viii.

espiritual. This work, though unfinished, is, in my view, the only part of the material from which Peers had intended to form *Studies of the Spanish Mystics*, IV that might be perceived as publishable almost as it stands.

In editing this essay, to which, since it lacked one, I have given the title 'Miguel de Molinos' *Spiritual Guide*', I have adhered as far as possible to Peers' original text, without modifying his words or expanding his observations, even in those passages to which he had meant to return, and in which sense and sentences remain incomplete. In the interests of clarity, however, I have not always adhered to the original punctuation, and, in particular, have reduced considerably the number of paragraphs. Peers quotes frequently from the *Guía espiritual* but invariably in English translation. The translation he has used is: Miguel de Molinos, *The Spiritual Guide which disentangles the Soul* ..., edited, with an Introduction, by Kathleen Lyttelton ... (London: Methuen, 1907). For the convenience of Hispanists, after every quotation of any length or particular significance, I have inserted, within square brackets, the original Spanish text. I have used square brackets also to indicate gaps in the text ([...]), and to signal my other editorial interventions. For the Spanish text I have used, and found invaluable, Miguel de Molinos, *Guía espiritual*, edición crítica, introducción y notas de José Ignacio Tellechea Idígoras (Salamanca: Universidad Pontificia de Salamanca/ Madrid: Fundación Universitaria Española, 1975 [1976]). I have provided notes: to clarify allusions or points of fact; to record notes and references made by Peers in pencil on the manuscript; to mention any deficiencies or to explain obscurities. Deciphering Peers' tiny handwriting correctly, as always, has been difficult. With this essential task I have had indispensable assistance from my colleagues, Ceri Byrne, Research Fellow of the University of Glasgow, and Adrian Allan, Archivist at the University of Liverpool.

Peers' views and interpretations of mysticism in Spain, as he himself realized, evolved during the several decades in which he conducted his researches and published his *Studies of the*

Spanish Mystics.[11] This essay on Miguel de Molinos was evidently written in the 1920s, at a period when Peers certainly regarded Molinos with disapproval as well as interest, and equated his *Guía espiritual* with 'the degradations of pseudo-mysticism'.[12] Had he lived to expand and revise his comments on 'Miguel de Molinos' *Spiritual Guide*', he might have offered different, and, in places, more positive interpretations of the beliefs and teachings of Molinos. Even as it stands, however, this piece of work provides a perceptive and still beneficial commentary on the mystical thought-content, consistently Quietist inclinations and persuasively elegant style of Molinos' *Guía espiritual*.

Seventy or more years after Peers' essay was written, the works of Molinos have yet to be given as much seriously critical attention as their significance deserves.[13] To all scholars concerned to understand the mystics of Spain, therefore, it is a matter for profound regret that *Studies of the Spanish Mystics*, Volume IV — meant to consider Quietism, and Molinos 'as he should be studied, in close relation to his contemporaries in Spain and elsewhere' — was destined never to be accomplished. Nevertheless, the numerous studies that he did compose have proved extensive and durable in their influence. Peers lived to achieve much more than, too modestly, he had hoped for:

> [to] interest a large and rapidly growing public in the works and movements ... studied, and [to] lay imperfect foundations for a history of Spanish mysticism which some more happily placed future writer may not find wholly without value.[14]

---

11 See his comment (1952) in *Studies of the Spanish Mystics*, III: 'A large proportion of the notes on which it [volume III] was based were made from twenty to twenty-five years ago ... Inevitably, ... my thought, and the standpoint from which I have regarded groups of writers, tendencies, and individual authors, have become modified in the interval' (viii-ix).

12 See *Spanish Mysticism: A Preliminary Survey*, 36.

13 Worth mentioning is the doctoral thesis of Trevor J. Boiling on *The 'Guía espiritual' of Miguel de Molinos and Passivity in Mystical Prayer* (University of Liverpool, 1987), 329 pp.

14 Preface to *Studies of the Spanish Mystics*, Volume III, ix.

II

Miguel de Molinos' *Spiritual Guide*[15]

Comparatively little is known of the life of Miguel de Molinos before he attained to the notoriety which still attaches to his name. He is said to have been born in Zaragoza in 1627, though the year is also given as 1628 and the place of his birth as Muniesa near Teruel.[16] He was a secular priest, and is known to have held the benefice of St Thomas, Valencia, after pursuing his studies at Coimbra (again this is uncertain) and being, either here or elsewhere, (he himself tells us this) a pupil of the Jesuits.[17] [...][18]

In the year 1662, Molinos went to Rome 'as procurator in the process of canonization of the servant of God Francisco Jerónimo Simón'.[19] [...] Molinos eventually took up his residence

15 Peers' essay — for which I have provided a title he would not have taken amiss — is written on lined pages taken from a school exercise-book.

16 Peers indicates in pencil, that Urbano and Lyttelton favour 1627, and asks if '?Urbano gives (Teruel) only' as the place of birth. Peers refers here to the edition of Miguel de Molinos, *Guía espiritual*, by Rafael Urbano (Barcelona, 1906). Lyttelton, as previously indicated, is Kathleen Lyttelton's edited translation, with introduction, of Miguel de Molinos, *The Spiritual Guide* (1907). Molinos was in fact born in Muniesa, 29 June 1628 (*New Catholic Encyclopedia* [Washington D.C.: The Catholic University of America, 1967], Vol. IX).

17 Brief references written in pencil indicate that Peers takes this information from Urbano: 'Urb.'; 'Urb.: it is said'; 'where. < Urbano'. Some of Peers' notes in pencil are, as here, written above the lines in the main text to which they refer; others are scribbled in the margin.

18 Peers leaves a space here, evidently for a later insertion. He continues to leave such spaces (which I have indicated by [...]) throughout the manuscript. Clearly, he had intended to fill these spaces, which vary in size, with additional facts and further observations.

19 Nicolás Antonio, *Bibliotheca Hispana Nova* [2ª ed.] (Madrid: Ibarra, 1783-88), I, 645. This is Peers' own bibliographical reference, to which, however, I have added date, place and publisher.

in Rome,[20] spending some time at the Discalced Carmelite convent of St Ana de Monte Cavallo and later living with the Discalced Augustinians at St Alfonso.[21] [...] He made firm and powerful friends, both by his social charm and by his evident spirituality. As a confessor he knew many well-born men and women, among them Queen Christina of Sweden,[22] then residing in the Italian capital. As a friend, he saw much of Cardinal Odescalchi, later (1676-1689) Innocent XI. [...][23]

The publication, in 1675, of Molinos' *Spiritual Guide* was carefully led up to by Molinos' friends. Fray Juan de Santa María,[24] a prominent Franciscan, made himself responsible for the book,[25] the text of which was preceded by the usual approbations: these were signed by the General of the Franciscans, a Carmelite [and] a Jesuit. [...][26]

To say that the book was successful from the point of view of its circulation is to use a mild expression. Molinos' teaching was well known, not only in Rome, and in Spain, but in many other countries. The size of the manual was conveniently small. Its style was highly attractive. Its subject matter, and above all its title, far from being (as the author pretended) 'mystical and unpalatable',[27] promised pleasant reading, with none of the meditations on uncomfortable subjects like death, judgment and

---

20 Peers notes in pencil that Lyttelton 'says 1669 or 70 "for private reasons"'

21 Peers begins this sentence with 'In Rome', then repeats the same phrase later in the sentence. I have deleted the first mention. A note in the margin identifies Urbano as the source for his facts. This sentence begins a new paragraph in the manuscript. But here, as elsewhere, I have altered Peers' punctuation, to improve, for the reader, the flow of comment and information.

22 Peers indicates that Lyttelton is his source for this fact.

23 Peers notes that he took this information from 'Larousse'.

24 Peers scribbles above the name of Fray Juan de Santa María: 'So Urbano. Lyt. gives Ital.'.

25 Peers notes in pencil here 'Not sure what his part was so left it vague'.

26 The source he gives is Urbano and adds '*cf.* Lyttelton 4[a]'. Peers leaves most of this page 3 of his manuscript blank, to insert further comments.

27 There is an abbreviated note in the margin referring to 'The A. to the Rdr [Address to the Reader] (Lyt.)'. The phrase cited indeed comes from Molinos' *A quien leyere*.

hell that such manuals written by Spaniards had included in the past.[28] Who that disliked penances, abstinences and confessions — who indeed that found life hard and religion difficult —[29] could refrain from buying a 'Spiritual guide that disentangles the soul and leads it by the inward way to the attainment of perfect contemplation and the rich treasure of inward peace'? [...][30]

The book was re-issued and translated again and again.[31] [...] Those in high places were no less favourable to the *Guide* than the public which read it in so many countries. The Archbishop of Palermo both recommended it and caused it to be read in his diocese. [...][32] Innocent XI, who in 1676 had succeeded to the Papacy, gave Molinos rooms in the Vatican and was as intimate with him as before.[33]

In the year in which he left Valencia for Rome (1662), Molinos had published there, under the name of Juan Bautista Catalá, a manual entitled 'The devotion of the good death with spiritual exercises of meditation'.[34] [...] After the *Spiritual*

---

28 A reference to himself in the margin — 'EAP' — suggests that Peers thought to look in his own books for examples of the sort of manuals he had in mind.

29 Peers writes in pencil possible alternatives to 'hard' ('severe?', 'full of trials?'), and to 'difficult' ('far from easy').

30 *Guía Espiritual que desembaraza al alma, y la conduce por el interior camino para alcanzar la perfecta contemplación y el rico tesoro de la interior paz* (Roma: Hércules, 1675). In a note in the margin Peers reminds himself to insert the title of the 1676 Spanish edition. The title of the 1676 Spanish edition, also by Fray Juan de Santa María (Madrid: Francisco Sanz, 1676), is identical to that of the Rome edition of 1675. Peers left a space at this point (Ms., p. 4) to insert other remarks.

31 Peers reminds himself, in a note, to add details here ' < Bibliog. when completed'.

32 There are large gaps on page 5 of Peers' manuscript — the page which begins 'The book was re-issued ... ' —. Clearly, he had meant to fill these gaps with additional information.

33 Notes in the margin reveal that Peers' source for this information was Lyttelton.

34 That is, *La devoción de la buena muerte* ...; the date of publication given by Nicolás Antonio, *op. cit.*, is, however, 1660 (*cf.* Paul Dudon, *Le Quiétiste espagnol Michel Molinos* [Paris: Gabriel Beauchesne, 1921], 26). In the margin Peers indicates that his information here is taken from Urbano.

Guide [there] was published in Italian a 'Brief treatise on daily communion', translated from the Spanish in which it had first been written. [...][35]

The turning of the tide of authoritative ecclesiastical opinion against the *Spiritual Guide* was slower than might have been expected. No doubt this was due to the proportion of good in Molinos' teaching, to the size of his following and to the care with which the way had been prepared for the book's appearance. The Dominicans appear to have turned [into] Molinos' enemies first, perhaps through the influence of their age-long feuds with the Franciscans, who had supported it. Jesuit enmity followed, as was natural, for although Molinos had Jesuit friends of great influence and had been associated with the Society, the exaggerations of orthodox mysticism which the book contained were the very antithesis of any tendencies to exaggeration which the Jesuits might have favoured. P. Segneri, with consummate skill, was chosen to lead the movement against Molinos: he was a man with a personality even more pronounced than his adversary, of intense energy and zeal, and of a sincerity and a spirituality as great and as evident as was his eloquence. At Florence in 1680[36] Segneri published a book of no greater dimensions than the *Spiritual Guide*, called *A Harmony between Labour and Quiet in Prayer* (*Concordia tra la fatica e la quiete nell'orazione*).[37]

Peers wonders whether '?a' would, in English, be preferable to the definite article in the phrase 'the good death'.

35 That is, *Breve tratado de la comunión cuotidiana* (Roma: Hércules, 1675). Peers reminds himself in pencil here to 'see Lyttelton, 3^{d}'. It should be noted that each of the last two sentences occupies a separate and otherwise blank page of Peers' manuscript (pp. 6-7). Clearly he had intended to elaborate substantially upon the facts given.

36 A note in the margin reveals Peers took this 'date and place < Lyt. 7'. He adds that 'Urbano has Bologna 1681'. In fact, Lyttelton has given the first edition, and Urbano a subsequent edition.

37 Peers adds a note here in pencil, above the title, that Lyttelton translated *fatica* as 'effort'. In another note in the margin — where he gives the Italian title of Segneri's work — he comments that 'Lyt. and Urbano agree here'. Below the title in English he scribbles a reminder to himself: 'For content *v*. Lyt. p. 7. But try to see self and Bigelow p. 19. Also what happened Lyt. 7-8'. Bigelow is: J. Bigelow, *Molinos the Quietist* (New York: C. Scribner & Sons, 1882).

[...][38] In January 1682 the attack on Molinos was renewed by the Archbishop of Naples, who appealed to the Pope for instructions as to how to deal with quietist teaching.[39] [...] The Inquisition at length took up the dispute, which was growing to serious dimensions, and set up a commission to examine the works of Molinos, Segneri and an Italian follower of Molinos called Petrucci.[40] [...] The result of the commission's deliberations was the condemnation of Segneri and the justification of Molinos and Petrucci, the orthodoxy of whose writings was definitely established. [...][41]

The Jesuits' new attempt was through Louis XIV, whose confessor, Père Lachaise, prevailed upon him to appeal to the Pope against Molinos. Innocent had, not many years since, condemned a collection of sixty-two propositions from Jesuit moralists and was probably in no way anxious to move in the direction which the French King suggested. However, he turned the matter over to the Inquisition, which, in May 1685, imprisoned Molinos (this order of procedure was the usual one) and in 1687 condemned him. On August 28th of the latter year a list of sixty-eight propositions was extracted from the writings of Molinos and of his followers, and each and all were declared heretical.

Molinos recanted his supposed errors. The ceremony, which took place on September 3rd 1687, was public and attended by [an] enormous multitude. But its details do not here concern us, and, as to what followed, it is sufficient to say that Molinos spent the rest of his life as a prisoner in a Dominican convent in Rome under strict rule. He is generally supposed to have died

38 Almost an entire page (Ms., p. 9) is left blank here — presumably in order to insert further information.

39 In a note in the margin Peers reminds himself where to find, for reference, the substance of this letter: '(< Heppe) Lyt. 8-9'. Heppe is: H. Heppe, *Geschichte der quietistischen Mystik in der katholischen Kirche* (Berlin: Hertz, 1875).

40 Peers puts a note in the margin to check 'Lyt. 9^b (Name of P's [Petrucci's] book'.

41 Most of these pages (Ms., pp. 10-11) are left blank presumably to take further inserted commentary.

on December 29th of the same year,[42] but only rumour speaks here with any confidence.[43]

It is no part of the intention of this book[44] to discuss the rights and wrongs of the disputes and intrigues which culminated in the condemnation of Molinos. Probably nobody to-day would feel very proud of them.[45] [...] Our aim in this chapter is to examine carefully the text of the *Spiritual Guide*, and, independently of anything that Molinos may have said or done, or that his followers may have said or done, to form an opinion of its teaching and to assign to it its place in the history of Spanish mysticism. Avoiding the editions which, confessedly or secretly, omit large portions of the book, we have used the ... edition of ... [...][46]

The *Spiritual Guide* consists of a prefatory note, a preface of some length, and three books. The first words of the text show the author in an attitude of self-defence which is extremely significant: 'There is nothing', begins Molinos, 'more difficult than to please all people, nor easier and more common than to censure books that come abroad in the world ... Kind reader, if thou understand not this (book), be not therefore inclined to censure it' ['No hay cosa más difícil en el mundo que agradar a todos, ni más fácil y usada que censurar los libros que salen a la

42 The year of Molinos' death is variously given in different reference books as 1692, 1695 and 1696. According to the *New Catholic Encyclopedia, ed. cit.*, IX, Molinos died in Rome 28 December 1696. Interestingly, in his notes for the projected *Studies*, Volume IV (see below, **Catalogue**, **VI**), Peers gives exactly this date of death, among other material that he needs 'to put in places'.

43 Peers ends the first section (I) of his article/chapter here.

44 A reference to the projected but never realized Fourth Volume of *Studies of the Spanish Mystics*, of which, as I have indicated, this essay/chapter was meant to form part

45 Peers reminds himself that a 'Gen. verdict' is needed here. He then leaves most of this page (Ms., p. 13) blank, clearly intending to return to elaborate this observation further.

46 Peers leaves spaces here to specify the edition used, and also a gap in which to insert a couple of additional sentences, to explain 'Why?' this edition. In the margin he notes that probably the edition of Madrid 1676 (of the B.Nac.) 'will be best'.

luz pública ... Si no le entiendes, lector amigo, no por eso lo censures' (*A quien leyere, ed. cit.*, 103)].[47] This said, he devotes the greater part of his address to the reader to a defence of the experiential nature of mystical theology. He himself has learned by experience what he proposes to expound and draws upon this experience rather than upon the 'speculative reading of books'.[48] He quotes 'the authority of some practical and experienced author, to show that the doctrine which is here taught is not singular and rare' ['alguna autoridad de autor práctico y experimentado para que se entienda que no es singular y rara la doctrina que aquí se enseña' (106)], but this 'very seldom'. Yet he somewhat inconsistently declares that 'he that shall condemn the doctrine of this book has no experience of mystical science' ['que no tiene experiencia de esta práctica y mística ciencia el que condenará la doctrina de este libro' (104)] — a bold claim! — and asserts that his doctrine is that taught by 'St Dionysius, St Augustine, St Gregory, St Bernard, St Thomas, St Bonaventura and many other saints and doctors approved by the Church'.[49]

Molinos lays great stress on one word in the title of his book: 'disencumbers' ['desembaraza']. His aim, he says, is not to write a treatise fully descriptive of contemplation. His experience as a director of souls has convinced him of the 'great need for removing the obstacles and taking away the inclinations, affections and allurements which wholly hinder their progress and obstruct the way to perfect contemplation' ['la grande necesidad que hay de quitarlas los embarazos, inclinaciones, afectos y apegos que totalmente las impiden el paso y el camino a la perfecta contemplación' (106)]. It is fair to add at this point that, though here and elsewhere he lays (as we may think)

47 In the margin Peers refers to 'A. to R. [Address to the Reader] Lyt. 49' — the English source of his quotation. I have added the text of the Spanish original here and elsewhere in square brackets. The excellent edition I have used, as previously stated, is: Miguel de Molinos, *Guía espiritual*, edición crítica, introducción y notas de José Ignacio Tellechea Idígoras (1975/76). All my in-text references are to this edition.

48 Above this quotation Peers identifies his source as 'Lyt. 53'.

49 Peers gives in the margin the source of all these quotations used in these two sections: Lyt. 53, 51, 51.

excessive stress upon the facility of contemplation, he points out that he is addressing himself 'not to all kinds of persons, but only to those who keep the senses and passions well mortified, who have already advanced and made progress in prayer and are called by God to the inward way' ['no ... a todo género de personas, sino solamente a aquéllas que tienen bien mortificados los sentidos y pasiones y que están ya aprovechadas y encaminadas en la oración, y llamadas de Dios al interior camino' (105)], and that, in this way, there are 'many and grievous pains and difficulties'.[50]

The preface to the book contains four 'admonitions' which follow lines familiar to readers of this study.[51] The first admonition draws the distinction between meditation, which is the way of beginners and pertains to the senses, and contemplation, which consists in 'pure faith' is 'detached, pure and interior' and the way of proficients. The second admonition develops this distinction. The third makes a further distinction, between 'imperfect, acquired and active' contemplation, and 'infused and passive'. The former may, with the consent of a director or the guidance of a book, 'be obtained by our own diligence, the Divine grace also assisting'[52] ['se puede alcanzar con nuestra diligencia, ayudados de la divina gracia' (114)]; the latter is given by God when He wills, without any labour or effort on the part of the recipient. The fourth admonition, a short one, lays down as 'the burden of this book' 'the uprooting of the rebellion of our own will, that we may attain to inward peace' ['que es desarraigar la rebeldía de nuestra propria voluntad para alcanzar la interior paz' (118)].[53]

The main part of the *Spiritual Guide* is distinctly less well arranged than its preface. The seventeen chapters of the first

50 Again, the source of all quotations used in this paragraph is given in the margin as: Lyt. 52, 51, and 52[b].

51 Peers wonders whether to write, instead of 'this study', 'these "Studies" ' — which seems, indeed, preferable, given that this chapter was to form part of a further volume of *Studies of the Spanish Mystics*.

52 Above the word 'assisting' Peers has written a reminder to himself to 'alter' this.

53 In the margin, throughout this paragraph, Peers continues to identify his source through a series of abbreviated references: L.[Lyt.]55, L.62 3rd and §20, L.65, L.66 (title).

book are said to deal with 'the darkness, dryness and temptations wherewith God purges souls, and with internal recollection' ['las tinieblas, sequedades y tentaciones con que Dios purga a las almas, y del recogimiento interior' (119)]. The familiar truths in connection with these themes are stressed again and again. The soul must keep ever in peace; must persevere in seasons of dryness; must not repine when it cannot meditate. As to recollection, both meditation and contemplation are allowed to be profitable: Molinos hence distinctly denies 'that the only true prayer is the contemplation by the soul of the exaltation and supreme Deity of God'.[54] Yet the goal to be aimed at is the latter (and here Falconi is both followed and quoted).[55] Thus, the soul, 'by placing itself in the presence of

---

54 Above the word 'Deity' Peers writes: 'lit. Divinity'.

55 Presumably Juan Falconi, *Lettera ... ad un religioso ... tradotta dalla lingua spagnuola nell' italiana* (Roma: Capodoro, 1674). See below, **Peers' Collected Papers on the Spanish Mystics. A Catalogue** — under **VI** (4). After this reference to Falconi Peers leaves a space to insert an example of a borrowing from Falconi by Molinos. And there is a note in pencil to remind himself to: 'Translate the first four lines of Ch. 13 (Lyt. pp. 100-1)'. The first lines of Libro I, cap. XIII are as follows:

> Has de ir a la oración a entregarte del todo en las divinas manos con perfecta resignación, haciendo un acto de fe, creyendo estás en la divina presencia, quedándote después en aquel santo ocio con quietud, silencio y sosiego, **procurando continuar todo el día, todo el año y toda la vida en aquel primer acto de contemplación por fe y amor**.
>
> (*Ed. cit.*, 173)

Interestingly, in *Studies of the Spanish Mystics*, II, chapter XII (which, as indicated above [note 9], Peers devotes entirely to Juan Falconi), Peers cites from Falconi a passage that, he says, was 'afterwards adapted and quoted by Molinos',

> that **every day, every week, every year and all thy life long, thou shouldst make this continuous act of contemplation, in faith and in love,** in a manner as pure and as spiritual as possible ... and that, having once surrendered and resigned thyself to the Divine Will ... **thy hours of prayer should not be filled with fresh acts but should merely continue that first act of faith and love already made**.
>
> (*Op. cit.*, 359)

Doubtless, this was also the passage from Falconi that Peers had particularly in mind here when referring to Molinos' debt to Falconi. Certainly, the

God, with perfect resignation, by the pure act of faith, dwells always in virtual and acquired contemplation'.[56]

The second book, which has [...][57] chapters, deals with 'obedience, indiscreet zeal and internal and external penance'.[58] This is the book most frequently mutilated by Protestant translators — in one edition omitted entirely — but it is essential to a full account of Molinos' teaching. It sets down, as the essentials of perfection, prayer, obedience, frequent communion and inward mortification. As to obedience, which is bound up with direction, [...][59] Frequent communion is one of the points in which Molinos was clearly a heterodox writer.[60] 'Frequent communion is the best preparation for the soul because one communion disposes her for another' ['la mejor preparación es comulgarse el alma con frecuencia, porque una comunión es disposicón para la otra' (Libro II, cap. XIII, 252)].[61] 'Exterior souls' may 'make their confession and retire from outward things' before communicating. But 'interior and spiritual souls ... have no need to prepare themselves, because their life is a continual and perfect preparation' ['las almas

similarities of wording and thought-content (my emphasis) are undeniable. In other passages in the *Guía espiritual* Molinos' debt to Falconi, as Peers observes, is openly acknowledged through direct quotation — see, for example, Libro I, cap. XIII, 173-74.

56 Marginal notes identify the source of his references as: L.69, *Passim*, L. Ch. 16, 112[d]. Keyed to the final quotation is the marginal note: 'Title of Ch. 14, Lyt. p. 105'. The title of chapter XIV of Book I is indeed: 'Se declara cómo, puesta el alma en la presencia de Dios con perfecta resignación por el acto puro de fe, va siempre en la oración y fuera de ella en virtual y adquirida contemplación' (179).

57 In his manuscript Peers has left a space here in which to insert (once verified) the number of chapters (in fact, eighteen) in the second book.

58 A marginal note reveals this is from the title of Book 2. Which is indeed the case: 'Del padre espiritual y su obediencia, del cielo indiscreto y de las penitencias interiores y exteriores' (199).

59 Peers has left a space in the manuscript, to be 'filled' with his observations on obedience.

60 Peers writes in pencil above this comment: '(this nothing to do w[ith] M[m] [?Mysticism] of course)'.

61 Here Peers refers in the margin to: Chap. 2 Lyt. p. 124; and, further down to: 125.

interiores y espirituales ... no tienen necesidad de prepararse actualmente, porque su vida es una continua y perfecta preparación' (Libro II, cap. XIII, 252)]. While this is dangerous doctrine, however, especially for those who think themselves more spiritual than they are, it should be noted that there is not in the actual text a shadow[62] of disrespect expressed for the Sacrament of the Altar, and no comparison of the reception of the Holy Communion with any other form of devotion, such as are found in Falconi. Penances which are indiscreetly severe are condemned, and, as in the chapter on Communion, the counsel of the director is to be followed strictly. These penances, however, are chiefly condemned because of the ill effect which they have on the character of the penitent. Penance in general is condemned neither as a principle nor as a practice, but on the contrary is described as 'good and holy and praiseworthy'. The most that is said against external penances is that they must gradually yield place to inward and spiritual mortification as the soul advances in this, 'because it is not good to spend the body and the spirit all at once' ['porque no es bien consumir el cuerpo y el espíritu a un mismo tiempo' (Libro II, cap. XV, 262)]. [...][63]

The third book of the *Spiritual Guide* has as its lengthy title: 'Of spiritual martyrdoms whereby God purges souls; of contemplation infused and passive; of perfect resignation, inward humility, Divine wisdom, true annihilation and internal peace' ['De los espirituales martirios con que Dios purga a las almas, de la contemplación infusa y pasiva, de la resignación perfecta, humildad interna, divina sabiduría, verdadera aniquilación e interior paz' (275)]. It begins by drawing a more heightened contrast than the author has yet done between what he terms the 'outer' and 'inner' way, — that is, the ways of meditation and contemplation respectively. The door[64] to the 'inner way' is not 'sensible delight or spiritual consolation' but

62 Peers inserts 'trace' below 'shadow', as a possible alternative.

63 Peers leaves space enough for a couple of additional sentences here. There is a note in pencil: ' ?more'. A series of references in the margin confirm that he continues to use Lyttelton: Ch. 4 L.128-9, L.129[d], 130[c].

64 Above 'door', Peers writes, as an alternative, 'gate'. And in the margin he gives his reference: Book 3, Ch. 3 Lyt. 144.

self-abnegation, or, as it is often called by Molinos, self-annihilation. This severe purgation has two forms: 'that of the bitter waters of afflictions, anguish, distress and inward torments' ['con amargas aguas de aflicciones, tentaciones, angustias, apreturas e interiores tormentos' (Libro III, cap. IV, 291)] (the Dark Night of the Soul) and, a 'more profitable and meritorious' one, 'that of the burning fire of enkindled love, a love impatient and hungry' ['con fuego ardiente de inflamado amor, impaciente y hambriento' (Libro III, cap. IV, 291)].[65] After describing each of these forms of 'spiritual martyrdom', Molinos returns to the more general subject of inward mortification, the necessity of which he emphasizes in a series of maxims not at all unlike those of St John of the Cross:[66]

> Thou wilt know thyself to be far from perfection, if thou findest not God in everything.
>
> [Conocerás que estás muy lejos de la perfección, si no hallas a Dios en todas las cosas. (Libro III, cap. VII, 308)]
>
> Know that pure, perfect and essential love consists in the Cross.
>
> [El puro, perfecto y esencial amor, sabrás que consiste en la cruz, ... (Libro III, cap. VII, 308)]
>
> The spiritual man who lives by God, and in Him, is inwardly contented in the midst of adversities of the body and soul.
>
> [El espiritual que vive para Dios y en Dios, en medio de las adversidades del cuerpo y del alma, está interiormente contento, ... (Libro III, cap. VII, 310)][67]

These maxims conclude with a paraphrase of the lines generally known as 'St Teresa's bookmark',[68] which Molinos renders, unexceptionably and indeed almost literally, thus: [...][69]

---

65 In the margin, referring to the first form of spiritual purgation, Peers writes here 'Des. [?described] in Chs. 4 and 5'. There is a reference, too, to p. 148[a], and, referring to the second form, he says 'Desc. in Ch. 6'.

66 Above the name of St John Peers writes: 'Ref. to M. [?*Mystics*, i.e. *Studies of the Spanish Mystics*] 2'.

67 There are references in pencil in the margin etc. to: Lyt. 159[a], Ch. 7, 159[c], 161[a].

68 Above this phrase Peers writes 'N. (Silva)'.

69 A space is left here in the manuscript, in which Peers had intended to write the lines to which he refers. There is here a reference in pencil to,

The following chapters continue the general theme, laying stress on self-depreciation and humility, a fresh series of maxims on humility emphasizing these counsels still further. A chapter on 'inward solitude' leads to a new, and loftier theme, that of 'infused and passive contemplation', which succeeds 'acquired contemplation' and is described as 'a complete repose' into which God leads the soul 'without its own knowledge', — a state, apparently, not unlike that of the Spiritual Marriage: [...][70]

This is a recurring, not a permanent state: the soul 'comes to herself again' from it and 'sometimes God grants this grace more than at other times'. Nor is it confined to those who have practised acquired contemplation: 'Sometimes He awaits not self-annihilation and self-abnegation of the soul, but ... gives this gift when He pleases' ['Unas veces se franquea más que otras, y no aguarda tal vez que esté el alma tan muerta y negada: que, como este don es gracia, le da cuando quiere' (Libro III, cap. XIV, 337)]. It may issue in increased illumination of the understanding or in increased ardour of the will. Two things must be avoided by the soul in this state 'activity of the spirit' and 'attachment', even to the state itself. It is given to very few to experience it, for it is 'the great perfection, the purest and most intimate union' ['la mayor perfección, ... la más pura y afectiva unión' (Libro III, cap. XIV, 339)], and is seldom bestowed save on the most spiritual.[71]

There now follow two chapters[72] of a more artificial kind, which abound in classifications of the spiritual states already

---

presumably, Lyttelton: 165[c] (§89). I assume that the passage to which Peers refers is the one that concludes Book III, chapter VIII, the last lines of which are: 'quien a Dios tiene, todo lo tiene; quien a Dios no tiene, todo le falta' (316).

70 Again Peers has left a space, intending to insert a specific quotation from the text. He reminds himself in a note, in pencil: 'Quote Lyt. 176. "There the Divine ... perfect union" All par. 129'. The brief quotations that he does include in this paragraph are from Libro III, chapter XIII, entitled 'Se explica que cosa sea la contemplación infusa y pasiva, y se declaran sus maravillosos efectos'.

71 There are references in pencil, in the margin etc.: 176[c], Ch. 14 Lyt. 178[a], 178[b], 178[c], 179[d].

72 Peers writes above in pencil: [chapters] 15 and 16.

outlined. There are 'two ways whereby the soul ascends to the felicity of contemplation and of perfect love: pleasure and desire' ['Dos son los medios por los cuales sube el alma a la felicidad de la contemplación y afectivo amor: el gusto y los deseos' (Libro III, cap. XV, 341)]. There are 'three steps of infused contemplation': satiety, inebriation and security. Six 'other steps of contemplation' are 'fire, union, elevation, illumination, pleasure and repose'. And 'many other steps of contemplation are ecstasies, raptures ... exultation, union, transformation' ['otros muchos grados hay de contemplación, como son: éxtasis, raptos ... exultación, unión, transformación'], which, says Molinos, 'I omit to explain, so as to give no occasion for their consideration, and also because there are whole books which treat of them' ['los cuales dejo de explicar por huir la especulación y porque hay libros enteros que tratan de estos puntos' (Libro III, cap. XV, 344)].[73]

There are four signs by which one may know the 'inward man'. Briefly, they are the direction of the understanding[74] and will toward God only; their turning to God at once when exterior occupations cease; the forgetting of outward things when prayer is begun; and the avoidance of them 'save when charity requires otherwise'. There are four effects of 'this secret intimate love': illumination, enkindling, sweetness (or fruition) and 'absorption of the faculties in God'. From this absorption arise two results: 'the first, a great courage to suffer for God; the second, a certain hope or assurance that the soul can never lose God, or be parted from Him' ['El primero, un grande aliento para padecer por Dios. El segundo, una cierta esperanza o seguridad, que jamás le ha de perder, ni de él se ha de separar' (Libro III, cap. XVI, 347)].

Finally, we are given three signs 'that a mind is purged'. The first sign is diligence, the contrary of neglect and sloth. The second is severity 'a strength of the soul against concupiscence together with an ardent love of asperity, lowliness and holy poverty' ['la severidad, que es una fortaleza de ánimo contra la concupiscencia, acompañada con ardiente

---

73 Notes in the margin refer to: Ch. 15 Lyt. 180[a], 180-1, 181[b], Lyt. 182.

74 Above this phrase Peers has written in pencil: '?express better?'.

amor de la aspereza, de la vileza y santa pobreza' (Libro III, cap. XVI, 347)]. The third is 'benignity, a sweetness of the soul'.

The next two chapters,[75] on 'Divine wisdom' ['De la divina sabiduría'], are notable only for their attack on 'men of learning, who lack the Spirit', the burden of them being the same contrast between acquired and infused knowledge, the latter of which is termed the 'mystical science' and its possessor 'the wise and truly mystical man'.[76]

Two chapters[77] then dwell on the nature of 'true and perfect annihilation' ['la verdadera y perfecta aniquilación'] and two more[78] on the 'high felicity of internal peace' ['la suma felicidad de la interior paz'] and the fewness of those that attain to it. [...][79]

Probably the first sensation of the reader who embarks upon Molinos' book with no pre-conceptions is the surprising beauty and appeal of its style.[80] He himself describes it as 'devout, pure and useful, without any ornament of polished sentences, ostentation of eloquence or theological niceties' ['devoto, casto y provechoso, sin exornación de pulidas frases, sin ostentación de elocuencias ni sutilezas teológicas' (*A quien leyere*, *ed. cit.*, 105)].[81] Menéndez y Pelayo remarks also, very justly, upon its concision and vigour;[82] to these qualities we may add a simplicity of construction, an absence of long quotations, and a

75 Above, Peers writes: '[chapters] 17 and 18'.

76 References in the margin continue in these paragraphs: 182-3, 183[b], 183-4, 184[b], 184-5, 187[b], 191[ac], 191[c].

77 Above, Peers writes: '[chapters] 19-20'.

78 Peers writes: '[chapters] 21-2'.

79 Peers leaves nearly a page (Ms., p. 24) blank here, evidently intending to develop this observation further. There is a note in pencil: 'Prob. say: The content of these will be fully discussed in next section. This ends the book'.

80 As before, I have used a double space to indicate where one section (II) ends and another (in this case, III) begins.

81 A note in the margin refers to 'Lyt. 51 A. to Rdr' ['Address to the Reader'].

82 A note in the margin refers to 'Het. Esp. p. 560 [i.e., to Menéndez y Pelayo's *Historia de los heterodoxos españoles*] (< Lyt. 42[n])'.

felicity of phraseology, all of which would make the book popular with religiously-minded people — not only with those who would read heavy tomes like the works of Luis de Granada and St John of the Cross, but also with those who preferred 'little books on prayer' like that of St Peter of Alcántara, or who, in the phrase of Malón de Chaide, would go about with the *Diana* in their pocket,[83] and would appreciate what could be read without effort of the understanding. The occasional rather cloying sweetness[84] of the *Spiritual Guide* is due rather to its content than to its style. One of the most attractive features of the book is its frequent and graceful use of metaphor: the figures themselves are usually (though not invariably) those common to most mystical writers, but their introduction is always suitable and the language in which they are clothed appropriate. A few examples may be quoted. [...][85]

It may safely be said that the content of a great part — probably the greater part — of the *Spiritual Guide* is wholly admirable, and admirably expressed. The author's claim that he was supported in his teaching by the greatest Christian doctors was, if exaggerated, at least not without justification.[86] St Augustine, St Gregory, St Bernard, St Thomas Aquinas and St Bonaventura are all represented in its pages; through it Dionysius and Gerson find their way once again into Spanish mysticism; and the most orthodox and most saintly of Molinos' predecessors in Spain, St Ignatius of Loyola, St Teresa and St John of the Cross are quoted or made use of more times than can easily be reckoned. In reading and re-reading the *Spiritual Guide* we have been especially struck with the evident attraction which the works of the Carmelite saints had for

83 There is a note in the margin: 'Ref M 1' — presumably a reference to *Studies of the Spanish Mystics*, I.

84 Peers writes in pencil above this phrase: '?alter???'.

85 Peers leaves a blank space consisting of nearly one page of his manuscript (p. 26), in which to insert the examples he has in mind. He adds in pencil a list of the pages from 'Trans. Lyttelton', which will supply him with the quotations required: '60 §13, 77 §23, 81 §32 (explain context), from §10 (to "broken"), 152 ll. 1-3, ?196 §199, 200 §213 end (if clear in orig[inal])'.

86 Peers wrote in pencil that the 'Ref. [is] above'.

Molinos. [...][87] And even if he were not able to call such notable witnesses to his defence — we have seen how he himself takes the defensive — we should be impressed by the truth and the nobility of much that he tells us.[88]

But one cannot praise anything nine-tenths of which is good if the remaining tenth be not commendable.[89] There is a leaven of error as well as one of malice and wickedness. And if the first page of a guide-book, which describes the initial stage of a journey, be inaccurate, it matters little if the remaining pages be wholly excellent, for the traveller will have strayed from his road and will have no occasion to profit by them. [...][90]

Molinos makes an antithesis[91] between what he calls the 'two sorts of spiritual persons, internal and external' ['Hay dos maneras de espirituales personas: unas interiores y exteriores otras' (Libro III, cap. I., 277)] which the great mystics never dreamed of. The latter class [...][92] We are, of course, familiar with this description of the Purgative Way, which Molinos here

87 Peers leaves a space, presumably intending to illustrate, through quotations, Molinos' debt and reference to St Teresa and St John of the Cross.

88 Peers adds a note in pencil here, only partially legible, to remind himself to 'Reread' something: 'Put in about ⅔ page'.

89 Peers puts a question mark above 'commendable' — a word with which he was not entirely satisfied.

90 The rest of the page (Ms., p. 28) is left blank for a later insertion. Peers, in a note added here in pencil, asks: '?Here cpn [comparison] of Mol. w[ith] Falc. [Falconi; *cf.* above, notes 9 and 55]. Say M [Molinos] better than F [Falconi] but no less dangerous — or even more so because of gter [greater] excellence and beauty of style'.

91 Above these words that begin the page (Ms., p. 29), there is a subheading in pencil, which reads 'Antithesis between inward and outward Spirituality'. Peers adds 'III', but must mean, in fact, section IV.

92 Peers leaves a space, intending to complete the sentence, with, he indicates, a quotation: 'quote Lyt. 139-40 to "and med^{n}" [?meditation]'. The passage he has in mind must be that which begins 'Estas buscan a Dios por afuera, por el discurso, imaginación y consideración; procuran con gran conato para alcanzar las virtudes muchas abstinencias, maceración de cuerpo y mortificación de los sentidos ...', and ends 'se deleitan de hablar continuamente de Dios, haciendo muy de ordinario fervorosos actos de amor, todo lo cual es arte y meditación' (Libro III, cap. I, 277).

terms 'the external way and the way of beginners' but we cannot assert with him that 'by it there is no arriving at perfection; nay, there is not so much as one step towards it' ['no se llegará por él a la perfección, ni aun se dará un paso' (Libro III, cap. I, 278)]. [...][93]

One of the dangers of the Quietists is that they made it appear that any person could attain to lofty mystical experiences and thus they (in effect, though not intention) lowered the standard of this. All sorts of people who felt moved by acts of resignation etc. would consider they had reached the lofty states described and would thereupon [?forsake ...] means of grace.

Molinos does not appear to say in so many words whether all *can* attain to infused contemplation or not. What he *does* say is that very few *do* attain to it and this fact he laments frequently:[94]

> Know that the souls which attain to this happy state are few, because few are they that are willing to embrace contempt and suffer themselves to be refined and purified ... There are many that enter this inward way, yet it is rare for a soul to go on in it.[95]
>
> [Pero sabrás que son pocas las almas que llegan a este dichoso estado, porque son pocas las que quieren abrazar el desprecio y dejarse labrar y purificar; por cuya causa, aunque son muchas las que entran en este interior camino, es rara la que pasa adelante, ... (Libro III, cap. II, 283)]

> O Divine Lord, how few souls are there in the world that serve Thee with perfection! ... O what a lack of souls is there who are

93 Peers indicates in the margin that the quotation is from: Lyt. 140. Peers leaves the rest of this page (p. 29) blank, presumably to make a later insertion.

94 These two paragraphs come under a subheading, '?Contemplation for all', and are scribbled in pencil — as if Peers was unsure of the wording, and meant to revise it later. The writing is difficult to read, and there are frequent abbreviations of words which I have given in full. I cannot claim to have deciphered this passage correctly in every particular. In the phrase, 'in effect, though not in intention', Peers gives 'result' as a possible alternative to 'effect'. More importantly, unable to read the key-word after 'thereupon' — which I have indicated by [?forsake ...] — I have resorted to mere conjecture.

95 Peers notes in the margin (correctly) that this quotation is from: III, 2. Lyt. 143.

> detached and wholly stripped! How few are the souls that are dead to themselves, alive to God and entirely resigned to His good pleasure! How few are those who are adorned with simple obedience, deep self-knowledge and true humility ... How few are willing to be led by the royal road of negation and the inward way![96]
>
> [¡Oh divino Señor! ¡Qué pocas almas hay en el mundo que os sirvan con perfección! ... ¡Oh, qué pocas almas se hallan desapegadas y totalmente desnudas! ¡Qué pocas almas hay muertas en sí y vivas para Dios, y que perfectamente se resignen en el divino beneplácito! ¡Qué pocas almas hay de sencilla obediencia, de profundo conocimiento de sí mismas y de humildad verdadera! ... ¡Qué pocas almas hay que quieran dejarse guiar por la vía regia de la negación e interior camino!
>
> (Libro III, cap. XXII, 374-75)]

The mystic's goal appears to be identified by Molinos with the higher, that is the infused, state of contemplation of which his own description has already been reproduced.[97] It terms the contemplation in question 'this passive state'. In it the soul is 'dominated and mastered' by God and 'put to sleep in a most sweet and placid rest' ['la adormece con suavísimo y dulcísimo sueño'].[98] But in it also God infuses into the soul light, love, strength and knowledge, and it is clearly stated that this is in preparation for the 'purest and most perfect union' ['la más pura y perfecta unión' (Libro III, cap. XIII, 334)], which, as its nature is not described, we must assume to be that of Heaven [...][99]

> ... the sweet, joyous and abundant riches of lofty contemplation and loving union.
>
> [... la dulce, suave y abundante riqueza de la alta contemplación y amorosa unión; (Libro III, cap. V, 302)]

---

96 Peers notes in the margin (again correctly) that this quotation comes from: III, 22; and refers us to [Lyt.] pp. 202-3.

97 In pencil here (Ms., p. 31) Peers adds the subheading: 'The Goal'. For the description referred to, see above, p. 127.

98 In the margin here Peers notes 'Lyt. 176^{c} *cf.* earlier trans. of passage'. This could be a reference to *The Spiritual Guide*, an English version printed in 1688 (based on the Venice edition of 1685), and reprinted with a foreword by Dugald Macfadyen (London: Hodder and Stoughton, 1928).

99 A space is left for an insertion here. There is also, before the quotations, a single line of comment (in pencil): 'Other phrases describing the Goal (attainment)'.

> ... By the way of nothingness thou must come to lose thyself in God (which is the highest degree of perfection).
> [Por el camino de la nada has de llegarte a perder en Dios, que es el último grado de la perfección; (Libro III, cap. XX, 366-67)]
>
> ... Those pure souls who ... long for annihilation and spiritual death.
> [... almas hay puras, ... que, ... anhelen a su negación y muerte espiritual! (Libro III, cap. XXII, 375)]
>
> The sixth [and last] step of contemplation is ... tranquillity ... The soul seems to rest in a sweet sleep, solacing itself and abiding in the loving Divine arms.[100]
> [El sexto es una ... tranquilidad ... que le parece al alma que, como en suave sueño, está solazándose y descansando en el divino y amoroso pecho. (Libro III, cap. XV, 343-44)]

The mystics' term of deification[101] is also used, but very sparingly and always fleetingly — 'the soul ... purged, transformed and deified', 'it is changed, spiritualized, transformed and deified' ['está trocada espiritualizada, transformada y deificada' (Libro III, cap. XIX, 364)]: never once does Molinos dwell on or develop this conception. [...][102]

In his insistence on obedience to an experienced director,[103] Molinos is in line with all his predecessors. He has some sharp comments on unpractised or unspiritual directors who 'for want of understanding the case' of those who are seeking to progress in prayer 'stop them in their course and ruin them', or, at best, 'leave them in greater perplexity and confusion'. [...][104]

---

100 In the margin Peers gives the precise references for these quotations, from Lyttelton: '156^{c}, 197^{a}, 203^{b}, 182^{b}'. After 203^{b} (keyed to 'Those pure souls ...') he asks: '(?Quote also)'. And (keyed to 'The sixth [and last] step') Peers asks: '?*Is* this the goal though'. The words '[and last]' in this quotation are words inserted and square-bracketed by Peers himself.

101 This phrase begins a new page (Ms., p. 32), at the top of which Peers has written: 'The goal (ctd.)'.

102 References are given above these quotes — which are: 91^{b}, 195^{b}. The rest of this page is blank, presumably because Peers intended to enlarge on this observation.

103 The word 'Director' is written at the top of the page (Ms., p. 33) which begins with this phrase.

104 A note in the margin reminds Peers: 'Develop < Bk [Book] II'. And he refers (as the source of his quotations here) to: [Lyt.] 72^{b}, 90^{b}. See, on this

As an earlier quotation will have made manifest, Molinos considers supernormal physical phenomena as beyond his province.[105] His attitude to them, however, is by no means clear and perhaps not consistent. In one place[106] he classes 'ecstasies and raptures' among the various 'steps' of contemplation, while elsewhere he makes 'internal communications, inward raptures and ecstasies' graces 'on which the soul leans and which it enjoys' to be 'purged away'[107] as much as 'attachments to natural and temporal advantages'. Elsewhere he adopts a middle position, classing the experience of 'raptures, or external ecstasies or vehement affections'[108] as 'a road liable to many illusions and to the danger of infirmities and of the torments of the understanding, whereby few attain to the summit of perfection' ['camino ... sujeto a muchas ilusiones, con peligro de enfermedades y fatigas del entendimiento, por cuya senda es raro el que llega a la cima de la perfección' (Libro III, cap. XIX, 362)]. [...][109]

Whatever part of Molinos may be [read] when compared [?...] with San Juan de la Cruz etc. certain[ly] he gives [the] impression of mere passivity by his frequent use of terms of negation.[110] [...] Phrases abound like 'clothe thyself with this nothingness' ['Vístete de esa nada'], 'we seek self whenever we emerge from nothingness' ['Nos buscamos a nosotros mismos siempre que salimos de la nada'], 'creep in as far as ever thou

---

subject, especially Libro II, caps. VI-VII. Most of this page is then left blank, indicating that Peers had intended to develop his thoughts further.

105 In pencil at the top of the page (Ms., p. 34) which begins with this sentence, Peers has written: 'Raptures etc.'. For the earlier quotation to which Peers refers, see above p. 128.

106 Above this word Peers identifies the place referred to: 182[c].

107 Above this phrase Peers writes: '86 (*cf.*, five, 145[c])'. And in the margin here Peers writes: 'This seems unorthodox M[m] [?mysticism]'.

108 References in the margin read: III 19, 193[b].

109 A space is left here too, for further comment.

110 This is the first sentence of a page (Ms., p. 35) which has a note or heading at the top: 'Faults of *SG* [*Spiritual Guide*] (1) Negation'. In this sentence, which is written in pencil, many words are abbreviated and some are illegible. I cannot claim to have read it correctly. After this, a line is left vacant in which Peers must have intended to write a further comment.

canst into the truth of thy nothingness' ['Éntrate en la verdad de tu nada'], 'by the way of nothingness thou must come to lose thyself in God' ['Por el camino de la nada has de llegarte a perder en Dios'], 'enclose thyself in nothingness' ['Si te estás encerrada en la nada'], 'only in nothingness reigns true and perfect dominion' ['sólo en la nada reina el perfecto y verdadero dominio'], 'knowing that thou art nothing, that thou canst do nothing and art worth just nothing, thou wilt quietly embrace passive aridity' ['Conociendo que eres nada, que puedes nada y que vales nada, abrazarás con quietud las pasivas sequedades'], 'by means of this nothingness thou must die to thyself' ['Por medio de esa nada has de morir en ti misma'], 'drown thyself in this nothingness' ['Anégate en esa nada'], 'consider nothing, desire nothing, will nothing, endeavour after nothing' ['no mires nada, no desees nada, no quieras nada, ni solicites saber nada'], 'endeavour to be overwhelmed in this nothingness, to lose thyself, to sink deep into it, if thou hast a mind to be annihilated, united and transformed' ['procura en esa nada sumergirte, perderte y abismarte, si quieres aniquilarte, unirte y transformarte'].[111]

These phrases, for convenience, are taken out of one chapter,[112] but they may be found almost anywhere in the later chapters of the book. Even granting that they are capable of an orthodox and reasonable interpretation, their very frequency would be apt to mislead those ignorant of the main lines of Molinos' teaching. And if it be urged that this is contained in the book, the reply is that the relation of the contemplative state contrasted with the practice of meditation to 'nothingness' is by no means clear to those who do not study the *Guide* with great care. In the Admonitions,[113] words and phrases occur like 'detachment', 'obscure knowledge', 'Divine knowledge', 'deprived of all that which the natural appetite requires' ['vacío de todo lo

111 In the margin near the beginning of this paragraph Peers has written, after III. 20, 'all [quotations] (in order)'.

112 All these quotations are, indeed, to be found in Libro III, cap. XX (*ed. cit.*, 365-68).

113 Peers asks, in pencil, above this word: 'Is this "Avisos"?'. In fact the word used by Molinos is 'Advertencias'.

que su apetito natural le pide' (*Advertencia* I, 109)], and it is not till comparatively late in the book that 'annihilation', 'self-stripping', 'passivity', 'nothingness' appear on every page. The natural conclusion to be drawn by the average not too careful reader is that those states are represented as the mystic's goal. [...][114]

E. Allison Peers†

University of Liverpool.

---

114 This essay, or chapter, is clearly unfinished for it does not end here. Peers leaves a space, and he writes in the margin: 'Consider and develop this'. Then he begins a new page (Ms., p. 37) with a new paragraph, and a sentence which, since it leads nowhere, I include (with bold emphasis) in this note, rather than in the main text:

> **Again what interpretation is likely to be put upon a passage like the following, considered as an account of the mystical progress.**

Peers left the rest of this page blank, in which to insert the passage referred to. And in the margin there is a scribbled note, difficult to decipher: 'That from III, 19, which §3 in M[olinos] (Lyt. p. 194)'. The third paragraph of Libro III, cap. XIX, which Peers evidently wished to quote, reads as follows: 'Haciendo el alma continuo progreso de su bajeza, debe caminar a la práctica de la aniquilación, que consiste en el aborrecimiento de la honra, dignidad y alabanza; porque a la vileza y al puro nada no es razón se le dé la dignidad y la honra (*ed. cit.*, 362). He never completed his evaluation of Miguel de Molinos.

III

Peers' Collected Papers on the Spanish Mystics
A Catalogue

Peers, Edgar Allison, Gilmour Professor of Spanish at Liverpool University, 1922-1952. **Notes, cuttings, pamphlets, offprints, drafts, correspondence, etc.** related to his publications **on the Spanish mystics**, including especially material for an unpublished **vol. 4 of *Studies of the Spanish Mystics*** (vols 1-3 published 1927-60). Sixteen boxes, *c.*5 linear feet, *c.*1920-60. Donated, in 1973, by Ivy L. McClelland, University of Glasgow, to the Department of Hispanic Studies, University of Liverpool. Transferred from the Department of Hispanic Studies in 1981 to Special Collections and Archives, Sydney Jones Library, the University of Liverpool. Ref. **Peers Collection**.

A catalogue of these **Papers** — prepared in 1982 under the direction of Mr Michael Perkin, Special Collections, Sydney Jones Library — is published here for the first time, to assist scholars researching into Spanish mysticism.*

I **Material relating to *Studies of the Spanish Mystics*, vols I-III, 1927-60:**

(1-18) Bibliography, index cards, notes. 18 bundles of slips.
(19-29) Named bundles of slips (11): M. Ágera, Antonio Arbiol, Juan de Bonilla (2), Juan Bretón, Andrés Capilla, Juan

* I am most grateful to Mr Perkin for a copy of this catalogue. It should be noted that some additional papers, relevant especially to Ramon Lull, which previously belonged to E. Allison Peers have come into my possession. These are: Peers' notes and typescripts; rare offprints from early periodicals; some eighteenth-century illustrations; news-cuttings; and letters (from the 1920s and 1930s) between Peers and Spanish and British scholars. I propose to donate these items to the University of Liverpool to enhance further the Peers Papers on the Spanish mystics held in the Sydney Jones Library.

de Cartagena, Juan del Espíritu Santo, Luis de León, Pedro Malón de Chaide.

II *Studies of the Spanish Mystics*, **vol. III, 1960:**

(1-3) MS notes and drafts on loose sheets from exercise-books. 3 envelopes.
(4-5) Index: draft in pencil; corrected typescript, 30 pp.
(6) MS notes and typescript bibliography.
(7) Typescripts.

III ***Santa Teresa. The Complete Works*, 3 vols, 1945:**

(1) Bibliography: index slips. 1 bundle.
(2) A-Z notebook: 'Sta. T. Peculiarities of diction'.

IV ***Santa Teresa.* Letters, 1951:**

(1-3) Notes, news-cuttings, pamphlet cuttings, drafts, corrected proofs. 3 envelopes.
(4 [1-111]) Letters: 111 letters to Peers, with a few drafts or copies of his replies (separately indexed).

V ***St John of the Cross. Complete Works*, 3 vols, 1934-35:**

(1) Notes, etc.
(2) Cuttings of reviews in periodicals and newspapers.
(3 [1-15]) Letters: 15 letters to Peers, with a few copies of his replies (separately indexed).

VI **Material relating to the projected vol. IV of *Studies of the Spanish Mystics*, not published:**

(1-3) 'Quietism': extensive MS notes, some grouped under names of individuals, some drafts, 2 extracted articles from journals, and plans: 'My first draft', 'My second draft'. 3 envelopes.
(4) Negative photostat copy of: Juan Falconi, *Lettera ... ad un religioso ... tradotta dalla lingua spagnuola nell' italiana*, Rome, 1674, with notes by Peers.
(5) MS drafts and notes for a study of Miguel de Molinos, probably intended for a vol. IV of *Studies*.
(6) 'Peers papers unpublished', 'Notes on Sta Teresa, S.J.X., and other mystics'. 11 packets.
(7) 'Peers papers unpublished'; notes on 'Quietists, Illuminists'. 6 packets.

(8) Quietism. Further notes.
(9) Quietism, etc. News-cuttings, extracts from reviews, offprints.
(10) Quietism. 2 letters to Peers (separately indexed).

VII Spanish mysticism and mysticism in general:

(1) Miscellaneous notes.
(2-6) Notes for a series of 5 lectures, in pink wrappers.
(7) 'Mysticism: cuttings', from newspapers and journals (some from an agency, Durrant's Press Cuttings).
(8) Carbon copy of an undergraduate thesis, Liverpool University, BA Hons. (Special Studies Spanish), 'Style in the *Vida* of Santa Teresa', by María de la Concepción Álvarez, with an appraisal by Peers.
(9 [1-267]) 267 letters mainly to Peers, but including some copies of his replies (with some unidentified items). Separately indexed.
(1-112) Letters to and from publishers:
- (1-56) Faber and Faber Limited. 1949-52.
- (57-58) Compañía Editora. 1952.
- (59-87) Student Christian Movement Press Ltd. (including royalty statements, agreements, publicity). 1946-51.
- (88-102) S.P.C.K. House. 1950-52.
- (103-112) Rockliff Publishing Corporation Ltd (including publisher's catalogue and publicity). 1950.

VIII Miscellaneous printed items:

(1-14) Offprints and cuttings of articles by Peers (not separately catalogued, but numbered according to the Selective Bibliography by H. B. Hall in the *Bulletin of Hispanic Studies*, XXX (1953), No. 117, 12-20.
(15-19) Booksellers' catalogues. 1923-48.
(20-23) Ephemera.
(24-51) Offprints, extracts and cuttings of articles by others, A-Z (separately catalogued).

Cervantes, Cardenio and Theobald

KENNETH MUIR†

University of Liverpool

As Allison Peers first made his name as an English scholar, and as I had the good fortune to be his colleague in his last years, it is not inappropriate for a Shakespeare specialist to contribute to this Volume in memory of a great Hispanist, especially as Shakespeare is known to have collaborated with Fletcher in a play twice performed at Court in 1612-13 — a play clearly based on the story of Cardenio in the first part of *Don Quixote.* The present article is a sequel to my chapter on the play in *Shakespeare as Collaborator* (London: Methuen, 1970) in which I considered the claim of Lewis Theobald that his play, *Double Falshood* (*sic*) was an adaptation of a manuscript he possessed of the Shakespeare play. He indignantly denied that Fletcher had any hand in it. A reconsideration of my chapter was prompted by a claim made by an antiquarian bookseller in July 1993 that a manuscript in the British Library (MS Lansdowne 807) was a missing *Cardenio* MS. This was an error. The MS had belonged to Warburton — one of the MSS which escaped the ravages of Betty his cook who used his MSS of unpublished plays for culinary purposes — and it had been published several times: 1824, 1875 (in an edition of Chapman, without claiming that Chapman was the author); 1909, in an early publication by the Malone Society, edited by W. W. Greg; and, as Professor Gary Taylor hastened to point out, it is to appear shortly in another edition and also in the Oxford edition of Thomas Middleton, of

† I record with sorrow the death of our friend and colleague, Kenneth Muir, 30 September 1996, in his ninetieth year (AM).

which he is the chief editor. The bookseller's error of attribution is easy to explain. One of the two plots of *The Second Maiden's Tragedy* (as it had been foolishly entitled by Sir George Buc, the licencer) was based on Cervantes' well-known novella, *El curioso impertinente*, read aloud by the Priest in *Don Quixote* (Chapters XXXIII-XXXV), interrupting those chapters concerned with the story of Cardenio.[1]

---

1 It will be remembered that in the novella a foolish husband, Anselmo, persuades his close friend, Lotario, to test his wife's fidelity by pretending to make love to her. Lotario, to his great distress, falls genuinely in love, and she with him. The play changes the name of Lotario to Votarius, but the names of the husband, of Camila/Camilla, and of Leonela, her lady-in-waiting, are retained. The conflict in the minds of the reluctant adulterers is brilliantly dramatized, but the melodramatic ending is less effective than Cervantes' story. Camilla accidentally kills her lover; Anselmo and Bellarius (Leonela's lover) are poisoned, but before they expire, Anselmo kills Leonela, and in the course of a fight between Anselmo and Bellarius Camilla runs between them and is spitted on both their swords. This carnage resembles that of Middleton's *Women Beware Women* (*c*.1621) in which all the main characters are killed.

Middleton's authorship of the play seems to be supported by this parallel, although it must be admitted that several of his contemporaries might have been responsible for the necrophilia of the other plot. More significantly, a very minor character, the contented cuckold, Sophonirus, is remarkably similar to Allwit in *A Chaste Maid in Cheapside*, performed in the same year as *The Second Maiden's Tragedy*.

Soph. I have a wife, would she were so preferd
I could be but her subject, so I'me now
I allowe her her owne frend, to stop her mowth
And keep her quiet, give him his table free,
And the huge feeding of his great stone horse
On which he rides in pompe about the Cittie
Only to speake to gallants in bay-windowes;
Marry, his lodging he paies deerly for.
He getts me all my children, there I save by't;
Beside I drawe my life owte by the bargaine
Some twelve yeres longer than the tymes appointed,
When my young prodigall gallant kicks up's heeles
At one and thirtie, and lies dead and rotten.
Some fyve and fortie yeares before I'm coffinde.
'Tis the right waie to keep a woman honest:
One frend is Baracadoe to a hundred

It is usually assumed that Shakespeare and Fletcher made use of Thomas Shelton's translation of *Don Quixote*, published a year earlier. They may have done; but Fletcher certainly and

---

And keepes em owte; nay more, a husbandes sure
To have his children all of one mans getting
And he that performes best, can have no better
I'me e'ene as happie then that save a labour.

Allwit The Founders come to Towne, I am like a Man
Finding a table furnish't to his hand
As mine is still to me, prayer for the Founder
Blesse the right Worhipfull, the good Founders life.
I thanke him, h'as maintain'd my House this ten yeares
Not onely keepes my wife, but 'a keepes me
And all my Family. I am at his Table,
He gets me all my children, and payes the Nurse
Monthly or weekely, puts me to nothing.
Rent, nor church duties, not so much the Scavenger
The hapiest state that ever Man was borne to.
I walke out in a morning, come to breakfast
Find excellent Cheere, a good fire in Winter,
Looke in my Coale-house about Midsommer-eeve
That's full, five or sixe Challome new layd up
Looke in my backe yard. I shall find a steeple
Make up with Kentish faggots, which o're-lookes
The Water House and the Wind-Milles. I say nothing
But smile, and pin the doore. When she lyes in
As now she's even upon the point of grunting,
A Lady lyes not like her, there's her imbossings
Embrodrings, spanglings, and I know not what,
As if she lay with al the gaudy shops
In *Gressams* Bursse about her, then her restoratives
Able to set up a Young Pothecarie
And richly stocke the Foreman of a Drug-shop.
Her Sugar by whole Loaves, her Wines by Rundlets.
I see these things, but like a happy Man
I pay for none at all, Yet Fooles think's mine.
I have the name, and in his Gold I shine.

A Chaste Maid in Cheapside was performed by Princess Elizabeth's men, the other play by the King's men, Shakespeare's own company. If Middleton wrote both, he must have used some of the same material for a rival company. The speech is more appropriate in a light satirical comedy than in a grim tragedy.

Shakespeare probably[2] could read Spanish. The two dramatists were naturally attracted to the theme of *Cardenio* at a time when forgiveness was the culmination of the tragi-comedies on which both dramatists were engaged. Imogen in *Cymbeline* forgives both Iachimo and her husband; Cymbeline forgives the kidnapper of his sons and is reconciled to Rome (so that universal peace could enable Jesus to be born); Hermione in *The Winter's Tale* forgives Leontes after he has suffered sixteen years of remorse, and Polixenes also forgives his murderous intentions. Prospero in *The Tempest* brings his enemies to his island, so that he can marry the son of one of them to his daughter and forgive even the unrepentant villains, Antonio and Sebastian. It will be remembered too that the forgiving of Proteus is the climax of *The Two Gentlemen of Verona* and that it was accompanied by one of Shakespeare's favourite devices, heroines played by boys disguised as boys, culminating in *Cymbeline* in which Imogen as Fidele wanders through most of the play.[3] The Cardenio story contains Dorotea's not very successful attempt to disguise herself as a boy.

However attractive and fashionable the Cardenio story appeared to Shakespeare and Fletcher, the dramatization posed several problems. In *Don Quixote* it is spread over a dozen chapters, and these are interspersed with unconnected episodes and, as we have seen, a whole novella. These deliberately tantalize the reader who wants to know the fate of the main characters. The reader is given clues — the dead mule, the abandoned luggage, the half-naked lunatic with incoherent rages interspersed with lucid intervals. The order of events is out of chronological sequence. We first meet Cardenio after the double betrayal has driven him mad; the nature of the betrayal is gradually revealed, and we are near the full explanation which will lead to a happy outcome. When Cardenio is given food he begins telling his story of Fernando's treachery and (as he thinks) of Luscinda's betrayal. He is

---

2 *Cf.* Kenneth Muir, 'Elizabethan Hispanists, Lope de Vega and Shakespeare', *Hispanic Studies in Honour of Geoffrey Ribbans*, *BHS* Special Homage Volume (Liverpool: Liverpool U. P., 1992), 91-96.

3 E.g. Portia, Nerissa, Jessica, Rosalind, Viola.

interrupted in his story and runs away — another teasing of the reader. He is next overheard by different auditors singing a courtly and sophisticated song and now perfectly sane. He again tells his story. They next encounter Dorotea, disguised as a shepherd boy. She has been secretly married to Fernando and bewails his desertion. Cardenio resolves to champion her cause, while leaving his own revenge to God. The arrival of Fernando and his recognition of Dorotea leads directly to his repentance and to everyone's forgiveness of him.

Another problem is caused by Cervantes' ambiguous attitude to the story. On the one hand he sympathizes with the lovers who suffer from their injuries at Fernando's hands; on the other hand he ridicules them more harshly than Shakespeare does the quartet of lovers in *A Midsummer-Night's Dream*. Cardenio, Luscinda and Dorotea seem to spend most of their time in floods of tears and the two women faint away on the slightest provocation. It is natural for Luscinda to faint at her wedding to Fernando and for Dorotea to faint when her would-be seducer has somehow got into her locked room; but when Luscinda's father agrees to wait a few days until Cardenio knows what the Duke wants him to do, and Luscinda also agrees, 'ella me lo confirmó', Cardenio tells us, 'con mil juramentos y *mil desmayos*'.[4] Shakespeare's heroines were made of sterner stuff. Rosalind in *As You Like It*, it is true, faints once at the sight of blood. The others never lose their senses. Imogen, for example, does not faint when she wakes up from her drugged sleep beside a headless corpse she thinks is her husband's. We may be sure that the dramatists of *Cardenio* would cut down the tears and swoons.

Another problem for the dramatists was the meagre information Cervantes provided about important characters. We are told little about Duke Ricardo and less about his elder son, who had inherited his father's virtues. We are told nothing about Luscinda's mother and too little about her father. The reaction of the Duke on discovering Fernando's secret marriage to a wealthy peasant's daughter is not

4 J. M. Cohen in his Penguin translation tones down somewhat Cervantes' satire. He renders Luscinda's agreement as 'made between fits of fainting'.

disclosed.

As *Double Falshood* was avowedly an adaptation, it is hazardous to try and determine for which alterations Theobald was responsible, and which he took over from the manuscript he claimed to have used. Nevertheless, it may be worthwhile to reconsider his version of the play in the light of what has been said above about the difficulties of dramatizing a deliberately confused narrative.

Critics are still divided about the respective shares of Shakespeare and Fletcher beneath Theobald's palimpsest. In *Shakespeare as Collaborator* I argued that Shakespeare's share was confined to the first two acts. I did not then — nor do I now — believe, as one critic argued, that IV.i and V.ii were pure Shakespeare, uncontaminated by Theobald's re-writing: to me they are Fletcherian.

In the first scene of Theobald's play[5] we are introduced to Duke Ricardo (Angelo) conversing with his elder son (Roderick) and they agree to send for Cardenio (Julio) to act as a companion to Fernando (Henriquez) and also as a restraining influence. As the Duke and Roderick take part in the denouement, it seems probable that these changes are part of the original play. In the second scene we meet Cardenio's father (Bernard) — a shadowy figure in *Don Quixote* — but in this scene Theobald's hand and method are only too visible. There are notorious plagiarisms from *Hamlet* and *Troilus and Cressida*.[6] Nevertheless, there are other passages which seem to many critics to be beyond Theobald's capacities and may be authentically Shakespearian.[7]

---

5 For convenience I have retained the names used by Cervantes, followed in brackets by Theobald's.

6 Stinting our Farewell kisses, cutting off
The forms of Parting, and the Interchange
Of thousand precious Vows with Haste too rude

Cf. Troilus and Cressida IV.3. 32-47. Theobald depends entirely on Shakespeare and reduces sixteen lines of great poetry to three lines of indifferent verse.

7 Patience! what else? My Flames are in the Flint.
Haply to lose a Husband I may weep;
Never to get one. When I cry for Bondage,
Let Freedom quit me.

In the third scene Fernando tries to seduce Dorotea (significantly re-named Violante), but she virtuously repulses him. Her resistance redoubles his determination to possess her. The scene contains five lines of which Theobald was apparently proud,[8] but much of the scene appears to be Shakespearian both in style and sentiment.[9]

In the first scene of Act II, Fernando, unable to gain his ends even by a promise of marriage, describes his rape of Dorotea. I doubt whether this scene was ever Shakespeare's. Although there is strong evidence that Theobald turned blank verse into prose, the dozen pentameters that can be disinterred are quite undistinguished.[10] In the next scene, however, in which the raped girl laments her shame and receives a cruel farewell message from the rapist, Shakespeare's hand has been surmised:

> O, wretched and betray'd! Lost Violante!
> Heart-wounded with a thousand perjur'd Vows,
> Poison'd with studied language and bequeath'd
> To Desperation. I am now become
> The Tomb of my own Honour: a dark Mansion
> For Death alone to dwell in.

---

8 Strike up, my Masters;
But touch the strings with a religious Softness;
Teach sound to languish thro' the Night's dull Ear,
Till Melancholy start from her lazy couch,
And carelessness grow convert for Attention.

9 e.g. Home, my Lord,
What you can say is most unseasonable; what sing
Most absonant and harsh: Nay, your Perfume,
Which I smell hither, cheers not my sense
Like our Field-violet's Breath?

10 See the long prose speech near the end of scene 1 from which one can extract several:

> Twas but the Coyness of a modest Bride
> Not the Resentment of a ravisht Maid.
> And is the Man yet born, who would not risque
> The Guilt, to meet the Joy?...
> Oh that a Man
> Could reason down this Feaver of the Blood
> Or sooth with words the Tumult in his Heart!

It seems likely that the rape was one of Theobald's ideas. A broken promise was regarded as less reprehensible in the aftermath of the Comedy of Manners than it had been a century before.

In the next scene (II.3), Fernando, while admitting that his conduct is murdering honour, is welcomed as a suitor by Luscinda's father, despite her passionate protests that she loves only Cardenio. Her father is motivated by the wish to marry Luscinda to the son of a Duke. This is revealed in an amusing scene when Camillo arrives to agree to the marriage of Cardenio and Luscinda. In the last scene of Act II the imprisoned Luscinda sends an urgent message to her lover, which he receives at the beginning of Act III. Luscinda, waiting for his arrival, at first assumes that he has not received her letter and finally convinces herself that he has plotted with Fernando to abandon her. The Luscinda in *Don Quixote* has no such absurd suspicion. It is true that Luscinda fears in I.2 that Cardenio will find another love at the Duke's Court, presumably teasing him, and that Cardenio feels that she 'plays the coy one', while he himself

> Like to a clime beneath Hyperion's Eye,
> Burns with a constant heart.

But the passage in Act III is probably by Fletcher and may be contaminated by Theobald's smug confidence in his understanding of female psychology.

Cardenio, in disguise, interrupts the marriage ceremony, challenging Fernando to a duel, and he is thrown out. There is one great difference between this scene and Cervantes' narrative; Cardenio does not hear Luscinda say 'I will' and cannot accuse her of betrayal. Whoever made the change presumably thought that Luscinda's apparent consent to marriage in Cervantes' tale was incredible in itself and a wicked deception of the reader.

The rest of the play is predominantly Fletcher's. In III.3 there is an important alteration, designed to heighten the importance of Roderick. Worried at the continued absence of Cardenio and Fernando he goes to Camillo to make enquiries. Camillo mistrusts a brother of the evil Fernando, but in the end Roderick succeeds in reconciling him with the remorseful

Bernard, and they go in search of Cardenio. Somewhat improbably, the plan is overheard by Dorotea who disguised herself as a Shepherd's boy.

In Act IV shepherds encounter the mad Cardenio, who is given some effective ravings in blank verse — here drama scores over narrative. The disguised Dorotea is persuaded to approach the lunatic who immediately becomes calm and recognizes that she is a woman. The Master of the Flocks has come to the same conclusion and, of course, lusts after her. She is saved by the opportune arrival of Roderick, who has arranged to meet Fernando, Luscinda having taken refuge in a nunnery nearby. Roderick agrees to help Fernando's plan to kidnap her, but lays down certain conditions. It is he who suggests the stratagem of gaining access to the nunnery by arranging a bogus funeral. In *Don Quixote* no stratagem is necessary as the doors of the nunnery are not shut.

Before this (in V.2) Cardenio overhears the disguised Dorotea singing two feeble songs, which he describes as heavenly. This scene has none of the glamour of the narrative version. Dorotea complains of the Master of the Flocks and when she mentions Fernando, Cardenio exclaims 'Ha!' and introduces himself. Whereas in *Don Quixote* he vows to champion Dorotea's cause, in *Double Falshood*, with a sickly sentimentality for which Theobald is clearly responsible, he proposes never to leave her and indulge Despair,

> So worn with griefs, steal to the Cave of Death
> And in a sigh give up our latest Breath.

In Act V all is ready for a happy ending. Roderick comforts the rescued Luscinda and Fernando begs her forgiveness. She declares that his well-dissembled passion

> Has gain'd you nothing but a deeper hate.

The disguised Dorotea plucks Roderick by the sleeve and tells him that Fernando had once loved her. He asks her to appeal to the Duke and to lead him to Cardenio.

In Scene 2, while the Duke is consoling Bernard and Camillo, Roderick arrives with Luscinda and Fernando who asks pardon of his father. Dorotea appears, still disguised, and Fernando denies ever having seen 'him'. Then Roderick produces the letter he wrote to Dorotea after the rape. Finally the disguised Cardenio enters with Dorotea as a woman. Fernando asks forgiveness, first of Dorotea, for whom his love is rekindled, then of Luscinda, and finally of Cardenio when he throws off his disguise and embraces Luscinda. Everyone forgives Fernando, and the Duke approves of the misalliance of Fernando and Dorotea because her father once saved his life in a boar-hunt.

> Tho' your Descent be low, call me your father.[11]

The play ends with these improbable sentiments.

What conclusions can be arrived at on the writing of *Cardenio*? Obviously they will have to be tentative because of the lack of the original manuscript (or MSS) which Theobald claimed to have seen. It seems probable that Shakespeare came out of retirement because his company had to celebrate Princess Elizabeth's betrothal. Hence his collaboration with Fletcher in *The Two Noble Kinsmen*, the younger man taking the larger share. No doubt they discussed the general outlines of the play as they would with *Cardenio*, but most of the scenes in that too would be allocated to Fletcher. They would agree that the roles of the Duke and his elder son should be used to start and round off the play. They would probably agree that Fernando should secretly marry Dorotea (but not rape her). In general they strengthened the parts of the parents of Cardenio and Luscinda but otherwise kept closely to the events described in *Don Quixote*. Theobald's alterations were mostly disastrous. Shakespeare's scenes were vandalized, as we have seen; but those of Fletcher, with whose style he was more sympathetic, were left relatively undamaged.

---

11 In an article entitled 'A Trick of Style' (*Shakespeare Studies*, VI [1970], 305-10) I examined the prevalence of internal rhymes in the later plays of Shakespeare, whether in the same or successive lines. In this article and in my edition of *Double Falshood* (London: Cornmarket Press, 1970) I showed that there were several examples in that play, the low percentage being explained by Theobald's re-writing of Shakespeare's scenes.

Conceits and Connections: Three Golden-Age Sonnets at Work

IAN MACPHERSON

Queen Mary and Westfield College, London

When the critic Anthony Burgess was asked in 1977 to select and justify his personal seven wonders of the world, he included among his choices the sonnet as a verse form, principally because:

> whatever extrinsic message is imposed on it, [the sonnet] always has the same meaning — non-verbal, though it needs words for its realisation. Or, to use the language of linguistics, the sonnet-phoneme can be heard only through the sonnet-allophone.[1]

In a discussion of three characteristic examples of what Burgess might describe as the sonnet-allophone, all taken from the Spanish Golden Age, my principal purpose here will be to concentrate, to some extent from a linguist's point of view, on one primary aspect of their composition: the conceits, wit and range of illustration which characterize and connect them, and through an examination of which a little more light might possibly be cast on our understanding of the Golden-Age sonnet-phoneme. The three sonnets are Luis de Góngora's 'La dulce boca que a gustar convida', Francisco de Quevedo's 'En crespa tempestad del oro undoso' and Sor Juana Inés de la Cruz's 'Verde embeleso de la vida humana'; my concern will be with artistic technique rather than argument or theme, with the way in which the linguistic, rhetorical and structural devices employed by these three very different poets operate in relation

1 *Sunday Times*, 16 October 1977, Supplement, p. 94.

to each other, and with how they underpin and enhance the message of the poems in which they figure.

Happily, recent criticism has done much to revise the view of Menéndez Pelayo and the legion of critics who have followed in his footsteps that the lyric poetry of the classical period in Spain can be dealt with by ringing categorizations of Góngora as a *culteranista,* dealing in an excess of learned polysyllables, and of Gracián and Quevedo as *conceptistas*, with a dislike of polysyllabic neologisms matched only by a marked penchant for the conceit.[2] It has now been established that the terms in question were unfamiliar to these writers in their own time, and it is not too difficult to demonstrate that the roots of *conceptismo* are to be found in a period long before Góngora, and that Góngora's *culto* poems would be a great deal less effective without the firm structure of poetic conceits which underpins them. I propose here to consider some of the common ground between the two men and then to focus on one of Sor Juana Inés' outstanding sonnets through the same critical lens, demonstrating the *concepto* and the literary allusion working together in three of the finest sonnets of the classical period to provide an extra artistic dimension.

Baltasar Gracián's much-quoted but less frequently fully understood definition of the *concepto* provides a convenient point of departure:

> [el concepto] es un acto del entendimiento, que exprime la correspondencia que se halla entre los objectos ... Esta correspondencia es genérica a todos los conceptos, y abraza todo el artificio del ingenio.[3]

Gracián saw the *concepto* as an act of the understanding that expresses a relationship between things, a metaphor which above all seeks to draw attention to an intellectual relationship between two objects or terms. As A. A. Parker marked out in his Presidential Address to the Modern Humanities Research

---

2 See especially Andrée Collard, *Nueva poesía: conceptismo, culteranismo en la crítica española* (Madrid: Castalia, 1967) and Paul Julian Smith, *Writing in the Margin. Spanish Literature of the Golden Age* (Oxford: Clarendon Press, 1988).

3 *Agudeza y arte de ingenio*, ed. Evaristo Correa Calderón (Madrid: Castalia, 1969), 2 vols; I, 55-56.

Association in 1982, this is a definition which has tended to puzzle non-hispanists, because it appears to be simply an explanation of ordinary metaphor.[4] We can see that for Gracián the *concepto* is in its essence an idea which the mind conceives, and in this sense is probably best rendered in English by a term like 'concept'. When the poet, subsequently applying his *ingenio*, his creative ingenuity, develops this idea by extending it to other interrelated ideas, and then, as Gracián recommends, later adds to it *agudeza*, or wit, this 'represents a superior level of thinking which achieves depth and intellectual sparkle, both of which give aesthetic pleasure of an intellectual kind'.[5] The *concepto* thus produced (and Gracián uses the term *concepto* for the end product as well as the initial idea, so that *concepto* in this wider sense signifies the combination 'idea + wit'), may reasonably be represented in English by the term 'conceit', in the sense in which it is used by present-day English-speaking literary critics.

This principle, whereby *concepto* (idea) is developed in the course of the sonnet into the infinitely more subtle *concepto* (conceit), can be demonstrated in Góngora's 'La dulce boca que a gustar convida':

La dulce boca que a gustar convida
un humor entre perlas distilado,
y a no invidiar aquel licor sagrado
que a Júpiter ministra el garzón de Ida,
amantes, no toquéis, si queréis vida;
porque entre un labio y otro colorado
Amor está, de su veneno armado,
cual entre flor y flor sierpe escondida.
No os engañen las rosas, que a la aurora
diréis que, aljofaradas y olorosas
se le cayeron del purpúreo seno;
manzanas son de Tántalo, y no rosas,

4 ' "Concept" and "Conceit": An Aspect of Comparative Literary History', *MLR*, LXXVII (1982), xxi-xxxv. The conceit, moreover, need not necessarily depend upon metaphor, but, as A. K. G. Paterson has pointed out, may be as readily generated by conceptual argument: ' "Sutileza del pensar" in a Quevedo sonnet', *MLN*, LXXXI (1966), 131-42.

5 ' "Concept"and "Conceit" ', xxvii.

que después huyen de el que incitan ahora
y sólo de el Amor queda el veneno.[6]

As is well known, Góngora's model is an Italian one: a sonnet composed by Torquato Tasso some eight years earlier and inspired by Leonora di Giberto Sanvitale, the stepdaughter of the Countess of Sala.[7] Góngora constructs a totally new first quatrain, in which he refers (line 2) to 'un humor entre *perlas* distilado'. The pearls are the lady's teeth, and here we have the basic concept which sets the sonnet in motion: an almost routine *metáfora* or *concepto* (the two terms are virtually synonymous in the Renaissance and the Golden Age). There is no question at this stage of the intervention of the *ingenio,* or the application of *agudeza*: the poet has simply marked out a correspondence between the terms *dientes* and *perlas,* employing a device in which only the second of the terms appears in the surface structure of his composition. It might be reasonable for the critic to inquire, before proceeding further, what the nature of this correspondence actually is. Is it an obvious parallel, for example, or could it be described as imaginative, ingenious, perhaps striking? Why write about teeth in terms of pearls at all? What, if anything, is gained by the device?

A degree of insight can be obtained by a componential analysis of the two terms. If the most obvious semantic features of 'teeth' and 'pearls' were to be set out in two columns, a pattern would emerge along the following lines:

---

6 Text, with spelling and punctuation modernized, from *Luis de Góngora, Sonetos*, ed. Birutė Ciplijauskaitė (Madison: Hispanic Seminary of Medieval Studies, 1981), 258. The date of composition is generally held to be around 1584, when Góngora was twenty-four years of age.

7 See J. P. Wickersham Crawford, 'Italian Sources of Góngora's Poetry', *RR*, XX (1929), 122-30. The sonnet, undervalued for many years as a pale imitation of Tasso, has been considerably rehabilitated by modern criticism such as that of Guiseppe Carlo Rossi, 'Rileggendo un sonetto del Góngora (e uno del Tasso)', *RFE*, XLIV (1961), 425-33, and Nathan Gross, 'Invention in an Imitated Sonnet by Góngora', *MLN*, LXXVII (1962), 182-87. A structuralist approach, stressing the dualism, eroticism and word-play, can be found in Katharine Kaiper Phillips, 'Structuralism and Some Sonnets by Góngora', *RR*, LXV (1974), 294-307 (299-303).

	Pearls		Teeth
	↓		↑
Distinctive features	*white*	↔	*white*
	precious	↔	*precious*
	round	↔	*round*
Associations	*glisten*	↔	*glisten*
	water	↔	*moist*
	oyster		*sharp*
	shell etc.		*smile* etc.

The three distinctive semantic features which teeth and pearls most obviously have in common are whiteness, roundness and preciousness and these overlapping characteristics, combined with the contextual evidence of the opening line of the sonnet — these 'perlas' are to be found not in the sea but in the mouth of a loved one — allow us in the second line to hear 'perlas' for the first time but to understand 'dientes'. The various associative features of the two terms (and I have suggested just a few from a potentially long list) are for the moment not relevant. There is nothing particularly ingenious about this device, nor is it by any means the first time that a poet has turned to it: it simply provides a reminder of a correspondence already familiar to those well-versed in these matters. It has the practical advantage, in a sonnet, of being concise and economical: the associations do not have to be spelled out or explained, and the poet capitalizes on a correspondence which he and his intended audience have in common.

The overriding importance of context is marked out when this is set alongside the elliptical four lines of 'Las flores del romero' in which Góngora exhorts the object of his affections not to shed tears:

> serénense tus ojos,
> y más perlas no des,
> porque al Sol le está mal
> lo que a la Aurora bien.[8]

8 Luis de Góngora, *Romances*, ed. Antonio Carreño (Madrid: Cátedra, 1982), 320. Gracián expresses particular admiration for these four lines: 'Por la disparidad, con sumo artificio, por ser el igual de los extremos, agradable pensamiento de don Luis de Góngora' (*Agudeza*, II, 85).

Again 'perlas' appear, but this time it is inconceivable to make the equation 'pearls = teeth', because the poetic context will simply not permit it. This is partly because the potential image of a young woman shedding teeth would offend the reader's aesthetic sensibilities and be at odds with all expectations and natural logic, but principally because the previous line has formally directed attention this time towards 'ojos': eyes shed tears, and 'perlas' this time inexorably generates 'lágrimas'. It is the context which has reordered the semantic components of 'perlas' for the reader, and on this occasion, alongside the distinctive feature 'round', the associations 'water' and 'glistening', suppressed in 'La dulce boca', have been brought towards the surface structure: this is what pearls and teeth have in common. The reader solves a potential problem unconsciously, by dipping just below the surface of the poem and matching off the relevant semantic features of the two terms involved. Góngora has introduced nothing novel here, since the correspondences were already familiar to the reader; his initial purpose, with this primary concept, is to remind the reader at this point in the poem that a young woman's tears are in some respects like pearls. It is the next two lines, where *agudeza* and *ingenio* are brought into play, which turn the embryonic concept into a full-blooded conceit:

porque al sol le está mal
lo que a la aurora bien.

'Perlas', tears, are like 'gotas de rocío', the morning dew (generated by the distinctive and associative features 'round', 'moist', 'glistening' which they have in common): this dew is appropriate to the 'aurora', the dawn (the girl's youth), but not to the 'sol', the full heat of day (her years of maturity). And the tears which are compatible with inexperienced youth are not appropriate to maturity. Mature women do not weep. Diagrammatically, the conceit can be represented as follows:

eyes	→	tears		**pearls**		morning dew				
		↓		↓↑		↓↑				
		round	→	*round*	→	*round*				
		moist	→	*moist*	→	*moist*				
		glisten	→	*glisten*	→	*glisten*				
						+ *dawn*	→	**dawn**	↔	**full sun**
								↓		↓
								youth	↔	maturity
										↓
										NO TEARS

Perhaps the most striking feature illustrated by this analysis is that only the four elements highlighted in bold type — 'ojos', 'perlas', 'aurora', 'sol' — appear in the surface structure of the *romance*. Those in medium type are implied, those in italics facilitate the process and the entire conceit is elaborated within the space of twenty-eight syllables. A series of progressive stepped links from metaphor to metaphor has involved the *ingenio* of the poet and the result, a combination of *concepto* + *agudeza* + *ingenio*, achieves what would still be described as a *concepto* by Gracián but which may properly be called a conceit in English. The reader has been required to exercise his intellect in the process of achieving understanding: he stands to gain intellectual, or aesthetic, pleasure from involvement in the creative process and above all is required to make a personal contribution towards the total impact of the poem. Mind as well as emotions have been engaged.

In 'La dulce boca que a gustar convida' Góngora has at his disposition the fourteen lines of the sonnet form in which to develop the initial concept. He takes as his model Torquato Tasso's sonnet 'Quel labbro che le rose han colorito', which already contains references to roses, the serpent and Tantalus, and the basic message is straightforward: love is bitter-sweet. The young lover is warned to beware of sweet temptation, or find himself left with just the bitter aftertaste of love. In reworking a well-tried theme Góngora turns to a closed form, the sonnet, and his range of reference is predictably the standard one for his times: he looks to the Bible and to Classical mythology to amplify and illustrate the main theme, not, as I hope to demonstrate, in order to obfuscate but in order to clarify. The cast list is expanded to include Jupiter, Ganymede and Cupid as well as Tantalus, because they are relevant, are drawn from the standard range of reference available to Góngora and his contemporaries, and, can, as Nathan Gross suggests, be 'integrated into an entirely new system of imagery expressive of a far more complex and subtle set of statements on the disillusions of life'.[9]

The theme of 'La dulce boca', while having its origin in and thus deriving its authority from Tasso's sonnet, is, as one might expect, not original in the modern sense of the word. Góngora, however, introduces a totally new first quatrain, in which the point of interest moves from the sensuous lower lip which inspired Tasso to the whole mouth. This allows the Spanish poet to present the concept which is to be the springboard for his version: teeth are pearls, at this stage no more than a simple juxtaposition of accepted notions. The range of reference with which this initial concept is elaborated can only be described as the obvious one for a writer of the Golden Age. What distinguishes Góngora's sonnet from less imaginative variations on this theme is the wit and invention which binds these elements together into a coherent and persuasive whole, the setting up of connections and links which, once traced, provide an artistically and aesthetically satisfying conceit. This sonnet is held together not by the surface structures but by the underlying components which generate them.

Teeth are pearls, for they share the features of roundness and moistness, and they glisten. Góngora now picks up one of the underlying semantic features — moistness — and develops it. The natural habitat of pearls is in shells, in water. An image is produced: the shell and the mouth have shape in common. In the shell/mouth lies *humor*, one of the four fluids of the body which in medieval physiology were held to determine the temperament of an individual. That *humor* suggests *licor*, the sacred liquor administered to Jupiter by his cup-bearer Ganymede. *Agudeza* links concept to illustration, progressively and logically, by one common semantic element in each case. In the second quatrain Góngora builds on this. The mouth has

9 'Invention in an Imitated Sonnet', 183.

lips. Lips are coloured, and their colour is red. Red symbolizes passion. Erotic love, now named as *Amor,* lies between them, armed with a dart. That dart is poisoned. Poison leads us to snake, concealed 'entre flor y flor', just as the tongue, potentially venomous and physically resembling a snake, lies 'entre los labios' of the loved one. The snake evokes the Garden of Eden, which generates the notions of Eve, Woman, sin, danger. *Amantes, no toquéis, si queréis vida.*

The first tercet, however, represents a false trail. The key words are 'diréis que ...': only the unwary might delude themselves into imagining that red lips lead to red roses. Roses are sweet-smelling (temptation, danger), and roses at dawn are covered in morning dew (evocations of the alternative *perlas* conceit); the invitation is to conjure up the moisture on expectant, tempting, feminine lips. But this is not the way of the world, and the first line of the final tercet brings the reader back to earth with a jolt and leaves him under no illusions: 'Manzanas son de Tántalo': for Góngora red lips lead, not to red roses, but to red apples. Women, if Góngora's warning is not heeded, will lead on the lover, tantalize him, dangle their forbidden fruits just out of reach of his questing lips, and love will hurt. The final word is 'veneno': only the poison on the tip of Cupid's dart will remain.

This sonnet has been much admired, and much anthologized. Its special attraction for me, however, is not the message, drawn from the Classical stockroom, but the poetic control and invention: the extraordinary coherence, economy and suggestiveness with which the metaphors are multiplied, the false trail laid and the final message thrust home. This is the sonnet form at work, in a convincing and coherent whole in which form and sense are completely complementary.[10]

---

10 David William Foster and Virginia Ramos Foster see the poem in a very different light: 'The sonnet is most assuredly a case in point of how literature has no relationship to logical, expository writing. For example, the reader is presented with at least three different sets of unrelated allusions: Jupiter and Ganymedes (associated with nonphysical, homosexual love); Love and his poisoned arrows, lying in wait like the prototypic snake in the grass; Tantalus and his frustrated appetites which may be to the point here but which traditionally are associated with a punishment by the gods for nonamorous reasons. A dominant characteristic of the poem is not only the

Quevedo's 'Afectos varios de su corazón fluctuando en las ondas de los cabellos de Lisi' has inspired some sensitive criticism in recent years, and I am indebted to the insights of Alexander Parker and Arthur Terry for many of the elements on which my analysis of its structure depends.[11] Quevedo contemplates the flowing blonde hair of the young woman he addresses, and his response is at once intellectual and emotional:

> En crespa tempestad del oro undoso,
> nada golfos de luz ardiente y pura
> mi corazón, sediento de hermosura,
> si el cabello deslazas generoso.
> Leandro, en mar de fuego proceloso,
> su amor ostenta, su vivir apura;
> Icaro, en senda de oro mal segura,
> arde sus alas por morir glorioso.
> Con pretensión de fénix, encendidas
> sus esperanzas, que difuntas lloro,
> intenta que su muerte engendre vidas.
> Avaro y rico y pobre, en el tesoro,
> el castigo y la hambre imita a Midas,
> Tántalo en fugitiva fuente de oro.[12]

The sense is not at all obscure. The poet, present at an intimate moment as Lisi unties her hair and allows it to fall

---

presence of these sets, but also the abrupt movement from one to another with little explanatory transition ...', *Luis de Góngora* (New York: Twayne, 1973), 74. The Fosters' belief that the relationship between Jupiter and Ganymede was a platonic one does not help to inspire confidence in their argument that Góngora's sonnet has no relationship to logical writing. Their incapacity to see beyond the surface structures, or to appreciate what the internal allusions have in common rather than how they differ, provides a healthy reminder of the dangers of responding to a Góngora sonnet without an awareness of the rhetorical and technical principles governing its construction.

11 A. A. Parker, 'La "agudeza" en algunos sonetos de Quevedo', in *Estudios dedicados a Menéndez Pidal* (Madrid: CSIC, 1952), III, 349-53, at pp. 351-53; A. Terry, 'Quevedo and the Metaphysical Conceit', *BHS*, XXXI (1958), 211-22. See also, for a more extreme view, Robert ter Horst, 'Death and Resurrection in the Quevedo Sonnet: "En crespa tempestad" ', *JHP*, V (1980), 41-49.

12 Text from Francisco de Quevedo, *Obra poética*, ed. José Manuel Blecua (Madrid: Castalia, 1969-81), 4 vols; I, 644.

free, contemplates the effects of this physical action upon his heart, and responds with love, admiration, longing and frustration. The concept is again simple, in the form of a metaphor which this time is produced by a visual image: Lisi's hair, flowing loose, evokes a stormy sea and the initial comparison generates a chain of surface images and illustrations which range through mythology: in apposition to the heart, Leander, Icarus, the Phoenix, Midas and Tantalus make successive appearances. The result is complex, and although the sonnet does have an immediate emotional impact, once again the effect is not to be complete until the reader has made his own intellectual and emotional contribution. Once this contribution has been made, Quevedo's sonnet has the same implacable logical progression and coherence as was evident in Góngora's 'La dulce boca':

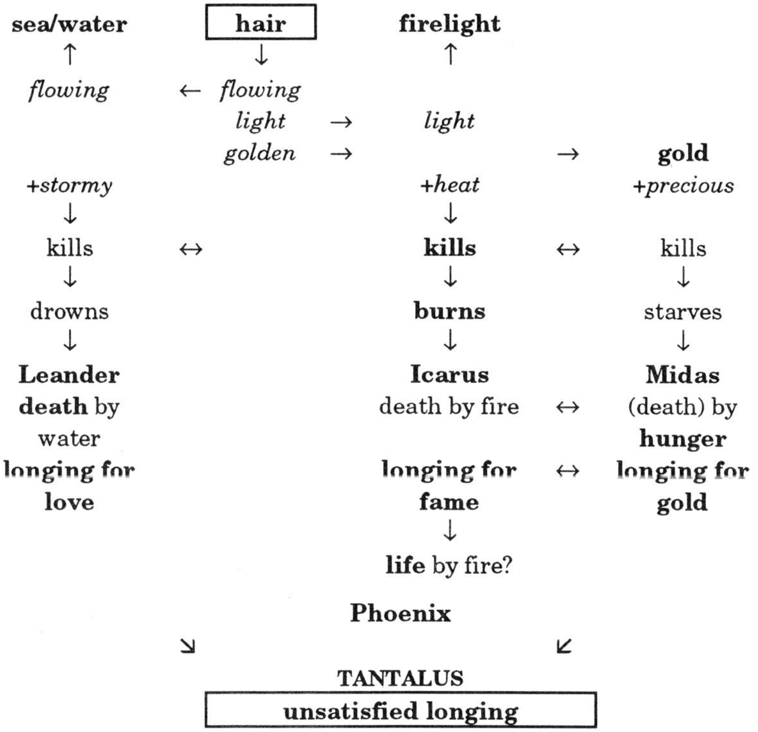

Lisi's hair, the point of departure, is flowing, light and golden. The first of these semantic features evokes the sea, and the addition of one further feature, 'stormy', brings to mind the sequence of ideas demonstrated by the first column: water, Leander, his love for Hero and his death by drowning in the Hellespont. The second element 'light' evokes the fire/light imagery of column three; this time the new component is 'heat' and the example of Icarus is brought forward to illustrate death by fire. The notion of death by fire generates the notion of possible life by fire, and Quevedo devotes the first tercet to opening up this idea via the example of the Phoenix. But, as with the Góngora sonnet, this proves to be a false trail: the Phoenix, regenerating itself from its own ashes, can only be an illusion now that all hopes which the heart may have once entertained are dead. The heart may try to imitate the Phoenix, but its immortality is out of reach. The first tercet loops back to Lisi's hair, and the last possibility of hope: its final semantic component 'golden'. This thought, however, with the addition of the feature 'precious' evokes the example of Midas demonstrated by column four, his lust for gold, his near-death by starvation and the frustration of his desires. Frustration and longing have been the elements common to three of the four exemplary cases so far brought forward as illustrations of the poet's predicament — Leander frustrated in love, Icarus in his ambition to soar to the heavens, Midas in his desire for untold riches — and any hope of eternity offered by the fourth, the Phoenix, has proved illusory. This brings Quevedo, inexorably, to his last line and to Tantalus, the prototypic illustration of frustration as the fruit is withdrawn and the water recedes from the mouth which reaches out towards them in unsatisfied longing. The destiny of the poet is to be hunger and unattained desire.

My aim in representing the formal structure of this sonnet to Lisi as I have done above has not been to reduce one of the finest poems of the Spanish Golden Age to an arid schema, and even less to suggest that Quevedo drew himself up a comparable table of correspondences before setting pen to paper, but rather to attempt a reconstruction of the way that the Golden-Age mind worked as it developed an idea. Góngora began by observing semantic correspondences between teeth and pearls, and Quevedo's point of departure was the correspondences between hair and water. Both can be described as concepts, but neither is in any way novel, exotic or mysterious. In both sonnets it is what happens next that matters: the *agudeza* and *ingenio* which are brought to bear on a web of connections and illustrations which build to form a complex and coherent whole, in every sense an elaborate conceit. This is poetic invention based on logic; the result aimed at, and achieved, is clarity. Relationships have not been invented or devised, but demonstrated.

One other key component of this sonnet, as Parker has shown, is the notion that Lisi's hair evokes all of these reactions not consecutively but simultaneously. Quevedo achieves his effects by the rhetorical technique of catachresis: 'crespa tempestad', 'oro undoso', 'golfos de luz', 'mar de fuego', 'fuente de oro'.[13] It will be immediately evident that each of these pairings represents the juxtaposition of an element from one of the columns set out above with an element from one of the others. If the senses respond initially with the impression of an extremely 'poetic' effect, then the logical processes subsequently applied will provide reassurance that it is also a coherent and intellectually satisfying one. Heart and head are in conflict; the sight of the lady's hair sets the poet on fire, while at the same time he has to swim against the torrent. The heart asks if passion is self-renewing, like the phoenix, and the head says no; the poet has the treasure of beauty close at hand, but the golden opening proves elusive and escapes, leaving him poor and hungry.

This is a poem which has been seen as a near-perfect example of Baroque tensions. A detailed structural analysis reveals that beauty of concept is totally matched in it by formal perfection of construction and form. There is no element in this sonnet which is not considered, relevant and coherent. Every conceit, every illustration, every catachresis is organically linked, via water, fire and gold, to the central themes of love, tension and frustration.

Sor Juana Inés de la Cruz's sonnet is also directed to Hope, but in a very different tone and with a very personal voice:

Verde embeleso de la vida humana,
loca esperanza, frenesí dorado,
sueño de los despiertos intrincado,

13 'La "agudeza" en algunos sonetos de Quevedo', 351-52.

como de sueños, de tesoros vana;
    alma del mundo, senectud lozana,
decrépito verdor imaginado;
el hoy de los dichosos esperado
y de los desdichados el mañana:
    sigan tu sombra en busca de tu día
los que, con verdes vidrios por anteojos,
todo lo ven pintado a su deseo;
    que yo, más cuerda en la fortuna mía,
tengo en entrambas manos ambos ojos
y solamente lo que toco veo.[14]

Again, the primary concept, although startling, is relatively straightforward: Sor Juana delivers an invective against Hope. She urges us not to trust in hope and not to live for tomorrow, which is an illusion; we are urged to live for the present moment, as she claims to do. She affirms a belief solely in the evidence of her senses, and not her intellect: 'y solamente lo que toco veo'. These are strange and wayward sentiments for a young woman who in 1667 entered the order of Discalced Carmelites as a novice and who from 1669 onwards lived out her life in Mexico City as a nun of the Hieronymite Order.[15] It is form rather than theme which primarily concerns us here however; and since Sor Juana Inés was a committed admirer of Góngora and an accomplished poet in a variety of styles, her work might well be expected to reflect some of the procedures observed in the first two sonnets.

One feature of this sonnet which leaps to the attention early is a certain spartan quality more reminiscent of the late fifteenth century than the seventeenth: there is no illustration of the main theme: the sonnet contains no biblical, Classical, or indeed any other type of allusion. And the second slight shock, when it is read alongside the first two sonnets considered, is that the spring-board which sets everything into motion is not a physical attribute, in the form of teeth or hair, which can be broken down into simple, easily-recognizable components, but

14 Text from *Sor Juana Inés de la Cruz. Obras selectas*, ed. Georgina Sabat de Rivers y Elías L. Rivers (Barcelona: Noguer, 1976), 630.

15 The story of her life, her loves and her work has attracted an outstanding full-length study from Octavio Paz: *Sor Juana Inés de la Cruz o Las Trampas de la Fe* (Barcelona: Seix Barral, 1982).

an abstraction: Hope. Sor Juana Inés, however, handles abstractions easily, through a very personal lens. Hope is green ('verde'), Hope is golden ('dorado'), Hope is rapturous ('un embeleso'), Hope is crazy ('loca'). These attributes are some distance from the basic semantic components which would have sprung to the mind of a linguist asked to undertake a distinctive feature analysis of Hope. On the other hand, the reader has not been required to undertake such a task on this occasion, since Sor Juana herself provides all four elements in the surface structure of the first two lines. Those first two lines also contain surprising juxtapositions of the type which lent themselves so readily to analysis in Quevedo: Quevedo's 'crespa tempestad' and 'oro undoso' would at first sight appear to be the basis for Sor Juana's 'verde embeleso' and 'frenesí dorado'. But whereas in Quevedo's sonnet the adjectives emerged as examples of catachresis — the epithets 'crespa' and 'undoso' properly belong to 'hair' but are transferred to 'storm' and 'gold' — with Sor Juana there is no question of transference: 'verde' and 'dorado' are simply two of the four components highlighted to represent Hope, and they are paired with the other two of her selection. The conceit is different in kind, and the impact immediate.

In the third line Sor Juana moves on to describe 'la esperanza' as 'el sueño de los despiertos intrincado'. This abstract notion of Hope as the tangled dream of the wakeful leads to another abstraction: Hope is green, Hope is golden, Hope is rapturous — but it is a dream. And that dream is no ordinary dream; it is the dream of the wakeful, and it is empty of one of its standard components: it is devoid of treasures. This leads, via two epithets for Hope, both abstractions — 'alma del mundo, senectud lozana' — to reality as Sor Juana saw it and the extravagant sixth line:

decrépito verdor imaginado.

Three elements come together to form the hendecasyllable. With the first word of the sonnet preparation has been made for the notion of greenery. Decrepit greenery introduces a paradox. Imaginary decrepit greenery offers another dimension for the paradox. The juxtaposition appears at first sight extraordinary and yet, within the context of the sonnet, nothing extraneous has been introduced. Sor Juana began with 'verde embeleso'; the 'sueño' of line three prepared the way for 'imaginado'; the 'senectud' of the previous line led directly to 'decrepito'. Hope is not really green: it is imagined greenery, a waking dream; it is decrepit greenery, for Hope has no future. And Sor Juana takes us out of the tangled maze of the quatrains via the two observations that Hope is the longed-for here and now of the happy, and that Hope always comes tomorrow for the unhappy. From this generality, a total inversion of the standard consolatory noises made by those who reassure the unhappy that a brighter tomorrow is on its way, Sor Juana turns to a characteristically independent-minded personal application: those with rose-coloured spectacles may well turn to a Hope created in the image of their own desires. Hope is not for the rational Sor Juana, capable only of a belief in the here and now: 'Y solamente lo que toco veo'.

This degree of concision, intellectual depth and emotional power is achieved, towards the end of the Golden Age, and within the technical restrictions of the fourteen lines permitted by the sonnet form, as a direct result of techniques firmly established over a long period of years by Sor Juana's literary predecessors. Here she discards illustration in favour of even greater condensation and density: this time the semantic components of hope are not the self-evident, nor what the reader and Sor Juana might be expected to have in common as a basic premiss, but those seen through this poet's lens (we may agree that hope is green, but will probably need to have it demonstrated that hope is mad). An awareness of the technical procedures underlying the use of the conceit should better equip the critic and the literary historian to respond to Sor Juana's very personal and idiosyncratic approach to the established norms and to respond sensitively and intelligently, as well as emotionally, to the effects achieved.

Of the three poets considered here, Sor Juana is probably the one who comes closest to Dame Helen Gardner's definition of the conceit as it relates to the English metaphysical poets:

> A conceit is a comparison whose ingenuity is more striking than its justness, or, at least, is more immediately striking. All comparisons discover likeness in things unlike; a comparison

becomes a conceit when we are made to concede likeness while being strongly conscious of unlikeness.[16]

The initial concepts which are the point of departure for the conceits of Góngora's 'La dulce boca' and Quevedo's 'En crespa tempestad' are not ingenious in the sense put forward by Dame Helen Gardner; they rather provide the common ground between poet and reader, as does the range of Classical reference. The ingenuity is there, but in the form of Gracián's *ingenio*: the marrying of the juxtaposed elements by the application of wit in order to form a coherent piece of persuasion, an aesthetically satisfying and intellectually stimulating whole. Sor Juana's conceits in 'Verde embeleso' are of a subtly different type: they emerge as just, striking and ingenious in the English sense of the word, and her development of the initial concept, while still operating within the accepted structural conventions of her time, both idiosyncratic and imaginative.

Stephen Booth reminds us that 'the sonnet is an especially poetic form ... It does what all verse does: it just does more of it', for it contains, he says, 'an unusually high number of systems of organization'.[17] I hope, by this close examination of those systems of organization in three of the most admired sonnets of the Spanish Golden Age, to have been able to demonstrate that an awareness of the underlying connections which determine their structure, and of the tight-knit causal relationships between their imagery and range of illustration, can contribute a great deal towards revealing their coherence, symmetry and structural perfection.

---

16 *The Metaphysical Poets* (London: Oxford U. P. [2nd ed.], 1972), xxiii.

17 *An Essay on Shakespeare's Sonnets* (New York/London: Yale U. P., 1969), 174.

Spain and its Literature

Part II

From the Dawn of Romanticism to the Twentieth Century

Sánchez's *Colección* and Percy's *Reliques*: The Editing of Medieval Poetry in the Dawn of Romanticism

ALAN DEYERMOND

Queen Mary and Westfield College, London

Laudemus viros gloriosos, et
parentes nostros in generatione sua.
(Ecclesiasticus 44: 1)

1 Sánchez's Achievement

Tomás Antonio Sánchez (1725-1802) does not stand at the beginning of hispanomedievalist scholarship. That glory belongs to the Marqués de Santillana, in whom Sánchez had an intense and abiding interest, or, if we confine ourselves to the editing of texts, to Gonzalo Argote de Molina, whose editions of *El conde Lucanor* (1575) and the *Libro de la montería* (1582) are the earliest attempts in Spain to publish scholarly editions of medieval texts.[1] But Santillana wrote a brief critical history of

1 These were not, of course, the first printings of medieval texts: the *Bocados de oro*, for example, was printed in 1495, but this and similar editions of thirteenth- and fourteenth-century works were intended as reading texts, they lacked apparatus of any kind, and showed no awareness that the texts were of a different epoch. On such editions, see E. P. Goldschmidt, *Medieval Texts and their First Appearance in Print*, Supplement 16 to *Transactions of the Bibliographical Society* (Oxford: Oxford U. P., for Bibliographical Society, 1943; 2nd ed., Meisenheim: Hain, 1965). Hernán Núñez's edition of Juan de Mena's *Laberinto de Fortuna* (first printed 1499) has an elaborate commentary, but again there is no sense that a work of an earlier age is being

poetry for another poet, and Argote de Molina's concept of an editor's task was very different from that of a good modern scholar: although he examined three manuscripts of *El conde Lucanor*, he did not know how to collate them (there are, I realize, comparable cases today), and although he provides some things that we should expect, such as an introduction and a glossary, he rearranges the *exenplos* on generic grounds.[2] To say this is not to disparage Argote's achievement. He undertook a task that no one had ever thought of undertaking in Spain: he took the first steps towards a published corpus of medieval literature, recognizing it to be so distinct from the literature of his own day that it needed historical and linguistic explanation. It is of course unreasonable to blame him for not applying to the editing of vernacular texts the methods and standards that his Italian contemporary Scaliger took for granted in the editing of classical Latin literature, since it had not occurred to anyone that they could or should be so applied.[3]

---

presented to the modern reader (Núñez was born a generation after Mena's death), and the relevance of the work is clearly contemporary: see Julian Weiss, 'Political Commentary: Hernán Núñez's *Glosa a "Las trescientas"* ', in *Letters and Society in Fifteenth-Century Spain: Studies Presented to P. E. Russell on his Eightieth Birthday*, ed. Alan Deyermond and Jeremy Lawrance (Llangrannog: Dolphin, 1993), 205-16. Florián de Ocampo published a substantially Alfonsine chronicle (*Crónica de España*, 1543), but it was one that had been through a series of reworkings, and his edition was a source of information for contemporary readers. Argote de Molina's position as the first to attempt scholarly editions of what he recognized as much earlier Spanish texts is thus secure.

2 This discovery was made by Alberto Blecua, and the evidence is given in his *La transmisión textual de 'El conde Lucanor'* (Bellaterra: Seminario de Literatura Medieval y Humanística, Univ. Autónoma de Barcelona, 1980), 79-82. He had earlier communicated the discovery to Enrique Miralles, who had used it, with full acknowledgement, in the introduction to his facsimile of Argote's edition, Biblioteca Hispánica Puvill, Literatura I (Barcelona: Puvill, 1978), 28-33, just too late to save me from imprudently concluding that Argote's order might reflect a lost manuscript tradition: 'Editors, Critics, and *El conde Lucanor*', *RPh*, XXXI (1977-78), 618-30.

3 See Anthony Grafton, *Joseph Scaliger: A Study in the History of Classical Scholarship* (Oxford: Clarendon Press, 1983-93), 2 vols. Lionel Gossman reminds us that the application to medieval vernacular literature of the standards used for the editing of classical texts is due to a few eighteenth-

Argote began the process of editing medieval Spanish literature, but Sánchez transformed it. His *Colección de poesías castellanas anteriores al siglo XV* (1779-90) was by far the greatest step forward that had ever been taken in hispanomedievalist editing, and nothing in the two centuries that have elapsed — not even such works of genius as Margit Frenk's *Corpus de la antigua lírica popular hispánica* or Brian Dutton's *Cancionero del siglo XV* — marks such an advance on what was available before as did Sánchez's four volumes.[4] The

---

century innovators:

> the literary heritage of the Middle Ages was not regarded with anything like the respect and awe granted to the works of classical antiquity, but continued to live and evolve until about the seventeenth century. (*Medievalism and the Ideologies of the Enlightenment: The World and Work of La Curne de Sainte-Palaye* [Baltimore: The Johns Hopkins Press, 1968], 225)

Sainte-Palaye was, Gossman says, the first to realize that medieval French texts 'posed the same problems and required the same kind of treatment from scholars as classical or medieval Latin texts' (225), and he quotes Sainte-Palaye's words in the *Mémoires de l'Académie des Inscriptions*:

> Je ne parle pas des livres Grecs et Latins, auxquels des Savans du premier ordre ne dédaignoient point d'employer leurs soins et leurs talens, afin qu'ils parussent avec toute la correction et la fidélité qu'ils méritoient; je parle de nos anciens auteurs François, pour lesquels nos premiers Imprimeurs ne se crurent point obligés d'emprunter des secours étrangers: persuadés qu'un manuscrit qu'ils avoient découvert, et dont l'écriture et la langue leur étoient en quelque façon familières, n'avoit pas besoin de plus grandes lumières pour en risquer l'impression, ils l'imprimèrent souvent sans avoir su ni le lire ni l'entendre. (225n)

4 *Colección de poesías castellanas anteriores al siglo XV: preceden noticias para la vida del primer Marqués de Santillana, y la carta que escribió al Condestable de Portugal sobre el origen de nuestra poesía, ilustrada con notas*, I: *Poema del Cid* (Madrid: Antonio de Sancha, 1779). The title in volumes II, *Poesías de don Gonzalo de Berceo* (1780); III, *Poema de Alexandro Magno* (1782); and IV, *Poesías del Arcipreste de Hita* (1790), instead of *preceden noticias [...] con notas*, continues: *ilustradas con algunas notas e índice de voces antiquadas*. In the first two volumes the editor is named as Thomás Antonio Sánchez, and in the last two Thomás becomes Tomás. (I modernize accents, and regularize the use of i/j, u/v, and c/ç, in quotations from Old Spanish, and modernize accents in quotations from eighteenth- and

magnitude of Sánchez's achievement may be measured in three ways:

1 Of the fourteen works that he edited (*Cantar de Mio Cid*, ten works by Berceo, *Libro de Alexandre*, *Libro de Buen Amor*, Santillana's *Carta*), at most three, and quite possibly only two, had previously been printed. One of the exceptions may be a phantom — Sánchez mentions a verbal report of an edition seen in a London bookseller's in 1786 — but one of the others was certainly accessible to him and the other may well have been.[5] Sánchez had the advantage of knowing the edition of Berceo's *Vida de Santo Domingo de Silos*, published by Fray Sebastián de Vergara in 1736, and used it as his base text, emending it by some readings from a fourteenth-century manuscript.[6] It had always been believed that Sánchez was the first to edit Santillana's *Carta*, but it has now been shown that an edition was printed in 1756, though never published, and is likely to have been known to Sánchez.[7] He also, as we shall see, had

nineteenth-century authors, throughout this article.)

5 'Don Gabriel de Sancha, cuyo manejo en libros, tanto por fuera, como por dentro es bien conocido, me ha asegurado que el año pasado de 86 vio en Londres en poder del librero Huith las obras de nuestro Arcipreste [de Hita], impresas en un tomo en 8. letra de tortis; y en otro de igual tamaño las prosaicas del de Talavera [...]' (IV, xxii). No subsequent scholar has been able to clarify this reference, though an occasional conjecture has been made: see *Libro de Buen Amor*, ed. Alberto Blecua, Letras Hispánicas LXX (Madrid: Cátedra, 1992), lii.

6 Vergara, *Vida y milagros de el thaumaturgo español [...] Santo Domingo Manso* (Madrid: Herederos de Francisco del Hierro, 1736), 230-308. See Sánchez, II, xxi. For the relation of MSS and editions, see Gonzalo de Berceo, *Obras completas*, ed. Brian Dutton, IV: *La vida de Santo Domingo de Silos*, Colección Támesis A, LXXIV (London: Tamesis, 1978), 18-25.

7 Francisco Aguilar Piñal, 'La primera impresión del *Proemio e carta* del Marqués de Santillana', in *Art and Literature in Spain 1600-1800: Studies in Honour of Nigel Glendinning* (London: Tamesis, 1993), 25-33. The editor was José Cevallos y Ruiz de Vargas, like Sánchez a Fellow of the Academia Sevillana de Buenas Letras. His edition was printed in the journal *Discursos Mercuriales*, but political reasons prevented the distribution of that issue (Aguilar Piñal, 27). Aguilar Piñal concludes that Sánchez must have known of the edition, since Cevallos read his critical annotations to the Academia on 1 June 1759, but that 'lo ignoró completamente en sus publicaciones, como hizo

the advantage of earlier transcriptions, some of them good, of most of his texts, and — in three cases and possibly more — a published account that included a few lines of text.[8] But for at least twelve of the fourteen texts in the *Colección* (and for twelve of the thirteen poetic ones) there was no earlier printed edition to serve as guide. In the eleven years that separated the publication of his first and fourth volumes, Sánchez wrought a transformation both vast and enduring. It was as if readers of Middle English, having had to make do with an edition of *The Book of the Duchess* and an account of *Piers Plowman* illustrated by quotations, had found in the late eighteenth century that they had access to scholarly editions of *The Owl and the Nightingale*, *Piers Plowman*, *Sir Gawain and the Green Knight*, and the complete works of Chaucer, all prepared for the press by the same man.

2 Sánchez was an innovator not merely in a Spanish context, but in Europe as a whole. Of all the great epics of medieval Europe, the *Cantar de Mio Cid* was the first to be published

---

con los descubrimientos de otros académicos sevillanos, que tanto le habían ayudado en sus trabajos epigráficos [...]' (27).

8 See Francisco Aguilar Piñal, 'Cándido María Trigueros y el *Poema del Cid*', *NRFH*, XXXIII (1984), 224-33. There are substantial quotations from the *Libro de Buen Amor* in José Luis Velázquez's *Orígenes de la poesía castellana* (1754) and in Esteban de Terreros y Pando's *Paleografía española* (1758). But from treatment of this kind, interesting and useful though it is, to a full edition is a long distance. Marcelino Menéndez y Pelayo, writing a century after Sánchez's death, described his achievement thus:

> pronto comprendió que la historia literaria exigía algo más que noticias tomadas al vuelo, y emprendió la reproducción textual de los mismos poemas, inéditos hasta entonces, y no sólo inéditos, sino olvidados y desconocidos, ya en librerías particulares, ya en los rincones de obscuras bibliotecas monásticas. [...] Sin más guía que el Glosario de Ducange se internó en las tinieblas de los tiempos medios. ('Dos opúsculos inéditos de D. Rafael Floranes y D. Tomás Antonio Sánchez sobre los orígenes de la poesía castellana', *Revue Hispanique*, XVIII [1908], 295-431 [325]).

Cf. what Lionel Gossman says of La Curne de Sainte-Palaye, a scholar a generation older than Sánchez (n. 3, above). Sánchez was not working in quite such isolation as Menéndez y Pelayo's words imply, but the estimate of his stature is a fair one.

in its entirety. Parts of the *Nibelungenlied* had, it is true, been published in 1757, but the first full edition of the poem did not appear until three years after Sánchez's *Cid.*[9] Grímur Jónsson Thorkelin transcribed *Beowulf* in 1787, while Sánchez was preparing his *Colección*, but Thorkelin's edition was not published until 1815. Count Alexei Musin-Pushkin's *Slovo o polku Igoreve* was published in 1800, but not until 1837, more than half a century after Sánchez, did Francisque Michel publish the first edition of the *Chanson de Roland.*[10]

3 Even more surprisingly, Sánchez was not finally superseded until nearly two centuries after his first volume appeared. This is, of course, a lasting reproach to the generations that followed him. As we shall see, the *Colección* did not have the impact for which its editor hoped, and Spain's early lead was not maintained. At a time when the Early English Text Society (1864) and the Société des Anciens Textes Français (1875) were building a sturdy foundation of scholarly editions financially accessible to any interested reader, there was no corresponding initiative in Spain. The Sociedad de Bibliófilos Españoles (1866) brought out some valuable editions of medieval texts, but as its name indicated it had a much wider chronological spread, and its lavishly produced volumes were inevitably expensive.[11] Spanish readers in the second half of the nineteenth century who wanted medieval texts had to turn to the Biblioteca de Autores Españoles, which did valuable work in providing for the educated general reader but, unlike EETS and SATF, was not designed to provide also for the scholar. Sánchez's

9 *Chriemhilden Rache, und die Klage; zwey Heldengedichte aus dem schvvaebischen Zeitpuncte: samt Fragmenten aus dem Gedichte von den Nibelungen und aus dem Josaphat*, ed. Johann Jacob Bodmer (Zyrich: Verlegens Orell, 1757). The first full edition was edited by Christoph Heinrich Müller (Berlin: C. S. Spener, 1782).

10 Menéndez y Pelayo makes the comparison with the editing of the French epic, 326-27.

11 There were also regional series for bibliophiles: see Homero Serís, *Manual de bibliografía de la literatura española*, I[.i] (Syracuse: Centro de Estudios Hispánicos, Syracuse Univ., 1948), 81.

Colección was amplified by Pedro José Pidal in 1841 with three more texts and by Florencio Janer with another nine in 1864, to form volume LVII of the Biblioteca de Autores Españoles.[12] Pidal and Janer almost doubled the length of the *Colección*, and it was in this form that Sánchez's editions (some emended by Janer) continued as the vulgate text of the thirteen poetic works that he had published. The admirable BAE policy of reprinting whenever stock of a volume was exhausted meant that readers were never without Sánchez's editions, though it is a pity that the date on the title-page is always that of the reprint, so that unwary readers have, over several generations, believed themselves to be using an up-to-date edition.

Had Allison Peers, while a first-year undergraduate, wished to turn from his studies of English to the *Cantar de Mio Cid*, the *Libro de Alexandre*, any of Berceo's works, or the *Libro de Buen Amor*, he would — unless he knew where to find specialist editions of a few of the texts — have had to turn to Sánchez. When he applied for the Gilmour Chair of Spanish at Liverpool, only the *Cantar de Mio Cid* and the *Libro de Buen Amor* were available in serious modern editions for students. As late as the 1960s and early 1970s, the University of London syllabus for the Special Subject on '*Mester de clerecía* of the thirteenth century' had to prescribe Sánchez, in his BAE garb, for most of the texts. The table below shows the editors and dates of the first scholarly edition, and the first serious edition for students, after Sánchez.[13]

12 Menéndez y Pelayo points out in the 'Advertencia preliminar' to his 'Dos opúsculos inéditos' that in these expanded editions not only are Sánchez's life of Santillana and his extensive notes to the *Carta* omitted, but 'además los prólogos están mutilados y los glosarios trabucados y confundidos' (332n). As far as I know there has been no detailed study of the textual history of BAE, LVII, but an investigation might prove interesting.

13 To give the bibliographical details of twenty-two editions, most of which are well known, would occupy an unjustifiable amount of space.

Cid	Vollmöller 1879[14]	Menéndez Pidal 1913
Alexandre	Morel-Fatio 1906	Cañas Murillo 1978
Santo Domingo	FitzGerald 1904	Orduna 1968
San Millán	Marden 1928	Dutton 1967
Santa Oria	Marden 1928	Dutton 1981 / Uría 1981
San Lorenzo	Marden 1930	Ramoneda 1980
Duelo	Dutton 1975	Dutton 1975
Sacrificio	Solalinde 1913	Dutton 1981
Loores	Dutton 1975	Dutton 1975
Signos	Dutton 1975	Dutton 1975
Milagros	Solalinde 1922	Solalinde 1922
Himnos	Dutton 1975	Dutton 1975
Buen Amor	Ducamin 1901	Cejador 1913

Thus for scholars the replacement of Sánchez did not begin until 1879, exactly a century after his first volume, and it ended only in 1975; for students it began in 1913 — one hundred and twenty-three years after the last volume of the *Colección* — and did not end until 1981. I doubt whether any other collection of medieval texts has had so long a shelf-life.

2 Percy and the *Reliques*

Fourteen years before the first volume of Sánchez's *Colección*, Thomas Percy published the three volumes of his *Reliques of Ancient English Poetry*.[15] It is known to many hispanomedievalists who are unfamiliar with English literature, because Ramón Menéndez Pidal named one of his most famous books after it: *Reliquias de la poesía épica española*; and he chose it as the starting-point of that book's introduction, under the heading of 'El título de este libro':

> En 1765 el capellán Thomas Percy, después obispo de Dromore, publicaba, con el título de *Reliques of Ancient English Poetry*, una

14 Damas Hinard's edition (1858) is too close to Sánchez's to be included in this list.

15 *Reliques of Ancient English Poetry, Consisting of Old Heroic Ballads, Songs, and Other Pieces of our Earlier Poets (Chiefly of the Lyric Kind), together with Some Few of the Later Date* (London: James Dodsley, 1765). My references will be to the two-volume Everyman's Library edition (London: J. M. Dent/New York: E. P. Dutton, n.d.) that I have had on my shelves for many years.

> antigua colección de baladas y cantos narrativos que en seguida se hizo famosa, influyendo poderosamente en los más grandes poetas de la época romántica.[16]

Percy's three volumes are in fact less like the *Reliquias*, and less like Sánchez's *Colección*, than Menéndez Pidal's words suggest. Not only do they, as their full title indicates, include a fair number of lyrics, but the chronological range is late-medieval to late-Renaissance (fifteenth to mid-seventeenth centuries). The chronological overlap with the *Colección* is thus minimal, and the generic overlap is virtually non-existent (it is restricted to some of the lyrics of the *Libro de Buen Amor* and some of those chosen by Percy). This is not the place to give a full account of the *Reliques*, which have been extensively studied. It is, however, necessary to summarize the basic information.

Thomas Percy (1729-1811) was born four years after Sánchez and outlived him by nine years. Like Sánchez, he was a priest, but whereas Sánchez chose a largely secular career as royal librarian and scholar (he was a Fellow of both the Real Academia Española and the Real Academia de la Historia), Percy made his career in the Church, spending his last thirty years as Bishop of Dromore, in Ireland.[17] His abundant scholarly and literary writings were produced in the leisure

---

16 *Reliquias de la poesía épica española* (Madrid: Instituto de Cultura Hispánica/CSIC, 1951), vii. This was not Menéndez Pidal's original choice of title: the printing of what was later to be *Reliquias* began in the mid-1930s, under the title *Epopeya y romancero, I: Textos referentes a la epopeya española*, but was interrupted by the Civil War (see *'Reliquias de la poesía épica española', acompañadas de 'Epopeya y romancero', I*, ed. Diego Catalán, Reliquias de la Épica Hispánica, I [Madrid: Cátedra/Seminario Menéndez Pidal/Gredos, 1980]). The Percy-derived title has thus spread to a series, and is now spreading further: Ángel Gómez Moreno, 'Nuevas reliquias de la cuaderna vía', *Revista de Literatura Medieval*, II (1990), 9-34. Menéndez Pidal was familiar with more than the title: he mentions (xvii) the circumstances of Percy's discovery of the manuscript.

17 The most extensive recent study is Bertram H. Davis, *Thomas Percy: A Scholar-Cleric in the Age of Johnson* (Philadelphia: Univ. of Pennsylvania Press, 1989). Davis had earlier written a shorter book on Percy's life and works: *Thomas Percy*, Twayne's English Authors Series 313 (Boston: Twayne, 1981).

time allowed by his ecclesiastical duties. One of Percy's strong interests was Spanish literature, particularly of the sixteenth century. He built up a library of the romances of chivalry read by Don Quixote, and he planned to use Shelton's translation as the basis for a thoroughly annotated volume that would remedy one defect that he had noticed in all English translations of *Don Quixote*: 'a *Key to the Satire*: None of them contains so much as an attempt (that I could discover) to point out the force of the ridicule'.[18] When Percy learned of John Bowle's detailed plans for an edition, he abandoned his own, but his status as the first British hispanist to contemplate a study of '*Don Quixote* as a Funny Book' deserves to be remembered.[19] So does the volume of translations of Spanish ballads (chiefly from Ginés Pérez de Hita's *Guerras civiles de Granada*) that he completed and took as far as page proof in 1775, but then, for unknown reasons, abandoned.[20] Smith suggests that Percy was dissatisfied with

---

18 Letter of 1762, quoted by A. Watkin-Jones, 'A Pioneer Hispanist: Thomas Percy', *BSS*, XIV (1937), 3-9 (6).

19 The title is, of course, not Percy's but P. E. Russell's: *MLR*, LXIV (1969), 407-40. For Percy's Cervantine studies see, in addition to Watkin-Jones's article, Thomas Percy and John Bowle, *Cervantine Correspondence*, ed. Daniel Eisenberg, EHT XL (Exeter: Exeter Univ., 1987), and Davis (1989), *s.v. Don Quixote*. I have not been able to see Gisela Beutler's doctoral thesis, *Thomas Percys spanische Studien: ein Beitrag zum Bild Spaniens in England in der zweiten Hälfte des 18. Jahrhunderts* (Bonn: the author, 1957). On Bowle, see also R. Merritt Cox, *The Rev. John Bowle: The Genesis of Cervantean Criticism*, UNCSRLL, XCIX (Chapel Hill: Univ. of North Carolina Press, 1971); *An English 'Ilustrado': The Reverend John Bowle* (Bern: Peter Lang, 1977); and 'The Library of the Reverend John Bowle: Revelations in English Hispanism', in *Studies in Honor of Gerald E. Wade*, ed. Silvia Bowman *et al.* (Potomac, MD: Studia Humanitatis, 1979), 23-34.

20 The page proofs were rediscovered a century and a half later, and the book was at last published: *Ancient Songs Chiefly on Moorish Subjects Translated from the Spanish*, ed. David Nichol Smith (London: Oxford U. P., 1932). The print-run for this edition was unfortunately so small that, as Eisenberg observes (vii), it is now harder to find than eighteenth-century editions of the *Reliques*. We clearly need a new edition, taking into account recent scholarship on Percy and specifically on his translations from Spanish (e.g. Shasta M. Bryant, *The Spanish Ballad in English*, Studies in Romance Languages 8 [Lexington: Univ. Press of Kentucky, 1973]). Davis (1989) comments on the volume, 213-14.

his translations (vi), Watkin-Jones that as he rose in the Church hierarchy he became nervous about his reputation (4).

3 The Genesis of the Two Collections

The first words of Sánchez's Prologue to his *Colección* suggest that it was born of a chance discovery, one of those fruitful accidents that change the course of literary history: 'Los años pasados cayó en mis manos una carta que con título de Proemio escribió el primer Marqués de Santillana [...]' (I, fol.*r). Although there is no reason to doubt the truth of the words, the impression that they give is misleading. The *Colección* is the result of a steadily developing plan of research, the culmination of a scholar's increasingly concentrated life: appointment as royal librarian in 1761 (what was then the Biblioteca Real is the present Biblioteca Nacional, not the Biblioteca de Palacio) gave both motive and opportunity for intensive bibliographical work (he collaborated with Juan Antonio Pellicer and Rafael Casalbón on a new edition of Nicolás Antonio's *Bibliotheca hispana nova*, published in 1788).[21] Bibliographical research both required a search for manuscripts and early printed texts and inspired the editing of those texts; what Gossman says of La Curne de Sainte-Palaye's time is largely true of the succeeding generation:

> In the vast and still fairly intact territory of medieval studies the encyclopaedic scholar was particularly at home, for the investigation of any single field required not only that the scholar be ready to branch out into many related fields, but that he be able to forge his own instruments of research. The development of the techniques and the tools of research was at this stage virtually identical with the research itself. (xi)

In Percy's case we really are confronted by a chance discovery that changed both the discoverer's life and the course of literary history. Percy tells us, near the beginning of the

21 The best and most extensive accounts that we have of Sánchez's life and works are still those of Juan Sempere y Guarinos, *Ensayo de una biblioteca española de los mejores escritores del reynado de Carlos III*, V (Madrid: Imprenta Real, 1789), 94-102, and Menéndez y Pelayo, 324-39. See also Francisco Aguilar Piñal, *Bibliografía de autores españoles del siglo XVIII* (Madrid: CSIC, 1993), VII, 482-85 (entries 3374-97).

Preface to the *Reliques*, that:

> The greater part of [the poems] are extracted from an ancient folio manuscript, in the Editor's possession, which contains near 200 poems, songs, and metrical romances. This manuscript was written about the middle of the last [i.e. seventeenth] century; but contains compositions of all times and dates, from the ages prior to Chaucer, to the conclusion of the reign of Charles I. (I, 3)

Elsewhere he gave more details: writing in 1769, he said that he found the manuscript when staying in Shifnal, Shropshire, at the house of Humphrey Pitt, uncle by marriage of a distant cousin of Percy's. 'I saw it lying dirty on the floor [of the parlour]: being used by the Maids to light the fires' (quoted Davis, 1989, 24). Pitt gave the manuscript to him (I, 6, with Pitt's information on its provenance, n. 3). Percy does not tell us the date of the discovery, but it was almost certainly during his period as a curate in Shropshire, 1751-56 (Davis, 24). In his Preface he says that:

> This manuscript was shown to several learned and ingenious friends, who thought the contents too curious to be consigned to oblivion, and importuned the possessor [i.e. Percy] to select some of them, and give them to the press. As most of them are of great simplicity, and seem to have been merely written for the people, he was long in doubt, whether, in the present state of improved literature, they could be deemed worthy the attention of the public. At length the importunity of his friends prevailed, and he could refuse nothing to such judges as the author of the *Rambler* and the late Mr Shenstone. (I, 3)

'The importunity of friends' is a familiar topos, but the work of Davis and others (e.g. Davis, 44-45) confirms that both Johnson and Shenstone were enthusiastic about the manuscript and — after initial opposition on Shenstone's part — about the possibility of its publication, and that their advice was frequently sought and readily given as Percy worked on the project.[22] During the decade or so that separated Percy's

---

22 Shenstone's initial opposition stemmed not from lack of appreciation of the manuscript's quality but from tactical opportunism; writing in January 1758 he said:

> Suppose then you consider your MS as an hoard of gold, somewhat defac'd by Time, from which however you may be able to draw supplies upon

discovery of the manuscript from the first edition of the *Reliques*, he was also busy with a variety of translations and compilations: Chinese (1761, 1762), Classical Latin (1762), Icelandic (1763), and Hebrew (1764). 1765, the year of the first edition of the *Reliques*, also saw the publication of his *A Key to the New Testament*.

Percy consulted widely while preparing the *Reliques*, partly because he was genuinely unsure of how best to proceed, partly because, as his plans evolved, he needed additional material, and partly, it seems, because he wanted some insurance in the dangerous world of eighteenth-century English literary criticism and scholarship (Pope's *Dunciad* attained its final form only some twenty years before the first of Percy's works appeared). His literary and scholarly contacts are acknowledged in the Preface, are frequently referred to in, for example, Davis' biography and Stephen Vartin's doctoral thesis on the *Reliques*, and are extensively documented in the nine volumes of *The Percy Letters* so far published and in some separate and smaller collections of correspondence.[23] Albert B. Friedman goes so far as to refer to 'the syndicate of scholars that assisted him during the years he was putting together his ballad book' (1233).

By far the most important of Percy's advisers was the poet

> occasion, and with which you may enrich ye world hereafter under more current Impressions. (Irving L. Churchill, 'William Shenstone's Share in the Preparation of Percy's *Reliques*', *PMLA*, LI [1936], 960-74 [964])

Once convinced that publication was desirable, Shenstone was Percy's most active helper.

23 Vartin, 'Thomas Percy's *Reliques*: Its Structure and Organization', unpubl. thesis (New York Univ., 1972); abstract in *DAI*, XXXIII (1972-73), 734-35. Another doctoral thesis on the *Reliques*, by Nicholas Groom (Univ. of Exeter), is near completion (information from Professor Malcolm Cook, January 1994). *The Percy Letters*, I-VI, gen. ed. David Nichol Smith and Cleanth Brooks (Baton Rouge: Louisiana State U. P., 1944-61); VII-IX, gen. ed. Cleanth Brooks and A. F. Falconer (New Haven: Yale U. P., 1977-88). Details of some other collections are given in the notes to Albert B. Friedman, 'The First Draft of Percy's *Reliques*', *PMLA*, LXIX (1954), 1233-49; and *Cervantine Correspondence*, ed. Eisenberg.

William Shenstone (1714-63), himself a talented anthologist.[24] Shenstone's advice was decisive, and only his early death prevented his appearance as joint editor of the *Reliques*.[25] The *Reliques* could never have been the kind of work that Sánchez's *Colección* would soon become—the nature of the folio manuscript acquired from Humphrey Pitt ruled that out, as did Percy's background and temperament — but Shenstone's influence widened the gap. Percy jealously guarded the folio manuscript (see Friedman, 1246), but its publication a century later, and the discovery of a first draft of the table of contents of the *Reliques* nearly a century after that, make it possible to see how the manuscript evolved into the three-volume printed anthology.[26]

The folio manuscript is an anthology, compiled in the mid-seventeenth century, and spanning nearly three centuries and several genres. Even had Percy edited the manuscript without adding anything, therefore, his edition would have been very different from Sánchez's fairly conservative use of single-work or single-author manuscripts, but Percy did not edit it in that way, so the difference was bound to be even greater. The first evidence for his intentions is the draft contents list (which Friedman dates tentatively at October-November 1761), 'carrying out in detail the general plans settled a short time before with Shenstone and Johnson' (Friedman, 1234). It has one hundred and sixty-six titles, against one hundred and seventy-six in the *Reliques*, but the difference is greater than

---

24 *Shenstone's Miscellany 1759-1763*, ed. Ian A. Gordon (Oxford: Clarendon Press, 1952).

25 'The plan of the work was settled in concert with the late elegant Mr Shenstone, who was to have borne a joint share in it had not death unhappily prevented him' (I, 6). See *The Percy Letters*, VII: *The Correspondence of Thomas Percy & William Shenstone*, ed. Cleanth Brooks (1977); Churchill, 'William Shenstone's Share'; Davis, Index, *s.v.* Shenstone; and Margaret M. Smith, 'Thomas Percy, William Shenstone, *Five Pieces of Runic Poetry*, and the *Reliques*', *Bodleian Library Record*, XII (1985-88), 471-77.

26 *Bishop Percy's Folio Manuscript: Ballads and Romances*, ed. John W. Hales and Frederick J. Furnivall, with [Francis J.] Child, William Chappell, *et al.* (London: N. Trübner, 1867-68), 3 vols. The first draft of the contents list was discovered in Harvard College Library, and is edited by Friedman, 1235-44.

that would suggest, since a considerable number of poems in the draft list were not printed, and others were brought in to take their place (Friedman, 1244 and 1247-48). A feature already noticeable in the draft list, and prominent in the *Reliques*, is that only a minority of the ballads in Pitt's folio manuscript were used, and to these were added many from other sources. Percy lists a number of sources in his Preface (I, 4-5), giving pride of place to Samuel Pepys's collection in the library of Magdalene College, Cambridge.[27] The Pre-Reliques (to use Friedman's term for the draft list) was a good deal closer to a work of scholarship as generally understood than is the published *Reliques*, whose stronger literary emphasis befits a work designed for the general educated public. Percy's original inclination was to print the texts from the folio manuscript more or less as they were: reworkings are rarely to be found in the Pre-Reliques (Friedman, 1247-48). It was only after lengthy persuasion by Shenstone that he changed his policy, convinced that the reading public would not willingly accept texts that seemed primitive and rough (Churchill, 967, 972; Friedman, 1247-48; *cf.* Davis, 103-04). His original determination to print the original manuscript version with any text that he reworked is clearly seen in the Pre-Reliques (Churchill, 967; Friedman, 1248), but is only occasionally reflected in the *Reliques*.[28]

---

27 Another important source was *A Collection of Old Ballads* (published 1723-25), and there seem to have been others not mentioned by Percy: for instance, Dianne Dugaw shows that Percy made use — perhaps substantial use — of chap-book ballads purchased from the printer Cluer Dicey, of Bow Church Yard, adding that:

> the exact relationship of the Dicey broadside ballads to their counterparts in the *Reliques* is impossible to determine. Percy, ever anxious to accentuate the scholarly seriousness of his work and to distance his 'reliques' from common streetsong fare, nowhere acknowledges his indebtedness to Dicey. ('The Popular Marketing of "Old Ballads": The Ballad Revival and Eighteenth-Century Antiquarianism Reconsidered', *Eighteenth-Century Studies*, XXI [1987-88], 71-90 [83])

28 *The Boy and the Mantle* is reworked in *Reliques*, II, 397-403, for 'Such readers as have no relish for pure antiquity' (II, 190), while the original text 'is printed verbatim from the old MS' (188) earlier in the volume (190-95). Percy did not, however, here mean by 'verbatim' what we should mean: Walter Jackson Bate finds that '9 of its 194 lines were altered for the purpose of

Similarly, Percy had intended to follow a chronological order (Sánchez was soon to plan his *Colección* on roughly similar lines), but Shenstone urged on him the inadvisability of alienating the reader by placing the oldest and most difficult poems at the beginning:

> throwing too many ballads together that were irregular in point of Metre, or subobscure in point of Language [...] at the beginning of your work, might perhaps be liable to give disgust. (Churchill, 971; *cf.* Friedman, 1248)

Instead, Shenstone convinced Percy that he should adopt what Palgrave, a century later, was to call 'the most poetically-effective order'.[29] Even so, Percy was nervous about the reading public's reception of late-medieval verse:

> In a polished age, like the present, I am sensible that many of these relics of antiquity will require great allowance to be made for them. Yet they have, for the most part, a pleasing simplicity, and many artless graces [...] To atone for the rudeness of the more obsolete pieces, each Series concludes with a few modern attempts in the same kind of writing [...][30]

---

clarification' ('Percy's Use of his Folio-Manuscript', *Journal of English and Germanic Philology*, XLIII [1944], 337-48). It may well be, therefore, that even at the Pre-Reliques stage Percy saw some degree of rewriting as his editorial function.

29 *The Golden Treasury of the Best Songs and Lyrical Poems in the English Language*, ed. Francis Turner Palgrave (London: Oxford U. P., [5th ed.], 1941; [1st ed. 1861]), xi.

30 Preface; I, 4. Similar anxiety was expressed in Spain a hundred years later: Florencio Janer, introducing the BAE volume that took Sánchez's *Colección* as its starting point, felt it necessary to apologize to his readers:

> Difícil será, por cierto, dejar en el presente tomo satisfecho el buen gusto literario de los suscritores a esta Biblioteca. Saboreadas, en volúmenes anteriores, las dulcísimas poesías de Garcilaso, Ercilla [...] y otros, que cultivaron el Parnaso español en no menos felices y abundosas rimas, la sequedad y rudeza de los orígenes de la poesía castellana ha de formar desagradable contraste con la fluidez y galanura de los poetas que alcanzaron nota de mejores. (*Poetas castellanos anteriores al siglo XV*, BAE, LVII [Madrid: Rivadeneyra, 1864], v)

Janer goes on to excuse the offence committed against good taste by printing 'los primitivos esfuerzos del idioma patrio' on Darwinian grounds: 'Sólo de este modo podrá apreciarse mejor la marcha progresiva, el admirable desarrollo de

4 The Reception of the *Reliques*

The strategy eventually adopted by Percy at Shenstone's urging proved both hugely successful and calamitous. The immediate success of the *Reliques* encouraged him to produce a second edition in 1767, only two years after the first; a third edition followed in 1775, and a fourth in 1794. There were reprints (including a pirated one in 1790-91 that suppressed Percy's name), selections, and adaptations, and the *Reliques* has seldom, if ever, been out of print in more than two centuries. Only Palgrave's *Golden Treasury* surpasses it in lasting popularity. Its literary influence was strong and enduring. It was quickly followed by eight similar anthologies (listed by Davis, 292). Sir Walter Scott wrote of the impression that it made on him in his youth:

> The first time I could scrape a few shillings together, I bought unto myself a copy of these beloved volumes; nor do I believe I ever read a book half so frequently or with half the enthusiasm.
>
> (Quoted *Reliques*, I, vii)

> [...] when the Reliques of Ancient Poetry were first put into my hands, an era in my poetical taste which I shall never forget. The very grass sod seat to which (when a boy of twelve years old) I retreated from my playfellows, to devour the works of the ancient minstrels, is still fresh and dear to my memory.
>
> (Letter to Percy, 11 January 1801, quoted Davis 314)

John Clare, in 1820, found the *Reliques* 'the most pleasing book I ever happend on' (Dugaw, 88). A few years earlier, in 1815, William Wordsworth had given his considered view of its influence:

> for our own country, its poetry has been absolutely redeemed by it. I do not think that there is an able writer in verse of the present day who would not be proud to acknowledge his obligation to the

nuestra literatura en su edad de oro' (*ibid.*). It is unlikely that a scholar who had taken the trouble to add very substantially to Sánchez's collection would believe this, but it is significant that, a century after Shenstone had persuaded Percy not to risk a scholarly approach, and in the year that the first volumes of the Early English Text Society were published, it should be thought prudent to say it. The primacy won for Spain by Sánchez had passed to scholars in other countries.

> 'Reliques'; I know that it is so with my friends; and, for myself, I am happy in this occasion to make a public avowal of my own.
> (Davis, 313)

Percy's influence on European Romantic literature, both direct and — mediated through Scott — indirect, was at least as great as his influence in England. And it was not only literature that was affected: H. R. Trevor-Roper shows how the writing of history was transformed, both in Britain and in Germany, by the Romantic movement, and he gives great weight to Percy in the origins of this transformation:

> Thomas Percy established a less brilliant but more lasting fame [than that of James Macpherson's Ossian]. With these two works, a new fashion was launched: a romantic cult of primitive society, primitive literature; and it was this cult which, transformed by political events unimagined in the 1760s, would help to create a new historical philosophy.[31]

Yet Percy presented the *Reliques* as a work of scholarship, and with good reason (it includes several extensive and thoroughly documented essays on aspects of literary history), thus exposing it to judgement by other scholars. An early objection was raised by Samuel Pegge in a paper read to the Society of Antiquaries and published in its journal *Archaeologia*; Percy protested to the Society in 1773 and demanded a retraction, though without success.[32] The most vehement and persistent critic of Percy's editorial practice,

31 *The Romantic Movement and the Study of History*, The John Coffin Memorial Lecture 1969 (London: The Athlone Press, Univ. of London, 1969), 2-3.

32 Jeremiah Milles, President of the Society, wrote to Richard Gough, its Director, on 24 February 1773:

> We had a right to read, as we have to print, whatever papers are delivered to us: Mr Pegge's paper was publick to the Society. Dr Percy as a member might have been inform'd of it and have answered it by another paper, in which case both would have been printed in the same volume. If he chuses to answer these objections in another channel, the Society neither ought nor can take any notice of them. Besides if we were to garble our papers and weigh the merits of them so nicely, we should very much check the spirit of enquiry and the communications of our members. (Joan Evans, *A History of the Society of Antiquaries* [Oxford: Oxford U. P., for Society of Antiquaries, 1956], 166).

however, was Joseph Ritson (1752-1803), who even called into question the existence of the folio manuscript.[33] The Percy-Ritson polemic continued over a number of years, and led to substantial changes in later editions of the *Reliques* (Davis, 279-92). Percy's revisions in successive editions are a tacit acceptance of the accuracy of some of Ritson's criticisms, and when, a hundred years after the publication of the *Reliques*, the printed texts were carefully compared with the folio manuscript, the results were devastating, and Ritson was vindicated.

John W. Hales — writing, we should remember, in the heady and confident first years of the Early English Text Society's life — says firmly that 'We know [Ritson] was right, that he said no word too much against the falsifications of originals that Percy indulged in' (I, xvii-xix, n. 2), and is bitter in his condemnation of Percy's method:

> There are 39 lines in [*The Child of Ell*]. There are 200 in the thing called the 'Child of Elle' in the 'Reliques'. But in those 200 all the 39 originals do not appear. Now and then one appears, always (with one exception) a little altered to fit it for the strange bed-fellows with which the polishing process has made it acquainted, its good manners corrupted, so to speak, by evil communications. On the whole, the union of the genuine and the false—of the old ballad with Percy's tawdry feebleness — makes about as objectionable a *mesalliance* as that in the story itself is in the eyes of the father. (I, 132-33)

33 Davis, 285-86. The accusation that Percy had hoaxed readers was false, but Percy's unwillingness to let Ritson see the manuscript—though understandable in view of the nature of the criticisms that Ritson was making — was a tactical error. Moreover, such an accusation was not self-evidently fanciful at a time when Macpherson's Ossian and Thomas Chatterton's *Rowley Poems*, at first acclaimed as the rediscovery of important medieval poems, had soon been exposed. Ritson was an antiquarian of great learning, copious production, and abrasive personality: see Bertrand H. Bronson, *Joseph Ritson Scholar-at-Arms* (Berkeley: Univ. of California Press, 1938), 2 vols. Percy was told by a friend in June 1789 that Ritson had failed to secure election as a Fellow of the Society of Antiquaries (Davis, 279; Evans does not mention the incident). Then, as now, rejection of someone who had got as far as a ballot was unusual.

> Before he learned to reverence [the MS], as he says, he scribbled notes over its margins and put brackets for suggested omissions in its texts. After he reverenced it, he tore out of it the two leaves containing its best ballad, *King Estmere*, which he had evidently touched up largely himself. (I, xvi)

It is true that Hales finds extenuating circumstances (the times in which Percy was working, his service in making late-medieval poetry known: xvii-xix, n. 2), and it is also true that the violence and sarcasm that break out from time to time ('That worthy prelate, touched by the beauty of it — he had a soul [...]', 132) repel the reader. Nevertheless, the overall effect is to establish a conclusive case against Percy on scholarly grounds.[34]

5 The Reception of the *Colección*

The reception of Sánchez's *Colección* was the mirror-image of that of the *Reliques*. In place of instant and resounding success among lovers of literature, an interest so small that the publication petered out; in place of growing scholarly doubts, culminating in Furnivall and Hales' damning verdict, the respect of succeeding generations of scholars. The publication of the *Colección* was made possible by the willingness of Antonio de Sancha, a scholarly printer and publisher, to invest money in the project:

> Ahora que ya poseo una mediana colección de poesías anteriores al siglo XV, he concebido esperanzas de darla a luz, mediante la generosa disposición con que se ofrece con su prensa y expensas Don Antonio de Sancha que tiene acreditado más su celo que su interés en otras muchas obras que ha publicado.[35]

---

34 Davis, surprisingly, deals with Furnivall and Hales only in a final note, concluding:

> The criticism, at times overwrought, was often on the mark. But while it led to a proper caution in accepting Percy's texts, it neither diminished his achievement nor rendered the *Reliques* any less delightful than earlier generations had found it. (334, n. 38)

35 *Colección*, I, fol. *4r. See Emilio Cotarelo y Mori, *Un gran editor del siglo XVIII: biografía de D. Antonio de Sancha* (Madrid: Cámaras Oficiales del Libro de Madrid y Barcelona, 1924 [offprint from *Bibliografía general española*

The increasing gaps between volumes (I, 1779; II, 1780; III, 1782; IV, 1790) were due not — as is usually the case — to delays by the initiator of the series but to financial difficulties caused by poor sales. Writing some years after the publication of volume III, Juan Sempere y Guarinos denounced the apathy of the reading public:

> Pero a pesar del mérito de la colección del Señor Sánchez, como el estudio de las antigüedades patrias, y mucho más el de la Historia literaria, está tan poco extendido, D. Antonio Sancha, que se había encargado de su edición, se ha visto precisado a suspenderla, por falta de despacho. ¡Cosa vergonzosa! que habiéndose encontrado quien diera generosamente mil doblones, para imprimir una mala colección de nuestras comedias, no haya otro que costee la de las Poesías anteriores al siglo XV, obra apreciable, hecha por un sabio, y de todos modos mucho más útil que la que se intitula, *Teatro español*. (V, 97)

He continues:

> Sé que el Señor Sánchez tiene materiales para muchos tomos, y aun el quarto, y quinto concluidos, y en disposición de poderse ya imprimir. El uno contiene las *Poesías de Juan Ruiz, Arcipreste de Hita* [...] El segundo tomo, que había de ser el quinto de la *Colección*, contiene las *Poesías de Pero López de Ayala* [...] (97-98)

There is no doubt that Sempere y Guarinos had seen these two volumes in manuscript: he gives several lines of information about, and quotes three stanzas from, both the *Libro de Buen Amor* and the *Rimado de palacio*. Whereas the information could have been pieced together from that given by Sánchez in vol. I, the stanzas must have come from the two volumes that he had ready for the press. A year after Sempere's reproachful words were published, Antonio de Sancha issued vol. IV of the *Colección*. I do not know whether Sempere's words bore fruit, or whether arrangements for the printing were already in hand. Whatever the explanation for the appearance of vol. IV, it is certain that no more followed, and that Sánchez's intentions were not fully realized.[36] Great as is his achievement in the

---

e hispanoamericana]).

36 Percy also had planned a further volume: 'I hope now in the Course of next Winter to prepare a 4th Volume of Reliques for the Press' (letter of 28 July 1775: Davis, 211). He was still contemplating a fourth volume in 1778

four published volumes of the *Colección*, his ambitions had been still greater:

> Los poemas que se publicaron por ahora, y el orden que se guardará según su antigüedad verdadera, o verosímil, será como se sigue: El poema del Cid Campeador: las poesías de don Gonzalo de Berceo: la vida de San Ildefonso escrita por el Beneficiado de Úbeda: las poesías de Juan Ruiz Arcipreste de Hita: las del Judío Don Santo: las de Pero López de Ayala: la Historia del Conde Fernán González: y unos versos de un tal Pero Gómez. También entrarán en esta colección, si se descubrieren a tiempo oportuno, el poema de Alexandro, los Votos del Pavón, y las poesías de Don Juan Manuel autor del Conde Lucanor. Y finalmente qualesquier poesías que los amantes de nuestra literatura quisieren comunicar, como sean anteriores al siglo XV. (I, fol. [*5])[37]

Thus the lack of support among the educated public — a public which seems to have shown interest in editions of Golden-Age works — prevented the publication not only of the *Rimado de palacio*, as Sempere testifies, but also of the *Vida de San Ildefonso*, the *Proverbios morales*, the *Poema de Fernán González*, the lines that Sánchez ascribes to Pero Gómez, and perhaps other texts that Sánchez found after 1779 (as he found the *Libro de Alexandre*).[38] Not until the 1840s, when Sánchez

---

(Davis, 223), but by 1780 the intention had waned (243), though it was not finally abandoned until 1807, when he was only a few years from the end of his long life (324). The resemblance to the history of the *Colección* is, however, much less close than it seems: Percy, unlike Sánchez, had an eager public, and the failure to produce a fourth volume of the *Reliques* was due to the pressure of other commitments and growing doubts as to whether old ballads were a suitable interest for a Dean of Carlisle, soon to be Bishop of Dromore (270). For another abandoned project, which had been planned in some detail in the 1770s, see Vincent H. Ogburn, 'Thomas Percy's Unfinished Collection, *Ancient English and Scottish Poems*', *ELH: A Journal of English Literary History*, III (1936), 183-89.

37 Colin Smith says that the *Colección* includes the *Libro de Apolonio* (*Poema de mio Cid* [Oxford: Clarendon Press, 1972], lxxxi), but this is an error, probably caused by momentary confusion with the texts contained in the expansions by Pidal and Janer. As will be seen, Sánchez does not even mention the *Libro de Apolonio* among the texts he knows.

38 The editions and studies, almost all of Golden-Age works, that were published in the period 1768-88 are listed by Ivy L. McClelland, *The Origins of the Romantic Movement in Spain* (Liverpool: Liverpool U. P., [2nd ed.] 1975),

had been in his grave for forty years, was there enough interest to support an amplified version of the *Colección*.

Yet, though the readers of Golden-Age literature in the last quarter of the eighteenth century were unwilling to subscribe in sufficient numbers to the *Colección*, a few readers were passionately interested in the texts that Sánchez published. Chief among these was Sánchez's younger contemporary Rafael de Floranes Vélez de Robles y Encinas (1743-1801).[39] Floranes, unlike Sánchez, was an amateur scholar, never holding an official post. His voracious reading and copious writing over an extraordinarily wide field led to virtually no publications during his lifetime, and though his scholarship was an essential resource for many of his contemporaries it was not recognized by election to one of the academies. Since Menéndez y Pelayo long ago gave an outline of his life and work (298-304), and Nicholas G. Round has recently reassessed him, it is unnecessary to say much more. It is, however, worth recalling, as a measure of his bibliographical knowledge, that he added three hundred authors to his copy — now lost — of Nicolás Antonio (Menéndez y Pelayo, 306). I should also draw attention to Menéndez y Pelayo's eloquent appraisal of the contrasting strengths and weaknesses of Floranes and Sánchez:

> La erudición de Sánchez [...] no era tan varia pero sí más profunda que la de Floranes [...] Era Floranes fecundísimo y fácil en producir, como quien se cuidaba poco del plan y menos del estilo. Su verbosidad irrestañable y desaliñada contrasta con la elegante sobriedad de Sánchez. [...] (324-25)
>
> Floranes se muestra más inventivo y original: Sánchez más cauto [...] Floranes yace enterrado bajo la mole inédita de sus obras. Sánchez, merced a un libro solo [...] ha conseguido perpetuar su nombre [...] (342)

We should also recall Round's statement that the more than eighty volumes of manuscript writings left by Floranes at his death 'have been used regularly — with slightly less regular

123-24.

39 See Menéndez y Pelayo, 'Dos opúsculos inéditos', 298-324; Nicholas G. Round, 'The Antiquary Reassessed: Floranes and the Liberal Tradition', *BHS*, LXVIII (1991), 107-23; Aguilar Piñal, *Bibliografía*, III (1984), 476-89 (entries 3906-4045).

acknowledgement — by generations of medievalists' (108) — and we should note in passing that the danger of having one's work published without acknowledgement of authorship is not confined to the long dead, as the authors of *tesinas* on *El Victorial* have recently discovered.[40]

Floranes was a born heckler: much of his work consisted of close scrutiny and copious annotation of the work of other scholars, and his correspondence with them extended throughout his working life. To have one's work subjected to this kind of scrutiny is an invaluable asset, but gratitude is not always the dominant emotion in the recipient. Sánchez was one of the recipients:

> D. Rafael Floranes, siguiendo su costumbre de apuntar, sobre los nuevos libros que adquiere para su uso, aquellas cosas que se le ofrecen quando los lee la primera vez, y juzga que pueden servir para confirmación, ampliación, o corrección de las noticias que contienen, habiendo leído el tom. I° de la colección de poesías antiguas del señor D. Tomás Antonio Sánchez, luego que salió a luz, advirtió por los márgenes sólo para su gobierno, y sin espíritu crítico, las especies siguientes. (Menéndez y Pelayo, 343)

What follows extends over more than fifty printed pages. As might be expected, some are shrewd corrections, some are comments that were reasonable when Floranes made them but have been invalidated by later research, and a few are clearly ill-founded. There is not necessarily agreement among today's scholars as to the category to which any given comment belongs: thus, whereas Sánchez dated the *Cantar de Mio Cid* at 'la mitad o poco más del siglo XII' (*Colección*, I, 223), a view later adopted by Menéndez Pidal, Floranes (356-62) anticipates the present

---

40 Some of Floranes' work was printed in the nineteenth century, notably the *Vida política y literaria del Canciller Mayor de Castilla D. Pedro López de Ayala*, written in 1779, which occupies vol. XIX (1851) and some of vol. XX (1852) of the Colección de Documentos Inéditos para la Historia de España. A good example of the value of Floranes' work to later scholars is his transcription of a substantial part of the *Cancionero de Martínez de Burgos*, now our only source for this lost *cancionero*. It is used, and fully acknowledged, by Dorothy Sherman Severin, *The 'Cancionero de Martínez de Burgos': A Description of its Contents, with an Edition of the Prose and Poetry of Juan Martínez de Burgos*, EHT XII (Exeter: Exeter Univ., 1976) (for Floranes, see viii-x).

majority view by arguing for composition in the thirteenth century. However, he chooses a date later in that century than anyone would now defend, concluding on the basis of the final lines that the *Cantar* was composed after 1221, and on other grounds that 1245 is the most likely date.[41] He anticipates Colin Smith by arguing that Per Abat is the poet, not merely the copyist (358-60), though his Per Abat is not a lawyer but precentor of Fernando III's Capilla Real.

Sánchez paid due attention to Floranes' commentaries, and his reactions, occupying nearly forty pages, are, like Floranes' notes, available to us in Menéndez y Pelayo's long article. It is impossible to know when, or over how long a period, he composed his replies to Floranes' points, but they took their definitive form in July 1792 (394), after the *Colección* had come to a halt. Round mentions his 'reasoned replies' (109), and the description is a fair one in terms of the arguments and evidence adduced by Sánchez. The tenor of the replies, however, sometimes reveals irritation rather than a wish for reasoned debate. Sánchez's first paragraph is supercilious: Floranes' 'muchas y muy curiosas advertencias', he says,

> se pueden reducir a tres clases; unas de poquísima consideración, como en ellas se verá; otras que bien examinadas no son tan justas como parecen; y otras que en lugar de advertencias son equivocaciones. (394)

Worse, he is at times sarcastic:

> gracias inmortales se deben dar al señor Floranes por el feliz descubrimiento del verdadero autor de la *Crónica General* de España, atribuida al Rey D. Alonso el Sabio, escrita de su orden. (416)

It is possible that this disagreeable tone may owe as much to disappointment at the *Colección*'s lack of wide support as to irritation at Floranes' heckling. Be that as it may, Sánchez's share of the debate, like Floranes', is full of interest. I do not

41 The early stages of the controversy, and the extent to which they foreshadow recent arguments, are documented by Miguel Magnotta, *Historia y bibliografía de la crítica sobre el 'Poema de Mío Cid' (1750-1971)*, UNCSRLL, CXLV (Chapel Hill: Dept of Romance Languages, Univ. of North Carolina, 1976), 17-23.

know whether similar exchanges exist for the other volumes of the *Colección*, or with other scholars.

6 Sánchez's Methods

A full study of Sánchez's editorial procedure and the sources of his editions would require much archival research, and would fill a book. The pages that follow are no more than a selective and summary treatment of some aspects.

As we have seen, the first impulse came from Sánchez's reading of Santillana's *Carta*. The realization of its importance as a document of Spanish literary history, and the decision to annotate it thoroughly, led to a search for manuscripts in the hope of resolving problems raised by Santillana's account, and thus to the realization that nothing short of a series of editions, with introductions and glossaries, would do:

> Desde que empecé a formar estas notas he tenido siempre un gran deseo de publicar una colección de nuestras primeras poesías para que el tiempo, los incendios, la polilla, y otros enemigos que tienen los códices, no acabaran con ellos y se perdiera del todo su memoria. Siempre he creído que un gran caudal de nuestra lengua, de nuestra historia, de nuestras costumbres y literatura antigua, yacía como mudo entre las tinieblas del más profundo olvido y abandono. Pero la dificultad de adquirir estos códices me había hecho desconfiar de la empresa, y me había ya reducido a estas notas y poner en ellas algunos extractos de poemas que poseía, y muestras que se me habían comunicado de otros, o que yo había sacado de los libros. [...] Yo [...] he cansado a los amigos solicitando códices, copiando algunos por mi mano, y costeando copias de otros que se han hecho por la agena, y cotextándolas después con los que han servido de originales. (I, fols $*4^{v}$-$[*5]^{r}$)

He announces his intention — duly carried out — of concluding each volume with a glossary, for immediate utility to readers of that volume, and promises that

> Todas estas voces se juntarán después en un tomo aparte en forma de diccionario, al qual precederán algunas observaciones que se van haciendo por las mismas poesías, sobre la lengua castellana. Veráse cómo se formó de la latina [...] (I, fol. $[*6]^{r}$)

This final volume of glossary and linguistic study, like volume V (*Rimado de palacio*) and those that were to follow it, was a casualty of the paucity of subscribers to the *Colección*.

The eleven-page introduction to the *Cantar de Mio Cid* discusses date, versification, language, and other matters. There are, surprisingly, hardly any notes to the text; although the number of notes increased in later volumes of the *Colección*, they were never as frequent as one might expect. This is one of the two ways in which Sánchez's approach to his task differs notably from that of twentieth-century editors (the other, to be discussed below, is his bowdlerizing of the *Libro de Buen Amor*).

Sánchez tells us that he was able, thanks to the good offices of Eugenio de Llaguno y Amírola, Secretary of the Council of State, to borrow the unique manuscript of the *Cantar* and transcribe it, 'lo que he hecho con la más escrupulosa puntualidad' (I, 220). Such words are, like Percy's 'verbatim' (n. 28, above), a hostage to fortune, and if the words are read as a claim that this is a paleographic transcription they are incorrect: punctuation is supplied, and there is a fair amount of regularization, and even occasional modernization, of orthography. I do not, however, think that such an interpretation of Sánchez's words is justified: 'copiar [...] con la más escrupulosa puntualidad' must have meant, in 1779, 'to copy very carefully', without making gratuitous alterations in the text. A comparison of three sections of twenty lines each with a facsimile of the manuscript reveals only one indisputable error of transcription.[42] This is in line 2002/1992, where the MS clearly reads 'coranado' but Sánchez has 'coronado'. There is, it is true, one point at which a reader is startled to find a word not generally present in modern editions: 'Burgeses e Burgesas por las finiestras son *puestas*' (l. 18/17). This is not, however, a gratuitous addition to the text: the word is there in the MS, though legible only with the utmost difficulty. Menéndez Pidal concludes that it was added by a later hand, and that later still it was altered to 'puestos' (III, 909). Editors up to and including Huntington generally accepted 'puestas' or 'puestos'; more recent editors have not; but although Sánchez's

42 The samples are lines 1-20, 1994-2003, and 3325-44 of Sánchez's edition (1-20, 1985-2013, and 3313-32 of Menéndez Pidal's paleographic edition). I have used the excellent colour facsimile in *Poema de Mio Cid*, ed. Hipólito Escobar Sobrino (Burgos: Ayuntamiento, 1982).

decision was almost certainly wrong, it was not irresponsible or careless. In the other case in which he includes a word not found in most modern editions, 'en su compaña LX. pendones *lebaba*' (l. 16), it is an interlinear addition accepted not only by Huntington but much more recently by Smith.

A much more serious issue is raised by a note added in 1792 by Juan Antonio Pellicer y Pilares to his revision of Juan Ruiz de Ulibarri's 1596 transcription. This note casts doubt on the provenance of Sánchez's edition:

> El original estaba en el lugar de Bibar. Húbole el Sr. Sánchez, por intercesión del Sr. Llaguno, Secretario del consejo de estado. Emendamos por él esta copia, y así ésta equivale al original, pero por él la publicó el referido Sr. Sánchez en sus Poesías antiguas, tomo 1.[43]

It is surprising that Sánchez, with the original in his hands, should edit the Ulibarri-Pellicer copy; a more plausible hypothesis is that having seen the copy, he went to some trouble to obtain the original in order to verify doubtful readings. The copy, before Pellicer's emendations, was seriously defective: Sánchez calls it 'una mala copia de este códice, la qual he leído y cotejado con su original' (I, 228-29), and its defects may be clearly seen in the page reproduced photographically by Roque Pidal y Bernaldo de Quirós (plate facing p. 10). Even so, Pellicer's assertion implies a complex chain of events: Sánchez sees the copy, secures the original and compares it with the copy, finding the latter to be seriously unsatisfactory; Pellicer (at Sánchez's request?) emends the copy; Sánchez, without acknowledging Pellicer's help (*cf.* Aguilar Piñal's statement that he did not always acknowledge the help of other scholars: n. 7, above), uses the emended copy as the basis for his edition. Menéndez Pidal is satisfied that Pellicer told the truth: 'La revisión que de la copia de Ulibarri hizo

---

43 Quoted by Menéndez Pidal, *Cantar de mio Cid: texto, gramática y vocabulario*, III, 2nd ed., Obras Completas de R. Menéndez Pidal, V (Madrid: Espasa-Calpe, 1946), 907. I have corrected the quotation against the photograph in Roque Pidal y Bernaldo de Quirós, *Los cantares de Mio Cid: noticias viejas y mozas del Códice único que los contiene y que hoy se reproduce íntegramente por medio de la fototipia* (Madrid: Comisión del Milenario de Castilla, Burgos, 1947), plate facing p. 12.

Pellicer nos explica algunas lecciones de Sánchez' (III, 908); this view is accepted by the *Cantar*'s latest editor, Alberto Montaner.[44] Since the question is important both for an assessment of Sánchez's editorial methods and also for his credibility, it deserves detailed investigation.

Volume II, containing Berceo's works, has more notes to the texts than volume I (though still fewer than one would expect), and a longer introduction: eighteen pages on Berceo and twenty-seven pages on the individual works (ranging from ten pages for the *Vida de Sán Millán* to half a page for the *Signos del Juicio Final*; the *Loores de Nuestra Señora* and the *Himnos* have no introduction). The seriousness with which Sánchez took his scholarly project is indicated by the page of corrections to volume I (II, xxiii-xxiv), though he seems to have allowed himself some relaxation: at the end of Berceo's works (II, 465-73) comes the *Loor de don Gonzalo de Berceo*, with its own introduction. As with the *Cantar de Mio Cid*, there was previous work on which Sánchez could draw, though this time it was both more abundant and more scholarly. As we have seen, Sánchez uses Vergara's 1736 edition of the *Vida de Santo Domingo* as the basis for his own, collating it with the mid-fourteenth century MS *H* and listing MS variants (99-102).[45] Vergara's publication aroused interest in Berceo, and two manuscript copies of the majority of the poems were made, the first (between 1741 and 1752) organized by Father Diego de Mecolaeta, Abbot of San Millán de la Cogolla, and the second (probably 1774-78) by Father Domingo Ibarreta.[46] Scholars have long recognized the value of the Ibarreta MS, and Mecolaeta's has recently been similarly valued, because these MSS derive directly from medieval ones temporarily or permanently inaccessible to later editors. Sánchez

44 *Cantar de Mio Cid*, ed. Montaner, introd. Francisco Rico, Biblioteca Clásica I (Barcelona: Crítica, 1993), 80.

45 Brian Dutton describes the list as 'algunas variantes muy someras', *Obras completas*, IV: *La vida de Santo Domingo de Silos*, 24.

46 For Berceo scholarship before Sánchez, see Daniel Devoto, 'Berceo antes de 1780', *RABM*, LXXIX (1976), 767-833, and LXXX (1977), pp. 21-54, 455-530, and 773-835. For Mecolaeta, see Brian Dutton, *A New Berceo Manuscript: Madrid, Biblioteca Nacional Ms 13149*, EHT XXXII (Exeter: Exeter Univ., 1982), v-xv.

acknowledges Ibarreta's help:

> El Rmo. Ibarreta que posee una copia moderna de ellas [Berceo's poems], se ha servido franqueármela para cotejar algunas que yo tenía, y copiar las que me faltaban. ¡Ojalá imitaran este exemplo de franqueza y generosidad otros muchos, que poseyendo códices antiguos, no hacen más uso de ellos que esconderlos, fomentar su vanidad, y la singularidad de tenerlos! (I, 121)
>
> Según la copia [of *Signos*] que se sirvió franquearme el Rmo. Ibarreta [...] (II, 273)

There is reason to think that Sánchez used Ibarreta's copy more extensively than these acknowledgements suggest, and that his editions of most of the poems (the Vergara-based *Santo Domingo* is the most important exception) are based on Ibarreta.[47] If this is the case, it does not lessen the force of Menéndez y Pelayo's judgement that the edition of Berceo's poems 'parece más esmerada que las otras' [in the *Colección*], but it does diminish Sánchez's reputation as a scholar.

Volume III, containing the *Libro de Alexandre*, moves further in the direction taken by the Berceo volume: the introduction occupies forty-one pages, and there are some two hundred and ten footnotes (chiefly explanatory, though with some references to the poem's sources), whereas the *Cantar de Mio Cid*, with one-third of *Alexandre*'s number of lines, has only eight footnotes. The introduction deals with the historical Alexander, his literary tradition in the Middle Ages (making special mention of Gautier de Châtillon's *Alexandreis* and one of the branches of the *Roman d'Alexandre*), the manuscript (MS *O*: the existence of the Paris MS would not be known for another hundred years) of the *Libro de Alexandre*, authorship (he accepts Juan Lorenzo de Astorga as author), date (mid-thirteenth century), content, metre, style, and language of the poem. A feature of special interest is that Sánchez comments

47 *Milagros de Nuestra Señora*, ed. A. G. Solalinde, Clásicos Castellanos XLIV (Madrid: La Lectura, 1922), xxvii-xxviii; Dutton, v. Solalinde hints broadly that Sánchez did not see the MSS he claimed to have seen: 'los dos códices que este erudito decía haber consultado' (xxvii), and:

> Si se lee con detención lo que Sánchez dice de estos manuscritos, conservados entonces en el monasterio de San Millán, se verá que no los describe ni habla de ellos especialmente [...] (xxvii)

(xiii-xiv, xxi-xxii, xxxiv) on the stanzas printed by Francisco de Bivar in the seventeenth century from the Bugedo MS, later lost, and that he concludes, after comparing them with the corresponding stanzas of MS *O*, that 'el de Buxedo era distinto del que posee el Excelentísimo Señor Duque del Infantado' (xiv), a conclusion that later scholarship confirms.[48] In view of the interest thus shown in the MS tradition, it is perhaps surprising that Sánchez seems unaware of the *Alexandre* stanzas quoted in *El Victorial* (Willis, xxii-xxv), though they were not widely known until Llaguno published his edition of that work in the same year as Sánchez's *Alexandre*. Although Sánchez's discussion of the *Alexandreis* and the *Roman d'Alexandre* (viii-xii) does not include a consideration of their relationship to the Spanish poem, he had already speculated on this question in the light of the Bugedo fragment, before he knew MS *O* (I, 96-98), and with the complete text at his disposal he goes on to a comparison of the Latin and Spanish poems, concluding that 'bastan los exemplos indicados para que se entienda que Juan Lorenzo teniendo presente el poema de Gualtero, no por eso dexó de hacer el suyo original' (III, xxiv). After the introduction to *Alexandre* there are corrections and additions to volumes I and II, and a twelve-page Life of Gonzalo de Berceo.

The manuscript was at that time in the library of the Duque del Infantado, who had a copy made for Sánchez and lent him the original so that he might compare them (III, xii). Comparison of two ten-stanza samples (889-98 and 1848-57) with Willis's paleographic edition of *O* shows, as with the *Cantar de Mio Cid*, regularization and occasional modernization of orthography, but a substantially correct presentation of the text. In two cases Sánchez seems to have emended the MS reading: 'minguaba' for 'mingua' (890b) and 'las aves' for 'la aves' (892b); in both cases, the emendation is required by the sense and is confirmed by the later discovery of MS *P*.

---

48 See *'El libro de Alexandre': Texts of the Paris and the Madrid Manuscripts*, ed. Raymond S. Willis [and C. Carroll Marden], Elliott Monographs in the Romance Languages and Literatures XXXII (Princeton: Princeton U. P./Paris: PUF, 1934), xxi-xxii. For Marden's share in the edition, see v, and Edmund L. King's statement in *RPh*, XXXIII (1979-80), 13.

Similarly, *P* confirms the emendation of 'garnidos' on linguistic grounds to 'guarnidos' (1851c). Sánchez's 'regajal' for MS 'regaral' (890c) is also confirmed by *P*. In two cases Sánchez has misread an abbreviation: '*contra*' is read as 'otro' (898b), and 'p*or*' as 'per' (1857b). Three other differences seem to be straightforward errors: 'solamente' for 'solament' (896a), 'oviesse' for 'huviese' (897d), and 'nen' for 'non' (898b). The comparison reveals a higher frequency of error than one would hope, but Sánchez's successful emendations must be offset against this, and Willis' judgement that his edition is 'regrettably full of errors' (xxv) overstates the case. Had it not been for the discovery of MS *P*, Sánchez's edition would still be usable as a reading text, though of course detailed literary study requires the rigorous transcription undertaken by Marden and Willis.

The edition of the *Libro de Buen Amor* that occupies volume IV — the last one published, though, as we have seen, not the last one prepared by Sánchez — has a shorter introduction (twenty-nine pages) and fewer notes than the developing pattern of the previous volumes leads us to expect, but the glossary is extensive (forty-five pages) and, like the previous ones, detailed. Discouragement in the face of the paucity of subscriptions may explain the absence of a feature found in volumes II and III: corrections and additions to previous volumes.[49]

The introduction to volume IV deals with Juan Ruiz's life (Sánchez takes literally the references to 'presión' and believes that the whole work was composed in prison, *circa* 1343), metre, the poet's literary knowledge, his *exempla*, his love poems, the manuscripts, and finally the relation of the Endrina episode to *Pamphilus* (pointed out to Sánchez by Juan Antonio Pellicer). A prominent feature is worry about the corrupting effect of

49 Compare:

> tal suele mostrarse el gusto y curiosidad de nuestros compatriotas en saber quiénes fueron sus antepasados, cómo hablaban, cómo pensaban, cómo discurrían los primeros autores de nuestra lengua, y qué ideas tenían de su poesía vulgar; que publicado un tomo en que todo esto se manifieste, queda poco deseo y menos calor para llevar adelante lo comenzado. (II, i-ii)

literature (xv-xvii), though the poet's moral purpose in the Endrina episode is affirmed, and his general intention defended in words that anticipate Jorge Guzmán's hypothesis:

> el Arcipreste en todos los casos de amor profano, sólo intenta satirizar los vicios de su tiempo, y descubrir las redes que los hombres solían armar a las mugeres; para que conocidas, se guardasen de ellas, para prevenirlas contra los artificios de las mensageras [...] (xvi)[50]

Yet Sánchez, priest as well as scholar, could not accept some of the more erotic lines of the *Libro*, or the poet's parody of sacred texts by putting Latin words into a vernacular erotic context: 'Reprehensible abuso hace el poeta de aquellas palabras' he writes (281) of 1672d, a line from the Clérigos de Talavera episode. There is no way of knowing whether he realized that the sacred texts were the means, not the target, of the parody; the mere use of the words in such a context was, understandably, offensive to him. So strongly did he feel that, although 'estas poesías no se dan al público con el fin de enseñar buena ni mala doctrina, sino [...] para averiguar [...] el estado que en aquellos tiempos tenía nuestra poesía vulgar [...]' (xvii), he felt obliged to suppress a few passages:

> de todo esto hemos suprimido una poesía entera, y varios pasages, no los menos festivos e ingeniosos, por no ofender a los que lean estas composiciones olvidados del fin con que se publican. (xviii)

The major suppression is the Pitas Payas story, with the stanzas that introduce it. However, the scholar reasserts himself:

> Para que el lector vea quántas coplas se suprimen siempre que ha parecido preciso suprimir algunas, se han dexado correr los números de ellas como si ninguna se suprimiese [...] (xviii)

The worry was one that this Catholic priest shared with his Anglican contemporary: 'great care has been taken to admit nothing immoral and indecent' (*Reliques*, I, 8). What is a little

---

50 See Jorge Guzmán, *Una constante didáctico-moral del 'Libro de buen amor'* (Santiago: Dpto de Estudios Humanísticos, Univ. de Chile, [2nd ed.] 1980). The first edition (a revision of a 1961 PhD thesis), was published in 1963. Although Guzmán's book is less often cited now, it aroused considerable interest, and won a good deal of support, at the time.

surprising is that Sánchez persisted in his suppressions in the face of reassurance by the Real Academia de la Historia. The Academia had asked Gaspar Melchor de Jovellanos for a detailed opinion, which was strongly in favour of publishing the *Libro* in its entirety, and its verdict was: 'el Consejo [...] dio licencia para que se imprima todo el texto del poeta, sin suprimir lo que había pensado el Colector' (xxxii). It is impossible to know whether Sánchez was influenced by this verdict: we know what he suppressed, but we do not know what he originally intended to suppress.[51] Janer says that he 'creyó [...] deber suprimir grandes trozos' (BAE, LVII, xxxv, n. 1), which seems excessive as a description of what Sánchez did. Be that as it may, he has been severely, and rightly, criticized: any scholar has a right not to edit an obscene or blasphemous or racist work, but scholarly editing and selective suppression do not go well together. Janer rightly restored the deleted passages. It should not be thought, however, that the exclusion of literary works from editions or studies is a thing of the past: Keith Whinnom said, in his inaugural lecture in 1967, that 'a whole tradition of writing [...] has continued to be ignored by modern Spanish editors and critics, as well as by the almost equally prudish foreign hispanists', and he went on to examine the consequences for scholarship.[52]

Sánchez based his edition on a copy of the Salamanca MS that had been made for him; he corrected errors in the copy by reference to another copy that had been made for the Conde de Mansilla, and filled gaps from the Gayoso MS (he explains his procedure, xix-xxii). Although aware of the existence of the Toledo MS, he seems to have made no use of it. His view is that *S* is

> mucho más copioso, aunque defectuoso en algo, que el de Gayoso. Cotejados los dos, se nota gran multitud de variantes, y que por lo

---

51 A list of the omissions is given by Mary-Anne Vetterling, 'The Rediscovery of the *Libro de buen amor*', *Dieciocho*, IV (1981), No. 1, 24-33, at p. 30.

52 'Spanish Literary Historiography: Three Forms of Distortion' (first publ. 1968), in his *Medieval and Renaissance Spanish Literature: Selected Essays*, ed. Alan Deyermond, W. F. Hunter, and Joseph T. Snow (Exeter: Exeter U. P. with *JHP*, 1994), 96-113 (104).

> común está más correcto y arreglado el de Salamanca; o porque el mismo autor le limó, o porque alguna mano diestra y antigua le retocó. (xix)

He observes that 'de los dos códices y del retazo de Toledo, no se puede formar uno completo de las obras del poeta' (xxii). Despite Sánchez's clear statement that he used copies of *S* except where he needed to fill gaps from *G*, Menéndez y Pelayo says that 'formó un texto ecléctico con los tres códices' (326). The resolution of this question would require a great deal of detailed comparison, since it is clear that Sánchez did not work directly with *S*. Until someone is prepared to undertake this arduous task, it seems prudent to accept Sánchez's assurance, since, while an editor who had relied on one MS and filled gaps from another might be tempted to claim that he had based his text on a critical collation of all three, few editors are likely to understate the trouble that they have taken.

7 Conclusion

Both Percy's *Reliques* and Sánchez's *Colección* are to some extent collaborative works, though in different ways: while Percy continually sought advice as well as manuscript and printed sources for his material, and changed his plans in the light of that advice, Sánchez was far more self-confident, relying on others for information and especially for copies of manuscripts but following unswervingly the plan that he had devised at the outset. Percy is generous in praising his advisers in his preface, though he may not have acknowledged all the suppliers of his material (see n. 27, above), and a picture of Sánchez's debts — an incomplete picture, according to Aguilar Piñal (n. 7, above) — emerges only gradually as one reads the prefaces to his editions. A surprising feature is Sánchez's preference — except in the case of MS *G* of the *Libro de Buen Amor*, and perhaps in that of the *Cantar de Mio Cid* — for working with recent copies, using the medieval MSS — if at all — to correct the copies. This preference was probably carried further than he acknowledges in the preface to volume I, in a passage quoted earlier that must now be repeated:

> He cansado a los amigos solicitando códices, *copiando algunos por mi mano*, y costeando copias de otros que se han hecho por la

> agena, y cotexándolas después con los que han servido de originales. ([*5r]; my italics)

It is hard to know whether pressure of work or uncertainty about his ability in paleography led Sánchez to rely primarily on copies. Percy, by contrast, uses originals whenever he can, but is not as much closer to modern scholarly practice as this may suggest, since his originals are of anthologies and chapbooks, always post-medieval MSS and printed texts.[53] Even so, this is one respect in which he seems more scholarly than Sánchez.

There are two other features of Sánchez's work that set him apart from the best scholarship of our own day (it would be foolish to take into consideration the store of knowledge and the technical resources that are available now and that scholars of Sánchez's time could not even have imagined). One is the suppression of some passages of the *Libro de Buen Amor* on moral grounds, and the other is the low frequency of explanatory and critical notes, even in the later volumes of the *Colección*. In all other respects he is a modern scholar, trying to do, with limited resources, what the best scholars try to do today. The task that he set himself, and that in large measure he accomplished, was to establish the most accurate possible text of the major Spanish poems before 1400, to introduce them with discussions of authorship, date, sources, manuscript tradition, language, style, and other features, and to conclude

53 There are, unhappily, signs that editors are in retreat from the manuscript: while some use their MSS more intensively and perceptively than ever before (I am thinking of codicological studies and the construction of stemmata, as well as the exploitation of technology for reading obliterated passages), others — especially graduate students in America, thousands of miles away from the MSS — rely, through economic constraints or by inclination, on microfilms. The most spectacular result so far is that two editors, having transcribed a two-volume incunable from the microfilm with which they were supplied, remained firmly convinced that they had been dealing with a manuscript. An increasing share of the responsibility lies with librarians who refuse to allow access to manuscripts, and insist that scholars work from published facsimiles: two or three years ago, for example, a student who was editing and translating the *unica* of the *Códice musical de Las Huelgas* was repeatedly refused access on the grounds that 'otros turistas' would want to see the MS if an exception were made for her.

with a detailed glossary. Flaws in his method and human weaknesses in the man have emerged in the course of the present study, but what I said of his achievement at the outset remains true. That achievement was well summarized by E. Allison Peers:

> a pioneer of modern scholarship [... His] *Colección* [...] stands alone in its class during the eighteenth century. [...] it is even more noteworthy for the manner of the presentation than for the matter. Prefaces, texts and glossaries display a regard for order and precision which, with the commendable modesty of the preface, convey above everything else the impression of a critical mind and of a sensitive and scholarly temperament.[54]

Such a man deserves a full biographical and literary study. Menéndez y Pelayo pointed to the need long ago (327). The example has been set by Gossman's book on La Curne de Sainte-Palaye and by Gies' book on Agustín Durán.[55] It is to be hoped that a medievalist with regular access to the Madrid archives will soon follow that example and thus lessen the painful contrast between the attention devoted to Percy by specialists in English and the neglect of Sánchez by hispanists.

Percy, though Sánchez's contemporary, seems of an earlier age in his subordination of scholarship to literary taste. Yet a concern for medieval poetry as poetry, not merely as historical evidence, unites them; it reminds us that they were working in the dawn of Romanticism, and it sets them apart from Enlightenment scholars of the previous generation, even from such an exceptional scholar as La Curne de Sainte-Palaye:

> On the whole, therefore, Sainte-Palaye was not interested in medieval literature as literature; he was interested in it as a source of information for the historian. The way he envisaged editing and publishing medieval literary texts reflects the historical orientation of his research. [... His] plan was to study the literary texts systematically and publish extracts from them containing 'tout ce qui paroîtroit de quelque usage pour l'Histoire,

54 *A History of the Romantic Movement in Spain* (Cambridge: Cambridge U. P., 1940), I, 40-41.

55 David Thatcher Gies, *Agustín Durán: A Biography and Literary Appreciation*, Colección Támesis A, XLVIII (London: Tamesis, 1975).

> pour les Généalogies, pour les Antiquités françoises et pour la Géographie'. (Gossman, 255-56)

Of course, as Gossman goes on to show, Sainte-Palaye was not blind to poetic quality, and of course Sánchez was much concerned with the value of his texts as historical and linguistic evidence. Nevertheless, the difference between the generations is a real one.

In the modernity of his scholarship, however, Sánchez (born in 1725) is much closer to Sainte-Palaye (1697) than to Percy (1729).[56] Here the decisive factor is not generation but temperament and background. Percy's *Reliques* sits uneasily between Sánchez's *Colección* and Palgrave's *Golden Treasury*, and whereas his original aim was closer to the former, Shenstone's influence moved him in the direction of the latter. He was an amateur scholar, Sánchez an ambitious professional. Sánchez's starting-point was the ferment of interest in medieval history and literature, the scholarly antiquarianism, that gripped Spanish intellectuals from the second quarter of the eighteenth century onwards: men like Velázquez, Sarmiento, Ibarreta, and Floranes were his predecessors and peers. Percy's starting-point was the literary world that felt the romantic attraction of the Middle Ages, an imaginative antiquarianism that could lead to excesses like the forgeries of James Macpherson and Thomas Chatterton.[57] To state the contrast thus is correct, but it risks unfairness to Percy in two ways. First, he was a scholar of wide interests and insatiable appetite for knowledge: the lists, given earlier, of his works and of the essays included in the *Reliques* make that abundantly clear. It is worth recalling, in particular, 'An Essay on the Ancient Minstrels in England' (I, 9-63), which anticipates the central doctrines of neotraditionalism — a matter to which I hope to

---

56 Sainte-Palaye seems, from Gossman's account, to be even more modern than Sánchez:

> He was probably the first scholar in France to study texts in the vernacular with the care that had hitherto been reserved for classical texts, combining exhaustive examination of all the elements of the tradition [...] with [...] careful internal criticism. (233-34)

57 See, for example, E. H. W. Meyerstein, *A Life of Thomas Chatterton* (London: Ingpen and Grant, 1930).

return. Secondly, we should recall Sir Walter Scott's words:

> It is no doubt highly desirable that the text of ancient poetry should be given untouched and uncorrupted. But this is a point which did not occur to the editor of the *Reliques* in 1765, whose object it was to win the favour of the public, at a period when the great difficulty was not how to secure the very words of the old ballads, but how to arrest attention upon the subject at all.
>
> (Bate, 337)

Percy aroused enthusiasm for medieval poetry; Sánchez did his best to provide sound texts for those already interested. Had there been a Spanish Percy, Sánchez's great *Colección* might have found a worthy response among his contemporaries, and we might now have more than the four volumes that reached print.[58]

---

58 I am greatly indebted to Professor Nigel Glendinning, Mr Brian Murphy, and Ms Carol Tully for bibliographical help. Professor David Hook, who gave up much time that he could ill afford so that I might have the material that I needed, deserves special mention.

Juan Antonio Pellicer and the Eighteenth-century Recovery of Early Spanish Literature

IAN MICHAEL

University of Oxford

In the last four decades of the eighteenth century, the Royal Public Library in Madrid, precursor of the Biblioteca Nacional, had a most remarkable staff of librarians (see Appendices 2-7 for the documentation, previously unpublished in its original form),[1] who between them produced a revival of scholarship and learning which led to numerous important publications. They were seized with a special enthusiasm for seeking out from the dusty shelves of monasteries and other archives the MSS of Spanish literature written before the fifteenth century, forgotten for the most part since the Marquis of Santillana's time. His *Carta e Prohemio*, indeed, acted as a spur to search for the texts he had possessed or mentioned. Much of the ground had been prepared for them by Nicolás Antonio (d.1684), and by Fr Martín Sarmiento (1695-1772), whom Menéndez y Pelayo later described as the

> ... tipo perfecto de la antigua erudición monacal, varón extraordinariamente noticioso, e incansable y férreo en el trabajo de leer y de extractar, [que] pasó la vida escribiendo, o mejor decir,

---

1 There is a full alphabetical list of the employees of the Biblioteca Real (not to be confused with the Real Particular) and a yearly list of the post-holders extracted from the documentation, together with portraits of fifteen of them, by Justo García Morales, 'Los empleados de la Biblioteca Real (1712-1836)', *RABM*, LIII (1966), 27-89.

> tomando apuntes, no para el público, sino por recreo propio y de sus amigos ...,[2]

though the learned Benedictine did not publish any of the texts.

Fr Sarmiento's enormous life-work of compiling references to the contents of old libraries and to early unknown MSS was continued by Juan Iriarte (1702-1771); his extensive annotations survive among the one hundred and ninety-eight boxes of the Iriarte Papers that once belonged to the Phillips Collection, which were brought in at Sotheby's Sale of the New Series, 6th part, on 16 June 1970, but which, through the good offices of Mr J. L. Gili, the publisher, bookseller and scholar, were sold privately on 25 June 1970 to D. Bartolomé March, in whose private library in Madrid they are now preserved. They contain numerous indices of Spanish private libraries (signs. 16/1/5, 16/1/7, 16/1/8, 16/1/9, 16/1/11), as well as copies made for Juan Iriarte at the Escorial of parts of Alfonsine works and even copies of entire texts such as Berceo's *Vida de Santa Oria*, prepared by Fr Mecolaeta at Silos all contained in the boxes of *Miscelánea Literaria*.

The author of the letter of February 1780, here published for the first time (Appendix 1), and which is full of scholarly news of the period, was D. Juan Antonio Pellicer y Saforcada, born at Encinacorba (Zaragoza) in 1738. Brought to Madrid in early youth, he there studied Latin and Philosophy, and later read canon and civil law at the University of Alcalá. In 1761, at the age of twenty-three, he was appointed to the post of *Tercer Escribiente* in the Real Biblioteca Pública, where he spent many years in the company of Juan Iriarte, Miguel Casiri, Tomás Antonio Sánchez and Rafael Casalbón preparing the *Adiciones y correcciones* to Nicolás Antonio's *Bibliotheca Hispana*, finally published in 1788.

His own special interest at this time was in translators, leading to the publication of his *Ensayo de una biblioteca de traductores españoles* ... (Madrid: Antonio de Sancha, 1778).

2 For an account of Fr Sarmiento's life, see Martín Sarmiento, *El porque sí y porque no*, eds. Michel Dubuis, Nicole Rochaix and Joël Saugnieux (Oviedo: FES XVIII/Lyon: Univ. Lumière II, 1988). *Cf. Historia de las ideas estéticas en España*, ed. E. Sánchez Reyes (Santander: Aldus [Edición Nacional de las *Obras completas* de Menéndez Pelayo], 1947), 5 vols; III, 264-65.

Later, when he had been elected to the Royal Academy of History, he developed a secondary interest in the history of Madrid:

Discurso sobre varias antigüedades de Madrid y origen de sus parroquias ..., (Madrid: Sancha, 1791).

Disertación histórico-geográfica sobre el origen, nombre y población de Madrid ... (Madrid: Imprenta de la Administración del Real Arbitrio de Beneficencia, 1803).

In 1797 he published an annotated edition of the *Quijote*, which led to considerable controversy, followed by a life of Cervantes in 1800, the year in which he responded with a pamphlet to the criticisms of his edition that had appeared:

Carta en castellano con postdata políglota: en la qual Don Juan Antonio Pellicer y Don Josef Antonio Conde ... responden a la carta crítica que un Anónimo dirigió al Autor de las Notas del Don Quixote ... (Madrid: Sancha, 1800).

This was followed by his *Examen crítico del tomo 1° de El Anti-Quixote publicado por D. Nicolás Pérez* (Madrid: Imp. de Sancha, 1806).

In 1793, when he had been promoted to the status of temporary librarian in the Real Biblioteca, he published a *Carta histórico-apologética que en defensa del Marqués de Mondéxar examina de nuevo la aparición de San Isidro en la batalla de las Navas de Tolosa* ... (Madrid: Sancha, 1793). In the same year, he penned a *relación* (here published in Appendix 8) of the present state of the Real Biblioteca Pública, no doubt after consulting with his colleagues (from the death of Juan de Santander in 1783 he had acted as secretary to the Junta de Bibliotecarios). From this lengthy account, one can deduce that he and his colleagues were possessed of that eighteenth-century desire to collect all human knowledge under the roof of one library, or, since that proved impracticable, in 'libraries without walls',[3] which in their case meant in particular *bibliotecas* or published collections of all Spanish writings of previous ages,

3 *Cf.* Etienne-Louis Boullée's project for the reconstruction of the Bibliothèque du Roi in Paris in 1785; see Roger Chartier, *The Order of Books. Readers, Authors, and Libraries in Europe between the Fourteenth and Eighteenth Centuries* (Oxford: Polity Press, 1994), 62-63.

and to make these works available for public use.

Pellicer's reference to the works of 'D^{n} Gonzalo de Berceo, poeta del siglo 13' (Appendix 1) reveals that in 1780 the general knowledge of medieval Spanish literature was extremely limited.[4] In the previous year Tomás Antonio Sánchez had been the first to publish the *Poema de Mio Cid*; now he had in the press the poems of Berceo (including some *Loas de Berceo* of his own inventive pen), and by 1790 he was to proceed to bring out the *Libro de Alexandre* and Juan Ruiz's *Libro de buen amor*. Not only do these librarians seem to have had a Romantic view *avant la lettre* of the 'primitiveness' of medieval literature, but this was combined with strong feelings of Spanish nationalism: Spain had had an early literature just as important as that of France, England or Germany, and it was their task to bring it to light.

---

4 One of the earliest eighteenth-century mentions of Berceo occurs in Luis Joseph Velázquez, *Orígenes de la poesía castellana* (Málaga: Francisco Martínez de Aguilar, 1754): 'El Poeta Castellano mas antiguo, de que tenemos noticia, nos sube del fin del siglo duodecimo, ò principios del decimotercio. Entonces vivia Gonzalo de Berceo, natural del Lugar de este nombre, y Monge en el Monasterio de S. Millan; de cuyo Archivo consta, que vivia el año 1211' (34), information which he reveals (n. 57) he has culled from Fr Sebastián Vergara's prologue to his edition of the *Vida de Santo Domingo de Silos* (Madrid: Herederos de Francisco del Hierro, 1736), which does not appear to have made much public impact, though it is cited by Fr Esteban de Terreros y Pando, *Paleografía española* (Madrid: Joaquín Ibarra, 1758), 24-25. Nicolás Antonio had erroneously thought that Berceo had lived in the time of Alfonso VI, *c.* 1080. I am much indebted to that great eighteenth-century expert, Dr Philip Deacon, for this and other important references; he has saved me from various errors. See also Daniel Devoto, 'Berceo antes de 1780', *RABM*, LXXIX (1975), 767-834.

APPENDIX 1

Holograph letter with bibliographical information from D. Juan Antonio Pellicer to the Bishop of Sigüenza [Juan Díaz de la Guerra].[5] Madrid, 17 February, 1780; Biblioteca Nacional, Madrid, MS Res. 227 (*olim* 18.692, núm. 50; sign. ant. Jj-148 [from the Osuna collection?])

[*fol. 1r*] +

Illmo Señor

Quien promete, cerca està de faltar, dixo un antiguo,[6] porque como la promesa està siempre executando, y la negligencia humana retarda por lo comun el cumplimiento de ella, imperceptiblemente se hace el hombre deliquente: y entonces es quando se da tormento al ingenio para que invente disculpas con que escusar su falta, las quales en lugar de minorarla, tal vez la agraban mas. Quantas pudiera acomular yo en descargo de mi prolixa tardanza en cumplir mi oferta: y en responder a la apreciabilisima que recibi de V.S.I.[7] con fecha de 7 de Nov^{e} del año pasado de 1779! aunque la respuesta de esta ya me acuerdo que la aligué, al cumplim^{to} de aquella; si ya no fue esto hacerme reo de dos delitos. Pudiera hacer merito de las obligaciones del oficio, de los cuidados domesticos, de los males de los hijos, de los de su madre, y aun de tal qual indisposicion de su padre: pudiera tambien representar la dilacion precisa en anotar en parte el Papel adjunto del P. Estrada,[8] empresa superior a mis fuerzas, y à que solo me determinè deseoso de hacer este tal qual merito mas con que pudiese desenojar à V.S.I. exponiendome à que se ria de mi charlatanería, o à que me mire con compasion, comparados lo arduo de la materia con lo pobre del sugeto. Pero mas quiero esperar el perdon de mi negligencia de la benignidad de V.S.I. que de la debilidad de mis

---

5 Juan Díaz de la Guerra, ob. de Mallorca, pr. 23.vi.1777, pos. 27.viii.1777, d. 29.ix.1800; see Quintín Aldea Vaquero *et al.*, *Diccionario de historia eclesiástica de España* (Madrid: CSIC, 1975), IV, 2476a, *s.v.* 'Sigüenza'.

6 *Cf.* Publius Syrus, Maxim 528.

7 'Vuestra Señoría Ilustrísima', the usual form of address to a Catholic bishop.

8 Fr Estrada's paper is missing in the BNM MS., but it was published fourteen years later: Fr Luis Estrada y Fr Lorenzo de Zamora, *Carta apologética por el mérito y arreglo de la célebre Biblia Regia de Arias Montano y sus versiones* (Burgos: Joseph de Navas, 1794).

disculpas. No dudo que ha de tener V.S.I. un buen rato en leer la Apologia de la Biblia de Arias Montano,[9] y que por ella y por la escasa luz que dan las notas en las que se trasladan facilmente mas señales de trabajo ageno que de propio. conocera V.S.I. las olas de contradiccion que cubrieron aquel varon *inanegable.*[10]

Quisiera saber recrear el espiritu de V.S.I. que le supongo tirante con los exercicios del estudio, y los de este santo t[*iem*]po, informando à V.S.I. de las novedades literarias que ocurren por aca; pero aunque pocas, escribire las que sè. Publicò mi compañero Dn Tomas Sanchez,[11] como V.S.I. habra visto, sus vegeces castellanas metricas, y como en las notas sobre la Carta del Marques de Santillana, q[*ue*] es el fundamento de la obra, se encuentra con el Rev^mo^ Sarmiento[12] que la

---

9 Benito Arias Montano (1527-1598), the famous sixteenth-century theologian, who was the first librarian of the Escorial Library and one of the Spanish participants in the Council of Trent, is chiefly known for the production of the Antwerp Polyglot Bible: *Biblia sacra Hebraice. Chaldaici. Graece et Latina. Philippe II Reg. cathol. pietate ...*, 8 vols, fol. mayor (Antwerpiae: Christophorus Planctinus, 1569-73).

10 *inanegable*: 'unsinkable'.

11 Tomás Antonio Sánchez (1725-1802) followed an ecclesiastical career, being master of the Colegiata de Santillana until 1761, when he was appointed one of the four librarians on the staff of the Biblioteca Real Pública (see Appendix 2) under the chief librarian, Juan de Santander, while Pellicer held only the post of *Tercer Escribiente.* He was temporary director of the Real Academia de la Historia in 1794-95, and elected member of the Academia de la Lengua. He was to collaborate with Pellicer and Rafael Casalbón in preparing the new edition of Nicolás Antonio's *Bibliotheca Hispana Nova* (1788). At the date of Pellicer's letter, Sánchez had just published the first of the four volumes, containing his edition of the *Poema del Cid*, of his *Colección de poesías castellanas anteriores al siglo XV* (Madrid: Antonio de Sancha, 1779-90), 4 vols. On Sánchez's *Colección* see, in the present volume, the article by Alan Deyermond. He was also a satirist who published under the pseudonym of 'El Bachiller D. Fernando Pérez' (*cf. Carta de Paracuellos escrita por D. Fernando Pérez a un sobrino que se hallaba en peligro de ser autor de un libro* [Madrid: Joaquín Ibarra, 1789]; etc.)

12 Fr Martín Sarmiento, Benedictine scholar known for his *Demonstración crítico-apologética del Theatro crítico universal ... de Fr Benito Geronymo Feyjoo* (Madrid: Vda. de Fco de Hierro, 1732), 2 vols. After his death the monks of his Order published his voluminous notes, in the words of Menéndez y Pelayo, 'en el estado en que las encontraron, y así se formó el volumen, algo desordenado, notabilísimo para su tiempo, y donde a vueltas de inexcusables errores hay adivinaciones históricas asombrosas': *Obras posthumas. Tomo 1°. Memorias para la historia de la poesía, y poetas*

explicò tambien en el primer tomo de sus obras postumas, y Sanchez coge à Su Rev^ma^ frequentemente puntos para la vanda; ha concitado contra sì la indignacion de todos los apasionados de aquel Padre eruditisimo; especialmente de sus hermanos los Monges de San Martin que se dice estan cargando los cañones para dar una rociada[13] à mi buen clerigo: ya se lo he advertido para que no le coja de improviso, porque duelen menos las pesadumbres quando se sabe que han de venir. Yo me alegrare que lleguen à rompimiento; que habra una de mazagatos.[14] Por lo demas presentara prontamente al Consejo[15] el segundo tomo que comprehende las Poesias de Dn Gonzalo de Berceo, poeta del siglo 13. Dn Josef de Castro,[16] otro compañero mio, està graduado de Coronista de la Gente iniqua y no santa: quiero decir que està para imprimir una Bibliotheca Rabinico-Hispana en castellano donde habla de los Judios Españoles añadiendo y corrigiendo a Wolfio y Bartolocci.[17] Dn Fran^co^ Cerda,[18] *vir magno tentus omaso*,[19] que por

---

españoles, dadas a luz por el Monasterio de S. Martín de Madrid (Madrid: Joaquín Ibarra, 1775) (no more published).

13 *rociada*: 'shower of missiles'.

14 *una de mazagatos*: 'a noisy wrangle' (prob. from Ital. *ammazzagatti*, *ammazzare*, 'kill'); *cf.* Cervantes, *Novelas ejemplares*, Clásicos Castellanos (Madrid: Espasa-Calpe, 1928), I, 273.

15 Probably a reference to the Council of Castile for permission to publish; Antonio de Sancha apparently financed the publication of Sánchez's *Colección* and various other works prepared by the royal librarians.

16 In 1770 don José Rodríguez de Castro, like Pellicer, held the post of *Tercer Escribiente* in the Real Biblioteca. A year after the date of Pellicer's letter, he published the first volume of his *Biblioteca española. Tomo 1°, que contiene la noticia de los escritores rabinos españoles desde la época conocida de su literatura hasta el presente* (Madrid: Imprenta Real de la Gaceta, 1781) (*Tomo 2°, que contiene la de los escritores gentiles y la de los christianos hasta fines del siglo XIII de la Iglesia* appeared in 1786). His work is still of interest for its quotations from MSS.

17 Fr Giulio Bartolocci (1613-1687) was a Cistercian orientalist who became professor of Hebrew at the Collegio dei Neofiti in Rome, where he prepared his monumental *Bibliotheca Magna Rabbinica* (Rome: Ex typ. Sac. Congregatio, 1675-1694), 4 vols. The fourth volume was completed by his pupil Fr Carlo Giuseppe Imbonati. The entire work was used as the basis of Johann Christoph Wolf's famous *Bibliotheca Hebraea* (Hamburg/Leipzig: Imp. C. Lieberzeit, 1715-1733), 4 vols.

18 Don Francisco Cerdá y Rico joined the staff of the Real Biblioteca as *Escribiente Zelador* on 13 January 1766. A year after Pellicer's letter he published his *Clarorum hispanorum opuscula selecta et cariora, tum latina, tum hispana ...*, vol. 1 (Madrid: Antonio de Sancha, 1781) (no more published).

esta obesitud en que coincidimos, y por razon de oficio, somos singularm[te] amigos sin envidia sea dicho de V.S.I. va à publicar una Coleccion de Opusculos selectos Latinos y Castellanos. Dn Tomas Yriarte[20] tiene ya impreso su Poema didactico de la Musica con elegantes y superfinas estampas: obra nueva en España, y aun en Europa dicen; y que ha merecido ya el elogio del Sr Abate Metastasio[21] que ha leido ya un exemplar, y entiende n[*ues*]tra Lengua, y de musica quanto es notorio: ha explicado su juicio diciendo que se acerca à lo maravilloso, y admirandose que Yriarte y él hayan coincidido en unas mismas observaciones y descubrimientos; pues el Metastasio parece va à publicar la Poetica de Aristoteles en italiano con notas concernientes à la Musica.

Sabidas son las guerras mas que civiles que ha traido entre si el Abate Pozi y Dn Juan Muñoz:[22] la impugnacion de éste: la respuesta

---

He is best known for his twenty-one volume edition of Lope de Vega's works (Madrid: Sancha, 1776-1779). There is a study of him by Ángel González Palencia, *Eruditos y libreros del siglo XVIII* (Madrid: CSIC, 1948), 2-167; see also Antonio Mestre, *Humanismo y crítica histórica en los ilustrados alicantinos* (Alicante: Univ. de Alicante, 1980), 94-120.

19 *Cf.* Horace, *Satires*, 2, 5, 40: '*pingui tentus omaso Furius*', 'Furius, fattened with cheap tripe', which Pellicer elegantly turns into part of a hexameter: 'a fat man with a large stomach'.

20 Tomás de Iriarte (1750-1791), Tenerife poet and nephew of Juan Iriarte (d. 23 August 1771) who was one of the four librarians in the Real Biblioteca by 1761. Tomás was appointed translator to the Secretary of State's office and engaged in contemporary polemics. His long didactic poem *La música* (Madrid: Imprenta Real de la Gaceta, 1779) was highly praised in a letter from Metastasio (reproduced in Juan Sempere, *Ensayo de una bibliografía española de los mejores escritores del reynado de Carlos III* [Madrid: Imp. Real, 1755-1789], 6 vols; VI, 204-05). He was also a well-known dramatist and translator of plays by French authors.

21 Pietro Metastasio (1698-1782), Italian poet and well-known operatic librettist, published a critical essay entitled *Estratto della poetica d'Aristotile e considerazioni su la medesina* in the last volume of his *Opere* (Paris: Veuve Hérissant, [2nd ed.] 1780-1782).

22 Fr Cesareo Pozzi's *Saggio de Educazione Claustrale per li giovani, che entrano nel Noviciati Religiosi* (Madrid: Antonio de Sancha, 1778), was savagely attacked by Juan Bautista Muñoz (1745-1799), the famous historian, in his *Juicio del tratado de educación del M.R.P. Cesareo Pozzi* (Madrid: Joaquín Ibarra, 1778 [reimpr. Barcelona: Gibert y Tutó, 1779, and Italian trans. Ravenna, 1779]). The Italian Benedictine replied in his *Apologia ... in difesa del suo libro Saggio di educazione claustrale ...* (Perpignan, 1780) (almost entirely in Spanish). Muñoz is best known for his *Historia del Nuevo*

de aquel: la censura de los Monges Benitos: los dictamenes diferentes de los que habian de determinar la question: la remision ultimamente de la obra de Pozi al Cuerpo de Curas Parrocos de Madrid, durante la qual resolvio el Sr Abate salir de España. Dicen que Su Santidad le ha concedido una pension; pero lo que en el dia corre es que en no sé que lugar està imprimiendo la Apologia de su obra, y respuesta à la censura de Muñoz, con la vida de este. Vn sacerdote Mallorquin llamado Dn Antonio Vila (creo que es de Mahon)[23] hombre habil, y que entiende el ingles y el hebreo, està trabajando una Encyclopedia Eclesiastica, obra de mucho tiempo y de muchos volumenes.

Celebro que V.S.I. recogiese en el viage esa preciosidad que se califica con ser de la aprobación y gusto de V.S.I. y a mi me dexa con hambre de saber lo que es.

En quanto à la Carta y Notas estimaré à V.S.I. las reserve, y comunique solamente con algun Amigo de confianza.[24]

N[*ues*]tro S^or^ gu[*ard*]e à V.S.I. muchos años como deseo.
Madrid y Febrero 17. de 1780.

B.L.M.[25] à V.S.I.
Su mas rendido Servidor
[*firma y rúbrica*:] Juan Antonio Pellicer/
[*Al*] Illmo Sor Obispo de Siguenza.

Mundo, tomo 1° (Madrid: Viuda de Ibarra, 1793) (no more published), and his famous Collection of Papers on American history is preserved in the Real Academia de la Historia, Madrid.

23 Antoni Vila i Camps (1747-1809), b. Ciudadela (Minorca), studied at Mahón, where he became doctor of theology, and went to become a tutor at Madrid, where he wrote a number of works. He became bishop of Minorca in 1797. He was in Rome in 1801, whence he was sent as negotiator to London, where a peace treaty was signed restoring Minorca to Spain. In July 1802 he was rewarded with the see of Albarracín, where the twenty MS volumes of his unfinished *Diccionario enciclopédico eclesiástico* are preserved in the Episcopal Library.

24 The need for secrecy reveals the atmosphere of animosity and personal rivalry that prevailed in the historical and literary circles of the time, the disputes among the religious orders being of course the most savage.

25 'Besa las manos'.

APPENDIX 2

Carta del Mayordomo Mayor al Contador General de S. M. Madrid, 26 de diciembre de 1761 (AGP [Archivo General de Palacio, Madrid], Cámara de Carlos III, Bibliotecas, Personal de Empleados, Caja 216/12).

Exmo S$^{r.}$

El Rey ha venido en nombrar para las quatro plazas de primeros escrivientes de Su Real Biblioteca à d^{n} Miguel Casiri, à d^{n} Thomas Antonio Sanchez, à d^{n} Raphael Casalbon, y à d^{n} Vizente Garcia dela Huerta;[26] para las de Segundos à d^{n} Juan Bautista Fernandez de Oteo, à d^{n} Joseph Parla, à d^{n} Juan Guerra de la Vega; para las de terceros à d^{n} Juan Antonio Pellicer, à D^{n} Juan Cubiè,[27] à d^{n} Joseph Rodriguez de Castro, y à d^{n} Justo del Zerro; y para los dos de Escrivientes Custodes, ò Zeladores a d^{n} Juan Joseph Lopez, y à d^{n} Phelipe Pantorrilla.

Participo à V. E. de orden de S. M. a fin de que, en consecuencia de lo que se sirviò de resolvèr en Decreto de 11 de este mes, que se comunicò à V. E. disponga se les forme à estos sugetos — el asiento correspondiente De Criados de Su Real Casa.

Dios gu^{e} à V. E. m^{s} a^{s} como d^{o}. B^{n} Retiro 26 de Diciembre de 1761.

[*firma y rúbrica*:] El Marq' de Campo de Villar/

[*Al*] Sr Marquès de Montealegre.

---

26 Today Huerta is probably the best known of these employees; see the recent study by Juan Antonio Ríos Carratalá, reviewed by Philip Deacon in *BHS*, LXIX (1992), 382-83.

27 Juan Cubié later published *Las mujeres vindicadas de las calumnias de los hombres* (Madrid: Antonio Pérez de Soto, 1768) and a *Semanario económico* (Madrid: Pantaleón Aznar, 1777), with information on science, technology and trade.

APPENDIX 3

+

Lista de los Individuos de la Real Bibliotheca, de S.M. (AGP: Expediente Personal: D. Juan de Santander, Cámara de Carlos III, Caja 975/54, No. 1: 12 de febrero de 1762)

Bibliothecario Mayor.
D[n] Juan Manuel de Santander.

Bibliothecarios.
D[n] Joseph Gutierrez.
D[n] Juan de Iriarte.
D[n] Manuel Martinez Pingarrón.
D[n] Leopoldo Geronimo Puig.

En 25 de Marzo de 1762 se despacharon titulos à estos individuos desde el Thess[ro], en adelante

Thesorero.
D[n] Juan Kelly.

Primeros Escribientes.
D[n] Miguel Casiri.
D[n] Thomas Sanchez.
D[n] Raphael Casalbón.
D[n] Vicente Garcia de la Huerta.

Segundos Escribientes.
D[n] Juan Bautista Fernandez de Otéo.
D[n] Joseph Parla.
D[n] Francisco Morán.
D[n] Juan Guerra de la Vega.

Terceros Escribientes.
D[n] Juan Antonio Pellicer.
D[n] Juan Cuvié.
D[n] Joseph Rodriguez de Castro.
D[n] Justo del Cerro.

Escribientes Zeladores.
D[n] Juan Joseph Lopez.
D[n] Phelipe Pantorrilla.

Porteros.
D[n] Diego Guedez.
D[n] Agustin de Anaya.
D[n] Phelipe Gonzalez: jubilado.

Impresor.
Antonio Perez de Soto.

Librero.
D^{n} Angel Corradi.
Enquadernador.
Antonio Sancha.

Madrid doce de Febrero de mil setecientos, y sesenta y dos años.
[*firma y rúbrica*:] Juan de Santander

El Pardo 3 de Marzo de 1762.
El Mayordomo Mayor.
Prevengase de Medico, y Cirujano, Decanos, de Familia, avisen a los de los respectivos Quarteles, asistan con puntualidad a estos Individuos, siempre que los llamen, respecto tenerlos S. M. admitidos por Criados de su Real Casa; y en su consecuencia se les despacharàn Certificaciones, que les sirvan de Titulos, conforme el Rey tiene mandado.

[*rúbrica ilegible*]

APPENDIX 4

\+

Lista de los Individuos que actualm[*en*]te sirven à S. M. en esta R[*ea*]l Bibliotheca segun el nuevo Plan y establecim[*ien*]to hecho por S. M. en 11 de Nov^{re} de 1761 (AGP: Cámara de Carlos IV, Caja 975/54, Personal de Empleados, Leg. 31, N° 2: 26 de junio de 1770)

	Bibliot^{rio} Mayor.
Murió en 23 de sep^{re} de 1783	D^{n} Juan de Santander.
	Bibliothecarios.
Falleció en 23 de Agosto de 1771	D^{n} Juan Yriarte.
Idem en ... de ... de 1777	D^{n} Man^{l} Mr̃z Pingarrón
	D^{n} Miguel Casiri.
	D^{n} Thomas Antonio Sanchez.
	Primeros Escrib$^{tes.}$
Pasò à Bibliotecario	D^{n} Raphael Casalbon.
	D^{n} Vicente Garcia de la Huerta.
	D^{n} Fran^{co} Moran.

	Seg^{dos} Escrib$^{tes.}$
	D^{n} Juan Guerra de la Vega.
	D^{n} Juan Antonio Pellicer.
	D^{n} Juan Cubie.
	D^{n} Joseph Rodr̃z de Castro.
	Terceros Escrib$^{tes.}$
	D^{n} Justo del Cerro.
Falleció en 28 de Agosto de 1771	D^{n} Juan Joseph Lopez.
	D^{n} Phelipe Pantorrilla.
Entró à servir à S. Mag^{d} en Plaza de Escrib^{te} Zelador en 28 de Nov^{re} de 1763	D^{n} Juan Domingo Cativiela.
	Escrib^{tes} Zeladores.
Entró en Plaza de Escrib^{te} Zelador el dia 28 de Nov^{re} de 1763 por nombram^{to} de S. M.	D^{n} Fran^{co} Ascensio.
Entró a servir por nombramiento de S. M. en 13 de Henero de 1766	D^{n} Fran^{co} Cerdá.
	Porteros.
Falleciò en 30 de Julio de 1771	D^{n} Agustin de Anaya.
Entró à servir en 1° de Marzo de 1763	D^{n} Fran^{co} Landa.
	Criado de la Bibliote$^{ca.}$
Entró a servir en 16 de Junio de 1766	Fran^{co} Garcia.
	Impresor.
	Antonio Perez de Soto.
	Librero.
	D^{n} Angel Corradi.
	Encuadern$^{or.}$
	Antonio Sancha

Y para que conste, lo firmo en dha R^{l} Bibliotheca, con declaracion de q^{e} desde prim^{o} de Henero de 1762, en que se puso en execucion el citado Plan han vacado varias Plazas que se han provisto y otras están suspensas; y los sugetos que han entrado de nuevo en las resultas, son los sig^{tes} d^{n} Juan Domingo Cativiela = d^{n} Fran^{co} Asensio = d^{n} Fran^{co}

Cerda = d^{n} Fran^{co} Landa, y Fran^{co} Garcia; los quales van inclusos en esta Lista donde les corresponde. Madrid 26 de Junio de 1770.

[*firma y rúbrica*:] Juan de Santander/

Nota.
Con fecha de 29 de Septiembre de 1770, se despachó Certificacion impresa para que les sirviese de titulo, à los veinte y quatro individuos, que comprehende esta Relacion, firmada del Sor Bibliothecario mayor, y ótra mas à D^{n} Phelipe Gonzalez Portero Jubilado de la misma Real Biblioteca. [*rúbrica ilegible*]

APPENDIX 5

+

Lista de los Individuos de esta R^{l} Bibliotheca segun el nuevo Plan y establecim^{to} hecho por S. M. que Dios guarde, en 11 de Nov^{re} de 1761 (AGP: Expediente Personal, Caja 975/54; Cámara de Carlos IV: Bibliotecarios, Personal de Empleados, No. 3; 26 de junio de 1770)

	Bibliot^{rio} Mayor.
Falleciò en 23 de Sep^{re} de 1783	D^{n} Juan de Santander.
	Bibliotecarios.
	D^{n} Joseph Ferñz Gutierrez.
Falleció en 23 de Ag^{to} de 1771	D^{n} Juan Iriarte.
Idem en ... de ... de 1777	D^{n} Manuel Mar̃tz Pingarron.
	D^{n} Leopoldo Geronimo Puig.
	Tesoro.
	D^{n} Juan Kelly.
	Primeros Escrib$^{tes.}$
	D^{n} Miguel Casiri.
	D^{n} Thomas Antonio Sanchez.
Ascendiò à la vacante de D^{n} Juan de Iriarte, p^{r} r^{l} Orn del 9 de Oct^{re} de 1772	D^{n} Raphael Casalbon.
	D^{n} Vicente Garcia dela Huerta.

Seg^{dos} Escrib$^{tes.}$

Murio en 4 de Mayo de 1767 — D^{n} Juan Bautista Ferñz de Oteo.

D^{n} Joseph Parla.

D^{n} Fran^{co} Moran.

D^{n} Juan Guerra de la Vega.

Terceros Escrib$^{tes.}$

D^{n} Juan Antonio Pellicer.

D^{n} Juan Cubie.

D^{n} Joseph Rodrz de Castro.

D^{n} Justo del Cerro.

Escribientes Zeladores.

Falleció en 28 de Agosto de 1771 — D^{n} Juan Joseph Lopez.

D^{n} Phelipe Pantorrilla.

Porteros.

D^{n} Diego Guedez.

Falleció en 30 de Julio de 1771 — D^{n} Agustin de Anaya.

D^{n} Phelipe Gonzalez ... Jubilado.

Criado de la Bibliot$^{ca.}$

Joseph Ximenez.

Impresor.

Antonio Perez de Soto.

Librero.

D^{n} Angel Corradi.

Encuadern^{or}

Antonio Sancha.

Y para que conste, lo firme en esta R^{l} Bibliotheca. Madrid 26. de Junio de 1770.

[*firma y rúbrica*:] Juan de Santander/

APPENDIX 6

Carta original de D. Juan Santander al Sr. D. José Guzmán, Mayordomo Mayor. Madrid, 30 de agosto de 1771
(AGP: Expediente Personal: D. Juan de Santander, Caja 975/54)

Muy S^{or} mio. Participo á VS^{a} como han fallecido tres Individuos de esta R^{l} Bibliotheca, es á saber d^{n} Agustin de Anaya, Portero, en 30 de Julio proximo de este año: d^{n} Juan de Iriarte, Bibliotecario en 23 de este mes, y asim^{o} en 28. de el d^{n} Joseph Lopez, Presbytero, y uno de los Escribientes. Quando estén provistas sus vacantes, avisaré á VS. de los sugetos q' las ocupen; y entretanto me repito a la disposicion de VS. rogando a Dios g^{ue} su vida m^{s} a^{s} como deseo.

Madrid 30 de Agosto de 1771.

Blm^{s} a VS. su mayor y mas at^{o} serv^{or}

[*firma y rúbrica*:] Juan de Santander/

S^{or} d^{n} Joseph Guzman.

APPENDIX 7

+

Lista de los Individuos dela R^{l} Bibliotheca, existentes en este presente año de la fha. (AGP: Expediente Personal: D. Juan de Santander, Caja 975/54; Cámara de Carlos III, Bibliotecas, Personal de Empleados; 25 de octubre de 1775)

Bibliothecario Mayor.

Muriò en 23 de Sep^{re} de 1783 — D^{n} Juan Manuel de Santander.

Bibliothecarios.

D^{n} Manuel Martinez Pingarrón.

D^{n} Miguel Casiri.

D^{n} Thomas Antonio Sanchez.

D^{n} Raphael Casalbon.

Oficiales Escribientes.
D^{n} Vicente Garcia de la Huerta.
D^{n} Francisco Morán.
D^{n} Juan Guerra de la Vega.
D^{n} Juan Antonio Pellicer.
D^{n} Juan Cubié.
D^{n} Joseph Rodriguez de Castro.
D^{n} Justo Pastor del Cerro.
D^{n} Phelipe Pantorrilla.
D^{n} Francisco Asensio.
D^{n} Francisco Cerdá.

en 10 de Marzo de 1783 le nombrò S. M. Ofiz^{l} de la Secr^{a} del Desp^{o} de Yndias

Portero.
D^{n} Francisco Landa.

Librero.
D^{n} Angel Corradi.

Enquadernador.
D^{n} Antonio Sancha.

Impresor.
D^{n} Antonio Perez de Soto.

Criado.
Francisco Garcia.

Madrid veinte y cinco de Octubre de mil setecientos setenta y cinco.
[*firma y rúbrica*:] Juan de Santander/

APPENDIX 8

Juan Antonio Pellicer, Estado de la Real Biblioteca de Su Majestad, 18 de octubre de 1793 (informe autógrafo) [Biblioteca Nacional, Madrid: Archivo Histórico, Cod. 0037, Doc. 01 (Sign. ant. Archivo Caja 1793, leg. 77/27)]

ESTADO DE LA R^{L} BIBLIOTECA DE S.M.

Ocupaciones y proyectos literarios en que pudieran emplearse sus Individuos en beneficio publico —

Por R^{l} Decreto de 11 de Dic^{e} de 1761. comunicado por el marques del Campo de Villar à D. Juan de Santander, Bibliotecario Mayor, se sirvio S. M. de establecer un nuevo Plan en su R^{l} Biblioteca, concediendola nueva consignacion, y aumentando el numero de sus individuos y sueldos. El numero de individuos era de 19: numero suficiente para el desempeño de las ocupaciones materiales y formales de la R^{l} Biblioteca, estando bien empleados, y no minorandose.

Pero en cumplimiento de la R^{l} Orden de 19 de Junio del referido año del 1761 en que manda y desea S. M. se establezca una Imprenta R^{l} unida à la misma Biblioteca, se propuso D. Juan de Santander para cumplirla mas plenamente hacer un Obrador de punzones y matrices. Como esta maniobra requeria muchos caudales, y no habia dotacion especial para ella, se valio del arbitrario de no proveer las plazas que iban vacando, ni los ascensos que resultaban de ellas, con cuyos productos y con otras economias y a fuerza de años se puso en estado este Obrador no solo de subsistir por sí, sin necesitar de auxilios agenos, sino de ser util y lucroso considerablemente à la R^{l} Biblioteca, como consta de las cuentas de su Tesorero.

Esta suspension de plazas empezò à verificarse desde el año de 1765. y de ella resultò minorarse notablemente el numero de los Individuos. Para restituir la Biblioteca à su antiguo estado, y aumentar el sueldo de sus plazas, en virtud de R^{l} Orden de 10 de Dic^{e} de 1782. se presentò à S. M. en Julio de 1783. un nuevo Plan, en que sin gravamen de la R^{l} Hacienda, se propone el aumento de la sobredotacion que se manda. Pero todavìa no ha tenido efecto este mandato ni esta propuesta. Sin embargo por una Orden interina de 25 de Mayo de 1789. se varió el numero, clase y sueldos de los Individuos, aunque à Costa de la misma antigua consignacion de la R^{l} Biblioteca, distribuida de otro modo. Los Individuos utiles para el desempeño de los ministerios y ocupaciones de esta R^{l} Oficina, incluso el Bibliotecario Mayor, son actualmente trece.

Estas ocupaciones deben ser de dos clases: una mas necesaria, que otra, aunque menos grata y gloriosa. La primera ocupacion es la de hacer cedulas y formar Indices de los libros, y suministrarlos al publico, cuyo servicio no puede verificarse como se debe sin Indices exactos y multiplicados, y por eso se encargan tanto en las Constituciones. De estos Indices hay que rectificar algunos de los hechos, y hay que hacer otros de nuevo. En la formacion especialmente de los Indices de materias, tanto de los libros impresos como de los MSS. (que tan utiles serian para el publico, y tanto facilitarian el camino à qualquiera que intentare escribir alguna obra) hay muy poco ò casi nada adelantado. Por otra parte el suministrar al publico los libros que pida, es tambien indispensable como se ha dicho; y en este ministerio se ocupan mas Individuos de los que deberìan: porque como el vaso de la Biblioteca no se fabricó para este destino, sino para servir de pasadizo ò transito desde Palacio al convento de la Encarnación, su forma es incomoda è irregular, sus piezas dilatadisimas, y aunque las principales son rectas, hay en lo alto y en lo baxo otras transversales por decirlo asi, de dificil manejo y uso. De donde resulta que es necesario distribuir por las salas en ciertas distancias mayor numero de Individuos para el servicio del publico: y estando cumpliendo con este ministerio solo pueden ocuparse en trabajos que sean compatibles con èl, como es el continuar en hacer cedulas à los libros MSS. genealogicos, y en proseguir igualmente las cedulas para formar el Indice de mas de 1600 volumenes de *Papeles Varios*, que coronan 77 Estantes, los quales contienen mas de 40 *mil* opusculos de diversas materias, parte impresas, parte mss. con un copioso numero de Alegaciones, de donde resultarìa grande utilidad, à los Letrados especialmente que hallarían ventilados los derechos de las principales casas y mayorazgos de España, y otros puntos curiosos y dificiles.

De estas ocupaciones menos cientificas por decirlo asi, solo se pueden reservar en el estado presente dos, ò à lo mas tres Individuos, à quienes se puedan encargar otros trabajos literarios, como se dirà adelante. Porque los destinados à las piezas de los MSS. aunque no sirven al publico diariamente, se ocupan en formar su Indice, que tienen bien adelantado, pues de los 31 Estantes, en que se contienen y donde hay cerca de 9 *mil* codices, y en ellos mas de 20 *mil* entre obras y opusculos, tienen ya hecho el Indice de 25, y por consiguiente faltan solamente 6. Estantes. Por otra parte el Oficial encargado del Monetario se emplea igualmente en hacer el Indice de las Monedas.

Este Monetario ò Museo corrio en otro tiempo por cuenta y al cuidado del P. Alexandro Panel, Maestro del Infante D. Luis, celebre Antiquario, que dexò muchos materiales MSS. para Indices, que existen en la R^{l} Biblioteca. En su tiempo se habia ya aumentado con la rica adquisicion del Monetario del Abate Rothelin, que compuesto de mas de 30. monetarios preciosos, se traxo de Francia el año de 1749. y se compró para la R^{l} B^{a} en 319 *mil* R^{s}. Despues se ha aumentado notablemente no solo con la adquisicion de los monetarios de algunos particulares, sino en especial con la del mencionado Infante D. Luis, que costo mas de 70 *mil* R^{s} y con la del Infante D. Gabriel, que se acaba de comprar en 300 *mil*. Estas adquisiciones hacen que el Monetario de la R^{l} B^{a} sea uno de los mas preciosos y abundantes de Europa, y una de las alhajas mas estimables de ella. Por esto manda S. M. que estè à cargo de un Bibliotecario, como persona de mas confianza, à quien se le debe dar un oficial ò Amanuense. Y si hubiese suficientes Individuos, convendria cumplir esta disposicion de S. M. no solo por obedecerle sino para que faltando uno, quedase otro instruido.

La pericia numismatica puede adquirirse en dos grados. El conocimiento de las monedas y el de sus series se adquiere no con mucha dificultad. El disertar sobre ellas es lo que requiere mucha noticia historica, erudicion selecta, combinacion atinada. El primer conocimiento bastaria para que un Bibliotecario ayudado del mismo oficial, y de los Indices numismaticos impresos, se pusiese en breve en estado de formar un Indice ò Inventario del de S. M. que bastase para saber lo que se contiene en el, y poder reconvenir si se echase menos alguna moneda ò alhaja. Pero si llegase el caso de publicar este Indice con la debida critica y erudicion correspondiente, ademas de necesitarse para esto de mayor pericia numismatica, se haria un servicio al publico, que cederia en honor del autor y de la misma Biblioteca, manifestando este tesoro; porque al fin los Monetarios son como la ciencia del otro Literato, de quien decia Persio que de nada le aprovechaba, si los demas ignoraban que sabia.

Las otras ocupaciones en que pudieran emplearse los Individuos de la R^{l} B^{a} si hubiese mayor numero, piden mas requisitos, son mas gloriosas y ceden tambien en beneficio del publico y en credito del Cuerpo. Estas consisten en reimprimir obras de gusto y utilidad, en publicar otras MSS. y en componer algunas propias. El desempeño de estos proyectos literarios requiere sugetos dotados de doctrina, de critica, de erudicion, de gusto y de estilo. No faltan en la Biblioteca. Y las obras en que pudieran ocuparse sus Individuos, son al parecer las siguientes.

1. Reimprimir correctamente y con oportunos prologos algunas obras apreciables de n[*ues*]tros mejores autores.

2. Publicar algunos codices de Antiguedades, como la *Via Militar* del Lic^{do} Juan Franco, algunas cronicas, historias generales y particulares de España, sus ciudades y familias: Viages, descubrimientos y conquistas de Indias: otros mss. pertenecientes a Buenas Letras, varia

erudicion, historia Literaria, à las artes y à la Botanica, como los Libros del Lic^do^ Bernabe de Cienfuegos, aunque este erudito ha variado modernamente. Todo con la debida correccion, examen, exactitud, cotejos, y prologos, ò notas oportunas.

3. Concluir y publicar el segundo tomo de la Biblioteca de D. Juan Yriarte, que solo imprimio el tomo primero. Los codices Griegos que posee S. M. se comprehenden en dos Estantes. Son en todos 230. La descripciòn de 125. se comprehende en el primer tomo. La de los 105 restantes se destinò para llenar el segundo. Yriarte hizo la descripción de todos los 230; pero juzgando que podria recibir mayor perfeccion, quando tratò de disponer el primer tomo para la prensa, volvió à reconocer los articulos de los 125. de que habia de constar, ampliàndolos, exòrnandolos, y amenizandolos. Habiendo fallecido sin perfeccionar toda la obra, entregó a la R[l] B[a] el Il[smo] S. D. Bernardo Yriarte, su sobrino y heredero, el material de los 105. codices restantes, de que se habia de componer el tomo segundo, pero sin extenderlo ni exórnarlo, como el del primero. Esta entrega se acompaño con una orden de S. M. para que se imprimiese en el ser y estado, en que le habia dexado su autor. Sin embargo de esto D. Juan de Santander quiso dar el encargo de arreglar y disponer este material segun el del tomo primero à D. Rafael Casalbon, pero este se escusò, prefiriendo el emprender por sí mismo y formar de nuevo la descripcion de los 105. Codices, desentendiendose del trabajo de D. Juan Yriarte, y dexandolo intacto. Era Casalbon un Bibliotecario docto, de vasta literatura, de conocida pericia en el Griego, y de notable desembargo en escribir Latin; pero de tan quebrantada salud que D. Juan de Santander le dispensó de la asistencia a la Oficina, y sin embargo trabajo mucho mas en su casa que si hubiera asistido a ella, pues reconocio 84. codices, haciendo de ellos una circumstanciada descripcion y examen critico, sin perjuicio de 6. volumenes en 4º que juntò de opusculos Griegos ineditos traducidos assimismo por èl en Latin. Todos estos trabajos, y los de Yriarte existen en la R[l] B[a]. Pero como D. Fran[co] Perez Bayer, Bibliotecario Mayor que fue de S. M. obligó à Casalbon à concurrir à la B[a] en medio de sus males, y por otra parte le suspendio del encargo de continuar la Griega sin atinar el Motivo, dexó la obra imperfecta sin embargo de haber sobrevivido tres años, que corrieron desde el año de 1784. en que entrò Bayer a ser Jefe de aquella Oficina, hasta el de 1787. en que fallecio Casalbon. Con que para concluir la Biblioteca Griega de Yriarte falta la descripcion de 21 Codices.

4. Utilizar en beneficio publico los MSS. del P. Andres Burriel. Este erudito critico fue destinado en t[*iem*]po de [Felipe V *tachado*] Fernando VI à la Biblioteca de la Sta Iglesia de Toledo y à los archivos de la ciudad con el fin de escoger y sacar copias de varias obras para

ilustrar la Historia Eclesiastica y Civil de España, su legislaciòn, su liturgia, sus concilios, las antiguedades y fundaciones de sus pueblos & c[a]. Muchas de estas copias desaparecieron; pero se conservaron no pocas, que despues de la muerte del autor, pasaron à la R[l] Biblioteca, donde existen. El edificio que el P. Burriel intentaba levantar con estos materiales, ya se frustrò, porque murio el architecto, y no dexò comunicadas sus ideas, trazas, ni plan. Pero supuesto que las copias son fidedignas, porque estan cotejadas por el Padre, y muchas ilustradas con notas, se pudieran colocar con algun orden y publicarlas como una Coleccion de Monumentos, al modo de las Colecciones de Martene, Achevy, Muratori y Montfaucon, para que fuesen como un archivo de donde se proveyesen n[*ues*]tros Escritores de documentos historicos y fidedignos.

5. Escribir de nuevo una Biblioteca Española, compendiando la de D. Nicolas Antonio, y trayendo su contexto hasta nuestro dias. Dividio la suya este celebre Biografo, como se sabe, en dos partes. Intitulò la una *Biblioteca Antigua*, incluyendo en ella los autores Españoles desde el t[*iem*]po de Augusto hasta el año del 1500, y procediendo por orden cronologico. Intituló la segunda Parte *Biblioteca Nueva*, incluyendo en ella los autores que florecieron desde el año de 1500 hasta el de 1684. en que murio, y en esta procedio por orden alfabetico, como mas facil y manual, supuesto que las Bibliotecas no son libros para leerse à pasto, por decirlo asi, sino que solo se acude à ellas por lo regular à consultar y leer un solo articulo, esto es, la vida y obras de un solo autor. Para su complemento deberian incluirse en él como se ha insinuado los autores que florecieron desde el año de 1684 hasta el presente. Deberian incluirse tambien en èl con mas estensiòn las Bibliotecas Arabico-Hispana, y la Hebraico-Hispana, ò las de los Escritores Arabes y Judios Españoles. Las fuentes de donde se debian tomar las noticias, eran del mismo D. Nicolas Antònio, del Sr Bayer, de los MSS. de S. M., de la copiosa coleccion de los libros impresos que hay en la R[l] Libreria, de las Bibliotecas modernas, publicadas despues de la muerte de D. Nicolas Antonio, asi de Ordenes Religiosas, como de provincias y reynos, como son las de los P[s] Dominicos por Echard y Quetif, la de los Carmelitas Calzados y Descalzos, la Augustiniana, la Franciscana de Fr. Juan de San Antonio, la Oriental de Barcia, la Lusitana de Barbosa, las de los Escritores del reyno de Valencia de Rodriguez y de Ximeno & c[a]. La Arabico-Hispana se pudiera corregir y aumentar por la de D. Miguel Casiri, y por el Codice ms. de los Filosofos Arabes; y la Hebraico-Hispana no solo por la MS. que dexò original D. Nicolas Antonio, y por la de Plantavicio, Buxtorfio, Ymbonati y Bartolocci, aunque reconocidas ya por D. Nic. Antonio, sino por la historia Judayca de Basnaga, y especialmente por la exacta y juiciosa de Wolfio, que no pudo ver D. Nicolas Antonio, y por los codices Hebreos

del Escorial. La formaciòn de esta obra requeria a lo menos quatro sugetos, literatos, poliglotos, de varia erudicion, de estilo correcto, y sobre todo muy instruidos en la Historia Literaria. Y por quanto una Biblioteca de autores Españoles se debe escribir para el uso de los naturales principalmente, parece debiera componerse en Castellano, aunque seria acertado traducirla tambien en Latin para noticia de los Estrangeros.

6. Publicar segun las Ordenes de S. M. el Codice Vigilano. Contiene este raro monumento de la Antiguedad Eclesiastica los Concilios, las Epistolas Decretales, el Fuero Juzgo, algunos opusculos de S. Isidoro y otros. Llamase Vigilano, por haber sido su principal copiante Velaó Vigila, monge del monasterio de Albelda. D. Fran[co] Xavier de Palomares, Oficial primero del archivo de Estado, le copio del caracter Gotico en que se escribio en el siglo X. al caracter Latino con suma perfecciòn en cinco volumenes de papel imperial de Holanda, dexando margenes espaciosas para notar en ellas las variantes que resultasen del cotejo con otros codices, que existen todavia de esta misma naturaleza, como son el Emilianense, el de Toledo, el Placentino y otros: todos puros y legitimos, sin los vicios del fingido Isidoro Peccator o Mercator, con que los Estrangeros han intentado desacreditar la Coleccion Canonica-Española. Esta copia de Palomares existe en la R[l] Biblioteca, que la satisfizo: pero falta todavia que cotejarla con el original para que sea fidedigna. El Fuero Juzgo ya no podria publicarle la Biblioteca, porque con orden de S. M. no informado de la que esta tenia, le saco de ella la Academia Española para imprimirla, y se la entregò con todos los trabajos criticos y variantes que habìa hecho sobre èl el P. Burriel, dexandose despojar de ellos la Biblioteca. Uno de los pensamientos de D. Juan de Santander fue publicar este Fuero Juzgo ilustrado por el P. Burriel, con la particular novedad de distribuir la impresion en tres columnas. En la I[a] se habia de colocar el texto Latino en caracteres comunes, y seria esta la primera vez que se hubiese impreso en España, porque las ediciones que corren dèl, estan hechas por estrangeros. En la II. el mismo texto Latino en Caracteres Goticos, para lo que se habian empezado à hacer algunas matrices. En la III. El mismo texto en Castellano, siguiendo la traduccion que mando hacer el Rey D. Alonso el Sabio.

7. Dar tambien à la prensa el Codice Arabe, que contiene la *Coleccion de Canones de la Iglesia de España*. Encontrose entre los MSS. del Escorial, de donde se traxo à los de la Biblioteca de Madrid, donde existe. Escribiose por los años de 1050. Traduxole al Latin D. Miguel Casiri por orden de S. M. habiendola copiado antes del original con el fin de publicarla con la version Latina. Comprehende los canones y decisiones tomadas de los concilios y decretales de los Sumos

Pontifices. Esta Coleccion de Canones se traduxo del Latin al Arabe en t[*iem*]po de la cautividad para el uso de la Iglesia de España. Acaso se hizo asi, porque se iba desusando el Latin, y prevaleciendo la Lengua Arabiga, que adoptaban los cristianos, cuyo vicio reprehende Alvaro Cordoves.

8. Ultimamente para mayor credito de la R^l^ Bilbioteca y de sus Individuos seria conveniente, que los que se sintiesen con caudal bastante presentasen al Bibliotecario Mayor el proyecto de alguna obra, la que hubiese mayor proporcion y analogia con sus estudios, gusto è inclinacion, para que prestandoseles los auxilios convenientes, la concluyesen, y se imprimiese à costos de la misma R^l^ Biblioteca, porque el honor y el interes son las alas con que se mueven los ingenios. Pero convendria que estas obras particulares fuesen reconocidas por el Cuerpo antes de imprimirse.

Madrid y Octubre 18 de 1793.

[*firma y rúbrica*:] Juan Antonio Pellicer

Luis Gutiérrez, Novelist and Impostor

MARTIN MURPHY

Oxford

The early nineteenth-century novel *Cornelia Bororquia*, once described by Menéndez Pelayo as 'muy miserable cosa', and by J. A. Llorente, the historian of the Inquisition, as 'una novela mal zurcida, muy inmoral y escandalosa', has recently been gaining in reputation. In 1973 Juan Ignacio Ferreras convincingly argued its artistic merits, and in 1987 Gérard Dufour republished the work with an introduction which throws much light on the hitherto obscure author.[1] Dufour shows that Llorente and Menéndez Pelayo were correct in identifying the anonymous author as a former Trinitarian friar named Gutiérrez who was executed at Seville in 1809 as a French spy. In the introduction to his *Anales de la Inquisición* Llorente wrote, 'En este año de 1812 se ha impreso en Madrid un librito dozavo intitulado Cornelia Bororquia segunda edición. Su autor (aunque no suena) parece haber sido Don F. Gutiérrez presbítero, ex-frayle apóstata que, habiendo huido de Castilla para librarse de las cárceles secretas de la Inquisición de Valladolid, huyó a Bayona de Francia, donde se sostuvo siendo redactor de la gaceta que allí había en idioma español antes de nuestra revolución; y entonces publicó por primera vez su Cornelia Bororquia'. Another source, the *Historia del Gazetero de Bayona extractada de la causa original e ilustrada con algunas notas por el Dr. D. J. M. D.* [Antonio Martínez, O. P.],

---

1 Gérard Dufour, *Cornelia Bororquia, o la víctima de la Inquisición* (Alicante: Instituto Juan-Gil Albert, 1987); *idem*, 'Andanzas y muerte de Luis Gutiérrez, autor de la novela *Cornelia Bororquia*', *Caligrama* (Palma de Mallorca), II (1987), 83-96; Juan Ignacio Ferreras, *Los orígenes de la novela decimonónica* (Madrid: Taurus, 1973), 268-81.

published in Seville in 1812, based on the police record of Gutiérrez's interrogation, gives his first name as Luis and his date of birth as 1772. The name Luis is confirmed by Menéndez Pelayo, whose information was derived from B. J. Gallardo, who was an eyewitness of the exhibition of Gutiérrez' corpse at Seville after his execution there in 1809.[2]

Dufour's critique of *Cornelia Bororquia* is exemplary, and he has gone some way towards reconstructing Gutiérrez's picaresque career, but he has not uncovered the whole story. This article will attempt to take the investigation further.

Cornelia Bororquia

The novel is in the form of a series of letters exchanged by the actors in a tragedy set in mid-sixteenth-century Seville at the height of the Inquisition's campaign against suspected Protestants. Dufour shows that the epistolary form mirrors that of Olavide's novel *El evangelio en triunfo, o historia de un filósofo desengañado*, published in 1797. In this recantation, which went into seven editions between 1797 and 1800, the most famous living victim of the Inquisition publicly repudiated his former opinions by defending the Holy Office and favourably contrasting its tribunals with those of revolutionary France. This *volte-face* shocked Spanish progressives, and *Cornelia Bororquia* is an attempt by one of them to set the record straight.

The plot begins with the disappearance of Cornelia, the eponymous heroine, daughter of the governor of Valencia. The father's suspicions fall on her lover Bartolomé Vargas, an enlightened young *sevillano*, and he writes to his friend Meneses in Seville, asking him to track down the young man. In fact the real abductor is none other than the Archbishop of Seville, who has conceived a secret passion for Cornelia and, having suborned her servant, has had her conveyed to the prison of the Inquisition, the more easily to assail her virtue. After Vargas fails in a rescue bid, the Archbishop is mortally

2 J. A. Llorente, *Anales de la inquisición de España* (Madrid: Imprenta de Ibarra, 1812), I, xxi-xxvi; M. Menéndez Pelayo, *Historia de los heterodoxos españoles* (Madrid: Suárez, 1932), VI, 28-29; *Historia del gazetero de Bayona* (Sevilla: Josef Hidalgo, 1802 [*vere* 1812]), BN Madrid, R/60358-40.

wounded by Cornelia while making an attempt on her honour, and dies begging her forgiveness. Vargas pleads for Cornelia's life with his brother Cipriano, the Inquisitor, but the latter rejects this appeal to his humanity, intent on bringing her to trial as a heretic. Having refused to recant, Cornelia dies bravely at the stake, and the story ends with the flight of Vargas and Meneses to asylum in Holland.

The bald outline of the plot might suggest a crude and tendentious piece of propaganda. *Cornelia Bororquia* is nothing of the kind. It is a novel of the eighteenth century, marked by economy and restraint, a *roman à thèse* of the Enlightenment, intended to illustrate the evils of religious intolerance and drawing its inspiration from Rousseau and Samuel Richardson. Though the epistolary form has the disadvantage of weakening the story line and reducing the hero, Vargas, to an impotent spectator of and commentator on events, it allows the author to set up a genuine theological debate. The letters between Bartolomé Vargas and his brother Cipriano, the Inquisitor, are crucial to the issue. Bartolomé argues that the Inquisition has distorted Christ's message by violating the right of the individual to spiritual privacy and by destroying the sacred ties of family and society — encouraging father to inform on son, neighbour on neighbour. If God allows the existence of religious plurality, he asks, how can his ministers presume to disallow it? In Letter XIV Cipriano dismisses these as worldly ideas picked up from English books. What matters is the salvation of souls, and to that end the Church must protect truth and eradicate error:

> Qué nos importa la ilustración y civilización de las demás naciones si al cabo sabemos que está cerrada para ellas la puerta del paraíso? ... Hemos nacido para morir, y nos debe importar muy poco que en este valle de lágrimas las cosas bayan bien o mal. Más vale ser esclavo y mortificado en este mundo que infeliz para siempre en el otro.

Cipriano goes on to challenge his brother's faith in human progress:

> Te he oido hablar varias veces del atraso en que se hallan entre nosotros las artes mecánicas y liberales, y ensalzar el ingenio e industria de los extrangeros.

The apostles, he declares, did not concern themselves with arts and manufactures:

> No dixeron a las naciones: Procuraos una buena legislación, labrad los campos, cultivad las artes, fomentad la navegación y el comercio &c. Bautizaos y creed: he aquí lo que predicaron con tan feliz éxito (III).[3]

The opposite extreme is represented by Meneses, who argues that Christianity itself must be vitiated, given its record of inhumanity and persecution, and he condemns religion as an instrument of social control and exploitation. Vargas himself is tempted to draw the same conclusion, but at the end of the novel he describes to Meneses in Letter XXVIII his meeting with a fellow-victim of the Inquisition, Casinio, a priest who for fourteen years has been living incognito with shepherds in the country (and who owes something of his conception to Rousseau's *vicaire savoyard).* When Vargas goes so far as to declare that the Christian religion is intrinsically corrupt, and has been so from the beginning:

> Nuestra religión siempre ha reynado por el terror, por la intolerancia y los crímenes. (149)

Casinio, the spokesman of evangelical Christianity pure and undefiled, protests that Christ himself forced no-one to believe: it is man who has betrayed Christ's message of spiritual freedom and has distorted the image of God, representing him as a tyrant rather than a father. Man, he suggests, gets the religion he deserves, and if Spain suffers under the yoke of religious tyranny it is because Spaniards have lacked the courage to defy it.

It is left to Meneses, at the end of the novel, to give rhetorical expression to the central paradox:

> O religión! religión! Quantos bienes has producido a los hombres! pero quantos males les has igualmente ocasionado! En tu seno halla el triste mortal asilo contra el vicio, consuelo en la adversidad, apoyo en las mayores afliciones: mas también con tu velo se cubre la maldad, en tu nombre corren arroyos de sangre y se autorizan los crímenes más enormes, con tu égida se defiende el poder arbitrario de los tiranos, con tus armas se enciende la guerra, se fomenta la discordia, se desahoga la venganza, y tú

3 References are to the Dufour edition (see note 1, item 1).

> sirves de sagrado pretesto [*sic*] para justificar las pasiones más horribles y vergonzosas (177).

It must be evident from these extracts that *Cornelia Bororquia* is a not ignoble novel. It might have been expected to find favour with Llorente as an eloquent critique of the Inquisition. What offended Llorente, however, was the author's unjustified claim that the story was based on historical truth. Since Llorente was a historian, not a novelist, and regarded himself as having exclusive rights to the history of the Inquisition, he was affronted by the author's use of novelistic licence. He was able to demonstrate that Cornelia Bororquia had never existed, but was a conflation of two separate historical characters, María Cornel and María de Bohorques, who suffered death at the hands of the Seville Inquisition in 1559. It was sufficiently damning, Llorente argued, to set down the factual record of the Inquisition without having recourse to fiction. Gutiérrez had cited Boulanger, Langle, Limborch and Marsollier as authorities for the historicity of his novel, but Llorente had no difficulty in showing this claim to be unfounded.

From the evidence so far cited, Luis Gutiérrez emerges as a gifted writer in whom idealism coexisted with disingenuousness. His later history confirms this first impression.

Editions of the novel

The first edition, entitled *Bororquia, o la víctima de la Inquisición*, was, as Dufour shows, first published in Paris in 1801. A copy is listed in the catalogue of the Bibliothèque Nationale but has disappeared from the shelves and has to be reconstructed from a French translation published two years later and dedicated by the translator to Lucien Bonaparte.[4] The second edition, 'revista, corregida y aumentada', published at Paris in 1802 under the altered title *Cornelia Bororquia*, was to become the standard text. It was reprinted in Paris in 1804 and

---

4 *Bororquia, ou la victime de L'Inquisition. Fait historique, traduit de l'espagnol, dedié au C. Lucien Bonaparte ... par le citoyen Duclos, professeur de langue espagnole et traducteur de plusieurs ouvrages en cette langue* (Senlis: de l'imprimerie de Tremblay, an XI — 1803). Since Gutiérrez was a teacher of Spanish and proficient in French, 'citoyen Duclos' is almost certainly his pseudonym. Lucien Bonaparte was French ambassador at Madrid in 1800.

(with a modified preface) at Madrid in 1812, under the regime of Joseph Bonaparte. The first edition was placed on the list of prohibited books as early as 1802 and under Godoy copies seem to have circulated clandestinely in manuscript.[5] There were at least five printings in Spain during the liberal triennium, but thereafter publication depended on the political climate. Altogether there were at least twenty-five editions of the novel in the course of the nineteenth century (not counting versions in Portuguese and German) and yet copies are extremely scarce in Spanish libraries, no doubt as a result of *depuración*. The Biblioteca Nacional in Madrid has only two copies, the earlier of which is the Madrid edition of 1812. However, four editions are to be found in a location understandably overlooked by Dufour: the Wiffen Collection in the library of Wadham College, Oxford. These include one of the only two extant copies of the Paris edition of 1802.[6] This, and the Paris edition of 1819 reprinted by Dufour, contains the full text of the author's preface which in all the Spanish editions was topped and tailed of its first two, and final, paragraphs.

In these first two paragraphs the author describes his work as a much expanded and improved reworking of the first edition which, though hurriedly put together ('compuesta e impresa en menos de un mes') had created a demand which exceeded supply. He also spells out the moral of the tale, which is a plea for religious toleration: 'Un gobierno debe permitir y proteger todos los cultos en su territorio, así como Dios los tolera a todos en la tierra ... El espíritu religioso es muy útil en las sociedades, pero es muy perjudicial quando se hermana con él la política'. In the final paragraph he cites the recently concluded Concordat between Napoleon and the Papacy as a model for Church-State relations: 'Ha sido mirado por las personas sensatas como una obra maestra de política capaz por sí sola de inmortalizar al héroe que le ha concebido' (61-64). In the Madrid edition of 1812 the word 'héroe' was altered to the more

5 A MS copy of the Paris edition of 1802 was advertised for sale in Catalogue 50 (1976) of the Dolphin Book Company, Oxford. Mr J. L. Gili informs me that it may have come from the Holland House library.

6 The other copy is at Heidelberg, in the University library. The Wiffen Collection also contains the Madrid edition of 1812 and that of 1846 (Imprenta de la Iberia).

anodyne 'rey'.

Besides the Madrid edition of 1812, the Wiffen Collection also includes a unique copy of a version published in London in 1819. Its full title is *Historia verídica de la Judit Española (Cornelia Bororquia), escrita por el presbítero Doctor Don Fermín Araujo, comisario del tribunal de la Inquisición de Valladolid. Publicada en Paris en 1803. Tercera edición corregida y aumentada por Don D. A. C. y G. Reimpresa en Londres en 1819.*[7] This adulterated version and the attribution to Fermín Araujo have been the source of much confusion and explain why many catalogues, including that of the British Library, still name 'Araujo' as the author of *Cornelia Bororquia.*

La Judit Española

The initials in the title conceal the identity of Don Diego Antonio Correa y García, a native of Tenerife, an army officer and prominent liberal who in 1814, after the restoration of Ferdinand VII, was arrested at Gibraltar and handed over by the British governor to the Spanish authorities, by whom he was imprisoned at Ceuta. His case was taken up by a number of Whig politicians, and after repeated appeals to the Prince Regent and to the British Minister in Madrid, and after several questions in Parliament, he was eventually released in 1816 and took up residence in London. William Walton, the translator of Puigblanch's *La inquisición sin máscara* supported him in his campaign to obtain an indemnity from the British government, and to this end he published a brochure entitled *Letter Transmitted to Ferdinand VII by Don Diego Correa, ex-Captain in the Spanish Army in that Imminent Crisis when the King was Proceeding to Destroy and Trample on the Political Constitution of the Spanish Monarchy ... with Various Documents and Papers Relative to his Imprisonment by General Smith, Governor of Gibraltar, who Delivered him to the Spanish Government ... Published by the Author in Vindication of his*

---

7 Palau 15106. The printer was E. Justins. There is a copy of an edition dated 1825 in the Bodleian Library. The BL copy was destroyed in the war.

Patriotic Character (London: E. Justins, 1819).[8] Correa may well have known Luis Gutiérrez to be the true author of *Cornelia Bororquia*, but as a liberal he would not have wanted to associate his name with that of a notorious *afrancesado* who had been executed by the Central Junta as a French spy. Hence his attribution of the work to 'Fermín Araujo'. Wiffen, in a note inserted into his copy of the book, suggests that Araujo may have been Gutiérrez's maternal name, and Fermín may have been his name in religion (Llorente calls him Don F. Gutiérrez). Was Correa correct in describing Araujo/Gutiérrez as an official of the Inquisition at Valladolid? Certainly the author of *Cornelia* evinces an accurate knowledge of the processes of the Inquisition, but Dufour could find no trace of either name in the records of that tribunal.

In Correa's hands Gutiérrez's novel became the vehicle for a violent attack on Ferdinand VII as the restorer of the Inquisition. In his *discurso preliminar* he names himself as one of those who had attempted to convert the king to a better way of thinking:

> Quando el Capitán Correa y los Generales Xauregui y el Empecinado manifestaron a Fernando sus errores políticos y religiosos ..., este estúpido rey cerró sus oídos a la voz imperiosa de la razón.

The classical economy and restraint of Gutiérrez's text is now marred by inflation and exaggeration, and vituperative footnotes keep hammering home the anti-clerical message, as at the end of Letter XII:

> El estado frailesco en España es el más idiota, más audaz y más artificioso de quantos se conocen en las naciones que los toleran, su Dios es su vientre, y su religión el vicio. Son las sanguijuelas de los pueblos fanáticos y las Harpías de la sociedad: enemigos irreconciliables de la razón y de la humanidad.

Almost every letter is filled out with emotive and partisan padding. The final *interrogatorio* between Cornelia and the Inquisitor, for instance, which in Gutiérrez's text is all the more effective for its brevity and conforms with known inquisitorial

8 The BL copy (1141 i 13.5) has an inscription on the flyleaf by the author to the Duke of Sussex. The latter, a younger brother of George III, patronized a number of liberal causes and was a prominent freemason.

procedure, is swollen to four times its original length. Some of the accretions to the text reflect the changed political circumstances of post-war Spain: the Inquisitor accuses Vargas of being a freemason as well as an atheist, and Cornelia defends him as a good constitutionalist. Gutiérrez's Inquisitor ends with the words 'Sois culpable: volved, volved al instante al calabozo'. Correa expands this to 'Nos los Inquisidores te declaramos culpable. Llevadla a otro mas estrecho calabozo, cargadla de más pesados hierros: su alimento será limitado basta que termine en un afrentoso espectaculo que hará temblar a los heréticos, apóstatas y tibios christianos corrompidos con las costumbres del siglo'.

Correa also appended to the novel a number of documents intended to reinforce the liberal polemic against the newly restored Inquisition. These included the text of various messages of congratulation sent to the Cortes on their abolition of the Inquisition in 1813, reprinted from the *Tribuno Extraordinario del Pueblo Español*, edited by Álvaro Flórez Estrada ('descendiente del celebre Pelayo'). This was followed by the *Oda a la Beneficencia* of Alberto Lista — not named — reprinted from the London journal, *El Español Constitucional*, with the annotations of its editor Pedro Fernández. Perhaps Correa refrained from naming Lista because of the latter's record as an *afrancesado*, but he described him as 'uno de los poetas nacionales más celebres, más sabios y más ilustrados'. Lista's poem, with its denunciation of the dark fanaticism now stirring again in Spain, was in keeping with Correa's message.[9]

La Judit Española was reprinted in London in 1825, but does not appear to have been used as the basis of any of the later Spanish editions of *Cornelia Bororquia*. However, it may have been one of the sources on which Blanco White drew for his novel *Vargas*, published anonymously in 1822. That was at any rate the opinion of William Walton, who knew both Correa and Blanco. In a letter to Luis Usoz y Río in 1855, Walton declared *Vargas* to be 'partly founded' on Correa's 'brochure'. Since Blanco moved in anti-clerical circles in Madrid between 1805 and 1808 he may already have come across Gutiérrez's novel in its original form there, or he may have found a copy in

9 The poem is reprinted in BAE, LXVII, 300-02.

the Holland House library, but it is certainly true that he is more akin to Correa than to Gutiérrez in the violence of his tone and language. Walton incidentally offers powerful testimony to Blanco's authorship of *Vargas*. At the time of its publication, he told Usoz, 'everyone conversant with Spanish affairs', including Lord Holland, considered him to be the author.

> Baldwin, the publisher of *Vargas*, in conversation, acknowledged the fact to me more than once, notwithstanding the disguise attempted in the preface. No other than a native and a *sevillano* could have written such a work. If I remember well, Blanco White gave me the copy in question, but at a subsequent period he regretted having written the novel, and endeavoured to suppress it and call it in.[10]

Popularizations of *Cornelia Bororquia*

Menéndez Pelayo recalled seeing a *copla de ciego*, based on the story of Cornelia Bororquia, being sold by hawkers in the street, 'pendiente de un cordel'. Dufour has traced a copy to the Bibliothèque Nationale: *Canción nueva de Cornelia Bororquia. Relación compendiada a modo de copla de ciego*, published in Barcelona by P. Maimó before 1848.[11] But the popular versions of the novel go back even further, to the liberal *trienio*, when the story became a weapon in the anti-clerical arsenal. The Hispanic Society of America has a verse adaptation of Letter XXXII, Cornelia's valedictory: *Epistola de Cornelia Bororquia a su amante Vargas escrita desde la capilla del Santo Oficio de Sevilla el mismo día que le metieron en ella. Puesta en verso por D. R. D. y C.* (Madrid: Imprenta de Dona Rosa Sanz, c/ del Baño, 1820).[12] The Archivo Municipal at Seville contains an even more interesting playbill, dating from January 1823. It reads:

---

10 ALS inserted in Usoz's copy of *Vargas* (BN Madrid, U/8795).

11 BN Paris, Réserve Yg 274-6, reprinted by Dufour, 209-14.

12 HSA 2817. The topicality of the publication is evident in the introductory *advertencia*, which refers to the 'tribunal bárbaro que no tenía otro código sino el capricho y la mentira, sostenido por un pueblo engañado, esclavizado e ignorante, y por unos legisladores que iban a la parte en sus lucrosas ganancias'.

> El ciudadano Tiburcio López, Primer Baylarín y Director de bayles de este teatro, ofrece al ilustrado Público Sevillano para el jueves 30 del corriente, día destinado a su BENEFICIO la función siguiente: Se abrirá la escena con una brillante sinfonía a toda orquesta, y seguidamente se representará por primera vez en este teatro el DRAMA en cuatro actos, titulado LA CORNELIA BORORQUIA, O SEAN, LOS HORROROSOS CRIMENES DE UN PRELADO SOSTENIDOS POR EL EXECRABLE TRIBUNAL DE LA INQUISICION, sacado de la historia verdadera. En la boca de los interlocutores Vargas, Meneses y el Conde de Bosque-espeso, se oirán las mas enérgicas reflecciones contra los abusos de tribunal tan tirano. Aun resuenan en los oídos de los amantes de la patria y de la humanidad toda, los ecos lisongeros de aquellas tan acaloradas discusiones en que los verdaderos sabios de nuestra nación sostuvieron y ganaron la abolición de un tribunal tan inicuo el año 12. Loor eterno a ellos y a los que tan dignamente les suceden. Viva la Constitución que nos libró de sus ominosos hierros.[13]

Luis Gutiérrez

A rough outline of the author's life may now be sketched. Menéndez Pelayo, who derived his information from Aureliano Fernández Guerra (who in turn relied on B. J. Gallardo) states that he was born at Valladolid and educated at Salamanca, and that he first made his name with a poem entitled *El chocolate*.[14] Gutiérrez later told his interrogators at Seville that he had fled to France about 1799 when his application for secularization was opposed by his Trinitarian superiors and refused by the Bishop of Pamplona. He settled at Bayonne, where he obtained secularization from the Bishop and earned his living initially as a teacher of Spanish. This is confirmed by the Mexican expatriate Fray Servando Teresa de Mier who met Gutiérrez at

13 Archivo del Ayuntamiento, Sevilla: Fondo Felix G. de León. I am grateful to Dr Manuel Moreno Alonso for obtaining a copy of this document.

14 This is not the Latin poem *In laudem potionis chocolaticae* which the old catalogue of the Hispanic Society of America wrongly attributed to Luis Gutiérrez (HSA 411/913). Palau (118725) puts the date of this MS at about 1700, and this is confirmed by the present Curator of the Modern Library of the HSA who informs me that the only watermark discernible is consonant with a date between 1660 and 1760.

Bayonne in 1802.[15] Mier and his friend Simón Rodríguez, *alias* Samuel Robinson, Bolívar's former tutor, also taught languages in Bayonne before moving to Paris. Some time later in 1802 Gutiérrez began publication of the *Gaceta de Bayona*, which managed to achieve some circulation in Spain despite being denied a licence by Cevallos. Eschewing politics, it professed to be concerned chiefly with the promotion of commerce.[16]

Dufour could find no record of Gutiérrez in the police files of the Département des Basses Pyrénées but he was able to trace his registration by the Paris police as a temporary resident in the capital between 8 November and 11 December 1807. He is described in the records as a language teacher from Bayonne.[17] Dufour assumes that Gutiérrez remained in Paris, but as long ago as 1909 Wenceslao Ramírez de Villa Arrutia quoted a document which shows that he returned to Bayonne and resumed his editorship of the Gazette. On 18 March 1808 an agent at Bayonne advised Madrid that Gutiérrez was now engaged as a propagandist for Murat:

> La supuesta circular del Gran Duque de Berg [Murat] es un amasijo hecho aquí entre el subprefecto, el comisario de policía y el malvado fraile trinitario apóstata redactor de la *Gaceta Española* de esta ciudad ... La *Gaceta de Bayona* está vendida a la policia e sirve de instrumento para estampar cuanto quiere y sugiere el Gobierno.[18]

It appears from this that Gutiérrez had a hand in the proclamation which Murat made to the Spanish nation from Burgos on 13 March. For the next three months his skills as a translator, interpreter and propagandist made him more useful than ever during the historic events which unfolded at Bayonne: the arrival of Napoleon, the forced abdication of the Bourbons,

---

15 Servando Teresa de Mier, *Memorias*, ed. Antonio Castro Leal (Mexico: Porrúa, 1971), II, 26.

16 Lucienne Domergue, *Tres calas en la censura dieciochesca* (Toulouse: France-Ibérie Recherche, 1981), 117-20; José Javier Sánchez Aranda, 'Napoleón y la prensa afrancesada en España', in *Les Espagnols et Napoléon* (Aix: Univ. de Provence, 1984), 86.

17 G. Dufour, 'Andanzas y muerte de Luis Gutiérrez'.

18 Wenceslao Ramírez de Villa Urrutia, 'La misión del Barón de Agra a Londres en 1808', *Revista de Archivos, Bibliotecas y Museos*, XX (Madrid, 1909), 315.

the proclamation of King Joseph and the convocation of a collaborationist Cortes. Unfortunately, copies of the *Gaceta* are hard to come by, but the Bibliothèque Municipale at Bayonne has a copy of the important issue of 1 July 1808 which bears the hallmarks of Gutiérrez's rhetoric. After listing the delegates to the Cortes, the editor launched into an encomium of the newly promulgated Constitution, laying particular stress on its historic recognition of the American colonies as an integral part of the Spanish nation and its provision for American representation in the Cortes:

> Esta innovación grande y saludable era solo propia de la época actual que se compone de prodigios, y debía resultar de las concepciones de aquel para quien no tiene volo el tiempo, ni obscuridades los intereses de los Pueblos, ni término las distancias, ni imperio las preocupaciones, y que no busca en lo que hay ni en lo que ha habido sino lo que puede y debe ser ... En lo sucesivo las Colonias no serán ya consideradas como hijas menores de la familia, destinados a vivir en provecho y baxo la vigilancia de sus hermanos mayores.

Under the enlightened rule of a Bonaparte, the editor continued, Spain had succeeded where Britain had failed, in averting the secession of its American colonies and inaugurating a new Spanish Commonwealth based on principles of justice and brotherhood:

> Aun quando la mudanza que acabe de verificarse en España no hubiera accarreado más que éste solo bien, bastaría para asegurar al Príncipe de quien emana derechos al reconocimiento del antiguo y nuevo mundo. ¡Quanto gusto y consuelo debe causar al ver el primer acto de la dinastía de Napoleón, consagrado a la reparación de las sinrazones e injusticias que han causado o hecho pesar las precedentes dinastías sobre sus colonias! ¡Qué diferencia, qué enorme diferencia de éste acto a los de la dinastía de Austria que las había abrumado y oprimido, y a los de la Borbónica que las había comprimido!
>
> El dar a las colonias arbitrios de fecundidad, es completar su descubrimiento, es hacer por ellas lo que hizo Colón por la Europa al descubrirlas, es en fin asociarse a la gloria de aquel grande hombre.[19]

---

19 *Gazeta de Comercio, Literatura y Política de Bayona de Francia*, No. 587 (1 de julio de 1808). My thanks are due to the Conservateur of the

Three weeks later, on 22 July, the *Gaceta* ceased publication, and two months after that its editor defected to London. The story of his 'mission', as told to his interrogators in Seville the following March, was not surprisingly regarded by Dufour as too fantastic to be credible, but it is fully corroborated by documentation in the Foreign Office and Canning archives.[20] The details lie outside the scope of the present article but may be summarized here. Posing as the 'Barón de Agra', Gutiérrez succeeded in convincing the Foreign Secretary, George Canning, that he was an emissary from the imprisoned Ferdinand VII, who wanted the British government to forward despatches to Mexico instructing the Viceroy to form a Regency in the New World. The 'Baron' had with him letters of introduction from Ferdinand and his brother, the Infante Don Antonio, a letter from Ferdinand to the Mexican Viceroy, and the text of the proclamation of a Regency — all forged. Canning gave the 'Baron' an advance of £1,000 and had a royal seal made to his specifications but after some hesitation insisted that before any instructions were sent to Mexico he should first report to the Central Junta. The 'Baron' reluctantly set out for Spain, but at Lisbon he was recognized, betrayed and arrested. Conveyed to Seville under conditions of the utmost secrecy, he protested under interrogation that his only intention had been to 'save America' and to foil French designs upon the Spanish empire. The central Junta at first suspected a British intrigue but finally concluded that Gutiérrez was the instrument of a French plot to divide Spain from America and to foster defeatism and confusion. Arraigned before a secret tribunal, the *soi-disant* Baron was sentenced to death and garrotted on the night of 14 April — his body being exhibited the following morning on a

---

Bibliothèque Municipale at Bayonne, M. Yves Chevalier, for letting me have a photocopy of this issue. There is a copy of No. 488, dated 17 July 1807, in the Biblioteca Nacional, Madrid (R/6248717).

20 The large dossier on Gutiérrez compiled at the time of his interrogation at Seville in the Spring of 1809 is in AHN Madrid, leg. 5438. The documentation of the case on the English side is to be found among the Canning Papers in the Leeds District Archives (bundles 45, 46, 46a) and in the Public Records Office (FO 72/64, 72/73, 95/7, 185/15-16). See my article 'Canning and the New World in 1808: The Tale of the Baron de Agra', *History Today*, XLIII (May 1993), 35-41.

platform in the Plaza de San Francisco.

The content of the real and forged correspondence of the 'Baron' is all of a piece with Gutiérrez's earlier known sentiments. 'Let us respect one another', ran the proclamation he wrote for the Regency, 'remembering that we are all children of one family, and that each one of us, whatever his caste, colour or origin, should contribute all that lies in his power towards the tranquillity, happiness and prosperity of our country'.[21] Or, again, when urging Canning (unsuccessfully) to abandon Spain as a lost cause and to transfer his support to a new, enlightened Spanish America, he put the rhetorical question:

> Ne serait-il point une tâche pour la nation anglaise de laisser crouer ces beaux et vastes pays dans la crasse de l'ignorance, du fanatisme et de l'incultivation? Pouvez-vous vous persuadir qu'une vieille politique ombrageuse et routinière puisse voir sans crainte, suspicion ou méfiance votre ascendant sur ces pays?[22]

Those are the tones of the author of *Cornelia Bororquia.*

Two days before his execution, Gutiérrez wrote a letter 'dans ma prison de Séville' to a friend in London, a Mr Sanders. It was intercepted by the authorities who at once wrote to the Spanish envoy in London with instructions to trace the correspondent. He was not found. The letter (reproduced in full by Dufour) reveals a Gutiérrez who is by turns candid, remorseful, defiant and attitudinizing:

> Je dois être une victime vouée a un monstre qu'on appelle *fanatisme* ... Il semble que la Providence a voulu me punir d'avoir trahi ma conscience, mes nobles sentiments et mes opinions libérales. La mort, mon cher Sandher's [*sic*], ne m'effraye point. Je me sens avec assez de fermeté et de tranquillité d'âme pour la souffrir, et je monterai a l'échafaud avec le noble courage de l'innocence.

These were words which, nine years earlier, Gutierrez had created for his fictional heroine, so they came easily to his pen. While admitting to the sin of pride in imagining that he could have saved America single-handed, he protested that though

21 PRO FO 95/7/6, *ff.* 672-85 (English translation), 658-71 (Spanish original).

22 PRO FO 95/7/6, *ff.* 731-34.

the means had been unworthy, the end had been a noble one. 'Adieu, mon cher Sandhers', he concluded: 'recevez pour la dernière fois mes tendres embrassemens. Ayez autant de fermeté à apprendre ma mort que j'aurai de courage à la supporter: banissez les regrets qu'elle va vous donner. Vous aurez toujours la consolation de dire que votre ami Gutierrez est mort innocent, et si vous lui donnez quelques larmes, que cela soit pour avoir été victime du fanatisme dans le 19e siècle'.[23]

Dufour suggests that this letter was a last desperate throw by Gutiérrez to save his life by hinting to his captors, for whose eyes the letter was intended, that he still had state secrets to reveal ('il est assez naturel pour un homme qui a quelque caractère d'ensevelir eternellement des secrets aussi importants'). If that were so, he would surely not have been so uncomplimentary about the Central Junta, whom he depicted to his English friend as benighted reactionaries, 'les quels ... n'ont pas l'air d'être bien versés dans la Politique et ses grands mystères'; nor would he have been so frank in expressing the hope that he might be rescued at the last moment by the arrival of the French in Seville. The circumstantial details of the letter and its tone both point to its authenticity. In his final paragraph Gutiérrez had some instructions for his friend Sanders concerning some manuscripts he had left at London in his keeping. Three bound volumes were to be sent to a M. Louis Fauche at Bayonne, to be at his disposition. One of these was evidently the manuscript of an unpublished novel, another draft of which had been found in Gutiérrez's possession at the time of his arrest, along with some verses in Spanish 'sobre asuntos libres e indecentes'.[24] These literary papers, Gutiérrez told Sanders, had caused him more trouble than all the other documents relating to his mission — no doubt because they incriminated him as an infidel and a libertine. But there was one other manuscript in London which Sanders was asked to burn but which the Central Junta would dearly have liked to get its hands on. It was entitled *Historia de lo acaecido en Bayona en 1808* and is likely to have contained valuable inside

23 Full text of this letter in G. Dufour, 'Andanzas y muerte', 95-96.

24 Pascual Tenorio to Martín de Garay, Lisbon, 2 February 1809 (AHN 5438).

information about the events surrounding the abdication of Ferdinand VII, of which his supposed representatives, the Central Junta, still knew next to nothing. It is not surprising that the Secretary of the Central Junta, Martín de Garay, should have written so urgently to his envoy in London instructing him to trace 'Mr Sanders' in order to recover this document.[25] Gutiérrez had written to his friend at '74 Winchester Street', but this address proved to be non-existent. Gutiérrez's command of English was evidently minimal, so the matter may be explained by a confusion or misunderstanding on his part. It is just possible that these unpublished works of Luis Gutiérrez are still lying undiscovered in a family archive.[26]

Though the letter to Sanders shows that *Cornelia Bororquia* was not the last of Gutiérrez's literary works, his greatest fiction was the one he played out in real life in London, Lisbon and Seville. After a lifetime of moral and political compromise, of playing second fiddle to those whom he regarded as his inferiors, he seems to have glimpsed an opportunity of redeeming himself and benefiting his fellow men by using the only gifts he possessed — duplicity, imagination and recklessness — in a utopian cause. America was the *tabula rasa* on which he would write what would be at the same time his masterpiece and a new chapter in the history of the world. He may have been exceptional in his *hubris*, but he was not the only *ilustrado* to make America the vehicle of his frustrated idealism, an Eden in which he might vicariously regain his innocence. The same idea may be found in Quintana's famous invocation of 'Virgen del mundo, América inocente', and in

25 Martín de Garay to Admiral Apodaca, 18 April and 13 June 1809 (Simancas E 8284).

26 Sanders cannot be identified with any certainty, but I venture the guess that he may have been the Scottish painter George Sanders (1774-1846), best known for his portraits of Byron. Gutiérrez knew little English and for obvious reasons shunned society while in London. However, he had some contact with the miniaturist commissioned by the Foreign Office to execute a portrait of Ferdinand VII to adorn the box containing the royal seal which was to be forwarded to Mexico. Sanders, being the leading miniaturist of the day, would have been the obvious choice for the task. It is perhaps not coincidental that he was later a friend of Blanco White and his brother Fernando. See V. Llorens, *J. M. Blanco White: Antología de obras en español* (Barcelona: Editorial Labor, 1971), 350.

Blanco White's vision of a time 'when the Arts, Science and Happiness which are about to be banished from Europe, will take shelter in the Spanish colonies of America and there thrive to the most glorious state of prosperity'.[27] Even Napoleon himself had dreamed such dreams. The Abbé de Pradt recalled how at Bayonne 'il parla, ou plutôt il *ossianisa* pendent longtemps sur l'immensité des trônes du Mexique et du Perrou, sur la grandeur des souverains qui les posséderaient et sur les résultats que ces établissements auraient pour l'univers ... Il fut sublime: je ne l'ai plus revu a la même hauteur'.[28] Gutiérrez claimed to have been privy to the discussions which took place between French ministers and he evidently saw himself as uniquely qualified, by reason of his inside information, to play the French at their own perfidious game. It is not inconceivable that his American dream may have owed something also to his conversations in Bayonne with those ardent and visionary advocates of American independence, Fray Servando Teresa de Mier and Simón Rodríguez.

Fate had decreed, however, that Gutiérrez should end his life not as the Barón de Agra but as Cornelia Bororquia, and he played out with some courage the part that he had written for himself. Not the least of the ironies attending his career is the fact that his fictional heroine went on to be celebrated as a 'historical' martyr of intolerance in the very city where, after an all too real death, he sank into oblivion.

27 Manuel Quintana, 'Oda a la expedición española para propagar la vacuna en America', in *Poesías completas*, ed. M. Dérozier (Madrid: Castalia, 1963), 301-06; Martin Murphy, *Blanco White: Self-Banished Spaniard* (London: Yale U. P., 1989), 125. See the further references cited by André Pons in his doctoral thesis for the University of Paris, *Blanco White et la crise du monde hispanique, 1808-1814* (Lille: Atelier Nationale de Réproduction des Thèses, 1990), I, 745, n. 142.

28 Abbé de Pradt, *Mémoires historiques sur la révolution d'Espagne* (Paris, 1816), pp. 112-13, 131-32.

Rivas and Tragedy: The Cases of *El Duque de Aquitania* and *Malek-Adhel*

DONALD L. SHAW

University of Virginia

In some earlier essays[1] we have glanced at certain eighteenth-century plays commonly classed as tragedies and at the relation of Rivas' initial attempts at tragedy to them. The conclusion of these studies was that the outlook of the Enlightenment, with its emphasis on reason, humanity, virtue and moderation, was intrinsically anti-tragic. As a result, there was a tendency to dramatize events which were merely unhappy or unfortunate rather than productive of genuine tragic emotion: love, for instance, in powerful individuals, breaking the bounds of reason, prudence or morality and threatening political stability, or else malignity, allied to ambition or vengefulness, sowing dissention and causing suffering. At best, we approach heroic tragedy; that is to say: plays which contain situations fraught with tragic potentiality, but in which this is offset by the nobility of mind, courage, devotion and magnanimity of a hero or heroine. The difference between heroic tragedy and traditional tragedy is, of course, that the former retains some degree of tragic pathos, while at the same time avoiding any serious challenge to the existential confidence of the audience.

1 D. L. Shaw, 'Dramatic Technique and Tragic Effect in García de la Huerta's *Raquel*', *Dieciocho*, IX (1986), Nos 1-2, 249-58; 'Montiano's *Athaulpho*', *BHS*, LXVIII (1991), 153-61; '*Ataulfo*, Rivas's First Drama', *HR*, LVI (1988), 231-42; and 'Acerca de *Aliatar* del Duque de Rivas', in *Entresiglos* (Roma: Bulzoni, 1993), II, 237-45.

We have argued that Rivas' *Ataulfo* and *Aliatar*, in so far as they qualify at all as tragedies, do so in the sense abovementioned. On the other hand, *Don Álvaro* is in a quite different category.

Rivas' evolution as a dramatist has been repeatedly discussed, notably by Peers, Boussagol, Lovett and Caldera,[2] but curiously, although all of Rivas' first five plays were called tragedies, there has been no satisfactory attempt to analyse them as such. It could be argued that such an examination is not without importance, in view of Ricardo Navas Ruiz's characterization of *Don Álvaro* as a 'tragedia moderna' based on the incomprehensibility of the human condition[3] and the arguments contained in Richard Cardwell's crucially important article '*Don Álvaro* or The Force of Cosmic Injustice'.[4] If, as Alborg, following Navas Ruiz and Cardwell, affirms, *Don Álvaro* is based on a view of fate which symbolizes 'la existencia como algo caótico y disparatado',[5] a view which now seems to be increasingly accepted, how does this fit with Rivas' earlier tragedies? Are we dealing here with a process of gradually intensifying insight in which fate is always the key-concept, as César de la Peña Izquierdo seems to argue[6] or should we agree with Caldera's dismissive remark: 'en comparación con el *Don Álvaro* las tragedias parecen ejercicios escolares'?[7] It is hoped that a brief examination of *El Duque de Aquitania* (1817) and *Malek-Adhel* (1818) will throw some light on the issue.

---

2 Edgar Allison Peers, *Ángel de Saavedra, Duque de Rivas: A Critical Study*, *Revue Hispanique*, LVIII (1923); Gabriel Boussagol, *Ángel de Saavedra, duc de Rivas, sa vie, son oeuvre poétique* (Toulouse: Privat, 1926); Gabriel Lovett, *The Duke of Rivas* (Boston: Twayne, 1977); Ermanno Caldera, 'De *Aliatar* a *Don Álvaro*. Sobre el aprendizaje clasicista del Duque de Rivas', *Romanticismo* (Genoa), I (1982), 109-25.

3 Ricardo Navas Ruiz, Introduction to his edition of *Don Álvaro* (Madrid: Espasa-Calpe, 1975).

4 *Studies in Romanticism*, XII (1973), 559-79.

5 José Luis Alborg, *Historia de la literatura española*, IV, *El romanticismo* (Madrid: Gredos, 1980), 497.

6 In Various Authors, *Homenaje a Ángel de Saavedra* (Cordoba: Instituto de Bachillerato Ángel de Saavedra, 1991), 73-107.

7 Caldera, *op. cit.*, 124.

We should note at the outset that practically all critics (in particular Peers and Lovett) follow Pastor Díaz[8] in preferring *Malek-Adhel* to its immediate predecessor, though even Peers, who deals with the early plays in most detail, gives no very convincing reason for this preference. Characteristically, he spends most of the time he gives to the two plays to reviewing their sources, as indeed does Boussagol. Adams, for his part, in a brief reference to the early plays, is chiefly concerned with the degree to which they mark stages in Rivas' gradual conversion to Romanticism,[9] while Caldera, after noting that the two plays under consideration here repeat the formula of *Aliatar*, concerns himself chiefly with aspects of expression. These critics and Lovett leave aside the question of whether the plays are what they purport to be, despite the fact that Rivas' changing conception of tragedy is obviously germane to the wider question of whether the major Spanish Romantic plays are tragedies and if so, what kind of tragedies they are.

The principal reason why *Malek-Adhel* is a far better play than *El Duque de Aquitania* is to be found precisely by comparing them as tragedies. Unless we regard the dramatization of unfortunate events in the lives of socially eminent personages as *ipso facto* tragic, *El Duque de Aquitania* is not a tragedy at all. Indeed it falls in this respect below the level of *Ataulfo* and *Aliatar* in the sense that we cannot even make out a case for it as a heroic or semi-heroic tragedy. It is in fact a moralistic melodrama, as is attested by Rivas' own description of it in the dedicatory verses quoted by Peers.[10] There Rivas calls it a 'moral ficción', which:

> Pinta el furor de las pasiones,
> la austeridad de la moral sublime,
> y la venganza atroz de los delitos.

This is not a formula for tragedy even in the broadest sense.

---

8 Quoted by Enrique Ruiz de la Serna in his prologue to Rivas' *Obras completas* (Madrid: Aguilar, 1945), lxxxv.

9 Nicholson B. Adams, 'The Extent of the Duke of Rivas' Romanticism', in Various Authors, *Homenaje a Rodríguez-Moñino* (Madrid: Castalia, 1966), 1-7. His remarks are too brief to do more than suggest that *Malek-Adhel* is the most Romantic of Rivas' plays before *Don Álvaro*.

10 Peers, *op. cit.*, 158.

The dramatic forces in conflict are, on the one hand, Eudón, the tyrannous usurping Duke of Aquitaine, and on the other his niece Elisa and her brother Reynal, the rightful heir to the Dukedom. Eudón has connived at the death of his brother, Reynal's father, the former Duke and has had Reynal himself immured in a dungeon in Jerusalem. Reynal, however, has escaped and returned in disguise to claim his inheritance and to revenge himself on his uncle. In between Eudón and Elisa/Reynal is the courtier Linser who is also in love with Elisa. Finding her in her brother's arms, however, he precipitates the crisis of the conflict out of mistaken jealousy. This is clearly not a tragic conflict, that is to say, a conflict between more or less equally justified forces. Eudón is revealed to be a cowardly usurper in the second scene of Act I, while Elisa emerges as a wholly innocent victim. Thereafter, in Acts II and III, Reynal is portrayed in a highly positive light as he prepares to stand up nobly against Eudón's tyranny,[11] calling on his father's former vassals to defend his rights, while at the same time saving his sister from a repugnant marriage. We are in the presence of a straightforward struggle between good and evil. By the same token, no-one in the play is called upon to make a rending internal decision and hence to undergo a tragic evolution of character. At worst, in the last act, Elisa is forced by Eudón to choose between marrying him or bringing about the death of her brother.

The structure of *El Duque de Aquitania* underlines its melodramatic conception. Act I is competently organized and dramatically effective. Eudón proposes marriage unsuccessfully to a startled and reluctant Elisa as the play begins. His explanation of his ignoble motives separates this opening scene from that of the arrival of Reynal (unrecognized by Eudón and Linser, but surely understood by the audience to be the young heir). With the false news of Reynal's death which the stranger brings, Eudón is overjoyed, but Linser is plunged into jealous despair at the now almost certain prospect of a marriage

---

11 Boussagol, *op. cit.*, 169 correctly points out that the play's 'phraséologie tyrannicide', which portends that of *Lanuza* in 1822, is of some significance. But, as he recognizes, *El Duque de Aquitania*, is about vengeance, not about tyranny.

between the Duke and Elisa. Now, however, Eudón leaves the stage for a full two acts; a worse mistake than the one Rivas had made in *Ataulfo*, where the forces in conflict are unwisely developed separately in Acts I and II. Here Rivas devotes the entire second and third acts to developing Reynal as the counterforce to Eudón. The obvious consequence is that even if one of the characters were to emerge as having potentially tragic stature, there would be insufficient time, in the last two acts, to bring it out adequately. As it is, the play remains static after Act I, except for the role of Linser, who proposes to Elisa at the end of Act II and symmetrically finds her in the arms of Reynal (whom he mistakes for a rival) at the end of Act III. Thus, instead of a tragic agent, we merely have a jealous tell-tale pushing on his master to revenge himself. In the last act, however, after Elisa has resisted pressure to save her once more imprisoned brother by marrying Eudón, a popular rebellion causes the deaths of both the latter and Linser.

Rivas has here abandoned the formula he had probably taken from García de la Huerta's *Raquel* of counterbalancing the tragic potentiality of uncontrolled passion, where the wellbeing of the state is at risk, with the grandeur of conduct of one or more of the characters involved. Instead he has fallen into the typically eighteenth-century trap of believing that tragedy could be used to reconcile the audience to explicitly moral values. Tragedy was thought to arise when the Enlightenment ideal of rational harmony and virtue governing society is threatened by passion and/or malignity on the part of a powerful and highly-placed personage. But for this to be the case, the figure involved must become aware of the disharmony his or her behaviour is creating and undergo a process of inner struggle between temptation and the dictates of conscience. By this means a measure of tragic pathos can be created, though only with difficulty. But nothing like this happens in *El Duque de Aquitania*, where harmony is restored by physical force. Virtue and right triumph, not because Eudón overcomes himself, but because Providence, according to the faithful Arnaldo, or ' el poderoso brazo/ del dios de las venganzas' (Act III, scene III) in the opinion of Reynal, has intervened to put matters right.

This is more important than it seems at first sight. When in

Act IV, scene VI, Reynal affirms:

> el Cielo
> que, benigno, a los buenos apadrina,
> me arrancará de la prisión ...

he is merely echoing what Elvira and García had repeatedly proclaimed in *Aliatar*. However, what triumphed in that play was not divine protection, but adverse fate, just as was to happen again in *Don Álvaro* where in Act I, scene VII, Álvaro declares 'Dios nos bendecirá desde su esfera' and Leonor later asserts that 'la voz del cielo' had drawn her to Hornachuelos! For that reason, we have argued, *Aliatar* has a special place not only in Rivas' development as a dramatist, but in the prehistory of Spanish Romantic drama as a whole. In *El Duque de Aquitania*, by contrast, the action is predicated on the idea of an ultimately harmonious Providential universe. It reveals what Rivas' later evolution was amply to confirm: that his ideology was inherently unstable. In *Aliatar* he had taken a hesitant but recognizable step towards the *cosmovisión* of the subversive Romantics. Now in *El Duque de Aquitania* he reverts to the notion of a fatherly world according to design, attempting, without success, to contradict *Aliatar* and to halt the process of insight which was leading him towards *Don Álvaro*.

Support for this interpretation of Rivas' can be found without difficulty in *Malek-Adhel*. The question here is not simply the extent to which the play exhibits Romantic characteristics. What is fundamental is to perceive the play as a tragic metaphor, what Matthew Arnold called 'a criticism of life'. Nothing more clearly illustrates the sterility of examining Romantic and pre-Romantic plays from the standpoint of whether they are realistically convincing in terms of plot-structure or characterization than Crespo's account of *Malek-Adhel*. It concludes that the play is 'la menos afortunada de las tragedias de Saavedra'.[12] Not only is this view at odds with mainstream critical opinion, but also, if the arguments just deployed about *El Duque de Aquitania* have any validity, it ignores the basic point that *Malek-Adhel*, in contrast to all Rivas' earlier plays, for the first time contains a really tragic

12 Ángel Crespo, *El Duque de Rivas* (Madrid: Júcar 1985), 60.

conflict and generates a sense of genuine pathos. If *Aliatar* had brought the question of fate to the forefront, *Malek-Adhel* focuses directly on the theme which was to be crucial to the last part of *Don Álvaro*: the struggle between love and religion. When Álvaro exclaims:

¡Señor ... esfuerzo
me dé vuestra santa ayuda!

and later in the same scene:

¡Oh Dios! ¿Me rehusa
Vuestra gracia sus auxilios? (Act V, scene VI)

we cannot appreciate the full force of his words unless we can put them into the context created by the earlier plays. In *Aliatar*, as we have mentioned, despite the confidence of the lovers that heaven will come to their aid, fate strikes them down. Troubled perhaps, in the more traditional part of himself, by what he had written in *Aliatar*, Rivas drew back in *El Duque de Aquitania* towards a more comforting metaphor of existence. But his choice of Mme Cottin's novel as the source for *Malek-Adhel*, seems to indicate that he was ready again to face a world-view in which Fate and Providentialism clash. The whole of Rivas' literary output up to 1841 attests this duality within his outlook. Peers was never more correct in all his many writings about Rivas than when, in *A History of the Romantic Movement in Spain*, he attributed the Duke's failure to become the leader of the Spanish Romantics to the fact that he 'alternated reactionary works so exasperatingly with progressive [ones]'.[13] It is the key to his literary personality.

Clearly, Rivas did not choose Mme Cottin's novel by chance. What evidently triggered his creativity in her story was that it contained something which he wanted to develop through the medium of a different genre. It was the open conflict between love and Christianity, with fate playing an indispensible role. This is the true stuff of tragedy. It expresses the awareness, intrinsic to all true examples of the genre, that the plight of the individual is tragic, not only because of external social constraints or ideological oppression, but because the human

13 Edgar Allison Peers, *A History of the Romantic Movement in Spain* (Cambridge: Cambridge U. P., 1940), II, 51.

condition itself is essentially conflictive and because human experience at the deepest level is not compatible with a harmonious cosmic explanation. Symbolic of the play's emphasis on pathos derived from unresolvable inner tension is the fact that it is Rivas' only play which begins with a genuine soliloquy.[14] Its function is to identify Matilde, from the play's opening, as a tragic victim and thus to prioritize at once the theme of her inner struggle, rather than using the initial scene conventionally to provide information needed by the audience. In addition, Matilde's soliloquy is highly effective in creating suspense. In less than forty lines we learn that the Christian princess has fallen in love with a Moslem prince and that her fate is to be decided that very day, hopefully through the intervention of a saintly prelate. As the curtain rises we are plunged into a situation in which human love runs directly counter to strongly held religious convictions, underscored by the 'symbolic space' in which the main part of the action occurs, the Palace of the Crusader kings, and by the atmosphere of religious conflict.

The innovative use of an opening soliloquy is only the first indication of the fact that *Malek-Adhel* is Rivas' first dramatically well-constructed play. In contrast to *Aliatar* and *El Duque de Aquitania* where the dramatic forces are developed separately from each other with grave detriment to the plays' tempo, here there is some form of outer confrontation and inner struggle in each act. Moreover, the plot as a whole is more organically integrated than in any of the previous plays. There are two sets of opposing forces in *Malek-Adhel*. On the one hand the lovers, bound together by a solemn oath, freely taken by Matilde after Malek had twice saved her life, are drawn asunder by their differing religious faiths. On the other, the consummation of their love is threatened by the decision of Ricardo (Richard the Lion Heart) to give Matilde in marriage to his comrade in arms Lusiñán. Thus a human level of conflict, based on political considerations, and one on a much deeper

14 Lisandro's complaints in the opening scene of *El desengaño en un sueño* are not a true soliloquy since they function in counterpoint with Marcolán's remarks. Even so, their purpose is similarly to present Lisandro as standing at an inner crossroads.

level, based on opposing religious beliefs, are deftly intertwined in each act and come together in the catastrophe when Lusiñán and his men-at-arms murder Malek for reasons connected both with jealousy and religious hatred.

In several major Romantic plays the fate-motif and the *plazo* are important elements. At the symbolic level they tend to reinforce one another as indications of life's hostility. Here they are already both part of the action, but in an undeveloped form, in the sense that, while it is an irony of fate that Matilde should be doubly indebted to — and deeply in love with — a Moslem, fate as such does not play an active role in the working out of the plot. Similarly, although Guillermo imposes a *plazo* of three days during which Malek must embrace Christianity, it is Lusiñán's hostility which brings about the Prince's death before the *plazo* runs out. Nevertheless, we must not overlook the fact that they figure in the plot, revealing by their presence that Rivas, after slipping back in *El Duque de Aquitania* towards the traditionalist mind-set with its desire for a re-integrating, authoritative, Providentialist world-view, was now moving cautiously forward towards once more bringing that world-view into question.

A problem with *Don Álvaro* when one looks at it as a tragedy is the disproportion which exists between Álvaro as an isolated human being and the ironically unjust fatality which he faces. He cannot really struggle against this opposing dramatic force, but only suffer its successive onslaughts. This situation is partly prefigured in *Malek-Adhel*, where the lovers are similarly at the mercy of circumstances which are too powerful for them to resist successfully. Hence, neither Matilde nor Malek can be said to undergo a tragic evolution of personality arising out of the need to make a tragic choice.[15] This is not a minor point: all the major Romantic plays operate like this. The individual is never allowed to rise nobly to the level of his or her destiny, but is instead inexorably crushed. Precisely for this reason the greatest Romantic plays, with the exception of Zorrilla's *Don*

---

15 Boussagol sees in this the play's basic defect as a tragedy. But his argument is self-contradictory. On the one hand he asserts that the play is Racinian, in that it deals only with the crisis of the situation; on the other, that Rivas does not allow himself enough time to develop the religious conflict.

Juan Tenorio, involve, as Navas Ruiz points out with regard to *Don Álvaro*, 'la negación de una imagen del mundo'. Such is the case also with *Malek-Adhel*.

If we compare its first act with Act I of *El Duque de Aquitania* we can already see that this is so. In the opening scene of the earlier play Elisa is already endangered by the combination of passion and *razón de estado* in Eudón, who pressures her to marry him without delay. But no sooner are we given the explanation for his impatience than the counterforce appears in the person of Reynal, who will eventually, against all odds, overcome both Eudón's lust and his tyranny. This is not just a question of juxtaposing the play's two dramatic forces. It prefigures and symbolizes the whole theme of the play, in which virtue is threatened but Providence promptly provides a remedy. In *Malek-Adhel*, on the other hand, the implication of the first act is quite different. Already in her soliloquy, we recognize Matilde to be in the grip of adverse circumstances and on the brink of emotional disaster. Scene II, in which we learn the full extent of her unhappy situation, reinforces and amplifies the effect. But then, instead of a counterforce appearing to sustain her, Ricardo enters and in his first speech heaps more misery on her by announcing that she must marry Lusiñán. A second blow has fallen on the head of the defenceless victim.

The respective structures of the opening acts of *El Duque de Aquitania* and *Malek-Adhel*, then, convey radically different messages. Bearing in mind the dramatic arrangement of *Ataulfo* and *Aliatar*, we could now expect the action of *Malek-Adhel* to languish, while Rivas, after removing Matilde from the stage, builds up the other dramatic force. Instead, with an irony that is as yet unsuspected by the audience, he not only opens Act II with Matilde on stage, but shows her hopes fulfilled by the arrival of the saintly bishop Guillermo, accompanied by Malek, who has not only found him in the nick of time but also, for the second time, saved his life. This is the high point of Matilde's fortunes in the play. Fate appears to have granted her wish to submit her case to Guillermo's arbitration and to employ his powers of persuasion to convert Malek. But no sooner have the two men appeared than Matilde's illusions begin to fade. Crespo writes dismissively of

Malek-Adhel because, in his view, the characterization is faulty.[16] However, attempts such as his to apply modern standards of psychological verisimilitude to Romantic plays are methodologically unsatisfactory. Guillermo is a medieval bishop whom one would expect to have an unbending hostility to the Moslem Malek. But this is not the point. Guillermo represents one of the horns of Matilde's dilemma, her sense of Christian duty, just as Malek represents the other: human love. Both are idealized in order to ensure that the conflict is fought out between equally justified forces. Guillermo has to be as intransigently Christian as Malek is Moslem or the tragic pathos of Matilde's situation would disappear. If there is an unconvincing element here it is Matilde's assumptions that Malek will be less persevering in his faith than she is in hers and that Guillermo's exhortations will inevitably prevail against the falsehood of Islamic belief. But love generates illusion.

The rest of Act II is a model of dramatic craftsmanship. It consists of four scenes, each of which performs a precise function within the mechanism of the plot. Now that Malek has returned and the lovers are reunited, the requirement is that the real conflict of the play, the struggle between human and divine love, must be muted or kept in reserve in preparation for its dramatic emergence to dominate the action near the end of Act III. Hence, in Act II scene ii this aspect of the drama is merely indicated, when Matilde, in return for a confirmation of her earlier oath to marry Malek or no-one, asks him pointedly whether he intends to destroy their chances of happiness by refusing conversion. But the conversation is cut short by the arrival of the jealous Lusiñán and the action swings over to the other side of the conflict. In symmetrical scenes Lusiñán defies Malek, establishing himself as the counterforce to the Moor at this level of the plot, but is then rejected by Matilde in a scene which decisively establishes the subordination of the rivalry of the two men to the rivalry of the two faiths. An interesting feature of these early plays is that Rivas' heroines never vacillate between two different claims on their affections. Rivas' women always know exactly which is their heart's choice

16 Crespo, *op. cit.*, 60.

and cleave to it implacably. It would be interesting to speculate about why the Duke seems to have been unwilling to envisage a situation in which a woman is simultaneously attracted to two different men. Lusiñán, at all events, never has a chance. Like Placidia in *Ataulfo* and Elvira in *Aliatar*, Matilde finds herself between two powerful lovers but, in spite of the dramatic potential implicit in such a position, she never for an instant allows this to affect her outlook or behaviour. Lusiñán's jealous passion has no role in the play other than to produce the catastrophe.

We now come to one of the play's most curious features. It will be recalled that in the third act of *Don Álvaro*, Álvaro and Carlos save each other's lives, before Carlos obliges his bosom friend and fellow-officer to kill him in a duel. We have argued in our introduction to the Castalia edition of the play (1986) that such a turn of events is too unrealistic to be anything but symbolic. Its function is to underline the ironic workings of fate. Precisely the same is true here in *Malek-Adhel*. No-one who reads the play as even a remotely realistic presentation of events can fail to overlook the apparently absurd situation which prefigures the technique of repetition that is so prominent in *Don Álvaro*. Malek not only saves Matilde's life twice, but also saves Guillermo's life twice! It is surely inconceivable that Rivas could have introduced this grotesquely unlikely detail into the plot for any other reason than the one which prevails in Act III of *Don Álvaro*. Malek is to be an impotent victim crushed between the millstones of love and religious fidelity. In order to emphasize not just the tragedy of his fate, but also its irony, Rivas makes the representatives of both love and religion, Matilde and Guillermo, owe their very lives to him, not once, but twice over. Nor should we overlook an additional irony. Before Guillermo's arrival, the Crusaders' Council had been about to sanction the marriage between Matilde and Malek-Adhel. Only after the bishop's remonstrances do the members change their minds. Thus is Malek rewarded for his magnanimity towards an enemy priest and for his success in finding him when the Christians had been unable to do so.

At the end of Act II Guillermo evades Hugo's question about Malek's religious position and the issue is left hanging until the pivotal sixth scene of Act III, when Guillermo's decision, endorsed by the Council, is announced. At this point the true tragic conflict in the play assumes its dominant position and thereafter gathers strength until the final catastrophe. The first five scenes of Act III, on the other hand, are devoted to Matilde's resolute defence of her love for Malek, in the face of her brother's opposition, Lusiñán's jealousy and penchant for violence, and Malek's anguished realization that Matilde is set on his conversion. By contrast, in Act IV, the first four scenes are the natural prolongation of scenes vi and vii of Act III: Matilde, already in despair at Guillermo's decision, receives an ultimatum from Malek and struggles to accept that the bishop's words express her Christian duty. After this, Ricardo and Lusiñán press the princess to accept a political marriage instead of clinging to the hope of Malek's conversion. For this they are sharply rebuked by Guillermo. In other words, taken together, Acts III and IV form a single dramatic unit in which the latent tragedy of the lovers' situation suddenly comes to the forefront of the play (Act III, scenes vi and vii; Act IV, scenes i-iv). These six scenes are the nub of the action. But they are enclosed and framed by scenes i-v of Act III and scenes v-vii of Act IV, which deal, not with the struggle between love and faith, but with the threat to Matilde and Malek from Ricardo and Lusiñán. The climax of Act IV is not one of despairing inner torment on the part of the lovers, but instead illustrates Lusiñán's inflexible determination to proceed with his intention to marry Matilde in spite of Guillermo's rebuke.

Why are Acts III and IV arranged like this? Rivas in 1818, writing under the despotically reactionary regime of Ferdinand VII, with whose censorship he had already had trouble, was on dangerous ground in *Malek-Adhel*. From a modern point of view, the section of the play between Guillermo's decision and the death of Malek should have been given over to the repercussions of the bishop's judgement, with both lovers torn between conflicting loyalties and the whole of Act IV generating a high level of tragic pathos. But, as we have seen, this is not at all what we find. Instead, the inner struggle of the two protagonists is played down and sandwiched in between two phases of the external struggle of Matilde against the pressure exerted by her brother and Lusiñán. This, and not the treatment of Guillermo, is the 'gran fallo' (in Crespo's words) of *Malek-Adhel*. It trivializes the play by shifting the emphasis just when we have reached the core of the action. But prudential considerations evidently prevailed. When Rivas in the early 1830s returned to the issue of human versus divine love at the end of *Don Álvaro*, he had in mind the much freer French theatre and was able to develop the conflict so memorably that it plays a major role in establishing the play as the central example of Spanish Romantic theatre. In 1818 he could only hint at what was to come.

The figure who is sacrificed on the altar of prudence is Malek-Adhel himself. Act V, like Act I, begins with a soliloquy, this time by Malek, in the second 'symbolic space' of the play, Montmorency's tomb, where the catastrophe occurs. All critics rightly mention this use of a tomb as paralleling the similar use of the Morosini family vault in Act II of Martínez de la Rosa's *La Conjuración de Venecia*, written ten years or more later. But we should not let this critical commonplace distract us from the irony suggested by this setting. Montmorency had died protecting Matilde; his tomb now becomes the scene of her most tragic experience. His sacrifice was powerless to prevent her future anguish. In the tomb, Malek reflects on the misery of his situation. But Rivas is careful not to bring human and divine love into open opposition. Instead Malek is made to refer to Matilde's religion, the source of his despair, in highly respectful tones. It all fits.

The problem of *Malek-Adhel*, we now see, is that when Guillermo in Act III invites Malek to abjure his religion or lose Matilde, Malek instantly refuses. When, on the other hand, Malek, in Act V, invites Matilde to set love above religion and flee with him (though remaining a Christian), she in turn dismisses the idea. Thus any tragic evolution of personality in either of them is precluded. We experience a certain impression of tragic pathos when Matilde confronts Guillermo in Act IV and more especially when she and Malek discuss their situation in the tomb in Act V. But these moments are only sporadic: both have already made their decision. The final outcome, the death of Malek, is not invested with any real sense of tragic inevitability and Matilde, instead of dying with him, ends the play on a note of symbolic reconciliation with the God who has presided over her anguish by retiring to a convent. Fernandine censorship would not have permitted any other outcome.

Similarly, there is no tragic error on the part of either of the lovers, unless falling in love is one. This, too, is not insignificant. Tragic error is not a factor in any of the major Spanish Romantic plays because the dramatists were not concerned with human failings which inadvertently set a tragic process on foot, but with innocent lovers crushed by an inexorably adverse human condition. So here, though Rivas had to tread carefully in his expression of the notion. None the less, for the first time in his theatre we find in *Malek-Adhel* a clash of equally justified forces accompanied by prominent elements of tragic irony. Rivas had at last set his foot on the path that would lead to *Don Álvaro*.

To conclude: *El Duque de Aquitania* and *Malek-Adhel* illustrate in the work of the same author the polarization of outlook which was to characterize the Spanish Romantic movement as a whole. Rivas' ambivalence is more visible than that of some of his more progressive minded contemporaries. But, as Derek Flitter has attempted to show,[17] the traditional world-view exerted great attraction even on Romantic writers who could see beyond nationalism and religion. In addition, the struggle between love and religion, timidly adumbrated in *Malek-Adhel*, was to remain crucial to Romantic sensibility until Zorrilla, as David Gies puts it, 'changes the equation', bringing high Romantic drama to an end in renewed respectability and popular orthodoxy.[18]

---

17 *Spanish Romantic Literary Theory and Criticism* (Cambridge: Cambridge U. P., 1992), *passim*.

18 'José Zorrilla and the Betrayal of Spanish Romanticism', *Romanistisches Jahrbuch*, XXXI (1980), 339-46.

More on *El moro expósito*

MARGARET A. REES

Trinity and All Saints University College, Leeds

'Ha declarado el autor su intento al componer el siguiente poema', wrote Antonio Alcalá Galiano on behalf of Ángel Saavedra in the preface to *El moro expósito*. 'No ha pretendido hacerlo *clásico* ni *romántico*, divisiones arbitrarias, en cuya existencia no cree'.[1] This statement has been as effective in warding off arguments between literary theorists as a referee blowing his whistle to prevent violence before the teams have even set foot on the pitch. In spite of Rivas' bid for neutrality, scholars have classed the work as Romantic. Indeed for Allison Peers *El moro* and *Don Álvaro* between them embodied what he saw as the two characteristic elements of Spanish Romanticism — revival and revolt — and each for him was a masterpiece.[2] One well-known critical battle has raged over the question of whether Saavedra was already 'a Romantic in all essentials'[3] before his exile in Malta brought him under the cultural influence of the British diplomat John Hookham Frere, or whether his patron's influence brought about a literary Saul of Tarsus conversion. Another controversy centres on French claims to have turned Rivas into a complete Romantic. *El moro* lends itself to this debate because it is not only long — an epic poem in twelve *romances* — but it was also long in gestation.

1 *El moro expósito*, ed. Ángel Crespo, 2 vols, Clásicos Castellanos 224, 225 (Madrid: Espasa-Calpe, 1982), I, 28. All references are to this edition, the numbers indicating volume and page, not canto and line.

2 E. Allison Peers, *Rivas and Romanticism in Spain* (London: Hodder and Stoughton, 1923), 13-14.

3 *Ibid.*, 39.

The first five *romances* were composed in Malta in 1829. In 1830 Rivas and his family sailed for France where he stayed until the amnesty of 1834. The tenth canto is dated Paris 1832 and the last was completed in Tours in 1833.

On the first issue Allison Peers is convinced, after analysing all Rivas' earlier works from the age of fifteen onwards, 'that the leaven of pre-Romanticism had long been at work within him, and that he was strongly disposed to receive Romantic influences, at about the time of his first emigration'.[4] (This period of exile was spent in Gibraltar and England in 1824.) Peers concludes: 'Rivas' Romanticism was a growth, and not the result of a conversion ... There is very little in the *Moro Expósito* which cannot be found in germ in the poems of 1806 to 1830'.[5] Critics as eminent as Menéndez Pidal have taken up the cudgels to defend Hookham Frere's role as initiator into Romanticism, a role upheld by the poet's brother-in-law, the literary critic Leopoldo Augusto de Cueto.[6]

As for the French claim to be the main influence on one of the landmarks of Spanish Romanticism, Gabriel Boussagol is one of the leading spokesmen. He sees a clear difference between the cantos written in Malta and those produced on French soil.

> Certes, il est loin de ma pensée d'attribuer à la seule influence française le renouvellement de la technique chez Rivas, et celui de sa vision poétique. Mais je ne puis croire que la nouveauté qui éclate dans certaines parties du *Moro* ... soit due au seul épanouissement de son génie, qui se serait produit, comme par enchantement, après son arrivée en France ... Quand il quitte Malte, notre poète compte vingt-trois ans d'activité et de production littéraires: le moins qu'on puisse dire de lui, c'est qu'il n'est plus un débutant. Mais il lui a fallu l'exemple des 'apôtres privilégiés, V. Hugo, A. Dumas, A. de Vigny' dont les oeuvres le 'fascinaient' ... N'avons-nous pas remarqué comme une coupure entre le Ve et le VIe romances? ... pourquoi ne pas constater

---

4 *Rivas and Romanticism*, 39.

5 *Ibid.*, 43.

6 Ramón Menéndez Pidal, *La epopeya castellana a través de la literatura española* (Buenos Aires: Espasa-Calpe, 1945).

> qu'entre le Ve et le VIe romances il y a eu le départ de Malte, l'arrivée à Marseille, le séjour à Orléans, à Paris, à Tours?[7]

When scholars of such eminence clash, the only prudent course would be to take cover so as to avoid being shot down in the cross-fire. Throwing prudence to the winds, it is tempting to put critical arguments out of mind for a while and to take another look at the text of *El moro.* It is true that Boussagol mentions revisions being made in the first five *romances* before publication but clearly, if their creator had swung suddenly from one literary ideology to another during the five years spanning their composition, the work could not have been completed, any more perhaps than Picasso could have painted *Les Demoiselles d'Avignon* in the same phase that produced *The Boy with the Dove.* Perhaps yet another glance at imagery, descriptions, characters, supernatural elements, humour, themes and motifs might reveal gradual change or — significantly — the absence of change.

Imagery is thought to be one of the clearest mirrors of a writer's innermost being. Here, in spite of Boussagol's opinion[8] that in the 'French' cantos classical phraseology had disappeared apart from certain formulas depicting natural phenomena, there seems to me no difference from the beginning of Canto I to the end of the last canto. Romanticism slipped the leash of the Age of Reason to let the creative imagination roam free, but from start to finish Rivas' similes and metaphors remain neo-classical and often stereotyped; the angle of comparison is narrow. In the first five cantos, written in Malta, the 'fire' of ambition burns (93), as does the 'volcano' of both a villain's and the heroine's passion (at least twice in the heroine's case) (91-92, 102, 106), as well as the 'flame' of love (56). Rivas, like many a born story-teller, has no qualms about repetition. The clouds form 'un velo' on many a page (e.g. I, 104), and night's mantle, surely tattered through centuries of use, is repeatedly drawn over the sky (I, 94, 125, 135, 243). Classical personifications have their own accustomed adjectives,

---

7 Gabriel Boussagol, *Ángel de Saavedra, duc de Rivas, sa vie, son oeuvre poétique* (Toulouse: Imprimerie et Librairie Edouard Privat, 1926), 446-47.

8 See *op. cit.*, 246.

used like Homeric epithets. 'La ciega Fortuna', for instance, makes her first appearance on page 39 before going on to overshadow the whole work. This does not mean that the imagery is not attractive. Nothing in nature, we are told, can surpass Kerima with her eyes like shining suns, her face of jasmine and rose, her throat of snow, breasts and arms of alabaster.

> No la hermosa azucena más lozana
> la blanca frente y el erguido cuello,
> reina de los jardines, alza en mayo,
> de la risueña aurora a los destellos;
>
> no más gentil orillas del arroyo,
> precursor de las flores, el almendro
> se mece ufano en tarde sosegada
> de las auras de abril al blando aliento. (I, 97)

By the time he wrote the second batch of cantos Rivas had been exposed to the growing vividness and originality of French Romantic imagery. One of the points at which the first performance of *Hernani* in 1830 almost ground to a halt, it will be remembered, was when the heroine had the temerity to address her beloved as 'mon lion brave et généreux', and readers of poetry were scandalized or elated by Musset's evocation of the moon 'comme un point sur un i'.[9] This exposure seems to me to have done nothing to renovate *El moro*'s imagery. Phrases like 'de su ambición la nave' (II, 193) and 'el astro de sus últimos amores' (II, 101) are still closer to Voltaire's language than to Hugo's. In the very last section Mudarra's hand at the wedding altar is 'fire', Kerima's is 'crudo hielo' (II, 344), and as she renounces her bridegroom for the convent the guests 'de mármol quedan' (II, 345). Perhaps the only metaphor that leaps out of the page, because it foreshadows Larra's horrendous portrayal of Madrid in 'Día de difuntos', is Nuño's reaction to Castile 'que un vasto cementerio era a sus ojos' (II, 65). *El moro* may be in verse, but Rivas' brilliant creative gifts are seen in his word-pictures rather than in the original imagery often associated with poetry from the Romantic period onwards.

---

9 'Ballade à la lune', *Contes d'Espagne et d'Italie*, 1830.

As for the delight he shares with Hugo in exotic vocabulary, this is present already in the Maltese cantos. The Moorish wedding 'en la hermosa luna de Giumada' has its 'almuedén', 'mezquita', 'atabales', 'añafiles', 'marlotas' and 'garzotas' (I, 51-52). In 1829 when these cantos were written, Hugo published *Les Orientales* and from this angle French and Spanish Romanticism were almost neck and neck in their progress.

It is when we turn to the pictorial passages for which Rivas is famous that a surprise lies in wait. Others may view the first canto differently, but it seems to me that the opening pages, including the exiled poet's invocation to his native Cordova, have no more colour or other sensuous detail than most neo-classical literature. Very little precise detail helps us to visualize the first dramatis personae to appear on stage. Zahira, for instance, is introduced as:

> Bella como el lucero refulgente,
> ...
> y cual la flor hermosa del desierto,
> melancólica siempre y retirada.
> ...
> reina de la belleza y de la gracia. (I, 42-43)

This might be the classical depiction of any eighteenth-century heroine, recording universal beauty and no specific detail, except for the one exotic Moorish touch of the comparison to a desert flower. The flowers in the gardens and woods are merely qualified as 'varias' (44). It is with the wedding scenes referred to above — still in the first canto — that colour, textures, scents and sounds envelop the reader in a plethora of riches that continues to the end of the epic. It is difficult to think of a reason for this monochrome beginning to a work full of brilliant colour, especially as Peers points out that from his earliest poems Rivas was a colourist (172-74).

Boussagol believes that the most often quoted passages were written in France,[10] but to my mind the Maltese cantos, after the first part of Canto I, are just as full of vivid word-pictures. 'Never, in Spain at least,' writes Peers, 'was there a writer with a more passionate love for colour, or with a better claim to be termed the painter-poet' (59). Not only colour but the interplay

10 See *op. cit.*, 447.

of light and dark conjures up gripping scenes, like that where the villainous Ruy-Velázquez and his two cronies are seen in a castle hall 'a la luz roja de la opaca tea'.

> ... Sus tres sombras,
> que la luz dibujaba en los sillares
>
> del muro, acaso vagas e indecisas
> al undular la llama, acaso estables
> y en gigantesca proporción ... (II, 208)

This is a skill already demonstrated in Malta with a gripping evocation of alternating fire and darkness in the night of terror that followed treacherous killing at the wedding (I, 172-74).

The impressive, large-scale crowd scenes that unfold from the first to the last cantos are not only richly hued historical tapestries of the type admirably executed by Romantics (in the thronging tableaux of Musset's *Lorenzacio*, for instance, or the banquet scene in Hugo's *Lucrèce Borgia*). One of the most striking characteristics about Rivas' scenes is the way in which he fills them with movement. Far from being static canvases, they are alive and bustling, carrying on the action rather than holding it up with a 'still'.[11] If the Romantics had possessed camcorders, they would surely have used them to obtain this type of effect. Hollywood itself would have been glad to have drawn for one of its teeming epics on passages such as:

> Parientes del Hagib, cien caballeros,
> con las marlotas de esplendente grana
> y con blancas gargotas los turbantes,
> corren de la ciudad calles y plazas
>
> en revueltos caballos berberiscos ... (I, 52-53)

Like a true Spaniard and ex-cavalryman, Rivas excels in capturing the movements of a horse in words (see II, 225 and 261).

One of the best known scenes of bustling activity, the preparation of a banquet, is like a Brueghel painting come to life. Chickens and hens dodge their pursuers between piles of

11 For further discussion of this point see Margaret A. Rees, 'Un consumado fabulador: el Duque de Rivas y *El moro expósito*', in *Atti del IV Congresso sul Romanticismo*, ed. E. Caldera (Genoa: Univ. of Genoa, 1988), 107-12.

firewood and jars; flames blaze under cooking pots; smoke billows; vegetables and pastry are prepared; birds are plucked; the fire tended; an old woman filches a black pudding by slipping it into her apron; a boy dips his finger into a honey jar; another surreptitiously samples the brandy. Meanwhile the housekeeper spins round in a dervish-like frenzy of activity, seasoning a stew, reprimanding servants, scalding the cat who was devouring half a pigeon, opening the wine cellar, bringing out the preserves, the towels and the silverware (II, 28-31). For Peers this figure, with her chestnut hair and costume of green, gold, blue, red and black, is too garish, but perhaps the loud colours were meant to be in character with this bustling factotum, as part of the affectionate caricature.

With their sights, scents, sounds and movements, the vast crowd scenes place *El moro*, from Canto I onwards, in the mainstream of Romanticism, with their abundant local colour. After the strange neoclassicism of the opening pages, Rivas paints individual portraits with the same specific detail. Already in Canto I we see Habiba dressed for her wedding in

> ... larga ropa rozagante
> de rica seda del color del alba,
> do brillan ...
> lazos de aljófar, flores de esmeraldas.

Her floor-length hair, more golden than the gold of Arabia, is decked with a rose garland. A veil of woven silver secured by a rich cameo and a head-dress of white plumes wave in the breeze. At her neck, round her arms and waist, on the border of her gown and on her sandals, pearls and sapphires shine (I, 55). No Romantic heroine anywhere could have wished for more fashionable bridal wear. Later, in France, Rivas pays just as much attention to a portrait of old age (II, 17-19). Throughout, characters with only a minimal role are given their visual identity. Giafar's false message is brought to Mudarra by 'un esclavo negro, / a quien de plata una bruñida argolla / cercaba en torno el atezado cuello' (I, 124).

The favourite motifs of Romantic writers certainly appear in the Maltese cantos as well as in those dating from France. In the second *romance* Mudarra stands by the dried-up 'fuente del Amir' at sunset, close to a moss-covered crag. Around him are the 'desnudas peñas' beloved by the Romantic movement, before him a panoramic view of a distant city with its gardens and palaces. Darkness falls on the autumnal scene until the moon rises slowly from thick clouds. The distant sounds of the city and the shepherds' voices on the plain die away. As the silence intensifies, the only sound is the rustling of dry leaves and the wings of night birds (I, 126-128). Puccini obtains the same spell-binding effect with his evocation of a city and a shepherd boy's voice in the last act of *Tosca*, though at dawn, not nightfall. Wild landscapes with crags and precipices, sometimes with attendant wolves, appear too in later cantos (II, 129 and 239-40).

Neither Espronceda nor Musset has the monopoly of moonlit nature. Habiba's wedding day ends, as Doña Sol's does in the last act of *Hernani*, in a palace whose surrounding gardens and woods are illuminated by the moon and by countless lanterns gleaming in the trees (I, 62-63). The appeal of Rivas' poetry is said to be visual rather than auditory, but lines in the next canto evoke the moon and nature with a music which brings Espronceda to mind. By moonshine, Mudarra

> dirigióse a un arroyo cristalino,
> que sobre guijas cándidas no lejos
> serpenteaba con murmurio manso,
> entre adelfas y frágiles helechos ... (I, 109)

Perhaps even more to Romantic taste was the depiction of ruins, and here *El moro* excels with an eighteen-stanza verbal reconstruction (II, 13-16) of the sights and sounds to be experienced in the deserted castle of the Laras. Apart from the wind howling, silence has fallen on the halls,

> silencio que tan sólo interrumpido,
> para mayor horror tal vez, se mira
> con el quejido en la espantosa noche
> del búho y del murciélago ... (15)

Gifted story-teller that he is, Rivas has the knack of creating the atmosphere of horror craved by readers of the 'new literature'. Towards the end of Canto V, before leaving Malta, he shows Kerima setting out at sunset on a stormy night when thunder roars like a lion. As she plunges into a wild path on the sierra, among pines and crags,

> un mar de fuego era el espacio a veces,
> a veces ciega noche, a que mezquino
> rayo de sol, muriendo en el ocaso,
> daba de horrenda luz pálidos visos.

Seeking shelter, she finds herself at the dreaded 'fuente del Amir': 'Un piélago de sangre es aquel sitio / a sus ojos, y en medio ve el espectro / de su padre feroz' (I, 266). Vengefully, the ghost calls down a curse upon his daughter. Even more horrific is the lengthy description of Giafar's corpse found swimming in its own blood, as a hungry wolf circles and a vulture flies off with blood on its beak (I, 233-235). Devotees of the horror novel or 'le bas romantisme' could ask nothing better, though the later cantos include a splendidly cinematographic scene full of sinister atmosphere. A panoramic view pictures the night as a whole, then the villain's castle in the distance. Moving in to a closer view, the camera of the verse lights on the vague shapes of guards on sentry duty, their weapons glittering. Torches are seen moving to and fro in the palace, then the focus moves to two windows, gleaming like wolves' eyes. Inside, Ruy-Velázquez, huddled in his cloak, paces up and down, throwing a huge shadow on the wall (II, 202-03).

Anyone wanting to make the case for French influence on *El moro* might point out that another prime Romantic theme — religiosity, the poetry of chapels and monastic buildings which is used to great effect in *Don Álvaro* — can be found only in the later *romances*. In a bright cameo of a scene Ruy-Velázquez enters a white-walled chapel glowing with torchlight. On a stone altar stands the statue of a black Virgin 'colorido / el rostro, y de oro y de trasflor las ropas', surrounded by 'siemprevivas, juncias, brezo y hierbas' and by wafting perfumes (II, 244-45). Far more detailed is the description of the monastery where the plot leads him (II, 260-64), but if Rivas is Romantic enough to add the horror-novel touch of a white-robed monk looking like a ghost, he is also Spanish realist enough to mention the 'discorde coro' whose voices 'por las cimbrias altísimas rimbomban', and the occasional cough is heard. French Romantic religiosity tends to exclude anything other than heavenly sounds from choir and organ. If the picturesque aspect of Christian worship does not figure in the earlier cantos from Malta, it could well be pointed out that this is because they deal predominantly with Moorish settings and beliefs, exotica which also entranced nineteenth-century readers.

For Boussagol, the 'French' cantos differ from the previous batch in their interplay of contrasts, the antithetical set of mind preached in Hugo's *Préface de Cromwell* as the only possible 'Weltanschauung' in the modern world. It is true that the first canto composed in France, Canto VI, opens with a long passage showing how totally unalike are Christian Burgos and Moorish Cordova, 'en todo cuán diversa y cuán distinta' (II, 10). Rivas sets against each other not only climate and architecture but also the sounds (the 'almuéden', the 'bullicio y alegría' of Cordovan squares; the harsh clangour of forges in Burgos, the 'monótono canto de los coros / de conventos, parroquias y capillas') in what reads like an exile's desperately homesick lament for Andalusia. This passage occurs in the later cantos, but the whole epic from its conception was based on the clash between two civilizations, as the sub-title — 'Córdoba y Burgos en el siglo décimo' — suggests. Already in Canto III Rivas makes a Moor underline the antithesis between 'La ignorancia y la rudeza / de aquel naciente reino, que, fundado / a fuerza de valor y de altos hechos, / hierro y ferocidad son sus ornatos' and 'nuestro florido y ancho imperio' (I, 149).

As far as descriptive techniques and themes are concerned, then, it seems to me that in 1829 Rivas in *El moro* and Hugo in *Les Orientales* were writing in parallel rather than as master and disciple. If we turn to look at the figures who people the Moorish and Castilian settings, surely *dramatis personae* conceived in a neo-classical mould could not, halfway through their gestation, have been transformed into Romantic heroes, heroines and villains? Boussagol believes something like this to have happened, with greater sentimentality in the style of Mme Cottin on display in the Maltese cantos, greater 'Sturm und Drang' in the French. If the divide had been extreme, it is difficult to see how the result would not have looked like those cardboard figurines cut in two so that children can amuse themselves by mismatching torsos and lower halves.

Mingling with the human actors is a truly Romantic horde of macabre spectres. In Malta Rivas and his family, so the story goes, first lived in a house with such a haunted atmosphere that the poet slept with a pistol on his bedside table. Whether or not this influenced him, Canto V has a horrific scene very like the Dance of Death in Espronceda's *El estudiante de Salamanca*. If anything, Rivas' blood-quaffing ghosts are even more fearsome than the capering skeletons that were to encircle the 'segundo Don Juan' (see I, 229-30). This is the same world of supernatural terror as Lewis' *The Monk* (1796), parts of Berlioz's *Symphonie fantastique* (1830) and Saint-Saëns' *Danse macabre* (1874). Rivas is superb in his ability to create spine-chilling atmospheres. In Canto IX he builds up a long crescendo of blood-curdling fear. The Moors who form young Lara's support group are rumoured to be not human but 'nigromantes', 'fantasmas', 'demonios'. As they circle the castle, 'alzan los pies del suelo, y por el aire / van como los cernaculos' (II, 214). In the next canto the villain's horse rears as a voice warns:

> 'tente ... ¿no adviertes, monstruo, que a su hermano
> socorro dando, en derredor se juntan
>
> los Infantes de Lara? ... ¿Seis espectros
> no ves? ... Pues tu caballo sí, y le asustan;
> por eso no se acerca.' (II, 301)

Spain with its bright, clear light may not in theory be a suitable home for the phantoms the nineteenth century loved to fear, but it is difficult to call to mind anything in Northern European literature which surpasses Rivas in this sphere.

On the human plane, the 'expósito' himself strikes me from the very outset as a blood brother of Hernani as well as of Don Álvaro. Perhaps at roughly the same time that Hugo was creating his mysterious outlaw to champion the French Romantic theatre, Rivas in Malta was conjuring up the image of his own hero, 'de presencia muy gallarda, / pero infeliz'. Tortured as he is by his mysterious background, like Hernani, 'ya la mano atroz de la tristeza / le rompe el corazón, le aprieta el alma' (I, 40). Canto I sees Mudarra, tortured mentally by 'espantosos espectros y fantasmas' of remorse, in a pose so archetypal that an illustrator could use it as the ideal source for the frontispiece of a study of the European Romantic hero.

> La espalda apoya a un solitario tronco,
> falto de fuerzas en tan gran borrasca,
> los brazos contra el pecho ahogado cruza,
> la frente inclina, y consternado calla. (I, 65)

The consuming love and self-hating death-wish which dominate so many of Hernani's ilk speak out clearly in his letter to his beloved.

> En dando cumplimiento al deber mío,
>
> la muerte buscaré: la muerte anhelo ...
> ¿Cómo sin ti vivir? Aborrecido
> te debe ser quien te privó de padre ...
> ¡Aborréceme! ... Sí, yo, yo a mí mismo
>
> me aborrezco también. (I, 250)

Kerima, whose likeness to Scott's Rebecca Allison Peers has noted,[12] is the very model of a demented Romantic heroine in the denouement, dramatically deserting her bridegroom for the cloister. Her appearance in the procession warns that she is a creature crazed by passion in the manner of Espronceda's Elvira, Giselle in the ballet or Lucia di Lammermoor in the opera. She is dressed 'con negligencia y abandono'. Her wild eyes, pallor, and even her way of moving and breathing make her seem 'cosa de otro mundo, / aparición o sueño vaporoso' (II, 340-41). Does she belong to the sisterhood of frenzied heroines only in the 'French' cantos? Ángel Crespo points out that in a much earlier canto the intensity of her jealous storm of emotion is already a sign of her mental fragility ('Introduction', xxix). Passage after passage describes her 'volcánico amor' (I, 243) and the intensity of all her emotions (e.g. I, 106-07, 244). She has only one thought: 'Mudarra nada más. Sí, de contino / le tiene ante sus ojos en mil formas, / en situaciones mil' (I, 257). She brings to mind Ophelia and Espronceda's Elvira 'una tarde que sola recorría, / con planta incierta y con los ojos fijos / en la tierra, su vergel' (I, 259). Later she runs through the countryside,

> desnuda el cuello, desceñida el cinto,
> suelta y volando a par de sus cabellos
>
> la blanca toca de delgado lino,
> ...
> y sus ojos brillantes y espantados. (I, 264)

---

12 See *op. cit.*, 98.

It seems that the passionate Romantic heroine was a fully fledged concept in Rivas' mind before his close encounter with the literary scene in Paris. *El moro* even has a second emotionally challenged woman. Elvida wanders the wild countryside, mad with grief for Gonzalo. Seen on a crag in winter, silhouetted against the moonlight, or wailing at night in the empty castle, she terrifies those who see or hear her (II, 140-43).

For good measure, we have two villains as black as anything in melodrama — 'el bárbaro Giafar' (I, 120) and Ruy-Velázquez, 'aquel demonio en carne humana' (II, 266). Eyes gleam with sinister light (I, 87) or are 'ojos de hiena' (I, 207); hearts are a 'horrible infierno' full of plots 'de sangre, de venganza, de exterminio' (I, 114). Bitter laughter contorts Giafar's features into a terrible sight (I, 123); as for Velázquez, that copybook villain, 'lumbre infernal resplandeció en su frente, / bañó su torva faz sonrisa horrenda' (I, 197). Rivas' sons must have had strong nerves if their bedtime tales included such characters. Again, these figures took shape before their creator left Malta. Even Romanticism's 'pathetic fallacy' can be seen in the early cantos. As the story is told of the infantes' dismembered heads, the seven memorial cypresses stir 'cual si tuvieran / instinto de tomar en tal momento / parte también en la solemne escena' (I, 209-10).

Like many a writer of his generation, Rivas displays his own emotions, such as the intensity of his feelings as the ghostly figures of the epic begin to take shape in his imagination (I, 38). Later, Romantic pessimism rears its head in a comment on the heroine's survival: 'Kerima sola fue más venturosa / (si es que quedar en este mundo es serlo)' (I, 94). Above all we hear the voice of the exile, living imaginatively in his homeland by recreating it in his verse. As the infantes' heads are to be taken back to Castile, he comments 'aun después de la muerte es gran desdicha / sufrir el peso de la extraña tierra' (I, 223).

Humour, believes Boussagol, is an ingredient in *El moro* which characterizes the cantos written in France, reflecting, as comic and tragic episodes intermingle, 'l'influence ... toute puissante du romantisme français' (247). It is true that the cartoon-like humour satirizing, for instance, the abbot and his monks figures in the French cantos (e.g. II, 270-76). Even the tragic drama of the last scene includes a reference to the archbishop's sermon 'que no fue corto' (II, 344). We seem at last to have come upon a facet of *El moro* which reflects contact with France. Yet a character created in Malta is portrayed in the same humorous light. Kerima has an old prattling nurse very like that in *Romeo and Juliet* (I, 100-02).

The reading of a text can be so subject to varying interpretations that it sometimes seems as if literary criticism is a fourth stage in the progression 'lies, damned lies, and statistics'. Yet it is perhaps possible to argue that the three characteristics Donald Shaw notes in his penetrating study of Romanticism — 'a negative view of life, love as the only real existential prop, and regular reference to adverse fate'[13] — are securely in place from the opening of *El moro*, as are the other traits I have examined. The idea of fate or 'el providencialismo' in Rivas's writings is crucial, and it forms the very spine of this work from start to finish. Just as obvious are the poem's fashionable medievalism and oriental exoticism. I have tried to suggest that, despite *El moro*'s long gestation and its exposure to the French literary world in the later stages, it is a unified whole. More important than critical debate is the fact that, despite lack of depth in the characters, the occasional platitude and the much debated abrupt ending, this is to my mind the eminently readable work of a master story-teller.

---

13 Donald L. Shaw, 'Spain / Romántico—Romanticismo—Romancesco—Romanesco—Romancista—Románico', in *'Romantic' and its Cognates / The European History of a Word*, ed. Hans Eichner (Manchester: Manchester U. P., 1972), 341-71, at pp. 357-58.

'The Bleeding Nun' and 'Our Lady of Paris'

J. E. VAREY

Queen Mary and Westfield College, London

In Chapter IV of Book V of *Notre-Dame de Paris* (1831), Victor Hugo describes the attack on the cathedral by the massed bands of the underworld. The gypsy Esmeralda has been plucked from the hangman's noose by the hunchback Quasimodo, and carried to asylum in Notre-Dame. The mob believes she is held prisoner and, set on rescuing her, attempts to take the cathedral by storm; Quasimodo, being totally deaf, is unable to comprehend the speech of defiance in which Clopin Trouillefou, the 'roi de Thunes', calls on the ecclesiastical authorities to surrender the young girl to him and his followers, and is equally determined to prevent their access. As the mob attacks the main doors with hammers and iron bars, Quasimodo hurls on them from above a great beam and a storm of stones; nevertheless, the attack is on the point of succeeding when, in desperation, he sets light to a pile of timber and melts sheets of lead, the molten metal pouring down through the mouths of two gargoyles onto the crowd before the great doors with deadly effect. The whole episode, built upon a failure of comprehension and communication, is replete with ironies: the builders' materials, intended for repair, are used for destruction; the massive beam which the hunchback hurls down in defence of the edifice is picked up and used by the attackers as a battering-ram; the discipline of the early stages of the assault degenerates into a determination to sack the cathedral. Hugo describes the scenes as follows:

> Tous les yeux s'étaient levés vers le haut de l'église. Ce qu'ils voyaient était extraordinaire. Sur le sommet de la galerie la plus

> élevée, plus haut que la rosace centrale, il y avait une grande flamme que montait entre les deux clochers avec des tourbillons d'étincelles, une grande flamme désordonnée et furieuse dont le vent emportait par moments un lambeau dans la fumée. Au-dessous de cette flamme, au-dessous de la sombre balustrade à trèfles de braise, deux gouttières en gueules de monstres vomissaient sans relâche cette pluie ardente que détachait son ruissellement argenté sur les ténèbres de la façade inférieure. À mesure qu'ils approchaient du sol, les deux jets de plomb liquide s'élargissaient en gerbes, comme l'eau que jaillit des milles trous de l'arrosoir. Au-dessus de la flamme, les énormes tours, de chacune desquelles on voyait deux faces crues et tranchées, l'une toute noire, l'autre toute rouge, semblaient plus grandes encore de toute l'immensité de l'ombre qu'elles projetaient jusque dans le ciel. Leurs innombrables sculptures de diables et de dragons prenaient un aspect lugubre. La clarté inquiète de la flamme les faisait remuer à l'oeil. Il y avait des guivres que avaient l'air de rire, des gargouilles qu'on croyait entendre japper, des salamandres que soufflaient dans le feu, des tarasques qui éternuaient dans la fumée. Et parmi ces monstres ainsi réveillés de leur sommeil de pierre par cette flamme, par ce bruit, il y en avait un qui marchait et qu'on voyait de temps en temps passer sur le front ardent de bûcher comme une chauve-souris devant une chandelle.[1]

This description is in tune with many of the recurrent motifs in the novel — the petrification of the human being and stone statues and carvings endowed with life, the contrast of darkness and light, the flood-tide assault of the mob on the symbol of authority (prefiguring the French Revolution of 1789)[2] — but there is another dimension to this description

---

1 Quotations are taken from *Notre-Dame de Paris*, ed. Jacques Seebacher and printed together with *Les Travailleurs de la mer* (Paris: Gallimard, 1975). This passage is at p. 417.

2 These motifs and the dichotomies inherent in them are skilfully analysed in recent critical studies, notably those of Victor Brombert, *Victor Hugo and the Visionary Novel* (Cambridge, Mass.: Harvard U. P., 1984), 49-85; Guy Talon, '*Notre-Dame de Paris*: La cathédrale dans l'univers hugolien', in *Victor Hugo 1: Approches critiques contemporaines*, ed. Michel Grimaud, *La Revue des Lettres Modernes*, (1984), Nos. 693-97, 139-55; Claudie Bernard, 'De l'architecture à la littérature: La topographie parisienne dans *Notre-Dame de Paris* de Victor Hugo', in the same volume, 103-38; and Ilinca M. Zarifopol-Johnston, '*Notre-Dame de Paris*: The Cathedral in the Book', *Nineteenth-*

summed up in the manner in which 'Le duc d'Égypte, assis sur une borne, contemplait avec une crainte religieuse le bûcher fantasmagorique resplendissant à deux cents pieds en l'air'. Whilst the 'démon qui passe et repasse devant le feu'[3] is recognized to be Quasimodo, and therefore a creature of flesh and blood, nevertheless the description is truly phantasmagorical, a term which demands further explanation and clarification.

The phantasmagoria is a development of the magic lantern perfected by Etienne Gaspard Robert, a native of Liège, born on 25 June 1763. He informs us in his *Mémoires* that the addition of *-son* is common in Flemish to distinguish a son from a father of the same Christian name, and once having become famous as Robert-son, he did not wish later to discard the addition. Robertson read philosophy at the University of Louvain but first attracted attention in his native city as an artist, winning a gold medal in a competition. He himself was later to paint the slides for his phantasmagoria. He became passionately interested in electrical experiments and in ballooning — Montgolfier had made his first successful ascent in a hot-air balloon in 1782 — and gave several scientific exhibitions in his native town before leaving for Paris. He remained in Paris for six years and then, after a brief visit to Liège, returned to revolutionary Paris, where he became friendly with Volta, Galvani and the Abbé Chappé, the inventor of the mechanical telegraph. Robertson was a founder member of the Société galvanique and published papers on electrical subjects; indeed, his performances about Europe were always accompanied by demonstrations of electrical phenomena and other pseudo-scientific entertainments. The first public demonstrations of the phantasmagoria took place in Paris in March 1796 in the Pavillon de l'Echiquier, but, after a visit to Bordeaux, Robertson transferred his apparatus to the former Couvent des Capucines, near the Place Vendôme, where his performances were highly successful and widely copied. In 1802 he was invited to visit Russia, and centred his activities for several years in that country, travelling around eastern and northern Europe and

---

Century French Studies, XIII (1985), 22-35.

3 *Notre-Dame de Paris*, 417-18.

undertaking balloon ascents in Hamburg, St Petersburg, Moscow, Riga, Archangel, Vienna, Stockholm, Copenhagen and other cities. He was finally to leave Russia in 1814 after the defeat of the Grande Armée. Returning to France, he became in later years manager of the Tivoli Gardens at Batignolles, on the outskirts of Paris, where he died in 1837. His *Mémoires* were published in two volumes in 1831-34. Robertson's sons, Guillaume Eugène and Dimitri, were also aeronauts.[4]

From the seventeenth century attempts had been made to suggest movement in magic lantern projections but, however quickly the slides were changed, it was not possible to ensure that an image remained constantly on the retina and thus appear to be endowed with motion, in the same way that the multiple still photographs of the cinema film, rapidly projected onto the screen, give the illusion of life and movement. Simple movements, such as eyes rolling in a face, were achieved by building up a slide from two or more thicknesses. If a face were painted on one element, and the eyes on another, then, by moving one in relation to the other, the eyes could be made to appear to roll in their orbits. These were known as slipping slides. But the phantasmagoria effect was both more subtle and more exciting. Robertson used a lantern on wheels, or moving on rails, which projected an image from behind the screen. As the lantern approached the screen, the image decreased in size, and as it moved away, the image became larger. Adjustments in the relative position of slide, mirror or lens were necessary in order to keep the image in sharp focus. Furthermore, the image was most brightly lit when at its smallest, and as it grew larger the brilliance diminished, a difficulty which Robertson was able to overcome. By multiplying the sources of light, Robertson produced multiple images, a result also obtainable by

---

4 The principal source of information on Robertson's life is his *Mémoires récréatifs, scientifiques et anecdotiques du physicien-aéronaute E. G. Robertson* (Paris: Chez l'auteur, 1831-33), 2 vols. There is a modern edition (Langres: Café-Clima Éditeurs, 1985). See also David Robinson, 'Robinson on Robertson', *The New Magic Lantern Journal*, IV (1986), 4-13; Marie-Françoise Christout, *Le Merveilleux et le 'théâtre du silence' en France á partir du XVIIe siècle* (Mouton: The Hague, 1965), 146-52; J. E. Varey, 'Robertson's Phantasmagoria in Madrid, 1821 (Part II)', *Theatre Notebook*, XI (1957), 82-91.

using one source of light together with multiple lenses. He also projected three-dimensional figures endowed with movement. These, when brightly lit and projected through multiple lenses in a phantasmagoria lantern or phantascope, could produce images which rotated and could be made to appear to advance towards or recede from the audience.

Robertson describes his theatre in the Couvent des Capucines as 'un lieu sombre, tendu de noir, faiblement éclairé par une lampe sépulcrale, et dont quelques images lugubres annonçaient seules la destination; un calme profond, un silence absolu, un isolement subit au sortir d'une rue bruyante, étaient comme les préludes d'un monde idéal'. After a long introductory harangue

> la lampe antique suspendue au dessus de la tête des spectateurs s'éteignait, et les plongeait dans une obscurité profonde, dans des ténèbres affreuses. Au bruit de la pluie, du tonnerre, de la cloche funèbre évoquant les ombres de leurs tombeaux, succédaient les tons déchirans de l'harmonica; le ciel se découvrait, mais sillonné en tout sens par la foudre. Dans un lointain très reculé, un point lumineux semblait surgir: une figure, d'abord petite, se dessinait, puis s'approchait à pas lents, et à chaque pas semblait grandir; bientôt, d'une taille énorme, le fantôme s'avançait jusque sous les yeux du spectateur, et, au moment où celui-ci allait jeter un cri, disparaissait avec une promptitude inimaginable. D'autres fois les spectres sortaient tout formés d'un souterrain, et se présentaient d'une maniére inattendue.[5]

Robertson was not content with producing images upon the screen of his theatre. At times he threw a figure upon smoke rising from a brazier, and to vary the effect he also used wax masks placed about the theatre or moved by stage-hands and lit from within by a dark lantern.

The dramatic effect of the spectacle is well described by Sir David Brewster, who witnessed in Edinburgh in 1802 a performance given by Philipstal, one of Robertson's imitators:

> The small theatre of exhibition was lighted only by one hanging lamp, the flame of which was drawn up into an opaque chimney or shade when the performance began. In this 'darkness visible' the curtain rose and displayed a cave with skeletons and

5 Robertson, *Mémoires*, I, 278-82.

> other terrific figures in relief upon its walls. The flickering light was then drawn up beneath its shroud, and the spectators in total darkness found themselves in the middle of thunder and lightning. A thin transparent screen had, unknown to the spectators, been let down after the disappearance of the light, and upon it the flashes of lightning and all the subsequent appearances were represented. This screen being half-way between the spectators and the cave which was first shown, and being itself invisible, prevented the observers from having any idea of the real distance of the figures, and gave them the entire character of aerial pictures. The thunder and lightning were followed by the figures of ghosts, skeletons, and known individuals, whose eyes and mouth were made to move by the shiftings of combined sliders [i.e. by means of slipping slides]. After the first figure had been exhibited for a short time, it began to grow less and less, as if removed to a great distance, and at last vanished in a small cloud of light. Out of this same cloud the germ of another figure began to appear, and gradually grew larger and larger, and approached the spectator, till it attained its perfect development. In this manner the head of Dr Franklin was transformed into a skull; figures which retired with the freshness of life came back in the form of skeletons, and the retiring skeletons returned in the drapery of flesh and blood. The exhibition of these transmutations was followed by spectres, skeletons, and terrific figures, which, instead of receding and vanishing as before, suddenly advanced upon the spectators, becoming larger as they approached them, and finally vanished by appearing to sink into the ground. The effect of this part of the exhibition was naturally the most impressive. The spectators were not only surprised but agitated, and many of them were of opinion that they could have touched the figures.[6]

The advertisements in the Paris press of Robertson's early performances do not give a very full picture of his repertoire. On 18 nivôse An VII [1798], for example, he advertised for the 21st of the month, 'Apparition de Spectres, Fantômes, et Revenans, offerts par les mêmes moyens qu'ont dû et pu employer la Pythonisse lorsqu'elle évoque l'ombre de Samuel, les trois sorcières, lorsq'elles apparurent à Macbeth, et les prêtres de Memphis, dans les mystères de l'initiation, etc.;

6 Sir David Brewster, *Natural Magic*, The Family Library, XXXIII (London: Murray, 1834), 80-82.

expériences sur le fluide galvanique'.[7] Much of his repertoire is revealed and commented upon in the *Mémoires*, but the fullest account of a specific series of performances is to be found in the *Diario de Madrid*, where Robertson performed in the Teatro del Príncipe from 22 January to 25 February 1821.[8] Robertson's repertoire in Madrid may be conveniently divided in two parts, the first consisting of the 'galería histórica', a portrait gallery of legendary heroes, such as Pelayo; figures of history and literature, such as Hernán Cortés and Cervantes; thinkers of the Enlightenment, such as Voltaire and Rousseau, and the Liberal heroes of the rising of 1820, Quiroga, Riego and Arco Agüero. In the imaginative part of the entertainment, heads were also used, but transformed by means of dissolving one slide into another, so that a portrait of a known individual could be metamorphosed into a skull. Other scenes were no less macabre, but more dramatic in nature.

The most important of these dramatic vignettes, from the point of view of the present article, is that of *La Nonne sanglante*. Robertson's first description of this scene in his *Mémoires* is very brief: 'Une nonne, victime de sa sensibilité, revient voltiger dans un cloître où son ami se livrait aux exercices de la piété.'[9] In explaining the manner of its performance, he gives us further details:

> APPARITION DE LA NONNE SANGLANTE. Le son d'une cloche lointaine se fait entendre. Au fond d'un cloître faiblement éclairé par les derniers rayons de la lune, apparaît une nonne ensanglantée avec une lanterne d'une main et de l'autre un poignard; elle arrive lentement et semble chercher l'objet de ses désirs, elle se rapproche tellement des spectateurs qu'il arrive souvent qu'on les voit se déplacer pour lui livrer passage.[10]

A further description of this scene gives some idea of the effect of Robertson's performances upon his contemporaries:

---

7 *Journal de Paris*, 18 nivôse, An VII. I am indebted to Dr Margaret Rees for the copies of advertisements from the *Journal de Paris* reproduced here.

8 Full details are given in my article in *Theatre Notebook*, referred to in note 4 above.

9 Robertson, *Mémoires*, I, 301.

10 *Ibid.*, I, 342.

> Cette jeune nonne, coiffée d'une guimpe que rivalise de blancheur avec les lis de son visage, elle vient, à pas lents, du bout de l'avenue d'un cloître. Les douleurs de sa vie mortelle sont empreintes sur son visage, mais sa vie céleste n'est pas détruite; ce front calme goûte déjà le repos et bientôt le bonheur. L'infortunée contemple cette figure qui répand autour d'elle tous les rayons d'une nouvelle et meilleure existence. Il se recueille, il espère, il transporte dans les régions éternelles, tandis que l'athéisme, qui étieint tout sous ses mains glacées, qui s'éloigne sans cesse, et du dieu miséricordieux et de la ligne ascendante, voudrait-on anéantir les tableaux mélancoliques, révélateurs, inspirateurs, et jusqu'aux mots de la langue qui ont une liaison secrète avec Dieu et l'immortalité.[11]

The slide of the nun, as painted by Robertson, still exists. The figure is dressed in white, the blood being very realistically represented. The nun is seen in two positions, and the image could thus be made to appear to move away from, as well as towards, the spectators.[12] This scene was presented by a mixture of front and back projection: the cloister was thrown onto the screen from the side where the audience was seated, and the slide of the nun projected by the phantasmagoria situated behind the screen. The nun would thus appear to walk down the cloister towards the spectators until she was apparently on top of them. The slide could then be quickly changed, and the nun, apparently spinning on her heel, would appear to retire down the cloister.

The immediate source of Robertson's scene, advertised in the *Journal de Paris* on 4 Germinal An VI (24 March 1798), was Matthew Gregory 'Monk' Lewis' *The Monk*, published in three volumes in 1796. In 'The History of Don Raymond', an extensive sub-plot, it is related that the young Agnes, in the charge of her aunt and uncle, Baron and Baroness of Lindenburg, is wooed by Raymond. Together they examine a drawing: the subject is a group of figures in the great hall of the

---

11 From an article by Mercier, reprinted in Robertson, *Mémoires*, I, 304-10, at p. 310. It is evident that Robertson was considerably assisted by audience participation in his entertainment.

12 *Conservatoire National des Arts et Métiers. Catalogue du Musée, Section L. Photographie, Cinématographie* (Paris: Conservatoire National des Arts et Métiers, 1949), 159 (No. 16527).

castle, terror-stricken at the sight of

> a female of more than human stature, clothed in the habit of some religious order. Her face was veiled; on her arm hung a chaplet of beads; her dress was in several places stained with the blood which trickled from a wound on her bosom. In one hand she held a lamp, in the other a large knife, and she seemed advancing towards the iron gates of the hall.[13]

Agnes explains that the drawing, in her own hand, represents 'the bleeding nun', a ghost that has haunted the castle for the past hundred years, making it 'scarcely habitable' by reason of her 'oaths and execrations'. After exorcism, she 'grew more tractable and well-behaved', and appeared only once every five years:

> On the fifth of May of every fifth year, as soon as the clock strikes one, the door of the haunted chamber opens. [Observe, that this room has been shut up for near a century.] Then out walks the ghostly nun with her lamp and dagger: she descends the stair-case of the eastern tower, and crosses the great hall.[14]

In order to escape from the castle, Agnes determines to disguise herself as the apparition. She appears in the moonlit garden of the castle; Raymond hurries her to his awaiting carriage, but the horses bolt as thick clouds obscure the sky, the wind howls, thunder rolls and lightning strikes. The carriage is overturned and Raymond hurled out, When he recovers consciousness he is in Ratisbon, and without news of Agnes. He is unable to sleep. The clock strikes one:

> Suddenly I heard slow and heavy steps ascending the stair-case. By an involuntary movement I started up in my bed, and drew back the curtain. A single rush-light, which glimmered upon the hearth, shed a faint gleam through the apartment, which was hung with tapestry. The door was thrown open with violence. A figure entered, and drew near my bed with solemn measured steps. With trembling apprehension I examined this midnight visitor. God Almighty! it was the bleeding nun! Her face was still veiled, but she no longer held her lamp and dagger. She lifted up her veil slowly. What a sight presented itself to my startled eyes! I beheld

---

13 Matthew Gregory ('Monk') Lewis, *The Monk* (London: Bell, 1796), II, 19-20.

14 *Ibid.*, II, 24.

> before me an animated corse. Her countenance was long and haggard; her cheeks and lips were bloodless; the paleness of death was spread over her features; and her eyeballs, fixed steadfastly upon me, were lustreless and hollow. [...] The visionary nun looked upon me for some moments in silence: there was something petrifying in her regard.[15]

The scene is to be repeated night after night. It is the true ghost who is visiting Raymond; by chance Agnes had been prevented from leaving her room, and it was the spectre who had accompanied Raymond in his carriage. A later explanation demonstrates that the ghost is that of Beatrice de las Cisternas, who had murdered her paramour, Otto von Lindenberg.[16]

In Book IX, Chapter I of *Notre-Dame de Paris*, Claude Frollo climbs towards the balcony where, unknown to him, Esmeralda is kept hidden by Quasimodo. When last he saw her, she was in the hands of the executioner, and he believes her to be dead:

> Il gravit lentement l'escalier des tours, plein d'un secret effroi que devait propager jusqu'aux rares passants du Parvis la mystérieuse lumière de sa lampe montant si tard de meurtrière en meurtrière en haut du clocher.
>
> Tout à coup il sentit quelque fraîcheur sur son visage et se trouva sous la porte de la plus haute galerie. L'air était froid; le ciel charriait des nuages dont les larges lames blanches débordaient les unes sur les autres en s'écrasant par les angles, et figuraient une débâcle de fleuve en hiver. Le croissant de la lune, échoué au milieu des nuées, semblait un navire céleste pris dans les glaçons de l'air.
>
> Il baissa la vue et contempla un instant, entre la grille de colonnettes qui unit les deux tours, au loin, à travers une gaze de brumes et de fumées, la foule silencieuse des toits de Paris, aigus, innombrables, pressés et petits comme les flots d'une mer tranquille dans une nuit d'été.
>
> La lune jetait un faible rayon qui donnait au ciel et à la terre une teinte de cendre.
>
> En ce moment l'horloge éleva sa voix grêle et fêlée. Minuit sonna. Le prêtre pensa à midi. C'étaient les douze heures qui revenaient. 'Oh! se dit-il tout bas, elle doit être froide à présent!'
>
> Tout à coup un coup de vent éteignit sa lampe, et presque en même temps il vit paraître, à l'angle opposé de la tour, une ombre,

---

15 *The Monk*, II, 60-62.

16 *Ibid.*, II, 86-90.

une blancheur, une forme, une femme. Il tressaillit. À côté de cette femme, il y avait une petite chèvre, qui mêlait son bêlement au dernier bêlement de l'horloge.

Il eut la force de regarder. C'était elle.

Elle était pâle, elle était sombre. Ses cheveux tombaient sur ses épaules comme le matin. Mais plus de corde au cou, plus de mains attachées. Elle était libre, elle était morte.

Elle était vêtue de blanc et avait un voile blanc sur la tête.

Elle venait vers lui, lentement, en regardant le ciel. La chèvre surnaturelle la suivait. Il se sentait de pierre et trop lourd pour fuir. À chaque pas qu'elle faisait en avant, il en faisait un en arrière, et c'était tout. Il rentra ainsi sous la voûte obscure de l'escalier. Il était glacé de l'idée qu'elle allait peut-être y entrer aussi; si elle l'eût fait, il serrait mort de terreur.

Elle arriva en effet devant la porte de l'escalier, s'y arrêta quelques instants, regarda fixement dans l'ombre, mais sans paraître y voir le prêtre, et passa. Elle lui parut plus grande que lorsqu'elle vivait; il vit la lune à travers sa robe blanche; il entendit son souffle.

Quand elle fut passée, il se mit à redescendre l'escalier, avec la lenteur qu'il avait vue au spectre, se croyant spectre lui-même, hagard, les cheveux tout droits, sa lampe éteinte toujours à la main; et, tout en descendant les degrés en spirale, il entendait distinctement dans son oreille une voix que riait et qui répétait:

'... Un esprit passa devant ma face, et j'entendis un petit souffle, et le poil de ma chair se hérissa.'[17]

Hugo's description is reminiscent of Agnes' drawing and story in *The Monk*, rather than the later visitation at Ratisbon, where the door opens with violence, the figure carries neither lamp nor dagger, and its face is corpse-like. Agnes had described the apparition as ghostly, descending a staircase and crossing the great hall; the drawing shows the figure as superhuman, veiled, and carrying a lamp and a dagger. However, several elements of Hugo's description recall rather the phantasmagorical performance of *La Nonne sanglante*. The tolling of the bell, the extinction of the lamp, the unnatural moonlight, and the gradual approach of the white-clad figure, taken by the cleric to be a spectre. When Dom Claude last saw Esmeralda she was at the foot of the scaffold, clad only in her shift, bare-headed and with a rope about her neck. As the

17 *Notre-Dame de Paris*, 360-61.

passage quoted indicates, she is now dressed in a white robe and wears a veil on her head. On rescuing her and after taking her to the place of refuge in the cathedral, Quasimodo has provided her with clothing offered by charitable ladies: 'Elle se hâta de se vêtir. C'était une robe blanche avec un voile blanc. Un habit de novice de l'Hôtel-Dieu'.[18] A rational explanation is thus provided for her clothing, but nevertheless Hugo has been at pains to attire his apparition in garments which echo those of the phantasmagorical nun, 'coiffée d'une guimpe qui rivalise de blancheur avec les lis de son visage'. The most striking difference is that the latter is covered in blood and bears a lantern in one hand and a dagger in the other. However, Esmeralda had seen her beloved Phoebus apparently stabbed to death and, whilst she is not so depicted in the present scene, Frollo recalls her in his nightmares as 'étendue sur le capitaine poignardé, les yeux fermés, sa belle gorge nue couverte du sang de Phoebus'.[19] The most striking similarity between the two scenes is the slow, deliberate advance of the spectral figure, 'une ombre, une blancheur, une forme, une femme', silent, with fixed regard, apparently larger than life, her white robe translucent in the moonlight, causing the priest to retreat before her advance. Robertson's scene is melancholy rather than terrible, and it is that aspect of the phantasmagorical scene which is mirrored by Hugo. It appears very probable that, whilst the source of the episode is to be found in Lewis' *The Monk*, Hugo, as he penned the description of the appearance of Esmeralda before the priest, viewed the original bleeding nun through the lens of Robertson's theatrical recreation.

If it is correct to see in this episode of *Notre-Dame de Paris* an echo of *La Nonne sanglante*, it is necessary to consider when Victor Hugo could have been present at a phantasmagoria performance. Hugo was born in 1802, when Robertson was already on his way to Russia. However, the latter informs us that his performances were quickly copied, in the first place by the brothers Aubée, who had been his assistants. Robertson

18 *Notre-Dame de Paris*, 364.

19 *Ibid.*, 380.

took out letters patent, but their protection covered only a brief period.

> Dès ce moment, la fantasmagorie devint un objet très commun; et exécutée par des fantasmagores de toutes les classes, Paris ressemble aux Champs-Élysées pour la quantité d'ombres que l'habitèrent, et ils ne tenait qu'à une imagination un peu métaphorique de transformer la Seine en fleuve Léthé; car les fantasmagores s'assemblèrent principalement sur ses rives, et il n'y eut pas de quai, ainsi que le dit quelque part Ducray-Duménil, qui ne vous offrit un petit fantôme au fond d'un corridor bien noir, au sommet d'un escalier tortueux. Les machines à fantômes furent même dès lors un objet de commerce pour Paris et Londres; les frères Dumortiez et les opticiens anglais en expédièrent plusieurs milliers dans toute l'Europe. Le moindre amateur de physique, dans toutes les contrées, eut sa fantasmagorie. J'ai trouvé de ces boîtes à chariot, fabriquées à Paris, dans le fond de la Russie, à Odessa, et depuis les frontières de la Sibérie jusqu'à l'extremité de l'Espagne, même à Ceuta.[20]

Hugo could thus have seen as a child an imitator of Robertson, but it must be remembered that he and his brothers led a somewhat nomadic life, following in the footsteps of their father, an officer in the forces of Napoleon. The family was in Italy in 1807-08. Mother and children returned to Paris in February of that year, whilst Léopold Hugo, now a General, was posted to Spain. The family was in Madrid in 1811-12,[21] when the three brothers attended the Real Colegio de San Antonio Abad. The academic year lasted from 1 September 1811 to 30 June 1812, and Victor Hugo is listed as studying mathematics, Latin, drawing, reading, writing and French.[22] It is therefore of

---

20 Robertson, *Mémoires*, 320-21.

21 Alain Decaux, *Victor Hugo* (Paris: Libraire Académique Perrin, 1984), I, 52-115; [Adéle Hugo], *Victor Hugo raconté par un témoin de sa vie 1802-1817* (Paris: Hertzel, n.d.). 28-126; for Madrid, see 108-26. According to this source, 'On ne leur avait pas, jusque-là [Bayonne], prodigué le théâtre. Leur mère y allait très peu, et ils n'y allaient jamais sans elle' (81-82); however, several visits to the theatre are recorded, in Bayonne and in Madrid.

22 *Diario de Madrid*, 11 October 1811. See also Geraud Venzac, *Les Premiers Maîtres de Victor Hugo*, Travaux de l'Institut Catholique de Paris 2 (Paris: Bloud & Gay, 1955), 19. According to Venzac, a photocopy of the relevant page of the *Diario de Madrid* appears as plate 4 of his *Origines religieuses de Victor Hugo*, a work which I have been unable to consult.

some interest to discover if the phantasmagoria was known at that time in Madrid. After Madrid, Hugo could have seen a performance at any time up to the 1830s, when, as Robertson informs us, the vogue for the phantasmagoria as an entertainment had spent itself. Robertson himself, says Roch in the introduction to the *Mémoires*, did not perform after his visits to Spain and Portugal in 1819-22.

In March 1797 François Bienvenu arrived in Madrid, performing in the Coliseo de los Caños del Peral, and, from October, in the Calle del Sartén, where he offered a mixture of pseudo-scientific and dramatic entertainments. In April 1798 he advertised:

> la vista de diversas figuras que representan estatuas hechas según las antiguas pinturas de Herculano en el reino de Nápoles; esta estatua aparece grande, pequeña, de grandeza natural, y se multiplica y mueve &c. Este es nuevo método de hacer aparecer las figuras nunca vistas en Europa, siendo de la invención del profesor Bienvenú.

Despite his claim, Bienvenu's performance appears to be a copy of Robertson's phantasmagoria, although lacking his dramatic presentation. In 1805-06, M. Martin, a Frenchman, offered performances of his phantasmagoria. On 1 January 1806 he advertised for 'una sala grande, y otra pieza para poder maniobrar con dicha máquina'. In March, on the point of leaving Madrid, he offered much of his equipment for sale. It appears that Bernardino Rueda took over the phantasmagoria, for on 11 March 1807 he advertised:

> las ilusiones de fantasmagoría, en las que aparecerán varios espectros, esqueletos, fantasmas, retratos de hombres célebres, como también la famosa tumba de Creux, sin que en nada varíe a lo que manifestó el año pasado Mr. Martin, dando fin con el chistoso *Baile de las brujas*, tan gracioso como aplaudido, en el que desde una se multiplicarán hasta lo infinito, intermediado todo con una excelente orquesta.

The repertoire — and therefore presumably that of Martin — is a clear echo of Robertson, particularly the *Baile de las brujas*, copied from Robertson's *Multiplication ou danse des sorcières*. Rueda advertised again in June 1809, but by October of that year the entertainment had passed into the hands of Josefa

Bañóblez and Juan González Mantilla, who offered 'El espectáculo extraordinario de fantasmagoría, que tanta aceptación mereció el año pasado, sin que en nada varíe de lo que presentó Mr. Marten [*sic*]'. In 1811 performances of the phantasmagoria were presented throughout the year as part of a miscellany which included acrobatics and shadow puppets. The company was headed by Valentín Corcuera. Although the names of the individual performers are not given, and the advertisements refer to 'una primorosa función de fantasmagoría nuevamente construida, que será diferente de cuantas se han presentado hasta el día', it is clear from the repertoire that this is Mantilla's, including the *Baile de las brujas*. The same company performed from 4 November 1811 to 2 February 1812. Mantilla was to give phantasmagoria performances in Madrid until 1836, and the *Baile de las brujas* continues to be advertised throughout his career. Robertson himself, as already mentioned, was in Madrid in 1820-22, performing in the Teatro del Príncipe in 1820-21, whilst a rival showman, the Italian Jenaro Benetorre Romanine, gave phantasmagoria performances in the Teatro de la Cruz. The repertoire of Robertson includes many pieces described in his *Mémoires*, but not the episode of *La Nonne sanglante*. Romanine's advertisements are not as specific as those of Robertson, but include many scenes reminiscent of Robertson; one of these is *El claustro de Fénélon*, which suggests that Romanine copied at least the cloister from Robertson's scene of the nun, with perhaps Fénélon appearing instead of the female figure.[23]

The direct influences of one genre on another are of course hard to prove. It is necessary to bear in mind that Hugo and Robertson may simply have found common sources of inspiration. Chapter VII of Book VII is headed 'Le Moine-

23 The details of phantasmagoria performances come from the pages of the *Diario de Madrid*; they will be published in full in J. E. Varey, *Cartelera de los títeres y otras diversiones populares de Madrid: 1758-1840. Estudio y documentos*, Fuentes para la Historia del Teatro en España VIII (London: Tamesis, 1996). See also J. E. Varey, 'Robertson's Phantasmagoria in Madrid, 1821', *Theatre Notebook*, IX (1955), 89-95; and XI (1957), 82-91; and *Títeres, marionetas y otras diversiones populares de 1758 a 1859*. Temas Madrileños XIX (Madrid: Instituto de Estudios Madrileños, 1959).

Bourru'. Captain Phoebus is followed through the night streets by a shadowy figure: 'Il courait alors par le monde je ne sais quelles histoires du moine-bourru, rôdeur nocturne des rues de Paris ...'.[24] The figure is that of Claude Frollo, contrasted with the young and handsome Captain Phoebus, whose very name suggests the sun (although Esmeralda is to discover how illusory this sun in reality is), and with Esmeralda herself, 'La creatura bella bianco vestita', a quotation from Dante which heads Chapter II of Book XI. The Moine-Bourru could be a distant reminiscence of Monk Lewis' *The Monk*, but the description of the recluse, la Gudule, in the Trou aux Rats suggests rather the black paintings of Goya:

> C'était un de ces spectres mi-partis d'ombre et de lumière, comme on en voit dans les rêves et dans l'oeuvre extraordinaire de Goya, pâles, immobiles, sinistres, accroupis sur une tombe ou adossés à la grille d'un cachot. Ce n'était ni une femme, ni un homme, ni un être vivant, ni une forme définie; c'était une figure; une sorte de vision sur laquelle s'entrecoupaient le réel et le fantastique, comme l'ombre et le jour.[25]

It is evident that Hugo's imagination had been stirred by a variety of influences. Undoubtedly one of these influences is that of the phantasmagoria. In Book IX, Chapter I, Claude Frollo, going in search of Esmeralda, pictures her and the gallows as two juxtaposed images:

> Il n'avait plus que deux images distinctes dans l'esprit: la Esmeralda et la potence. Tout le reste était noir. Ces deux images rapprochées lui présentaient un groupe effroyable, et plus il y fixait ce qui lui restait d'attention et de pensée, plus il les voyait croître, selon une progression fantastique, l'une en grâce, en charme, en beauté, en lumière, l'autre en horreur; de sorte qu'à la fin la Esmeralda lui apparaissait comme une étoile, le gibet comme un énorme bras décharné.[26]

As the daylight fades he crosses the Seine by boat and, when the boatman leaves him on the Cité, stares into the waters:

> Le bercement monotone du bateau et le bruissement de l'eau avaient en quelque sorte engourdi le malheureux Claude. Quand

24 *Notre-Dame de Paris*, 288.

25 *Ibid.*, 219.

26 *Ibid.*, 354.

le batelier se fut éloigné, il resta stupidement debout sur la grève, regardant devant lui et ne percevant plus les objets qu'à travers des oscillations grossissantes que lui faisaient de tout une sorte de fantasmagorie. Il n'est pas rare que la fatigue d'une grande douleur produise cet effet sur l'esprit.

Le soleil était couché derrière la haute Tour de Nesle. C'était l'instant du crepuscule. Le ciel était blanc, l'eau de la rivière était blanche. Entre ces deux blancheurs, la rive gauche de la Seine, sur laquelle il avait les yeux fixés, projetait sa masse sombre, et, de plus en plus amincie par la perspective, s'enfonçait dans les brumes de l'horizon comme une flèche noire. Elle était chargée de maisons, dont on ne distinguait que la silhouette obscure, vivement relevée en ténèbres sur le fond clair du ciel et de l'eau. Ça et là des fenêtres commençaient à y scintiller comme des trous de braise. Cet immense obélisque noir ainsi isolé entre les deux nappes blanches du ciel et de la rivière, fort large en cet endroit, fit à dom Claude un effet singulier, comparable à ce qu'éprouverait un homme qui, couché à terre sur le dos au pied du clocher de Strasbourg, regarderait l'énorme aiguille s'enfoncer au-dessus de sa tête dans les pénombres du crépuscule. Seulement ici c'était Claude qui était debout et l'obélisque qui était couché; mais comme la rivière, en reflétant le ciel, prolongeait l'abîme au-dessous de lui, l'immense promontoire semblait aussi hardiment élancé dans le vide que toute flèche de cathédrale; et l'impression était la même. Cette impression avait même cela d'étrange et de plus profond, que c'était bien le clocher de Strasbourg, mais le clocher de Strasbourg haut de deux lieues, quelque chose d'inouï, de gigantesque, d'incommensurable, un édifice comme nul oeil humain n'en a vu, une tour de Babel. Les cheminées des maisons, les créneaux des murailles, les pignons taillés des toits, la flèche des Augustins, la Tour de Nesle, toutes ces saillies que ébréchaient le profil du colossal obélisque, ajoutaient à l'illusion en jouant bizarrement à l'oeil les découpures d'une sculpture touffue et fantastique. Claude, dans l'état d'hallucination où il se trouvait, crut voir, voir de ses yeux vivants, le clocher de l'enfer; les mille lumières répandues sur toute la hauteur de l'épouvantable tour lui parurent autant de porches de l'immense fournaise intérieure; les voix et les rumeurs que s'en échappaient, autant de cris, autant de râles. Alors il eut peur, il mit ses mains sur ses oreilles pour ne plus entendre, tourna le dos pour ne plus voir, et s'éloigna à grands pas de l'effroyable vision.

Mais la vision était en lui.[27]

27 *Notre-Dame de Paris*, 355-56.

I have already quoted above the description of the attack on the cathedral in which Hugo also uses the term 'phantasmagorie'. Seen from above by Esmeralda, the attack appears to be a battle between witches and gargoyles:

> L'aspect de la place, la vision que s'y agitait, le désordre de cet assaut nocturne, cette foule hidieuse, sautelante comme une nuée de grenouilles, à demi entrevue dans les ténèbres, le coassement de cette rauque multitude, ces quelques torches rouges courant et se croisant sur cette ombre commes les feux de nuit que rayent la surface brumeuse des marais, toute cette scène lui fit l'effet d'une mystérieuse bataille engagée entre les fantômes du sabbat et les monstres de pierre de l'église.[28]

As described frontally by Hugo, the effect is rather that of fire and darkness, with the figure of Quasimodo silhouetted against the flames: 'il y en avait un qui marchait et qu'on voyait de temps en temps passer sur le front ardent du bûcher comme une chauve-souris devant une chandelle'.[29] The reference to the bat flitting across the scene could well be a direct recollection of a Robertson technique, for in the more elaborate of his horror scenes we are told that 'd'autres fantômes, des chauves-souris, etc. allaient et venaient sur la toile en tous sens; ils étaient produits par une plus petite lanterne maintenue par des courroies sur la poitrine d'un autre opérateur, qui jouait ainsi le rôle de support et manoeuvrait avec ses deux mains libres les tableaux de l'appareil optique'.[30] On 6 January 1810 Mantilla advertised in the *Diario de Madrid* that 'saldrá un mochuelo que volará por toda la pieza', and 'la primorosa y nueva escena de *Las aves nocturnas*, en la que los espectadores advertirán que dichas aves se les acercan a la vista, y creyendo que verdaderamente lo son, irán a separarlas con la mano, y desaparecerán de un lugar a otro'.

The word phantasmagoria quickly acquired in all languages a second sense of, to quote the *OED*, 'a shifting series or successions of phantasma or imaginary figures, as seen in a dream or fevered condition, as called up by the imagination, or

28 *Notre-Dame de Paris*, 457.

29 *Ibid.*, 417.

30 H. Fourtier, *La Pratique des projections* (Paris: Gauthier-Villars, 1892-93), II, 89.

as created by literary description'. It is in this secondary sense that Hugo uses the word in *Le Dernier jour d'un condamné* (1829), where the narrator describes how 'cette fantasmagorie des juges, des témoins, des avocats, des procureurs du roi, passait et repassait devant moi, tantôt grotesque, tantôt sanglante, toujours sombre et fatale'.[31] It is evident, however, that in *Notre-Dame de Paris* Hugo used the term in a more precise sense, and I hope to have demonstrated that he saw and recollected elements of the performances of Robertson or of one of his imitators. In particular, it appears reasonable to suppose that the episode in which Esmeralda, dressed in white, progresses in mysterious fashion towards the spectator (in this case, Dom Claude), growing larger than life as she advances in the moonlight, is a reflection of the scene of *La Nonne sanglante*, adapted to Hugo's purpose, and that it is not the case that the novelist and the showman are separately interpreting the common source of the episode in *The Monk*.

Robertson often insists, both in the *Mémoires* and in the advertisements of his performances, that the phantasmagoria can play an important part in the banishment of superstition. Despite this insistence on the rational — a legacy of the Enlightenment — he was quick to exploit the vogue for the weird and the gloomy among his contemporaries. He also consciously aimed, as the Romantic writers were to do in Hugo's day, at an intermingling of 'des scènes tristes, sévères, bouffonnes, gracieuses, fantastiques'.[32] Robertson's performances are an indication of the importance of popular entertainment as a link between the neo-Gothic and the Romantic, and in Spain the phantasmagoria, certainly from 1806, and possibly from 1798 through the performances of Bienvenu, introduced Spanish audiences to themes and motifs which were to become typical of Romantic writers writing some three decades later.

31 Victor Hugo, *Le Dernier Jour d'un condamné. Claude Gueux* (Paris: Hertzel, n.d.), 43.

32 Robertson, *Mémoires*, I, 283.

Bécquer, autor de *Doña Manuela*

JOAN ESTRUCH TOBELLA

I. B. 'Sant Andreu', Barcelona

La autoría de *Doña Manuela*, periódico satírico dirigido contra la Unión Liberal, ha sido tradicionalmente atribuida a Bécquer, pero no se ha podido demostrar de manera clara. Los especialistas no se ponen de acuerdo sobre el tema. R. Pageard considera verosímil la atribución, mientras otros destacados estudiosos, como D. Gamallo Fierros, R. Brown y R. Benítez, no la aceptan.[1]

Antes de entrar en la cuestión de la autoría, realizaremos una breve descripción del periódico. El único número apareció en Madrid el 26 de setiembre de 1865, con el subtítulo de 'periódico político'. Consta de cuatro hojas, y anuncia una periodicidad semanal. Todos los artículos son anónimos, y sólo aparece el nombre del editor responsable, Celestino García. Especial interés tiene el dibujo de portada, firmado por Francisco Ortego, conocido dibujante satírico de ideas republicanas, amigo de Gustavo y Valeriano.[2] Representa a

---

1 R. Pageard, *Bécquer. Leyenda y realidad* (Madrid: Espasa-Calpe, 1990), 393; R. Benítez, *Bécquer tradicionalista* (Madrid: Gredos, 1971), 30; R. Brown, *Bécquer* (Barcelona: Aedos, 1963), 275. En cuanto a D. Gamallo Fierros, inicialmente, en su introducción a Bécquer, *Páginas abandonadas* (Madrid: Valera, 1948), 45, aceptaba la autoría becqueriana de parte de *Doña Manuela*, pero, tal como señala R. Brown, once años más tarde la negó al tener conocimiento del mentís del poeta en *Las Noticias*.

2 Francisco Ortego es, probablemente, el autor de una serie de acuarelas pornográficas de orientación antimonárquica y anticlerical que, firmadas con el seudónimo SEM, han sido atribuidas a Gustavo y Valeriano Bécquer y publicadas con el título *Los borbones en pelota*, ed. R. Pageard, L. Fontanella y M. D. Cabra (Madrid: Ediciones El Museo Universal, 1991).

'doña Manuela', es decir a Manuela Bargues, la esposa de O'Donnell, rodeada de siete personajes, presumiblemente los ministros del gobierno presidido por el general, que aparece a la derecha de su esposa, mirándola embelesado.[3] También se puede reconocer a Posada Herrera, ministro de Gobernación y gran organizador de las elecciones. La actitud de la dama es enérgica, como si estuviera dando órdenes a su esposo y a los ministros. El dibujo se corresponde con las insinuaciones que se vierten en el editorial, y que comentaremos más adelante.

Aparte del editorial de presentación, integran el número diversos artículos, todos ellos dirigidos a satirizar a la Unión Liberal. 'Dos en uno' ataca a Posada Herrera y al ministro de Hacienda, Manuel Alonso Martínez. Aparece también una mención burlesca a José Luis Albareda, ex-director de *El Contemporáneo*: '... el unionismo de ayer, de hoy y de mañana, tres tiempos distintos que el Sr Albareda ha hecho *contemporáneos* ...'. Este ataque se corresponde con los que contra *El Contemporáneo*, que se había pasado al unionismo, se lanzaban desde *Los Tiempos*, diario al servicio de González Bravo en el que Bécquer trabajaba como redactor.[4]

'Cuestión previa' trata el tema de la censura, que *Doña Manuela* considera un serio peligro para su supervivencia. La labor del censor se describe así:

> La ley de imprenta tiene, como complemento necesario, un fiscal, que es su artículo más importante, un comentario de carne y

---

En nuestra opinión, se trata de una atribución escasamente fundada. Véanse J. Estruch, 'Los Bécquer, ¿pornógrafos y republicanos', *Ínsula* (Mayo 1992), núm. 545, y 'Nuevos datos sobre SEM', *El Gnomo*, II (1994).

3 Todos los testimonios coinciden en señalar su amor por su esposa: 'Sencillo en sus costumbres, D. Leopoldo O'Donnell puede citarse como modelo de esposos' (M. Ibo, *Apuntes para la historia de D. Leopoldo O'Donnell* [Madrid, 1867], 81); 'Amante de su familia, hijo cariñoso, marido fiel' (C. Navarro, *O'Donnell y su tiempo* [Madrid, 1869], 269); 'O'Donnell, hombre de una dulzura grande y de sencillez patriarcal en sus afectos, la amaba tiernamente y la ponía en las niñas de sus ojos azules. Decían gentes maliciosas que la temía. Temía todo lo que pudiera desagradarla, que es el temor de los enamorados' (B. Pérez Galdós, *O'Donnell, Episodios Nacionales*, III [Madrid: Aguilar, 1974], 995-96).

4 Véase J. Estruch, 'El compromiso político de Bécquer', *Cuadernos Hispanoamericanos* (1991), núm. 496, 101-08.

hueso que esgrime implacablemente su lápiz rojo, trazando todos los días el croquis de la libertad de pensamiento. Este funcionario pesa ocho ministros y cuesta un ojo de la cara.

No deja de ser llamativo que Bécquer, probable autor o inspirador del artículo, describa en estos términos un cargo que tan sólo hacía tres meses él había ocupado gracias al nombramiento efectuado por su protector González Bravo. No menos chocante resulta la referencia al coste económico del cargo, cuando el poeta había disfrutado como censor de un sueldo de 500 pesetas mensuales, que entonces era 'uno de los mayores del Estado español'.[5] En el artículo aparecen también nuevas pullas contra diversos ministros y contra Albareda: 'No se contemporanizará como el señor Albareda y secuaces, ni hará de su consecuencia una virtud póstuma a prueba de embajadas'. Se alude aquí al nombramiento de Albareda como embajador en La Haya, con lo que se insinúa que es el 'premio' a su 'traición' al partido moderado.

'El reconocimiento' es una breve e ingeniosa pieza teatral que tiene como protagonista a un unionista en busca de una colocación en un ministerio. Este sainete podría ser atribuido a Miguel Ramos Carrión, autor teatral posteriormente muy conocido, y que, según Gómez Aparicio,[6] colaboró con Bécquer en *Doña Manuela*.

Completan el número una serie de textos jocosos, en prosa y en verso, posiblemente escritos por Eduardo de Lustonó, periodista satírico que Gómez Aparicio considera otro de los colaboradores de *Doña Manuela*. Destaca esta parodia de los conocidos versos (268-72) de *El estudiante de Salamanca*, de Espronceda:

Hojas del árbol caídas,
juguetes del viento son;
las credenciales perdidas
¡ay! son brevas desprendidas
de la higuera de la Unión

5 Gamallo Fierros, *op. cit.*, 49. Véase también R. Montesinos, *Bécquer. Biografía e imagen* (Barcelona: RM, 1977), 82.

6 *Historia del periodismo español* (Madrid: Editora Nacional, 1967), I, 507.

Las metáforas utilizadas en esta parodia no resultan muy originales, puesto que el *Diccionario de los políticos* (1855) define 'situación' así: 'Higuera que produce muchas y sazonadas brevas; [...] Debajo de sus ramas hay siempre numerosos grupos de golosos con la boca abierta, esperando que caiga alguna'.[7]

Examinaremos ahora el contexto político y las circunstancias personales de Bécquer en el momento en que apareció *Doña Manuela*. El 21 de junio de 1865, al caer el gobierno Narváez, sustituido por O'Donnell, Bécquer perdió el cargo de censor de novelas. La pérdida del sueldo hizo que el poeta tuviera que buscar otras fuentes de ingresos. Colaboró asiduamente en *El Museo Universal* y siguió trabajando en *Los Tiempos*. Desde las páginas de este diario se realizaba una intensa campaña contra el gobierno unionista y en especial contra los 'angélicos', es decir los que, como los periodistas de *El Contemporáneo*, habían abandonado las filas moderadas para entrar en la Unión Liberal.

Es entonces cuando surge la operación 'Doña Manuela', detrás de la cual estaba probablemente González Bravo, que en su juventud había practicado el periodismo satírico en *El Guirigay*. Con esta operación se pretendía desprestigiar a O'Donnell en el terreno de lo personal. Los rumores que circularon por los ambientes políticos de la capital indicaban que Bécquer era el director de la nueva publicación. Además del análisis del editorial de presentación, que examinaremos más adelante, así parece confirmarlo el hecho de que los colaboradores del periódico fueran amigos suyos: Ortego, Ramos Carrión, Lustonó. Ortego era dibujante, director y editor de *El Fisgón*, periódico satírico en el que colaboraban varios amigos de Bécquer: Lustonó, Eusebio Blasco y Juan de la Puerta Vizcaíno. Este último había intervenido en *La historia de los templos de España*. Casi todos ellos escribían también en *Gil Blas*, periódico satírico de orientación republicana. El punto de reunión de estos periodistas satíricos era la tertulia del café *El Suizo*, en la que participaba Bécquer.

Las relaciones entre el poeta, reconocido seguidor de González Bravo, y estos periodistas demócratas no son tan

---

7 J. Rico y Amat, *Diccionario de los políticos* (Madrid: Narcea, 1976), 300-01.

extrañas como puede parecer a simple vista. En la época existían fuertes lazos entre los asalariados de la pluma, jóvenes procedentes de provincias que se abrían paso en el mundo del periodismo, que por sus estrechos vínculos con la política, con frecuencia era la plataforma para alcanzar alguna colocación gubernamental. El agitado y cambiante escenario político determinaba que los periódicos tuvieran una vida inestable, y para afrontar los inconvenientes de esa inestabilidad, los periodistas mantenían una actitud solidaria y gremial que muchas veces quedaba por encima de la militancia partidista.[8]

Así parece haber ocurrido en el caso de *Doña Manuela*, cuya orientación antiunionista permitió que Bécquer contara con la colaboración de sus amigos republicanos. Para González Bravo, el enemigo principal no eran los republicanos, sino los unionistas, con los que se disputaba el gobierno. De ahí que la prensa controlada por él no dudara en atacarlos mucho más que a la oposición que se situaba fuera del sistema. Por eso *El Español*, uno de sus periódicos, acogía coplas satíricas contra O'Donnell de Manuel de Palacio, redactor de *Gil Blas*. Y, del mismo modo, los hermanos Bécquer colaborarán, entre octubre de 1865 y febrero de 1866 en *Gil Blas* con unas caricaturas antiunionistas.[9] Este mismo periódico defendería a Bécquer cuando, siendo de nuevo fiscal de novelas, fue criticado por los sectores más conservadores.[10]

La suerte corrida por *Doña Manuela* es un buen ejemplo de la situación que acabamos de describir. El periódico murió con el primer número debido a la intervención del gobierno, que reaccionó con dureza ante un ataque que desbordaba los estrechos márgenes establecidos por la ley de imprenta. Tal reacción era previsible, puesto que se trataba de un ataque político que incidía directamente en el ámbito de lo privado. En

8 B. Pérez Galdós, en *Fortunata y Jacinta*, ed. F. Caudet (Madrid: Cátedra, 1983), II, 15, describe así la atmósfera que reinaba en los cafés: 'Allí brillaba espléndidamente esa fraternidad española en cuyo seno se dan mano de amigo el carlista y el republicano, el progresista de cabeza dura y el moderado implacable'.

9 R. Benítez, 'Los hermanos Bécquer en *Gil Blas*', *Ínsula*, (1972), núm. 311.

10 R. Benítez, 'El periódico *Gil Blas* defiende a Bécquer, censor de novelas', *Hispanic Review*, XXXVI (1968), 35-43.

efecto, para cualquier lector de la época estaba claro que 'Doña Manuela' era Manuela Bargues, la esposa del general O'Donnell. El título del periódico, el dibujo de portada y las insinuaciones vertidas en el editorial venían a decir que el general, el gobierno y la Unión Liberal estaban manejados por ella, lo cual, en una época de dominio absoluto del hombre en la esfera pública, era un recurso ridiculizante de primer orden, un insulto. De ahí que el asunto saliera del ámbito de la política y se convirtiera en un escándalo que atentaba contra el honor personal del general O'Donnell.

Según informó la prensa de la época, el encargado de vengar la afrenta fue Aureliano Vinyals, uno de los hijos que Manuela Bargues había tenido de su primer esposo, el comerciante catalán Ignacio Vinyals.[11] El hijastro de O'Donnell hizo diversas gestiones para identificar al responsable del periódico y desafiarlo para batirse en duelo. No debió de serle muy difícil, pues el escándalo tuvo que ser la comidilla de los mentideros de la capital. *Los Tiempos* publicó el 30 de setiembre un comunicado en el que afirmaba que ninguno de sus colaboradores había participado en *Doña Manuela*, deplorando al mismo tiempo que se hubiera amenazado al director de ese periódico. Es probable que el comunicado fuera un primer intento de Bécquer de alejar el peligro que se le venía encima. Pero no fue suficiente, puesto que el 13 de octubre *Las Noticias*, dirigido por su amigo Rodríguez Correa, publicó otro comunicado en el que desmentía rotundamente los rumores que le atribuían la dirección de *Doña Manuela*:

> Habiéndose dicho en algunos círculos que yo formo parte de la redacción del periódico *Doña Manuela*, o que lo he inspirado, me encuentro en el deber de desmentir una especie que ignoro cuál haya podido ser su fundamento. Abrigo la esperanza de que ninguna de las personas que me conocen darán crédito a un falso rumor que me perjudica, cargándome con la responsabilidad moral

---

11 Según indica M. Ibo, *op. cit.*, 80, O'Donnell se casó en 1837 con Manuela Bargues, viuda del comerciante catalán Ignacio Vinyals, de quien había tenido dos hijas y el citado Aureliano. Pageard, *op. cit.*, 393, afirma que Aureliano Vinyals era yerno de O'Donnell, pero el general no tuvo hijos.

de escritos cuya índole condeno y cuyo género repugna a mi carácter.[12]

El mentís es terminante e inequívoco, pero al mismo tiempo suena a forzado, a convencional. Parece el resultado de un acuerdo con la parte ofendida para evitar el duelo. No es casual que aparezca como intermediario Rodríguez Correa, que en 1858 había trabajado en *El Reino*, periódico unionista. El amigo de Bécquer, bien relacionado con los ambientes unionistas, era la persona indicada para mediar entre ambas partes y evitar que el asunto tuviera trágicas consecuencias. A pesar de esos indicios, y a falta de otras pruebas, el mentís sería suficiente para creer que el poeta nada tuvo que ver con *Doña Manuela*. El análisis detenido del editorial de presentación permite, sin embargo, comprobar que existen en él suficientes concordancias con otros textos becquerianos como para que podamos atribuir al poeta su autoría. Para ello reproduciremos el editorial modernizando la ortografía y la puntuación, aclarando las referencias a personajes y situaciones y señalando las concordancias más importantes.

Advertencia[13]

Deseando darse a conocer al público *Doña Manuela*, advierte a sus lectores que ésta será la primera y única vez que salga a prueba por las calles.

Esta señora será *recogida*,[14] aunque detesta las *recogidas*, porque su quebrantada salud no le permite callejear con frecuencia.

Doña Manuela aprovecha esta ocasión para poner en conocimiento de sus numerosos amigos que desde el próximo número publicará en sus columnas un folletín titulado 'La

12 *Obras completas* (Madrid: Aguilar, 1969), 1228.

13 En la prensa de la época, éste era el título de una sección introductoria en la que se daban avisos a los lectores, se comentaban los incidentes del periódico con la censura, etc.

14 Juego verbal: 'recatada, honesta' y 'secuestros de la prensa ordenados por el gobierno'.

tertulia,[15] o cuadros de la vida airada', dibujados por uno cuyo corazón vale por *doce*.[16]

... ...

Con el permiso de la fiscalía vamos a tener el gusto de presentar a nuestros suscritores a *Doña Manuela*.

Lo general, tratándose de periódicos, es que éstos sean presentados a quienes les favorecen.

Nosotros vamos a proceder en razón inversa, precisamente para huir de todo lo que huela a *general*,[17] que en estos momentos podría parecer alusión.

¡Ser presentados a *Doña Manuela*! ¡Ahí es nada lo del ojo!

Ser presentados a *Doña Manuela* en la situación[18] que atravesamos equivale a clavar la rueda de la fortuna, a heredar un tío en Californias (sic), a sacar el premio gordo de la lotería.[19] Y de todas estas ventajas van a disfrutar nuestros suscritores en el mero hecho de serlo.

¡Cuántos unionistas de los que aún permanecen en los limbos del favor les envidiarán la fortuna!

Pero '¿quién es *Doña Manuela*?'—preguntarán algunos, deseosos de saber si en efecto la ganga de ser presentados a esta señora es tan grande como dicen.

¿Quién es *Doña Manuela*? He aquí una pregunta a la que no es del todo fácil contestar.

El asunto tiene algo de teológico.

Tratemos de ser claros.

---

15 Parece aludir a la tertulia que Manuela Bargues celebraba habitualmente en su casa. De acuerdo con lo que se dice más adelante, se insinúa que en esa tertulia se decidían las cuestiones de gobierno. A. Fernández de los Ríos, primero colaborador y después enemigo de O'Donnell, alude a 'los rumores, no ya sobre los hombre políticos, sino sobre las mujeres políticas' (*Luchas políticas en la España del siglo XIX* [Madrid: 1880], II, 456). El título del folletín anunciado podría también aludir a la afición de Manuela Bargues por los folletines truculentos: 'Gustaba doña Manuela de la lectura de folletines, y se deleitaba con los más excitantes, de acción enmarañada y liosa' (B. Pérez Galdós, *op. cit.*, 1020).

16 Más adelante se menciona a 'los doce apóstoles de espada', probable alusión al grupo dirigente de la Unión Liberal, en la que los militares tenían mucha influencia. Entre los generales unionistas figuraban: Concha, San Miguel, Serrano, Ros de Olano, Dulce, etc.

17 Evidente juego verbal entre 'lo general' y 'general' (O'Donnell).

18 En el argot político de la época, *la situación* designaba al gobierno.

19 Clara insinuación de que Manuela Bargues otorgaba prebendas.

Doña Manuela es el verbo vicalvarista[20] hecho mujer.[21]

Es el punto del *círculo*[22] del cual parten y al cual convergen todas sus irradiaciones.

Es el principio y el fin: el *alpha* y el *omega*.[23]

Su espíritu flotaba en el caos de la política sobre el haz de las aguas sin nombre[24] antes que el Programa de Manzanares[25]

---

20 La Unión Liberal era designada también como vicalvarismo, nombre derivado de Vicálvaro, pueblo de las cercanías de Madrid en el que en junio de 1854 se pronunciaron los generales O'Donnell y Dulce contra el gobierno del conde de San Luis.

21 Bécquer utiliza esa expresión, tomada de San Juan, 1, 14, en *Cartas literarias a una mujer*: '[La mujer] es, en una palabra, el verbo poético hecho carne', *Obras completas*, 620. También aparece en el artículo 'Dos en uno': 'Pagar es un verbo que se hizo nómina para redimir las ambiciones impacientes de ciertas conciencias valetudinarias, verbo cuya trasfiguración gramatical, vulgo conjugación, es sumamente peligrosa en boca sobre todo del señor ministro de Hacienda'.

22 Juego verbal: 'asociación política' y 'circunferencia'.

23 *Cf. La creación*: 'Brahma es el punto de la circunferencia: de él parte y a él converge todo. No tuvo principio ni tendrá fin' (*Obras completas*, 303). La expresión se basa en el Apocalipsis, 1, 8 y 22, 13.

24 Esta imagen, tomada del Génesis, 1, 2, aparece también en *Cartas literarias a una mujer*: '... las aguas de oro que flotan en la imaginación [...] pensamientos que nadan en su caos' (*Obras completas*, 624) y *Apólogo*: 'Brahma se mecía satisfecho sobre el cáliz de una gigantesca flor de loto que flotaba sobre el haz de las aguas sin nombre', (*Ibid.*, 394). Esta descripción de los orígenes de la Unión Liberal se corresponde con otro artículo (R. Benítez, *Bécquer tradicionalista* [Madrid: Gredos, 1971], 29), en el que Bécquer recurre al mito del nacimiento de Minerva y a la versión bíblica de la creación del mundo. Por otra parte, la imagen de algo vaporoso flotando 'sobre el haz de las aguas' es muy frecuente en Bécquer: '¿Ves allá, entre los espesos cañaverales, encenderse una llama ligera y cárdena, que vacila y corre sobre el haz de las fétidas aguas del pantano?' (*Obras completas*, 83); '... los fuegos fatuos que corren sobre el haz de las aguas infectas' (*Ibid.*, 141); '... los fuegos fatuos que cruzan como exhalaciones sobre el haz de las lagunas' (*Ibid.*, 161); 'Corren como llamas azules y ligeras sobre el haz de los pantanos' (*Ibid.*, 218); 'Ven a mecerte en las ramas de los sauces, sobre el haz del agua' (*Ibid.*, 268); '¿No habéis visto [...] levantarse [...] del haz de un pantano [...] un jirón de niebla que flota lentamente en el vacío ...?' (*Ibid.*, 365).

25 El Programa de Manzanares (6 de julio) fue el manifiesto de la sublevación de Vicálvaro, en el que O'Donnell se comprometía a llevar a cabo una serie de medidas progresistas. El manifiesto atrajo el apoyo popular a los sublevados, que habían sido militarmente derrotados por las tropas

sacase el mundo de Vicálvaro de la nada de una rebelión vencida.

Doña Manuela, pues, era antes de la Unión Liberal, es en la Unión y seguirá siendo cuando la Unión haya desaparecido.

Porque, como dicen los demócratas,[26] la idea no muere, y *Doña Manuela* no es una mujer, es una idea.

Esto parecerá a nuestros lectores ininteligible; por nuestra parte fuerza es confesar que también se nos antoja algo confuso, y sin embargo, abrigamos la esperanza de que nos hemos de entender sin comprendernos.

¡Maravillas de la teología!

Volvamos a *Doña Manuela*.

Doña Manuela dijimos que era una idea: es más que una idea, es un símbolo.

El pueblo castellano, entusiasta del valor heroico, sintetizó una época en un hombre, y tuvo al Cid con el Romancero en que se reflejan sus glorias.

El pueblo alemán, en su ansia de ciencia y de maravillas, creó a Fausto,[27] que tuvo por cantor a Goethe.

El vicalvarismo, que tenía algo de mujer por la índole de su carácter,[28] sus defectos y sus pasiones, deseoso de encontrar una fórmula, subió al Tabor del presupuesto,[29] y ante sus doce

---

gubernamentales, y les permitió derrocar al gobierno. Por eso en el texto se habla de 'una rebelión vencida'.

26 Miembros del partido demócrata, en el que destacaba Francisco Pi y Margall.

27 *Cf.* 'La soledad': 'El pueblo ha sido, y será siempre, el gran poeta de todas las edades y de todas las naciones. / Nadie mejor que él sabe sintetizar en sus obras las creencias, las aspiraciones y el sentimiento de una época. [...] El soñó a Fausto' (*Obras completas*, 1187). *Cf.* también 'Solar de la casa del Cid en Burgos': '... el Cid, la más acabada y perfecta figura entre las varias de que la Historia nos ha consignado el nombre y el pueblo se ha encargado después de completarla con todos sus detalles ...' (*Ibid.*, 993); '... este mismo lujo de detalles, hijos de la imaginación del pueblo, revelan poderosamente la vitalidad del personaje [el Cid] que palpita a través de sus creaciones, que son como un ropaje espléndido tejido por los romanceros ...' (*Ibid.*, 994).

28 R. Pageard (*op. cit.*, 318) señala que la caracterización femenina de la Unión Liberal se encuentra ya en un artículo atribuido a Bécquer, fechado en 1862.

29 Parodia basada en la transfiguración de Jesús ante sus discípulos (Mateo, 17, 1-13; Marcos, 9, 2-13 y Lucas, 9, 28-36). La alusión al presupuesto alude a las corruptelas y el reparto de prebendas que la oposición atribuía a la Unión Liberal. En un artículo de *Los Tiempos*, diario moderado del que Bécquer era redactor, también se recurre a referencias bíblicas: '... esa

apóstoles de espada, se trasfiguró en *Doña Manuela*, que tuvo a *La Correspondencia* por órgano.[30]

Y nació la Unión Liberal, partido hembra, con sus infidelidades de *boudoir*, sus caprichos de *toilette*, sus coqueterías de salón y sus pequeños odios femeninos.

Tenemos, pues, una mujer que es un partido, o lo que es igual, un partido que es mujer.

He aquí explicado sencillamente por qué el pueblo, sintético y pintoresco en sus expresiones, al ver que la Unión gasta y triunfa, dice que 'es *Doña Manuela*, que satisface a nuestra costa sus caprichos y sus fantasías'. He aquí explicado asimismo por qué en las columnas de los periódicos, en las mesas de los cafés, en los salones de los círculos y en los corros de las plazas,[31] al tener noticia de una nueva calaverada política, de una traición, de un despilfarro o de un resello,[32] exclaman las gentes: 'Aquí anda la mano de *Doña Manuela*'.

Y a favor de esta figura retórica, el nombre de *Doña Manuela* cunde y se propala de un extremo a otro de la península, no faltando quien, creyéndola una mujer de carne y hueso, que come y bebe, que anda y respira, asegura haberla visto, hoy en el teatro, ayer en el paseo, el otro en el salón de alguna embajada extranjera ...

Fenómenos de la imaginación.

Doña Manuela, tal como se la finge el vulgo, no existe.

En vano es, pues, que el fiscal, armado del sangriento lápiz,[33]

---

agrupación de hombres de tan distintas y opuestas procedencias, que en mala hora tomó el nombre de Unión Liberal, que no tienen lema fijo, más que su adhesión al presupuesto, ¿qué se proponen? ¿qué? Saborear de nuevo las ollas de Egipto' (Véase J. Estruch, *art. cit.*, 104).

30 *La Correspondencia* fue fundada en 1848 por Manuel María de Santa Ana, que le dio una orientación independiente. Pero en 1859, durante el gobierno de la Unión Liberal, fue arrendada a Ignacio José Escobar, futuro marqués de Valdeiglesias, que la puso al servicio de la Unión Liberal.

31 Una descripción parecida de los ambientes políticos de la capital se encuentra en *Desde mi celda*, ed. D. Villanueva (Madrid: Castalia, 1985), 111: '... las redacciones, donde hierven las ideas que han de caer al día siguiente como la piedra en el lago, y los círculos de la opinión pública, que comienzan en el casino, siguen en las mesas de los cafés y acaban en los guardacantones de las calles'.

32 En el argot político de la época, designaba el cambio de partido por motivaciones interesadas.

33 *Sangriento* tiene doble sentido: 'cruel' y 'de color rojo'. El lápiz rojo era utilizado por el censor para señalar lo que no podía publicarse. En un

siga con mirada inquieta el caprichoso curso de nuestra inocente pluma, pronto a descargar sus iras sobre ese nombre si por casualidad lo encuentra en nuestro periódico; en vano que los satélites de la Unión quieran rodear ese fantasma de mujer de una atmósfera de inviolabilidad que aquí no ha alcanzado ni a las cosas más altas; sus iras y sus afanes sólo podrán servir para confirmar en su error al vulgo, y que éste pregunte con tono misterioso: '¿Conque en efecto hay una *Doña Manuela*?'

Por nuestra parte no hemos de contribuir al engaño. Volvemos a repetirlo. *Doña Manuela* es una mujer mítica, es una concepción ideal, un símbolo.

Reunid en un haz todas las debilidades, los errores, los absurdos, los odios y las miserias de la Unión, colocadlo delante de un espejo, y la imagen que se refleje en el cristal podrá daros una idea de su tipo.

Trazad en un periódico, día por día, la historia de las mistificaciones, las pequeñeces, las ilegalidades y los contrasentidos de la situación que atravesamos; barajad en sus columnas los rasgos de la ambición y el descreimiento,[34] de la nulidad y el amor propio, del descaro y de la envidia, y ese periódico en que se encuentre reflejado el espíritu del vicalvarismo tendrá que llamarse como se llama el que hoy ofrecemos al público: *Doña Manuela*.

Conclusión

Aunque los datos externos — sobre todo el mentís de Bécquer — están en contra de atribuir al poeta toda participación en *Doña Manuela*, el análisis intrínseco proporciona elementos más que suficientes para atribuirle, cuando menos, el editorial, y, por

---

pasaje del artículo 'Cuestión previa', que hemos reproducido anteriormente, se habla del fiscal, 'que esgrime implacablemente su lápiz rojo'.

34 Aunque A. Fernández de los Ríos (*op. cit.*, 375), dice que O'Donnell era escéptico en materia religiosa, afirmando que 'no era creyente en la comunión católica', aquí *descreimiento* no parece referirse a la religión, sino al hecho de que la Unión Liberal se nutría de tránsfugas de otros partidos. En *Los Tiempos* se utilizan con frecuencia referencias religiosas para aludir a esta cuestión: 'La Unión Liberal [...] se alimentó con los incrédulos, ateos y tránsfugas de todos los partidos, [...] sembrando el ateísmo político ...' (2 de Junio, 1865); '... esos descreídos, esos escépticos, esos ateos políticos ...' (24 de Junio, 1865); '... esa agrupación prostituida, formada de los tránsfugas y de los apóstatas de todos los bandos ...' (29 de Junio, 1865).

tanto, la dirección del periódico, con lo que se confirman los rumores que circularon entonces. Dadas las repercusiones que alcanzó el escándalo, conscientemente provocado por los inspiradores del libelo — probablemente González Bravo — no es extraño que Bécquer se viera obligado a publicar el rotundo mentís, única forma de evitar un duelo con el hijastro de O'Donnell.

Además de proporcionarnos una visión inédita de la personalidad del poeta, la autoría becqueriana del editorial nos demuestra claramente dos cuestiones: primero, que Bécquer participó activamente en la agitada vida política de su tiempo y que, por tanto, es ilusoria su tradicional imagen de poeta angelical, alejado de la prosaica realidad social; segundo, que Bécquer, hasta cuando escribía libelos políticos, era un gran escritor, puesto que seguía utilizando su personal estilo, el mismo que hallamos en lo mejor de su obra. Sabíamos que Bécquer había escrito — y no de manera fugaz — prosa política,[35] pero ahora podemos comprobar que tiene una gran calidad. El editorial de *Doña Manuela*, lleno de maliciosas alusiones, expresiones irónicas e ingeniosos juegos verbales, constituye una pieza magistral de la sátira política, y puede y debe figurar al lado de sus mejores textos.

35 Llama la atención que la crítica haya ignorado este aspecto de la obra becqueriana, que el poeta no ocultó. Así, en *Desde mi celda* (*ed. cit.*, 110-11), habla de su trabajo como cronista parlamentario de *El Contemporáneo*, y su amigo R. Rodríguez Correa declara en el prólogo a las *Obras* de Bécquer (reproducido en *Rimas*, ed. J. C. Torres [Madrid: Castalia, 1982], 206): 'Escribió mucho y en géneros diferentes, como zarzuelas, traducciones, artículos políticos ...'.

'Hoy es siempre todavía': la plasticidad del ayer en los poemas de Antonio Machado

LUIS CAPARRÓS ESPERANTE
Universidad de La Coruña

> Un día tornarán, con luz del fondo ungidos,
> los cuerpos virginales a la orilla vieja.
>
> ANTONIO MACHADO

El tiempo es tema tan evidente en la lírica de Antonio Machado, tan estudiado además, que habría que disculparse por tentar terrenos tan transitados con algún ánimo de originalidad. Por ello, para aviso de transeúntes apresurados, debo precisar antes cuáles son mis objetivos y cuáles no. Mi principal objetivo es hacer evidentes algunos procedimientos de simbolización con un claro valor constructivo, esto es, algunos recursos literarios que le sirven a Antonio Machado para construir poemas ... más que sobre el tiempo, poemas saturados de temporalidad. No son objetivos de este trabajo, sin embargo, dos aspectos de la temporalidad estrechamente relacionados con lo anterior: el puramente teórico o filosófico y el histórico.

La fórmula machadiana de la poesía como 'palabra esencial en el tiempo' ha tenido un considerable éxito, aunque no haya sido siempre bien entendida.[1] Machado señalaba con ella un

---

1 La bibliografía sobre este aspecto es abundantísima, como es lógico. Sin ánimo alguno de exhaustividad, podrían señalarse: P. Cerezo Galán, *Palabra en el tiempo: poesía y filosofía en Antonio Machado* (Madrid: Gredos, 1975); P. de A. Cobos, *Humor y pensamiento de Antonio Machado en sus*

aspecto favorito del pensamiento filosófico de su tiempo, que desde Bergson alcanzaría una cumbre en el *Sein und Zeit* de Heidegger: el conflicto entre esencia y existencia. Para nuestro caso, como acabo de señalar, esos aspectos teóricos solamente importan como trasfondo metafísico de los poemas, que son el centro real de interés. Para Machado se trataría, por tanto, de hacer poemas a partir de una paradoja: la de salvar del tiempo el mismo tiempo. Pues bien, éste será el auténtico eje de este estudio: la cristalización de símbolos personales para expresar la concurrencia *en* el poema, sobre el plano del presente y desde la primera persona, de diferentes tiempos vivos, alejados entre sí. Y con 'tiempos vivos' quiero expresar que no se trata de recuerdos fosilizados, por así decirlo, sino de una voluntad de revitalización del pasado personal, con todas sus consecuencias. La poesía, en realidad, es la única vía para salvar lo esencial del pasado, para vencer los rígidos condicionantes de la existencia, que es tiempo en orden inflexible, sucesión inalterable, flecha lanzada al futuro.

Evidentemente, sería muy fácil señalar tal o cual comentario anterior — muchos, tan brillantes — a tal o cual poema de los aquí seleccionados. No me preocupan demasiado las inevitables coincidencias, pues el objeto último de estas páginas es mostrar la coherencia, casi diría, el sistema — recurrente, organizado, previsible — con que Antonio Machado temporaliza sus poemas. Y se trata de mostrarlo, además, en su desarrollo lógico ... desde el último al primer libro.

---

apócrifos (Madrid: *Ínsula*, [2ª ed.] 1972); M. Di Pinto, 'Antonio Machado e la poetica del tempo', en *Introduzione allo studio della poesia spagnola contemporanea* (Nápoles: Liguori, 1966), 45-51 y 121-38; E. Frutos Cortés, 'Ser y tiempo en la poesía', *Ínsula*, LV (1950), núms. 1-2; R. Gullón, *Una poética para Antonio Machado* (1970) (Madrid: Espasa-Calpe, 1986); P. Ilie, 'Verlaine and Machado: The Aesthetic Role of Time', *Comparative Literature*, XIV (1962), 261-65; J. López Morillas, 'Antonio Machado y la interpretación temporal de la poesía' (1961), en *Antonio Machado*, ed. R. Gullón y A. W. Phillips (Madrid: Taurus, 1973), 251-66; J. Marías, 'Machado y Heidegger', *Ínsula*, XCIV (1953), núms. 1-2; R. L. Predmore, 'El tiempo en la poesía de Antonio Machado', *PMLA*, LXIII (1948), 696-711; R. Sáez, 'Sens et conscience du temps dans l'oeuvre d'Antonio Machado', *Les Langues Néo-latines*, (1977), núm. 223, 75-90; etc.

I

Comenzaremos por el final. Esto nos lleva a uno de los últimos días de febrero de 1939, allá en la Cataluña francesa. Antonio Machado ha muerto — acaban de enterrarlo — y en un bolsillo de su gabán aparece 'un pequeño y arrugado papel', escrito a lápiz, con varias notas y versos.[2] En una de esas notas está la variante a uno de sus poemas a Guiomar, aquel amor tardío y clandestino, que había quedado al otro lado de la Península, en Portugal, con toda la guerra por medio:

> Y te enviaré mi canción:
> 'Se canta lo que se pierde',
> con un papagayo verde
> que la diga en tu balcón. (*Poesía y prosa*, 732)[3]

Donde pone 'Y te enviaré', el poeta ha corregido por 'Y te daré': 'Y te daré mi canción ...'. Volver sobre este poema de su *Cancionero apócrifo*, como el ahora viejo y agotado Machado acaba de hacer, y, además, hacerlo para no alterar sustancialmente el poema, podría pensarse que es algo gratuito, si no obsesivo. Claro que del verbo 'enviar' al verbo 'dar' hay un evidente deseo de presencia, que matiza su utilización en tiempo futuro. Pero no es esa precisión semántica lo importante, o no debía de serlo para él. Lo importante sería volver al diálogo con la amada enemiga, y eso es lo que el poema — siempre abierto — le acaba de permitir.

Pero en el raído gabán del poeta aparece también un texto lírico nuevo, brevísimo, un verso solitario: 'Estos días azules y este sol de la infancia' (*Poesía y prosa*, 836). La tentación de leer este verso en relación con el poemilla anterior es inevitable ...

'Se canta lo que se pierde', dice el verso central — éste,

2 La noticia procede de su hermano José, en *Últimas soledades de Antonio Machado (Recuerdos de su hermano José)* (1940) (Madrid: Forma, 1977). José Machado señala que estos textos están escritos con un lápiz que él mismo le había dejado, pocos días antes.

3 Cito los textos de Antonio Machado, en todos los casos, por la edición de Oreste Macrì, Antonio Machado, *Poesía y prosa* (Madrid: Espasa-Calpe/ Fundación Antonio Machado, 1988), 2 vols. La referencia al número de página acompaña la cita entre paréntesis.

incorregible — de la redondilla revisada. Ahí está expresada la angustia del tiempo, que es el acicate del poeta, según había dejado escrito él mismo, tiempo atrás. Bueno, no él mismo ... o no exactamente. Fue Juan de Mairena, el heterónimo machadiano, quien mediante una interrogación lo había afirmado, con pirueta de profesor de Retórica ... y de Gimnasia: 'Porque, ¿cantaría el poeta sin la angustia del tiempo?', se preguntaba Mairena (*Poesía y prosa*, 1936). La poesía, en fin, como había repetido tantas veces, es 'palabra en el tiempo' o 'palabra esencial en el tiempo'. Pero sobre todo, la poesía es 'diálogo del hombre con el tiempo' (*Poesía y prosa*, 1802, 1937 ...).

Lo que vibra en el verso final — en realidad, su último poema — es, desde luego, la emoción del tiempo — casi diría, la emoción del tiempo recobrado. Sin embargo, para hacer evidente todo aquello que guarda, conviene destacar sus circunstancias. Esos días azules de febrero — aquellos concretos que el poeta ha fijado en su último verso — suceden a otros días concretos, los de finales de enero de 1939, que no fueron azules, sino fríos y lluviosos. Como se sabe, en uno de esos días de enero don Antonio Machado ha cruzado su penúltimo límite, su penúltima frontera. Quizás recordaría, al escribir el verso, cómo su madre preguntaba, camino de Francia y del exilio, si faltaba mucho todavía para alcanzar Sevilla ... Los días prometen ahora la primavera, una primavera mediterránea y azul, y Antonio Machado puede soñar con haber alcanzado Sevilla, su sol de la infancia. Nos suena el verso como un desahogo. Desde su perspectiva, Machado ve una etapa más en su búsqueda del origen, como si su vida hubiese sido un largo viaje hacia un patio sevillano perdido.

¿A qué viene todo esto? O planteada la pregunta en otros términos: ¿está todo esto en el verso? ¿Es legítimo leer en él todo lo anterior? El verso realmente — materialmente — nos da poco. Sus palabras no son más que un esbozo, un par de pinceladas, seguramente el arranque de un poema que se iba escribiendo mentalmente, frente al paisaje, y que no dejó más rastro al llegar el día 22 de febrero, cuando el poeta cruzó la frontera definitiva. Pero, si lo vemos desde la perspectiva correcta, ese verso no está solo: es también el último verso del gran poema que forma el conjunto de su producción. Y desde luego, mal que le pese a la crítica inmanentista, sin todos estos datos señalados — cotextuales y vitales — apenas encontraríamos emoción en esas pocas palabras — emoción legítima, se entiende. Claro que tampoco la habría en el hermosísimo y largo poema a José María Palacio, el 'buen amigo' — fechado en abril de 1913 — si nosotros, lectores, no supiésemos que en el Espino está el cementerio de Soria, donde sobre el cadáver de Leonor, muerta en agosto del año anterior, llegaba entonces la tardía primavera de las tierras altas.

Sin embargo, el verso mismo, en su materialidad, nos ofrece pistas para rescatar algunas de las claves literarias que producen la emoción. Primero está el léxico: 'días azules', 'sol', 'infancia' ... Muchos, muchísimos versos de Antonio Machado juegan con palabras cercanas a éstas. La infancia, concretamente, es el espacio poético del paraíso, según un tópico repetido en la mejor literatura de nuestro siglo. 'Mi infancia son recuerdos de un patio de Sevilla' decía aquel otro conocidísimo alejandrino con que se autorretrata el poeta, al comienzo de *Campos de Castilla*. Pero no es ésa la clave, evidentemente. En el caso del alejandrino final, son los adjetivos demostrativos los que aportan toda la fuerza expresiva. '*Estos* días azules' llevan fecha, la subrayan incluso: 1939. Pero '*este* sol de la infancia' vuelve más densa y compleja esa datación.

Los demostrativos empleados indican proximidad, presencia. Aquí, como se ve, sirven además para hacer presente lo que está ausente. Podríamos decir, de modo más exacto, que sirven para hacer co-presentes situaciones o cosas de por sí naturalmente alejadas. *Este* sol, que brilla ahora, al final de todo, es también *aquel* sol que brillaba entonces, cuando todo comenzaba. Es éste y es aquél. Comienzo y final absolutos, de imposible concurrencia en el plano de la experiencia real, aparecen así unidos irónicamente en el verso, gracias exclusivamente a la poesía.

El procedimiento literario descrito, esa concurrencia y fusión de tiempos vividos — opuesta a la 'espacial' y secuencial de la experiencia — ha sido una técnica constante a lo largo de la obra de Machado, desde el primer libro — *Soledades* (1903) — hasta el último verso de 1939, que acabamos de ver. Y todavía más. El vehículo favorito para esa catársis temporal, realmente mágica, lo constituyen un puñado de imágenes rescatadas de la memoria profunda de Machado, precisamente la infantil: un patio cerrado, un limonero, y bajo él, una fuente con agua corriente ... Hay más elementos en la escena, pero los anteriores son los fundamentales. Son imágenes que él rescata de su recuerdo del palacio de los duques de Alba, de aquella casa de las Dueñas, en Sevilla, donde nació y donde pasó parte de su niñez.

Esas imágenes infantiles, en cuanto se constituyen en símbolos literarios, son polivalentes. Antonio Machado puede usarlas para hablar de su amor a Guiomar, cuando ya anda por la cincuentena pasada, o bien para expresar la voluntad de abrir su poesía a otros rumbos, cuando compone su segundo o tercer libro, mucho antes. El principal valor de esas imágenes consiste en su fuerte impregnación temporal. Cuando las emplea, sea cual sea su contexto, logra teñir de temporalidad experiencias humanas muy diversas, y con ello, gracias a la especie de perspectiva o escala temporal que ellas aportan, consigue darles auténtico calado, esa hondura sentimental que él cifraba — y hay que destacarlo ahora — en las coplas de Jorge Manrique.

'Este sol de la infancia ...' es, por tanto, un sol sevillano, el sol que iluminaba el patio de la casa de las Dueñas. De nuevo salta al labio el citadísimo verso: 'Mi infancia son recuerdos ...'. Sigamos por ahí, tirando de ese mismo hilo, que nos lleva desde el futuro al pasado.

II

Y vayamos diez, quizás veinte años antes. En *Nuevas canciones* (1917-1930) arranca de un modo similar, con el mismo uso del demostrativo, un soneto autobiográfico. Es un poema que ya comentó Bousoño, de un modo brillante, como ilustración de su idea de la superposición temporal en la lírica.[4] El sol se hace ahora luz. '*Este* sol de la infancia' se convierte en '*esta* luz de Sevilla ...'. Leamos, mejor, el soneto completo:

---

4 Carlos Bousoño, 'Tiempo futuro sobre tiempo presente: en Antonio Machado', en *Teoría de la expresión poética* (1952) (Madrid: Gredos, [5ª ed. aum.] 1970), I, 304-08.

Esta luz de Sevilla ... Es el palacio
donde nací, con su rumor de fuente.
Mi padre, en su despacho. — La alta frente,
la breve mosca, y el bigote lacio —.

Mi padre, aún joven. Lee, escribe, hojea
sus libros y medita. Se levanta;
va hacia la puerta del jardín. Pasea.
A veces habla solo, a veces canta.

Sus grandes ojos de mirar inquieto
ahora vagar parecen, sin objeto
donde puedan posar, en el vacío.

Ya escapan de su ayer a su mañana;
ya miran en el tiempo, ¡padre mío!,
piadosamente mi cabeza cana. (*Poesía y Prosa*, 666)

Desde el principio, como se ve, el eje fundamental de los versos recorridos está en la percepción subjetiva del tiempo, que gracias a la poesía no tiene por qué seguir una única y tiránica dirección, como sí sucede en la vida. 'Esta luz de Sevilla ...', arranca el primer cuarteto, con una sensación engañosa de inmediatez. 'Ya escapan de su ayer a su mañana', comienza el último terceto. La paráfrasis del poema podría ser: ya escapan de su ayer los ojos del padre, aún joven, hacia el hoy del hijo, ya viejo y canoso. Pero la clave del poema no es tan sencilla, porque el movimiento dominante no es ése, sino el de la voz poética, la del hijo viejo que marcha, a contracorriente del tiempo, hacia el padre joven.[5] Dos tiempos, naturalmente separados, se funden así de manera paradójica, sobre direcciones prohibidas, por así decirlo.

---

5 Bousoño marca las semejanzas del procedimiento con la metáfora, aunque, como él dice, se trata de una superposición de 'dos esferas que la realidad mantiene separadas' sin establecer comparaciones entre ellas (*ibid.*, 306). En realidad, Bousoño niega cualquier movimiento: 'La misión del procedimiento, en este caso, es transmitirnos, con intensidad difícilmente superable, la impresión del "fugit irreparabile tempus", la impresión de la instantaneidad del vivir y el correlativo sentimiento de melancolía. ¿Cómo lo hace? Diríamos que *suprimiendo* las zonas intermedias entre la juventud del padre y la vejez del hijo, pero con tal ímpetu que los dos hechos, que en realidad andan muy lejos de ser sincrónicos, se superponen en una imaginaria simultaneidad: el padre es joven, repito, cuando el hijo es *ya* viejo' (307).

Me gustaría añadir que en el soneto, esa vivencia — subjetiva — del tiempo aparece de un modo inmediato, más expresivo que conceptual. A pesar de ello, creo que el poema no alcanza el nivel de otros machadianos, pues aun así, pesa más en él el brillo de la idea sorprendente que la pura y desnuda emoción lírica. Claro que por eso mismo sirve perfectamente para destacar el procedimiento seguido, como lo demuestra el ejemplo de Bousoño. En cualquier caso, ya va siendo momento de leer otras citas de Juan de Mairena, que he ido reservando hasta ahora. Una de ellas es la continuación de aquella anterior, la que decía ...

> Porque, ¿cantaría el poeta sin la angustia del tiempo, sin esa fatalidad de que las cosas no sean para nosotros, como para Dios, todas a la par, sino dispuestas en serie y encartuchadas como balas de rifle, para disparadas una tras otra? Que hayamos de esperar a que se fría un huevo, a que se abra una puerta o a que madure un pepino, es algo, señores, que merece nuestra reflexión. En cuanto nuestra vida coincide con nuestra conciencia, es el tiempo la realidad última, rebelde al conjuro de la lógica, irreductible, inevitable, fatal. (*Poesía y Prosa*, 1936)

La poesía vence esa fatalidad. O al menos, ésa es su misión, piensa Machado. De este modo, la poesía puede contradecir el 'irreparabile tempus' de Virgilio, que tantas veces ha citado. Mairena mismo añade, en otro lugar:

> Cierto que lo pasado es, como tal pasado, inmodificable; quiero decir que, si he nacido en viernes, ya es imposible de toda imposibilidad que haya venido al mundo en cualquier otro día de la semana. Pero esto es una verdad estéril de puro lógica, aunque nos sirva para hombrearnos con los dioses, los cuales fracasarían como nosotros si intentasen cambiar la fecha de nuestro natalicio. ¿Algo más? Que siempre es interesante averiguar lo que fue. Conformes. Mas, para nosotros, lo pasado es lo que vive en la memoria de alguien, y en cuanto actúa en una conciencia, por ende incorporado a un presente, y en constante función de porvenir. Visto así — y no es ningún absurdo que así lo veamos —, lo pasado es materia de infinita plasticidad, apta para recibir las más variadas formas. (*Poesía y prosa*, 2018)

Me he propuesto hablar solamente de recursos líricos, no de ideas o teorías que puedan ser abstractas y no tener directa correspondencia en la práctica poética. Pero no es éste el caso.

La idea no es estéril — como sí la lógica — por utilizar las mismas palabras de Mairena.[6] Esa plasticidad del pasado, a que alude Mairena, se alcanza en el espacio del poema mediante la fusión de tiempos. La proyección del pasado como futuro, que encontramos en el último verso del gran poema machadiano, recorre toda su obra. 'Hoy es siempre todavía' (*Poesía y prosa*, 627) afirmará un brevísimo poema de *Nuevas canciones*, en un solo espesísimo verso. Y más tarde, en una canción con fecha de 1924, escribirá 'del Hoy que será Mañana, / del Ayer que es Todavía' (*Poesía y prosa*, 664).

La misma idea resuena en el poema CLXIX, incluido en *De un cancionero apócrifo* (1924-1936) con el título 'Últimas lamentaciones de Abel Martín':

Hoy, con la primavera,
soñé que un fino cuerpo me seguía
cual dócil sombra. Era
mi cuerpo juvenil, el que subía
de tres en tres peldaños la escalera.
— Hola, galgo de ayer. (Su luz de acuario
trocaba el hondo espejo
por agria luz sobre un rincón de osario.)
— ¿Tú conmigo, rapaz?
— Contigo, viejo.

6 Es obligado citar a Aurora de Albornoz, 'El problema de la identidad personal', en *La presencia de Miguel de Unamuno en Antonio Machado* (Madrid: Gredos, 1968), 277-310: 'Dentro de la lógica temporal de Abel Martín, el filósofo sabe que "*A* no es nunca *A* en dos momentos sucesivos [...]". Pero esto dentro de la lógica, dentro del mundo del pensamiento. Mas a través del sueño y del recuerdo — o del sueño del recuerdo — todo es posible, hasta encontrar el yo que fuimos' (286). Aurora de Albornoz también comenta la concreta cita de Mairena que acabamos de ver: 'Como indiqué, creo hallar [en esa cita] una presencia, un comentario, mejor, a algunas ideas de Unamuno: es unamuniana la de la imposibilidad de modificar el pasado; lo es la de la posibilidad de transformar el pasado en porvenir. Mas hallamos un sabor del más auténtico machadismo en ese deseo de creación del yo en el pasado partiendo de la pura imaginación. Es decir: lejos de desesperarse por no poder cambiar lo que ha sido, el poeta halla una solución: crear un pasado que no fue' (290-91).

Soñé la galería
al huerto de ciprés y limonero;
tibias palomas en la piedra fría,
en el cielo de añil rojo pandero,
y en la mágica angustia de la infancia
la vigilia del ángel más austero.

La ausencia y la distancia
volví a soñar con túnicas de aurora;
firme en el arco tenso la saeta
del mañana, la vista aterradora
de la llama prendida en la espoleta
de su granada.

¡Oh Tiempo, oh Todavía
preñado de inminencias!
tú me acompañas en la senda fría,
tejedor de esperanzas e impaciencias.

(*Poesía y prosa*, 714-15)

Con este poema aparece una modalidad de concurrencia temporal nada rara en la poesía de Machado, y desde luego, más sofisticada que la anterior, pues los dos protagonistas pasan a ser uno solo, desdoblado en dos tiempos. Anotada esta especificidad, creo que buena parte de los versos se comentan solos, si se contemplan a la luz de cuanto vamos recorriendo y de lo que aún recorreremos: esa coincidencia del 'rapaz' con el 'viejo' — que se relaciona con la 'ilusión cándida y vieja' del poema VII, que luego se verá — el inevitable 'huerto de ciprés y limonero' — que con notas simbólicas muy parecidas, se proyecta desde la infancia —, la referencia a 'la ausencia y la distancia', con su peculiar modelización plástica de lo ausente, que también se verá después ... En fin, todo ello podemos resumirlo por ahora en esa llamada final al Tiempo, al concreto Todavía, tendido como saeta al futuro y 'preñado de inminencias'.[7]

Esto mismo, aunque de modo aun más complejo, volvemos a encontrarlo en uno de los poemas amorosos a Guiomar, donde

7 Aurora de Albornoz (*op. cit.*, 282) cita este poema como ejemplo de sus reflexiones sobre la personalidad problemática en Antonio Machado, y liga ese proceso de recuperación del yo de ayer machadiano con la novela proustiana y con los diferentes yoes pasados de Unamuno, el real y el ex-futuro.

escribe estos versos:

> [...] Todo a esta luz de Abril se transparenta;
> todo en el hoy de ayer, el Todavía
> que en sus maduras horas
> el tiempo canta y cuenta,
> se funde en una sola melodía,
> que es un coro de tardes y de auroras [...]
>
> (*Poesía y prosa*, 729)

'El tiempo canta y cuenta' escribe aquí, pues el tiempo es el sujeto poético por excelencia.[8] Y acaso podría bastarnos con esa referencia al 'hoy de ayer', y aun más, al 'Todavía' — con mayúscula — que florecen y se funden en '*esta* — demostrativo — luz de Abril'. Pero este poema a Guiomar, que comienza por una precisión cronológica — 'hoy te escribo en mi celda de viajero' — ofrece más centros de interés:

> Hoy te escribo en mi celda de viajero,
> a la hora de una cita imaginaria.
> Rompe el iris al aire el aguacero,
> y al monte su tristeza planetaria.
> Sol y campanas en la vieja torre.
> ¡Oh, tarde viva y quieta
> que opuso al *panta rhei* su *nada corre*,
> tarde niña que amaba tu poeta!
> ¡Y día adolescente
> — ojos claros y músculos morenos —,
> cuando pensaste a Amor, junto a la fuente,
> besar tus labios y apresar tus senos!
> Todo a esta luz de Abril se transparenta;
> todo en el hoy de ayer, el Todavía
> que en sus maduras horas
> el tiempo canta y cuenta,
> se funde en una sola melodía,
> que es un coro de tardes y de auroras.
> A ti, Guiomar, esta nostalgia mía.
>
> (*Poesía y prosa*, 729)

8 'Canto y cuento es la poesía' — dice en otro lugar —: 'Se canta una viva historia, / contando su melodía' (*Poesía y prosa*, 663). El tiempo sabe cantar historias y sabe contar melodías. Del mismo modo, y mucho antes, la canción de los niños que aparecía en el poema VIII de *Soledades. Galerías. Otros poemas* tenía 'confusa la historia / y clara la pena' (*Poesía y prosa*, 95). Toda una poética de la nostalgia ...

Los tres apóstrofes, con sus respectivas personalizaciones — 'tarde viva y quieta', 'tarde niña' y 'día adolescente' — conducen en el flujo de los versos hasta '*esta* luz de Abril', o mejor dicho, es *esta* luz de Abril — presente — la que contiene y transparenta todos los presentes del ayer. Es así un Todavía. O el 'Hoy de Ayer', de este poema, es también aquel 'Hoy es Siempre Todavía', antes visto. Ahí está el sentido final del poema: cómo toda honda experiencia sentimental, sea o no gozosa, 'se funde en una sola melodía, / que es un coro de tardes y de auroras'.

Y en ese Todavía, que cruza el presente amoroso de un don Antonio Machado bien maduro ya, se dibuja al fondo una fuente: 'cuando pensaste a Amor, junto a la fuente'. En seguida volveremos con esa fuente, que es fuente modernista. En el caso concreto de este poema a Guiomar, como ya señaló Valverde, el espacio de los versos hace posible una cita amorosa en el ayer, ambos aún niños, en torno a la simbólica fuente del jardín.[9] Una vez más, solamente la poesía puede ofrecer el regreso al ayer, ahora como un encuentro donde se suman dos ayeres diferentes, el del viejo poeta, cuando no era viejo, y el de su amada imposible, ay, cuando no era imposible ...

Antes citaba la extraña confluencia del espacio mítico de la infancia con el del amor — y el amor maduro, además. Lo acabamos de ver. Y el primer poema de estas mismas 'Canciones a Guiomar' nos sitúa aun más cerca del semillero

---

9 Vid. *Nuevas canciones y De un cancionero apócrifo*, ed. José María Valverde (Madrid: Castalia, 1971), 85: 'En [el poema] IV [de las *Canciones a Guiomar*] le hallamos solo, enviando a la amada un mensaje serenamente desesperado: su amor parece ahora sobre todo reviviscencia de un pasado que no fue suyo, la nostalgia de un tiempo en que "Guiomar" era muchacha, pero el poeta no estaba allí. El hoy es un "Todavía", y el amor de ahora resucita ese pasado imposible, queriendo ir a contracorriente del tiempo, hacia una unión en el ayer'. Sin embargo, no puedo seguir a Valverde, por todo cuanto vamos viendo, en su valoración final: 'En conjunto, el poema es algo hermético y enigmático: el lector echa de menos las informaciones concretas que le permitan seguir el sentido del poema, su tema, sin quedarse fuera. Por eso, quizá sea uno de los menos afortunados de toda la obra de Antonio Machado, por su tono sibilino y por su imaginería de sueño, carentes de la clave necesaria' (*ibid.*).

sentimental y lírico de estas imágenes temporales. Lo transcribo:

> No sabía
> si era un limón amarillo
> lo que tu mano tenía,
> o el hilo de un claro día,
> Guiomar, en dorado ovillo.
> Tu boca me sonreía.
>
> Yo pregunté: ¿Qué me ofreces?
> ¿Tiempo en fruto, que tu mano
> eligió entre madureces
> de tu huerta?
>
> ¿Tiempo vano
> de una bella tarde yerta?
> ¿Dorada ausencia encantada?
> ¿Copia en el agua dormida?
> ¿De monte en monte encendida,
> la alborada
> verdadera?
> ¿Rompe en sus turbios espejos
> amor la devanadera
> de sus crepúsculos viejos? (*Poesía y prosa*, 726-27)

No es fácil seguir la idea del poema ... Guiomar ofrece al poeta — ambos, personajes literarios, por supuesto — un limón. Pero ese limón ofrecido desborda bien pronto su inmediatez de 'limón amarillo' — segundo verso — y abre otras dimensiones.

Nada es lo que parece, afortunadamente — que diría Mairena.[10] El limón que tiende Guiomar, con sonrisa enigmática, pudiera ser 'el hilo de un claro día / [...] en dorado ovillo' — versos cuarto y quinto — es decir, el hilo de Ariadna para este machadiano laberinto de los tiempos, o bien el hilo que enlaza las cuentas de un collar de imágenes plásticas sucesivas. Todo es ya interrogación en el poema hasta el final.

Quizás es tiempo, 'tiempo en fruto' o 'tiempo vano / de una bella tarde yerta' — versos ocho y once. ¿Y por qué y cómo va a ser tiempo un limón? ¿Qué asidero objetivo justifica el símbolo

---

10 O como decía Antonio Machado — no éste, sino el heterónimo muerto en Huesca: 'Confiamos / en que no será verdad / nada de lo que pensamos' (*Poesía y prosa*, 691).

del limón, tan arbitrario? Vale que el limonero sea símbolo amoroso en la lírica popular, pero que sea tiempo ... Claro, nos asaltará de nuevo el verso del autorretrato: 'Mi infancia son recuerdos de un patio de Sevilla, / y un huerto claro donde madura el limonero' (*Poesía y prosa*, 491). Bien. Admitido esto, y siguiendo esa lógica poética, quizás el limón no sea sino ausencia, algo así como la huella de una larga ausencia, 'dorada ausencia encantada' — verso trece. Este 'limón amarillo' aludiría, por tanto, al 'huerto claro donde madura el limonero'. Lo haría, si no presente, al menos inminente.

Quizás, del mismo modo y por las mismas razones, el buen limón amarillo no sea algo material, sino 'copia en el agua dormida', reflejo inmaterial en el agua de una fuente, de aquella fuente que ya nos hemos encontrado varias veces ... Y si antes la hemos dejado reservada, con ella también reservaremos ahora este limón reflejado en el agua.

Y nuestro poema concluye sin aparente respuesta: si anunciará ese limón 'alborada verdadera' o 'crepúsculo viejo' ... Posiblemente — podemos pensar nosotros — el limón ha de sumar todas esas dimensiones temporales, no excluyentes en un plano lírico, como parece claro después de los poemas anteriores.

III

Dejemos a este Machado cincuentón, que espera en Segovia la llegada del fin de semana, y sigamos camino. Nos vamos a detener ahora en un lugar preciso — Lora del Río, parada del ferrocarril entre Sevilla y Córdoba — y en un concreto día, el 4 de abril de 1913. Machado tiene ahora treinta y ocho años. Estamos, por tanto, en la época de *Campos de Castilla.*

Campos de Castilla, aunque pase por ser el centro de su producción lírica y reúna — en sus sucesivas ediciones — tonos y temas anteriores y posteriores, no deja de ser un libro bastante singular. Con él — y resumo ideas muy repetidas — Antonio Machado pretendía romper amarras con lo que consideraba el espacio claustrofóbico del Simbolismo, que habría dominado su producción anterior.[11]

Pues bien, en un poema de ese libro — el CXXV — con ese lugar y fecha precisos — Lora del Río, 4 abril 1913 — Antonio Machado nos permite acercarnos a sus incertidumbres poéticas de aquellos momentos, siempre oscurecidas para el lector por las vitales. No hace un año todavía que se ha muerto Leonor y que él ha abandonado Soria. Está, por tanto, en la frontera sentimental entre dos mundos físicos, la campiña andaluza y las tierras altas sorianas. Y está también en la frontera entre dos expresiones literarias, la simbolista — cerrada sobre sí misma como el huerto simbólico de la infancia — y la que se quiere objetiva y abierta a lo plural y social — la metáfora española de los campos castellanos.

En ese momento de incertidumbre y debilidad que el poema busca reflejar, la voz poética quisiera tender puentes — puentes líricos — entre todo aquello que ha acarreado hasta su presente: la 'Castilla del desdén y de la fuerza' — verso ocho — junto a recobradas 'imágenes de luz y de palmeras' — verso doce — las 'grises peñas, / y fantasmas de viejos encinares' — verso quinto — junto a 'imágenes de grises olivares / bajo un tórrido sol que aturde y ciega' — verso veinticinco ... Este Antonio Machado que reniega del Simbolismo en busca de una nueva expresión, abierta y natural, reclama ahora, mediante este sujeto poético, el hilo que consiga aunar experiencias tan diferentes: 'mas falta el hilo que el recuerdo anuda / al corazón, el ancla en su ribera'.

Y hacia el centro del poema, como un espacio singular frente a esos dos, sobre todo por su dimensión simbólica, reaparece el patio de Sevilla, con sus limones:

> [...] y en un huerto sombrío, el limonero
> de ramas polvorientas
> y pálidos limones amarillos,
> que el agua clara de la fuente espeja,
> un aroma de nardos y claveles
> y un fuerte olor de albahaca y hierbabuena [...]
>
> (*Poesía y prosa*, 549)

Son limones reflejados — espejados, de modo más exacto — en el agua de la fuente, como aquéllos que le ofrecerá Guiomar,

11 Vid. la reciente — y necesaria — edición de Geoffrey Ribbans (Madrid: Cátedra, 1989) para un análisis actualizado de estas cuestiones.

veinte años más tarde. Pero sobre todo, son un eco consciente de su primer libro, y hasta un eco concreto de uno de sus poemas, el VII de *Soledades. Galerías. Otros poemas*, que en seguida voy a analizar.

Aquí no bastará con apuntar la reaparición de la imagen infantil. En relación con lo visto hasta ahora, este destello es engañoso. En el poema de *Campos de Castilla* el patio con su limonero es, por así decirlo, una imagen náufraga. El patio y el limonero se resguardan del aire abierto de los *Campos de Castilla* o de los correlativos campos jienenses entre imaginarios paréntesis. Leamos, mejor, el poema completo y observemos cómo los seis versos mantienen tozudamente su singularidad, a diferencia de lo que venía sucediendo en los otros poemas vistos:

En estos campos de la tierra mía,
y extranjero en los campos de mi tierra
— yo tuve patria donde corre el Duero
por entre grises peñas,
y fantasmas de viejos encinares,
allá en Castilla, mística y guerrera,
Castilla la gentil, humilde y brava,
Castilla del desdén y de la fuerza —,
en estos campos de mi Andalucía,
¡oh, tierra en que nací!, cantar quisiera.
Tengo recuerdos de mi infancia, tengo
imágenes de luz y de palmeras,
y en una gloria de oro,
de lueñes campanarios con cigüeñas,
de ciudades con calles sin mujeres
bajo un cielo de añil, plazas desiertas
donde crecen naranjos encendidos
con sus frutas redondas y bermejas;
y en un huerto sombrío, el limonero
de ramas polvorientas
y pálidos limones amarillos,
que el agua clara de la fuente espeja,
un aroma de nardos y claveles
y un fuerte olor de albahaca y hierbabuena;
imágenes de grises olivares
bajo un tórrido sol que aturde y ciega,
y azules y dispersas serranías
con arreboles de una tarde inmensa;

mas falta el hilo que el recuerdo anuda
al corazón, el ancla en su ribera,
o estas memorias no son alma. Tienen,
en sus abigarradas vestimentas,
señal de ser despojos del recuerdo,
la carga bruta que el recuerdo lleva.
Un día tornarán, con luz del fondo ungidos,
los cuerpos virginales a la orilla vieja.

(*Poesía y prosa*, 548-49)

Aparentemente estamos ya muy lejos del verso de 1939: 'Estos días azules y este sol de la infancia'. 'Tengo recuerdos de mi infancia', dice ahora, explícitamente. 'Cantar quisiera', dice también. Pero no puede, concluye. O no ahora. Sin embargo, ¿hasta qué punto son su patria de la infancia esas vegas sevillanas o los campos de olivos jienenses, cuando Machado vivió su infancia — y sólo ella — en Sevilla, alrededor de ese huerto con limonero? Un huerto con limonero que, como vemos incluso en este último poema, no se deja ligar con el conjunto de esos 'despojos del recuerdo' o con su 'carga bruta'.

Pero la clave no es biográfica, sino literaria. En realidad, desde ese punto de vista literario, existirían aquí dos discordancias fundamentales. Una tiene que ver con el procedimiento utilizado para dar credibilidad al conflicto temporal. En este poema, a diferencia de los casos anteriores, Machado no funde experiencias emocionales alejadas sobre el plano del presente, según el esquema señalado al principio. Poco tiene que ver si con ello consigue alcanzar la queja final sobre la distancia entre el recuerdo y la emoción, que convertiría ese desajuste en algo esencial al poema. En realidad, esa característica del tratamiento machadiano del tiempo, la con-fusión de planos temporales, parece ahora imposible por cuanto supondría también una indeseable con-fusión de lenguajes poéticos. Como hemos ido viendo, el simbólico limonero de la infancia está tan lejos de los muy rotundos olivos andaluces como de la adjetivación histórica que dedica al paisaje de Castilla — 'mística y guerrera', 'gentil, humilde y brava', 'del desdén y de la fuerza' ...

Y aquí entra la otra discordancia, que es fundamental. La otra discordancia es de lenguaje. Para lograr una nueva expresión, necesaria para los nuevos contenidos que busca,

Antonio Machado se ve impelido a rechazar el lenguaje literario asociado al Simbolismo, el de su libro anterior, y él mismo — sin la necesaria distancia — llega a identificar totalmente *patio sevillano recordado* con *jardín modernista* tópico. Esto es algo que subyace, inevitablemente, en la imagen, pero esa identificación, aunque justa para sus libros anteriores, resulta más dudosa a medida que Antonio Machado va construyendo su propia voz, su propio mundo lírico y sentimental ...

Aun así, me asombran los dos últimos versos del poema, también desligados del conjunto en tono, contenido y hasta métrica. Me asombran, porque a pesar de cuanto acabamos de ver, en ellos se anuncia proféticamente el desarrollo de la imagen. Es decir, el poeta señala el momento en que la imagen, resobada por su cercanía al lenguaje poético del fin de siglo, pueda volver a él intacta, ungida en lo más profundo de su ser con la auténtica emoción original, como cuerpo aún virgen. Pero cuando eso suceda, encontrará las orillas de un poeta viejo: 'Un día tornarán, con luz del fondo ungidos, / los cuerpos virginales a la orilla vieja'.

Yo, al menos, entiendo así esos versos.[12]

IV

Vayamos ya de una vez al origen de esta larga secuencia, que arrancaba en un futuro día azul de 1939. Ahora estamos en 1903, en el momento de *Soledades*. Machado tiene veintiocho años y profesa de simbolista convencido, al menos en su obra. No falta mucho, sin embargo, para que comience su huida del Simbolismo. Entre tanto, la poesía de Machado rebosa de fuentes y de parques melancólicos.

12 Es algo diferente la interpretación de Antonio Sánchez Barbudo, *Los poemas de Antonio Machado. Los temas. El sentimiento y la expresión* (1967) (Barcelona: Lumen, [4ª ed. aum.] 1989), 263-64. Para él, estos versos, 'bastante oscuros y modernistas', aludirían a la 'esperanza, tal vez, de que todos esos recuerdos de su tierra recobren un día el "alma" ' o bien a la 'esperanza remota de recobrar la inocencia, aquel encanto, aquel pasmo de sus días infantiles'. Es ya imposible seguir al crítico cuando, ahí mismo, añade: 'Lo de volver "con luz del fondo ungidos", da a esos cuerpos — que no se sabe exactamente qué cuerpos sean — un aire espectral; y la esperanza queda así pospuesta hasta el día del Juicio Final, poco más o menos'.

El 'limonero / de ramas polvorientas / y pálidos limones amarillos', recién visto, aparece por vez primera — si no me equivoco — en el que será poema VII de *Soledades. Galerías. Otros poemas*, cuya primera versión conocida es de esa fecha temprana, 1903, aunque no alcanza a ser incluido en el libro de ese año. Me detendré de un modo especial en este poema, puesto que permite observar, por encima de estilemas o tópicos de época, cómo Machado, en su etapa plenamente simbolista, buscaba ya su expresión más característica de lo temporal.[13]

Cuando el poema apareció por vez primera, en julio de 1903 y en la revista *Helios*, llevaba este título: 'El poeta visita el patio de la casa en que nació'. De momento, convendrá saber que el poeta suprimió esa precisión autobiográfica al incorporarlo a la segunda versión del libro, en 1907.[14] Claro está que nosotros no podemos confundir ingenuamente este patio lírico, el mismo donde antes vimos pasear a su padre, joven aún, con lo que debió de ser aquel patio real, con su misma fuente ... Entre el patio real y el patio lírico se entremezclan muchos otros patios, jardines y fuentes puramente literarios, como vamos a ver.

Desde la primera lectura, salta a la vista la presencia de motivos simbólicos recurrentes en el Modernismo, lo que en seguida habrá de punzar su mala conciencia poética: ambientación decadente, rumor de agua de fuente o parque melancólico. No voy a insistir en estos valores ... Baste decir que son símbolos, y símbolos abiertos. Es decir, permiten la acumulación de matices semánticos, y según cuál sea su contexto, se actualizarán unos u otros y con uno u otro valor. Por lo pronto, el tan manido *parque* o *jardín* simbolista se convierte en este poema VII en *patio*, un patio que a medida que avanza el poema se vuelve más y más familiar, asociado a la madre. La referencia a la hierbabuena y la albahaca — que se

13 El lector de este artículo entenderá que ahora, a diferencia de los ejemplos anteriores, no transcriba el poema entero (*Poesía y prosa*, 432-33), pero esto se justifica y compensa por la inclusión en el texto de numerosas citas parciales.

14 También suprime Machado, con buen criterio, los dos versos iniciales de la versión temprana: 'El suelo de piedra y musgo; en las paredes / blancas agarra desgreñada higuera ...', que diluían el protagonismo del limonero en ese lugar privilegiado del poema. Véanse las notas de Geoffrey Ribbans en su edición de *Soledades. Galerías. Otros poemas* (Madrid: Cátedra, 1983).

mantiene en el poema visto de *Campos de Castilla* — sería una marca de esto. En ese patio aún simbolista — pero ya individualizado — se alza el limonero, que será símbolo personal hasta los días de la Guerra.

El poema se desarrolla en varias etapas, cada una de ellas asociada a la recurrencia de la determinación temporal 'tarde clara, casi de primavera'. Pero esa expresión se modifica sutilmente según la voz poética penetra más y más en su realidad profunda, en su espesor cronológico, como iremos viendo.

En un principio, se da una presentación del escenario, en tiempo presente:

> El limonero lánguido suspende
> una pálida rama polvorienta
> sobre el encanto de la fuente limpia,
> y allá en el fondo sueñan
> los frutos de oro ... [...] (*Poesía y prosa*, 432)

Es una imagen que ya nos resulta familiar, con los limones reflejados en el agua, como si soñasen en el fondo. A esta primera impresión, inmediata, corresponde la primera aparición de la recurrencia: 'Es una tarde clara, / casi de primavera'.

En el verso noveno aparece por fin la primera persona, el 'poeta' a que hacía alusión el título en *Helios* — poeta como sujeto poético, no como autor. El poeta busca, y su búsqueda se plasma en una sucesión anafórica de versos en proceso de concretización:

> [...] y estoy solo, en el patio silencioso,
> buscando una ilusión cándida y vieja:
> alguna sombra sobre el blanco muro,
> algún recuerdo, en el pretil de piedra
> de la fuente dormido, o, en el aire,
> algún vagar de túnica ligera [...]
> (*Poesía y prosa*, 432)

En estos versos se recorren las ideas de *ilusión*, *sombra*, *recuerdo* y, asociado a 'vagar de túnica', *fantasma*, acaso *mujer fantástica*. Habría que destacar, sobre todo ello, la imagen contradictoria que se desprende del sintagma 'ilusión cándida y vieja', que tendrá su correlato, versos más abajo, en 'fragancias vírgenes y muertas' y que, en realidad, viene a ser proyección sobre la frase de la estructura temporal del poema completo.[15] Lo *nuevo* — cándido — y lo *viejo*, adjetivos aplicados a un único sustantivo, a un solo objeto, aparecen, de este modo contradictorio, como algo co-presente: la niñez, desde el hoy, es niñez ya vieja, pero sin dejar de ser niñez.

Esa búsqueda, a partir del verso quince, alcanza un primer resultado: el recuerdo. Pero antes incluso de que aparezca el recuerdo, lo hace la conciencia — puramente sentimental — de que es posible burlar las leyes del tiempo:

> [...] En el ambiente de la tarde flota
> ese aroma de ausencia,
> que dice al alma luminosa: nunca,
> y al corazón: espera.
>
> Ese aroma que evoca los fantasmas
> de las fragancias vírgenes y muertas [...]
>
> (*Poesía y prosa* 433)

'Dorada ausencia encantada' será el limón que habrá de tenderle Guiomar treinta años después. Treinta años antes, flota ya, y con similar sinestesia, 'ese aroma de ausencia'.[16] La ausencia, en estos poemas machadianos, tiene siempre bulto, tiene forma, como corresponde a algo que no acaba de irse jamás, que se prolonga indefinidamente en *todavía*. Más que vacío es hueco, es literalmente ausencia de algo, de algo que deja ahí su molde, su color dorado o su aroma, y que, por tanto, reserva su posible regreso en el poema, su presencia rescatada.[17] Solamente el poeta puede intuir el cuerpo

15 Y recuérdense los versos finales del poema de Lora del Río, donde se daba una concurrencia semejante. A ellos podrían sumarse los del poema CLXIX, donde se unían también el 'rapaz' y el 'viejo'.

16 El sintagma aquel funde, en torno al sustantivo 'ausencia' — ya comentado — dos apelativos de este poema: 'frutos de oro' y 'frutos encantados'.

17 Recordemos, a este propósito, la expresiva referencia a 'la ausencia y la distancia', del poema CLXIX, visto antes. 'La ausencia es la forma más pura de la temporalidad', señala Octavio Paz, a propósito de Antonio Machado, pero referido a su lírica amorosa ('Antonio Machado' [1951], en *Las peras del olmo* [Barcelona: Seix-Barral, 1983], 170). Y Claudio Guillén, a propósito del poema 'A José María Palacio', todo él construido sobre la percepción plástica de lo ausente, escribe: 'Entre el olvido completo (o el vivir hacia un futuro) y la nostalgia (del pasado) se sitúa la emoción de la ausencia, que es percibir, no ya

desplazado y, sobre todo, solamente él puede re-presentar el ayer, joven y viejo a un tiempo, como esas muy decadentes 'fragancias vírgenes y muertas' del último verso citado.

En esta frontera lírica — y toda lírica es frontera — el corazón y la razón son adversarios, como ya señalaba la cita anterior de Juan de Mairena. Ese aroma de ausencia 'dice al alma luminosa: nunca'. Es el muy traído y llevado *never more*, del poema *The Raven*, de Poe, que a menudo cita Machado implícitamente en sus poemas. Para la luz, para la razón, no hay camino de vuelta hacia el ayer, nos despeñamos inevitablemente hacia el futuro. Pero el sentimiento, en cambio, ofrece esperanza — y la poesía es sentimiento para Machado. Ese mismo 'aroma de ausencia' que dice 'nunca' a la razón, dice 'al corazón: espera'. La poesía es camino de reencuentro — vital, cordial, físico — con el ayer.

Por eso, la segunda aparición de la recurrencia dedicada a la 'tarde clara, casi de primavera', trae nuevos matices. Era antes una escueta frase: 'Es una tarde clara, casi de primavera'. Aparece ahora como apóstrofe personalizante: 'Sí, te recuerdo, tarde alegre y clara, / casi de primavera'. Fijémonos que se ha colado entre medias ese adjetivo 'alegre', que tiñe de precisa afectividad la afirmación antes seca y melancólica. En realidad, todavía se trata de dos tardes diferentes: ésta y aquélla, la vieja y la niña, tan alegre. Pero esta separación va a durar poco.

¿Qué sucede? Sucede que el recuerdo asciende, casi proustianamente, del centro mismo de los objetos evocados, y desde la recuperación del recuerdo, todo en el poema se desboca.[18] La recuperación tiende a hacerse concreta. Aparecen verbos en pasado, y sobre todo, el anterior 'aroma de

---

lo que fue, sino lo que no es. Entre la elegía y el canto de esperanza — ambos susceptibles de expresión directa — se interpone el estilo alusivo. Estilo que permite a Machado resolver el problema planteado por Mallarmé en *Le nénuphar blanc*: "... résumer d'un regard la vierge absence" '. Tomo la cita de su 'Estilística del silencio (en torno a un poema de Antonio Machado)' (1957), en *Antonio Machado*, ed. R. Gullón y A. W. Phillips (Madrid: Taurus, [2ª ed.] 1979), 460.

18 *Cf.* Geoffrey Ribbans, 'Recaptured Memory in Juan Ramón Jiménez and Antonio Machado', en *Studies in Modern Spanish Literature and Art presented to Helen F. Grant*, ed. Nigel Glendinning (Londres: Tamesis Books, 1972), 149-61.

ausencia' se hace el ya muy preciso 'perfume de la hierbabuena y de la [...] albahaca':

> [...] tarde sin flores, cuando me traías
> el buen perfume de la hierbabuena,
> y de la buena albahaca,
> que tenía mi madre en sus macetas [...]
> (*Poesía y prosa*, 433)

Y en esa recuperación, los limones reflejados en el agua, con que comenzaba el poema, serán la clave mágica que salva el pasado *en* el presente del poema:

> [...] Que tú me viste hundir mis manos puras
> en el agua serena,
> para alcanzar los frutos encantados
> que hoy en el fondo de la fuente sueñan ...
> (*Poesía y prosa*, 433)

¿Habrá que explicar la extraordinaria concentración de significados en estos cuatro versos? El niño que el poeta fue confundía de modo ingenuo el limón con su reflejo, identificaba el efecto óptico con los limones reales. Y claro, el niño hundía sus manos en el agua para cogerlos ... ¿Absurdo? No. Lo que era ingenuidad en el niño es voluntad consciente en el poeta. El uno y el otro, el niño y el poeta — cándido y viejo, él mismo — han visto esos limones y creen en ellos, en su realidad ...

Son, literalmente, unos limones que 'sueñan', proyección del sueño del contemplador sobre lo contemplado, con todo lo que el sueño implica en Machado: fermentación del poema, ruptura de la lógica temporal ... Pues bien, insisto en la lectura literal de los versos citados, sin olvidar el tránsito sutil que en ellos se da desde el verbo en pasado hasta el verbo en presente. La voz poética viene a decirnos, exacta y literalmente, que 'ayer hundí las manos de niño para rescatar este concreto reflejo de mi hoy'. En ese punto se confunden los tiempos, como se funden las manos del niño y del hombre, identificados en el sueño.[19] Así,

19 No comparto la interpretación de Carlos Bousoño, quien lee estos versos como expresión del deseo frustrado, algo exactamente contrario a lo que aquí se defiende: 'El hombre mira, requiere, desea; pero desea en vano; jamás alcanza su propósito, su afán, como el poeta nos dice, entre otros sitios, en el poema VII, a través de un símbolo disémico' ('El símbolo en la poesía de Antonio Machado', en *op. cit.*, I, 252).

los dos últimos versos del poema son casi previsibles: 'Sí, te conozco, tarde alegre y clara, / casi de primavera'.

Como se ve, permanece el adjetivo 'alegre' y cambia solamente el verbo del apóstrofe: del 'te recuerdo' anterior pasamos al 'te conozco' actual, verbo que expresa este encuentro, esta síntesis de la tarde recordada y la tarde actual. Por tanto, en las tres apariciones del sintagma y en sus modificaciones se resumen buena parte de los significados del poema: '*Es una* tarde clara, / casi de primavera' > '*Sí, te recuerdo*, tarde *alegre y* clara, / casi de primavera' > 'Sí, te *conozco*, tarde alegre y clara, / casi de primavera'. Leído desde la perspectiva temporal continuada: *esta* tarde > *aquella* tarde > *ésta* y *aquella* tarde.

Cuando don Antonio, viejo y agotado, escribía su verso final, en aquel hoy lejano 1939, podría sumar a la primera tarde la luz de otras tardes innumerables. Todas ellas estarían irremediablemente bajo el primer sol, el tozudo sol original, el auténtico. Bergson, a quien voluntariamente he preferido dejar fuera, supo cristalizar en conceptos algo muy sentido por los artistas contemporáneos de Machado. El tiempo vital, el vivido, es diferente al tiempo espacial de los relojes. En realidad, podríamos decir nosotros, la dirección real y profunda que sigue el tiempo del poeta — y quizás, la de todo hombre — es opuesta a la aparente. Don Antonio Machado, como Marcel Proust — a quien, curiosamente, no acaba él de entender — cifrará su destino poético en ese puñado de imágenes aún puras que descansan en lo más hondo de la memoria. Hacia la mirada del niño que fue, camina el poeta. Hacia el origen, hacia 'estos días azules y este sol de la infancia'.

V

Con eso podría concluir. Sería un final más o menos redondo, pero en realidad sería también engañoso y literario, demasiado literario. Lo queramos o no, es imposible olvidar otros jardines y fuentes, más convencionales, no teñidos de esta temporalidad plástica, pero en cualquier caso anteriores a los de Machado, a ese origen poemático citado y datable ... aunque no sean anteriores al jardín y la fuente realmente vividos por Machado niño.

Buena parte de los significados vistos dependen de ese repertorio simbólico de época. En el imaginario simbolista, el parque o el jardín cerrado va asociado a la fuente, muchas veces con una estatua alegórica. Todo ello se sitúa en una determinación temporal de signo marcadamente melancólico, crepuscular: sea el final de la tarde o sea el final del verano o el pleno otoño. En Antonio Machado, aunque la tarde siga siendo el momento favorito, el mes será abril, en plena primavera, para realzar el contraste entre voz melancólica y naturaleza exaltada. El jardín es espacio subjetivo e interiorizado para el simbolista, como puedan serlo las habitaciones y las ventanas, desde donde se escruta lo externo y hostil. Así, decir el jardín es como decir la topografía de la propia alma, cerrada sobre sí misma. El agua de la fuente, en el centro de ese espacio interior, podrá reunir diferentes significados, según corra alegre y cantarina — como el tiempo o como la vida — o bien monótona y repetida — con esa abulia tan querida por el decadentismo. En coherencia con lo anterior, el agua puede también expresar la muerte, si está estancada, si no fluye. El agua, por insistir en este símbolo, puede contrastar también con la piedra o mármol de la fuente, que puede sostener una estatua.[20]

Ese acoso del tópico generacional explica el rechazo posterior de algo aparentemente tan unido a su biografía sentimental. Hay aquí una paradoja que bien podría aplicarse a otros escritores, sea cual sea su época, si dispusiésemos de una futura Estética de la Producción, tan necesaria hoy, aunque aún no exista. Lo que nos parece tan personal, tan teñido de sustancia biográfica en Antonio Machado — el patio, el limonero, la fuente — se construye en su obra a partir de un buen número de elementos tópicos del imaginario modernista, nada personales, por así decirlo. De este modo, el patio sevillano viene a ser la apropiación — o legitimación sentimental y lírica — de un tópico de época: el jardín con su fuente melancólica.[21]

---

20 Son muy numerosas, como es lógico, las referencias bibliográficas sobre estos y otros símbolos de época. Para nuestro caso, puede ser de utilidad el estudio de José María Aguirre, *Antonio Machado, poeta simbolista* (1973) (Madrid: Taurus, [2ª ed. aum. y corregida] 1982).

21 *Cf.* Rafael Ferreres, *Verlaine y los modernistas españoles* (Madrid: Gredos, 1974), donde se enmarca bien la recepción del poeta que casi siempre

El tránsito es visible en su propia obra, como sucede con el poema VI de *Soledades. Galerías. Otros poemas*, inmediato al que acabamos de ver y también de 1903, pero mucho más amanerado, y donde la idea se expresa de modo mucho menos sutil:

> [...] La fuente cantaba: ¿Te recuerda, hermano,
> un sueño lejano mi canto presente?
> Fue una tarde lenta del lento verano.
> Respondí a la fuente:
> No recuerdo, hermana,
> mas sé que tu copla presente es lejana.
> Fue esta misma tarde: mi cristal vertía
> como hoy [...] (*Poesía y prosa*, 431)

No es éste, a pesar de la comunidad de ideas, el mismo patio sevillano que hemos ido viendo, e incluso el sujeto del poema podría ser otro poeta, acaso Verlaine, cuyo influjo es decisivo para la cristalización del parque melancólico en tópico modernista.[22] Todavía se ve más clara esa raíz puramente

---

se asocia a este tópico literario. En lo que afecta al caso concreto de Antonio Machado, véanse, de Geoffrey Ribbans, *Niebla y Soledad: aspectos de Unamuno y Machado* (Madrid: Gredos, 1971) y su artículo 'Antonio Machado's Attitude to Symbolism', en *Waiting for Pegasus: Studies on the Presence of Symbolism and Decadence in Hispanic Letters*, ed. R. Grass y W. R. Risley, (Macomb, Il.: Western Illinois U. P., 1979), 39-56.

22 Este poema VI sufre una honda transformación en su paso de uno a otro libro. El profesor Ribbans, a quien quiero agradecer desde aquí sus comentarios, me señala que esa primera versión reforzaría el contraste que he señalado antes con el poema VII. A este propósito, vienen muy a cuento las sugerencias de Aurora de Albornoz (*op. cit.*, 283-84): '¿Qué significan, entonces, esos paseos por los solitarios parques, por los jardines, más que una búsqueda intencionada, pensada, querida, del yo de ayer? Es muy cierto. Y ya en un poema de principios de siglo — el núm. VI de *Poesías completas*, el conocido "Fue una tarde clara, triste y soñolienta" ... — la búsqueda de su yo de ayer se convierte en el problema central'. Albornoz alude aquí a la 'clara influencia verleniana' y cómo 'a través del jardín — verleniano y modernista — el problema de la identidad personal está claramente planteado' (284, y vid., sobre Verlaine, mi nota anterior). Aunque me parezcan de una gran finura crítica las opiniones de Albornoz, creo no obstante que la idea no ha madurado en el poeta lo suficiente como para justificar ese sentido nítido, casi definitivo que ella le da. Ése es el planteamiento de mi trabajo. Por ello, prefiero quedarme con la parte más dubitativa del análisis de Albornoz, donde

literaria de la imagen si consideramos otro poema, 'La fuente', cuya primera versión apareció en *Electra*, en 1901, y que sería eliminado de la segunda versión de *Soledades*. Ahí tenemos una convencional fuente modernista 'y cerca de ella — dicen dos de sus versos — el amarillo esplende / del limonero entre el ramaje obscuro' (*Poesía y prosa*, 742). La referencia es engañosa, porque no es éste, pese a las apariencias, el patio familiar, y no lo es, sencillamente, porque aún no lo ha inventado Machado. La prueba está algunos versos más abajo, cuando añade:

> [...] En las horas más áridas y tristes
> y luminosas dejo
> la estúpida ciudad, y el parque viejo
> de opulento ramaje
> me brinda sus veredas solitarias [...]
>
> (*Poesía y prosa*, 981)

Es fácil recordar a poetas cercanos a Machado, como el Juan Ramón Jiménez de *Arias tristes*, coetáneo de *Soledades* (1903). De ahí son estos versos, que el propio Machado llegará a citar en algún poema suyo:

> [...] Mi jardín tiene una fuente
> y la fuente una quimera
> y la quimera un amante
> que se muere de tristeza [...][23]

O bien, casi más cerca, los de su hermano Manuel en *Alma* (1902):

> [...] ¡Jardín sin jardinero!
> Viejo jardín,

---

se pregunta: '¿No era su yo de ayer lo que buscaba el poeta [...]? Buscaba muchas cosas el joven poeta que se creía viejo y quería revivir el pasado. Buscaba el mismo jardín y la misma fuente, a una hora determinada—la tarde—de un verano lento; buscaba recobrar un instante perdido, al intentar vivirlo de nuevo. ¿Para qué? Acaso no lo sabía aún el joven autor de *Soledades*; o ¿sabía ya que era a sí mismo de unos años atrás a quien buscaba, sin poder hallarlo, sin poder hallarse?' (284). Esa última interrogación de Albornoz resume el desenlace de mi trabajo.

23 Juan Ramón Jiménez, *Arias tristes* (1903), ed. Aurora de Albornoz (Madrid: Taurus, 1981), 122.

viejo jardín sin alma,
jardín muerto. Tus árboles
no agita el viento. En el estanque, el agua
yace podrida. ¡Ni una onda! El pájaro
no se posa en tus ramas [...][24]

Como es lógico, ese repertorio finisecular de símbolos, a fuerza de repetidos, se hacen cada vez más obvios y menos simbólicos. Están, por así decirlo, lexicalizados. Todo esto es válido para el primer Antonio Machado, el de 1903, aunque esos símbolos no llegan a agotar el sistema global de su libro, donde actúan otros interrelacionados, como son el sueño, el espejo, el camino, la galería o la noria, que lo enriquecen. Sin embargo, habría que marcar la inflexión que se produce en *Soledades. Galerías. Otros poemas*, de 1907, donde esos símbolos se revisten de nuevas formas, más complejas e individualizadas, y de este modo llegan a adquirir un valor propio en el sistema lírico del poeta.[25]

Hay, no obstante, poemas del primer momento — del *Soledades* de 1903 — que expresan con indudable calidad una misma conciencia melancólica del tiempo, aunque no sean tan personales. Me gustaría citar el XXXII del mismo libro, un poema de tono parnasiano que no es momento de comentar, aunque nos permitiría profundizar en las raíces de la imagen:

Las ascuas de un crepúsculo morado
detrás del negro cipresal humean ...
En la glorieta en sombra está la fuente
con su alado y desnudo Amor de piedra,
que sueña mudo. En la marmórea taza
reposa el agua muerta. (*Poesía y prosa*, 449)

Aquí aparece completamente traspasada la raíz vivencial de la imagen, ya puro objeto literario y extremo opuesto del verso de 1939. De este poema XXXII — y de su extraordinaria concentración de significados — se podría hablar largo y

24 'El jardín gris', en *Alma*, ed. Pablo del Barco (Madrid, Cátedra, 1988), 92.

25 Véase para esto, entre muchos posibles trabajos — como el ya citado de Aguirre — las magníficas aproximaciones de Cesare Segre, 'Sistema y estructura en las *Soledades* de Antonio Machado' y 'Las variantes de las *Soledades*', en su *Crítica bajo control* (Barcelona: Planeta, 1970), 103-50.

tendido, o mejor dicho, se ha hablado largo y tendido, como lo demuestra la abundante polémica crítica que ha merecido.[26] Pero subsiste en él, pese a todo su valor, un hálito de convencionalidad, de imaginería añeja, que en cambio ha conseguido vencer su retoño poético, el patio sevillano.

Cuando Antonio Machado publica *La Guerra* (1937), última recopilación de sus poemas y artículos — ahora tocados por la urgencia del momento — el contrapunto al acento cívico de su voz lo pondrán las ilustraciones de su hermano José, quien prende de esas páginas la huella del ambiente andaluz perdido, de aquellos patios con fuentes y limones añorados, de todo aquel sol de la infancia ganado por fin como legítimo recuerdo tras larga lucha con la palabra.[27] El reflejo de los limones sí vence al tiempo, o mejor, se instala sobre el tiempo y consigue vivir fuera del que era su tiempo original, lejos de su retórica desgastada, como un pez que viviese después de pescado, o por seguir con la imagen, fuera del agua estancada y muerta del simbolismo tardío ...

La imagen no es mía, claro está, ni siquiera de Machado, sino del viejo maestro Mairena. Él sí tiene la última palabra, un final nada engolado, que va, además, de algo tan poco lírico como son los pescados:

> La poesía es — decía Mairena — el diálogo del hombre, de un hombre con su tiempo. Eso es lo que el poeta pretende eternizar, sacándolo fuera del tiempo, labor difícil y que requiere mucho tiempo, casi todo el tiempo de que el poeta dispone. El poeta es un pescador, no de peces, sino de pescados vivos; entendámonos: de peces que puedan vivir después de pescados.
>
> (*Poesía y prosa*, 1946)

---

26 Deben destacarse las interpretaciones contrapuestas de Carlos Bousoño y Rafael Ferreres. *Cfr.* Carlos Bousoño, *op. cit.*, I, 209-21; Rafael Ferreres, 'Sobre la interpretación de un poema de Antonio Machado (XXXII)' (1954), en *Los límites del Modernismo* (Madrid: Taurus, 1964), 111-28. Vid. también José María Aguirre, *op. cit.*, 337 ss.

27 Debo agradecer a Gonzalo Santonja la referencia a *La Guerra* y a los dibujos de José Machado. Fue el profesor Santonja quien, después de oír un resumen de este trabajo, me llamó la atención sobre este dato plástico, que reforzaría el acento hondamente autobiográfico — y ya no dominantemente literario — de los últimos versos.

Alvaro Cunqueiro, Britain and Ireland

COLIN SMITH†

St Catharine's College, Cambridge

While Cunqueiro's sensibility was formed in the languages, people and landscapes of his native Galicia, his fund of information and of literary inspiration knew no frontiers. He was unable to travel much until late in life, but his voyages in books ranged very widely and are reflected in the settings — often purely notional, as it were, rather than geographically authentic — of his own narratives.[1] As a child and youth he read voraciously whatever came to hand and absorbed the materials and the techniques of tales told in the family and outside it. He remarked that 'Toda la infancia la pasé a la escucha', that is, in the Galician tradition, and also of interest for our purposes, that 'Me gustaría incluso contar como dicen que contaban los antiguos celtas de Irlanda, con pruebas por delante [...]. Me gustaría abrir mi libro y que de entre las páginas saliera el puñal o la cadena, la perla o la rosa que figuran en ellas'.[2] No doubt his early formation equally in two

† I record with sadness the recent and unexpected death (16 February 1997) of our friend and colleague, Colin Smith.

1 Cunqueiro was himself entirely clear about this. In an interview published in *El País* on 27 June 1979 he confessed of *Las mocedades de Ulises* that although it 'aparentemente se desarrollaba en Grecia, era Galicia la que estaba en el trasfondo'. Equally, in *As crónicas do sochantre* he said in an *Epílogo para bretones* added to the Castilian version that he had never been to Brittany but had travelled only in 'esta Bretaña que yo descubro en mí': such, doubtless, is the pan-Celtic sentiment of any good Celt.

2 This and a great deal else of interest by Cunqueiro was recorded on

languages — he and his four siblings spoke Galician to their mother, Castilian to their father — was a fine preparation for a man who was to be a consummately artistic writer of both. To his school French and Latin he eventually added a reading knowledge of several other languages, including English, to the extent of being able to translate for publication poems from very varied originals (sometimes aided by intermediate versions in French, etc.), including works of Hölderlin, Yeats, Lawrence, Pound, Pasternak and Cavafis.[3] In early days he often depended for his reading of foreign prose materials upon published Spanish and sometimes French translations. He expressed special devotion to Shakespeare (who will figure much in this paper), Dickens, Stevenson, the Irish O'Casey and others of the Abbey Theatre, Shaw and other Anglo-Irish writers. One of this last group was to be of altogether special importance in Cunqueiro's formation, as he acknowledged with deep gratitude.

Edward John Plunkett, Lord Dunsany, 18th baron in the Anglo-Irish ascendancy and possessor of a castle in County Meath, was born in 1878 and died in 1957. His early association with Yeats, Lady Gregory and others of that great period in Dublin led on to a varied literary lifetime and to some fame, but it is fairly safe — and sad — to say that he is largely forgotten today. Cunqueiro was offered a full page in *El País* of 8 July 1979 in which to remedy this on the centenary of

---

tape by his friend the novelist Elena Quiroga — *santanderina* by birth but Galician by adoption — and quoted with much else within the very interesting survey which Doña Elena delivered as her *discurso de recepción* on being admitted to the Real Academia Española on 8 April 1984, a memorable occasion which the present writer was fortunate to attend; published as *Presencia y ausencia de Alvaro Cunqueiro* (Madrid: Real Academia Española, 1984). The quotations are respectively on pp. 19 and 13.

3 This was a permanent activity of Cunqueiro's, the results appearing in the newspaper *El Faro de Vigo* and other journals. The scope and quality of the translations are assessed by Xesús González Gómez, 'Tradutor de mil poetas', in number Extra 2 of *A Nossa Terra* of Vigo, December 1984, 33-35, an issue republished with changes in December 1991 (to mark the tenth anniversary of the writer's death), 26-28. Some eight hundred translated poems were published in *El Faro de Vigo* alone, many under pseudonyms. Among the English-language poets translated by Cunqueiro, in addition to those mentioned, were Blake, Keats, O'Casey, Eliot and Sylvia Plath.

Dunsany's birth 'con un año de retraso' and to acknowledge the extent of his debt. Lord Dunsany's family history seems to have fascinated the Galician quite as much as his writings:

> Una familia de soldados, y en los ratos libres, de salteadores de caminos. Se acusó a los Dunsany de saber fabricar espesas nieblas para que en ellas se perdiesen los viajeros que iban y venían a Dublín, para mejor asaltarlos y robarlos. Y en las consejas populares irlandesas aparecen los Dunsany nocturnos en las encrucijadas, acompañados en sus fechorías de espectros de sus antepasados.[4]

We are almost in the world of Cunqueiro's *As crónicas do sochantre* (1956).[5] Genealogical fantasies akin to Cunqueiro's own in his narratives are there too: 'Los Dunsany, burlándose de los sesudos genealogistas ingleses y de los reyes de armas de Su Graciosa Majestad, mandaban pintar árboles familiares fantásticos, que llegaban hasta Harold Godwinson, el último rey sajón de Inglaterra. [...] También estaban los Dunsany emparentados con un hada y con varios fantasmas'. All this Cunqueiro would have discovered long after reading Lord Dunsany's early work *A Dreamer's Tales* (1910) in translation as *Cuentos de un soñador*. Of this book he wrote: 'Para servidor, fue durante los últimos años de la adolescencia [Cunqueiro was born in 1911] un compañero inseparable y, en cierto modo, un libro decisivo en la dirección que tomaría mi obra literaria'.

The translation was published in the *Biblioteca de la Revista de Occidente* at Madrid in April 1924, and included the ten-page introduction by the Irish poet and playwright Padraic Colum. The translation is anonymous, though attributed (without details or arguments in support) in one reference

4 A phrase such as 'aparecen los Dunsany nocturnos' shows that Cunqueiro's newspaper style was just as richly evocative as that used in his literary narratives. In his excellent book *Alvaro Cunqueiro ou os disfraces da melancolía* (Vigo: Galaxia, 1984), 104-05, Anxo Tarrío Varela briefly mentions this particular trait, citing 'Orestes llegaba nocturno a la ciudad', 'Pasaba nocturna la nave en que viajaba Amadís', and 'Penélope saldría vespertina a la ventana', among other examples. The shade of Góngora was hovering close, one suspects.

5 References are made to Galician originals where these have the priority, and to Castilian texts in other cases.

work to Ortega. Two of the translated stories were separately published in the *Revista de Occidente*, *Poltarnees* in number 2 (1923), and *Carcasona* in number 3 (1924). At this point one has to ponder. Cunqueiro in the same essay wrote that

> Muchas cosas que vienen en *Los cuentos de un soñador* pasaron a mi universo mítico: la lejana ciudad de Carcasona, a la que nunca se llega ... Lord Dunsany tenía un decir abundante y fácil, muchas veces profundo, y siempre capaz de crear, con un breve párrafo, la atmósfera de misterio que sus personajes precisaban para vivir. En esto tenía que ver con los otros irlandeses de su tiempo, con Synge, con Lady Augusta Gregory, con Yeats, pero también con la tradición popular irlandesa.

This statement must clearly be respected, but it must be said that to this native reader of modern English, Dunsany's *Tales* may still have their attractions as themes for the imagination but that stylistically they are not great work, seeming strangely wooden and inexpressive for all their soaring flights of fancy, though not without ample traces of the poetical and archaic and especially the biblical which have much force. The Castilian translation is fluent and entirely acceptable, but it seems unlikely that Cunqueiro can have learned any technical aspect of his writing from it. The original and hence the translation have no hint of the lightness of touch, the irony, and humour which were to characterize Cunqueiro's narrative prose. It is then as a general stimulus to the youthful imagination and as the opening of a door onto worlds of fantasy that one must see Dunsany's *Tales* as they affected the Galician. Particularly to be noted are Dunsany's fondness for settings in abandoned cities and deeply rural landscapes, his capacity for effortless transformations, and especially his sense of timelessness according to which everything that has ever existed in fact or in fiction still exists — lives — today. All of these are important features of Cunqueiro's art. It is, however, the case that Cunqueiro was careful not to borrow any settings or personages or plots directly from Dunsany, or even to allude to them in his own narratives: so rich was his own varied store that he had no need to. This becomes apparent as Cunqueiro explores Dunsany's qualities in the *El País* essay: 'Hay ocasiones en las que enciende una lámpara ante nosotros y nos enseña paisajes del alma que hasta entonces el alma no pudo soñar nunca'. In an eloquent verse tribute to the Anglo-Irish writer, he says 'Soñóu todas as cousas invisibles ...'.[6] As to the form of the narrative, Cunqueiro devised his own, both the brilliant use of the framework-story in *Merlín e familia* (1955) and *As crónicas do sochantre* (1956), and the greatly varied novelistic modes of *Las mocedades de Ulises* (1960), *Si o vello Sinbad volvese ás illas* (1961), *Un hombre que se parecía a Orestes* (1969), *Vida y fugas de Fanto Fantini* (1972), and especially *El año del cometa* (1974).

Cunqueiro's summary, that of a lifelong *dunsanyano* as he confesses, that 'En fin, la de Lord Dunsany es una obra riquísima y compleja, que hace de él uno de los más grandes escritores de este siglo', is, alas, not borne out among readers and critics in Britain and Ireland today. Even Cunqueiro late in his life and with (at last, after years of relative obscurity) an established national reputation, failed, he says in the same piece, to interest publishers in commissioning Castilian translations of other titles from among Dunsany's numerous works. One should then ponder on the productive accident by which someone — possibly Ortega himself? — read and liked Dunsany's *Tales* and patronized a good translation. Which Spaniard in Dublin or London in (say) 1923 happened to pick a not very new small book off a shelf in a bookshop, read it in a railway carriage or in bed, and mailed it to a friend in Madrid? Alternatively, which literary-minded member of the British Embassy in Madrid — still handling Irish affairs in about 1920 — met Ortega or one of his colleagues at a party and suggested the translation? We can probably know no more of this than we can about many other productive accidents much further back in literary history. What we can urge is the need to know more about details of translation and the circulation and readership of translations, in view of the creative influence which these may sometimes unexpectedly have had. Torrente Ballester has acknowledged the influence of Chesterton and Wilde, among many others. Cunqueiro mentions Stevenson

6 *Lord Dunsany: Epitafio*, in *Alvaro Cunqueiro: Obra en galego completa* (Vigo: Galaxia, [2nd ed.], 1991), 4 vols; I, 169.

beside (though not necessarily in the same category as) Dickens. Gillian Gayton in a notable contribution began on the task of discovering what J. L. Borges — a native reader of English, of course, though he may have known translations too — owed so unexpectedly to his admired G. K. Chesterton, a declaration which so puzzled French and Spanish critics who had scarcely heard of him.[7]

Cunqueiro's first published narrative, *Merlín e familia*, may be claimed at least vaguely as 'British' in its remote origins, however extended and diffuse were the medieval continental versions of the Arthurian materials. In this Cunqueiro tries to see (as he was to do with Ulysses and Orestes) what elements from heroic and romantic myth might be worth saving for disbelieving moderns. The result forms a great contrast with T. H. White's *The Sword in the Stone* of 1938, a contrast wholly to Cunqueiro's benefit despite the great *succès d'estime* which White's book enjoyed and perhaps enjoys. One of Cunqueiro's masterstrokes was to omit Arthur, though he must have pondered the omission. Not only is the King absent — dead, or waiting out there in the misty West — but none of the personages thinks of questioning Merlin about him. Of Guinevere, 'Decían que era viuda dun grande rei que morréu na guerra, e que tivo a noticia por un corvo, cando estaba en Miranda probando un peite de ouro'. Guinevere herself is somewhat marginally present, a tall, elegantly ageing widow occupied in the less onerous sort of domestic tasks. Merlin was believed by the servants to cherish a passion for the Queen, naturally of the most purely platonic kind. The setting is wholly Galician, in and around Merlin's house, Miranda (in 'fact', the house of the writer's grandparents in Riotorto, which enchanted him as a boy); but the implication throughout is that this setting — woods, fields, rivers, a battlemented castle in the middle distance — is as primitively Arthurian and western-British as one could wish for. Among the tales included in the Merlin-framework, told by

7 Gillian Gayton, 'J. L. Borges and G. K. Chesterton', *Actas del VI Congreso Internacional de Hispanistas* [Toronto, 1977] (Toronto: Dept of Spanish & Portuguese, Univ. of Toronto, 1980), 312-15. She quotes Borges: 'Tout ce que j'ai fait est dans Stevenson, Poe, Wells, Chesterton'.

or about visitors from remote parts to Miranda, is that of Lady Tear, bride of Lord Sweet of Marduffe, situated some thirty leagues from Windsor (which 'E un lugar mui venteado' and so named). There are brief appearances by the widow of the Bishop of Liverpool, the doctor Master Hairy who had trained at Edinburgh (whose medical curriculum is detailed), the musician Master Flute, and the Duke of Lancaster.

Cunqueiro devoted a whole new appendix to Merlin's life when he produced the Castilian version in 1957. A lawyer from the court in Cardiff has appeared to question Felipe de Amancia, in his boyhood servant to Merlin and now the narrator of the story as a ferryman in his old age, about any descendants or property that the magician (who is not dead, but was last reported in Rome on his way to Jerusalem as a pilgrim) might have left in Galicia. With a fine disregard for national sensibilities, Cunqueiro defines the lawyer as 'un caballero inglés', and later names him as James Craven. What follows is a merry amalgam of our islands. Mr Craven wears a tartan cloak ('un macferlán a cuadros verdes y negros', recalled elsewhere by Cunqueiro as Sherlock Holmes' typical garment, which later turns out to be a piece devised for a quick-change artist) and a cream-coloured bowler hat also of varied potential. His permanent position is that of 'escribano procurador de la ciudad y deanato de Truro en Cornualles, con cursiva patentada'. We proceed to learn of the birth of Merlin in 'un claro que hay en el antiguo bosque de Dartmoor, en la Grande Bretaña', to a woman who had fled from Ireland 'que siendo soltera, había concebido de un botonero que la enamoró estando ella asomada a una ventana'. A separate chapter, 'Auto de la mujer barbuda', then tells the story of this woman and of attempts to remedy her hirsute condition, with rich details of a timeless Ireland stranger than anything imagined in folktales. It has, among other marvels, 'el rey Chluas Haistig, o sea, Oreja Chata, que era uno de los más notorios entre los doscientos cuarenta y siete reyes que había por entonces en Irlanda'. After early schooling at Longwood, whose admirable curriculum is detailed (it included 'alquimia por don Gabir Arábigo'), Merlin left fully qualified to study medicine at Montpellier, but not before completing essential tasks, including forging Arthur's magic sword 'Plantata' with a secret anti-rust recipe, and using his skill at military engineering to build the moat at Persse Castle. There, among the Breton 'damiselas' who served the old Countess and to whom Merlin gave a class on Thursdays, was the youthful Guinevere. Merlin's subsequent career was largely continental and eventually Galician, but he made one more trip to Ireland to claim his mother's inheritance. As for Guinevere she, having lost her Breton rents in the French Revolution and feeling death approaching, 'quiso ir a morir a su país natal de Gales, en un pequeño huerto vecino a las ruinas de Persse Castle'.

If it should be thought that Cunqueiro resolved that he could not fit Arthur into his re-creation of Arthurian myth with a humanized, domestic, and certainly unheroic Merlin at its centre, his judgement was surely correct. Arthur, however, was to have his day — a melancholy, even tragic one — in Cunqueiro's last book, *El año del cometa.* The dream-city which Paulos has created — its secret name, which we eventually learn, is Lucerna, rich in resonances — is eventually threatened, and armies and generals are needed for its defence. Paulos visits King David, King Arthur and Julius Caesar to seek help. The visit to the Roman is prefaced with six lines of Yeats: 'Our master Caesar is in the tent / Where the maps are spread ...', which is indeed how Paulos finds him.[8] If Caesar is heroic historical reputation, Arthur is all myth, and his central heroic aspect is unsustainable for Cunqueiro and for moderns generally, as the writer had already shown to be the case with Orestes. Paulos finds Arthur in bed and almost deserted in his palace at Camelot. Around the courtyard are papier mâché figures of horses, and the same are being prepared to represent the now absent knights of the Round

8 Elena Quiroga (see note 2) quotes from notes for a lecture by Cunqueiro about his playing truant from class in the Instituto de Lugo in order to read in the library Burckhardt and the anthology of English verse edited by Yeats, in which he was delighted to discover that the Irish poet 'había puesto en ella, como un poema, aquel ardiente párrafo que Pater dedica a la Gioconda'. The genuineness of Cunqueiro's emotion is not to be doubted, but his memory was not quite perfect. He left the Lugo Instituto in 1927, and *The Oxford Book of Modern English Verse, 1892-1935*, edited by Yeats, was not published until 1936 (Oxford: Clarendon Press). Pater's text does indeed figure in this, as the first item of the anthology.

Table. The King is attended by a dwarf, Próspero, and at intervals by Guinevere, who when Paulos pays a courtesy visit to her in her remote rooms, proves to his surprise to be flirtatious in an elegantly aristocratic way. Arthur is incapacitated by a complaint at once painful and ridiculous, which his doctor, Avicenna, is unable to cure. Paulos' plea arouses the King to action: he dons (still in bed) his war helmet and promises — swears — to come to the aid of Lucerna, but the reader surmises at this point, and knows at the end of the book, that just as the noble myth is unsustainable, the well-intentioned promise cannot be kept, and Paulos' city will perish in the collapse of his dream. There is even worse to come as the episode concludes. As Paulos crosses the courtyard on leaving, a woman wrapped in a cloak approaches him to ask for a small payment for the 'Guinevere show' he had been privileged to attend: 'diez reales'. Paulos suspects that the cloaked woman was Guinevere herself: '¡Mal andaban las finanzas de Bretaña!'. This is surely a vibrant echo of Dulcinea's request to Don Quixote in the dream-sequence of the Cave of Montesinos for 'media docena de reales, o los que vuesa merced tuviere'. Just as Cervantes saluted and ironically adjusted heroic myth, Cunqueiro for his times salutes them both and makes his own adjustments.

Imaginative play with myths and settings of the Celtic world of which Cunqueiro was so firmly a part was one thing. Play of the same kind with Shakespeare was tolerable on any score, a reflection of the permanent influence which the dramatist had upon the Galician's imagination, but to go beyond this into a radical rewriting was quite another matter, as will be seen. In the first category, references to and evocations of Shakespearian personages and scenes abound in Cunqueiro's work. Sometimes it is merely an echo of names, as when Arthur's dwarf is Prospero, or when in *Las mocedades de Ulises* Laertes appears both as a charcoal-burner and as King of Ithaca, father of Ulysses. In *Orestes*, Filón el Mozo, the official dramatist of the city, is writing a play entitled *El caballero de Olmedo*, and in *Ulises*, *King Lear* is in performance in the theatre. In *As crónicas do sochantre* the itinerant coachload of ghosts, mistaken by the people of Comfront in Brittany for a company of Italian actors they are expecting, assume fleshly form and begin to perform *Romeo e Xulieta, famosos namorados.* Only Juliet of the principals has time to appear: in Scene IV, before night falls, the actors revert to their skeletal form (Juliet's hand as she reads a letter from Romeo showing the first signs), the audience cries that this means the plague has reached Verona from Siena, and the show ends in chaos as a sudden wind destroys the backdrop. In *Orestes* there is a brief hint, again, of a *Función de Romeo y Julieta.*

The second category is very different. It consists of *O incerto señor Don Hamlet, príncipe de Dinamarca*, written in the autumn of 1958 and published in 1959. It has achieved several editions and, in recent years, performances. The work is in prose. There are three acts, each divided into scenes. The personages are Hamlet, the new King Halmar, his spouse Queen Gerda; Ophelia, Laertes and Polonius; with some prominence, the company of visiting players, including Pantalone, Harlequin, Columbina, and others; also a few students, and (in a way replacing the Ghost) a Chorus, consisting of 'xente, sombras e voces de Dinamarca', which has a major role. There is a brief preface — '¡Benvidos a Elsinor!' — and, in an edition of 1974,[9] an appendix of six pages headed 'Notas' of considerable interest. These are partly designed to respond to criticism, which there had evidently been (probably by word of mouth, since I know of none in print) of Cunqueiro's temerity in appearing to challenge or modify Shakespeare: the writer might do what he wished with Arthurian materials, misty and multiform and multilingual from early times, but with a universally known and canonical text such as that of Shakespeare the matter was different. Cunqueiro declares: 'Rogo que se acepte que estas liñas [that is, his play] están escritas cunha humildade sin reservas' (87). A few pages later we find:

> O que máis me amolóu, hai que decilo, foi, cando esta peza se publicóu en 1959, que máis dun, entre nós, non soio non vise que había nesta peza unha esencial novidade no que toca ao máis segredo do suceso Hamlet, sinón que tomase o meu *Don Hamlet* coma unha simple parodia do *Hamlet* de Shakespeare, que eu, que

---

9 *Don Hamlet e tres pezas máis* (Vigo: Galaxia, 1974).

> teño dende a mocidade por tomo de cabeceira o das obras do grande dramaturgo e altísimo poeta, non a escribiría ... (91)

Certainly nobody has ever accused Cunqueiro of arrogance or insensitivity.

The essence of the new text based on this 'suceso Hamlet' came to the writer as a 'revelación' 'coma un lóstrego', after lengthy meditation: 'Eu tiñalle dado moitas voltas no maxín á traxedia de Shakespeare, e din na teima de que había algo no máis fondo do conto que non tiña sido usado polo dramaturgo inglés' (87). The discovery was that 'o Usurpador [his King Halmar] era o verdadeiro pai de Hamlet. Entón, todo cadraba millor' (87). Within the play, in Act I, scene ii, the Chorus reveals the fact to the Prince: 'Teu verdadeiro pai é el Rei novo'. Hamlet violently denies it, naturally, but thereafter proceeds with a growing conviction that he has been told the truth. This entry of overtly Oedipal myth and psychology into the play transforms the basis of the Shakespearian original into something completely new. Hamlet kills King Halmar at the end of the play-within-a-play (III.vi), but the following scene III.vii between Queen Gerda and her son Hamlet brings us close to the denouement. It takes place in the presence of the Chorus which, according to the stage-direction, 'Arrodea á parexa real. Coma un enxamio de vésporas fungadoras'. The Queen in seductive tones ('¡Eres mui fermoso, Hamlet!', and later, '¡Deixaréi sempre a porta entreaberta!') and with much physical contact produces something between fascinated desire and barely-controlled outrage in her son, who finally stabs her to death.[10] After reflections by Polonius and the Chorus, Hamlet, with a rope already round his neck, makes a final

---

10 Scene III.vii was apparently written at the same time as the rest of the play, but was evidently thought much too alarming to be printed in the first edition in 1959, being included in that of 1974. The work would seem very lame without it, and Cunqueiro's new hypothesis would not have been carried to any conclusion. In these same notes in the 1974 edition, Cunqueiro refers to a 1970 study by Georges Dumézil of a Norse saga: 'Dumézil fai notar que, nas historias eddicas de incesto, é a muller quen toma a iniciativa, quen seduce ao irmán ou ao fillo'. Cunqueiro was greatly interested in the Nordic origins of the Hamlet story as first set down by Saxo Grammaticus.

brief speech before hanging himself from the battlements, as a great wind blows through the castle and the curtain falls slowly.

Critics and friends seem to have been disturbed by the very radical departure in Cunqueiro's writing which *Don Hamlet* represented. He had been thought a good poet and an excellent writer of lightly humorous fantasies, a purveyor of high-quality escapist literature: why should he suddenly meddle in tragedy, Oedipal complexes now taken with utmost seriousness, potential incest, murders ...? Cunqueiro's lengthy appendix to the 1974 edition of the play is his justification: his devotion to Shakespeare was permanent, but for him something in *Hamlet* was not quite right, the moment of revelation came, and he wrote his play. Critics have since amply concurred with the justification.[11]

In any case, Cunqueiro had already shown, in *Merlín* (1955), the obsessional power wielded by a remarkable offshoot of Shakespeare's *Hamlet*: the painting *Ophelia in the Stream* by Millais, exhibited in 1852. At the time Cunqueiro can have seen only a reproduction, since he had not then visited London (the painting is in the National Gallery). The Galician story is that of *O espello do mouro*, which fills less than seven pages of *Merlín*. Alsir the Moor was an exotic but welcome figure when he appeared in Miranda with strange merchandise which included compasses, rare essences and books (among these being 'a Novela do peido do Demo, que escribíu mosiú Gui Tabarie'). Thus far, and for a while yet, we are in Cunqueiro's typically light-hearted world of fantasy. The Moor, however, needs to consult the magician Merlin about a small magic mirror of Italian make, which he had acquired at the Tilsit fair. In Elsinore he had sold it to one 'doña Ofelia, que é canto hai que ver en condesiñas de quince'. Ophelia had awoken one night screaming, disturbing the whole castle. Among the many images shown in the mirror — only between dusk and

---

11 A first volume of *Monografías* of the *Boletín Galego de Literatura*, edited by Anxo Tarrío Varela in 1992, is wholly dedicated to Cunqueiro. Its section 'Cunqueiro autor dramático' (89-127) includes two papers on *Don Hamlet*, by Ricart Salvat Ferré and Xoán-Luis Marín Escudero, and a third by M. C. Ríos Panisse on the writer's early dramatic efforts.

midnight on Saturdays — was that of Ophelia in the stream, which had occasioned the girl's distress. Next day Alsir, who had been innocently unaware of the mirror's evil powers, returned the purchase price and went for an audience with Prince Hamlet. The Prince, discovered 'aloumiñando unha calivera', offers some very Shakespearian reflections on the incident and orders the Moor to remove the mirror from the kingdom. Merlin, who recognizes the mirror as one he had himself originally made, though defectively, for the government of Venice, smashes it in a mortar and 'mistouróu os mil anacos con sal i un allo zamorano'. Merlin did not care to tell Alsir before his departure that the prediction of the mirror had been realized, that Ophelia already lay drowned in the stream.

Cunqueiro seems not to have known, or at any rate seems not to refer to, Tom Stoppard's play *Rosencrantz and Guildenstern are Dead*, of 1966, but he was to be consoled — from Britain, too — if he had any lingering doubts about his boldness in rewriting *Hamlet*. In 1969 Christopher Booker had much the same idea about the play:

> The most puzzling and powerful of all Shakespeare's plays is *Hamlet*. Like all his tragedies, it describes the unfolding of a fantasy cycle, perhaps more profoundly and explicitly than any. And yet what is the offence against nature for which Hamlet must die? It is not some obvious crime like Macbeth's, or delusion like Othello's. On the face of the story, in fact, it is that he *cannot* [author's emphasis] commit an offence; he cannot revenge his father by killing his uncle. But if we accept that in some way Claudius and his father are the same, and that it is his subconscious urge to 'kill' his father and 'marry' his mother that he cannot fulfil, then we see why the play exercises such an extraordinary and subtle hold over our own subconscious minds ...[12]

Cunqueiro translated the above, and more, in the appendix to the 1974 edition of his *Don Hamlet*, making clear his own priority with this idea but also (we may assume) breathing a grateful sigh for this wholly independent support from a British writer. He cites in further support the novel *Aquelarre*

12 Christopher Booker, *The Neophiliacs* (London: Fontana, 1969), 329 (not 349 as Cunqueiro has it).

by Carlos Rojas in which the personage Antonio Escuín, a schizophrenic who imagines himself to be Hamlet, 'advirtió, [...] como por vía de iluminación o corazonada retrospectiva, que Claudio, no el difunto rey, era su verdadero padre'. But Rojas, Cunqueiro adds, knew his *Don Hamlet* before writing the novel.

The extraordinary breadth of Cunqueiro's daily reading in older and contemporary literature, including journals in English, may be gauged from the wealth of materials assembled in a collection such as *El envés*, consisting of more than a hundred pieces (there must be thousands awaiting reprinting) originally published in *El Faro de Vigo*, which he edited.[13] All are in the writer's distinctive literary style, and many could have served as the basis for the kind of short stories which are fitted so elegantly into the frameworks of *Merlín* and *Sochantre*, or could have served as digressions and tales in novels such as *Ulises* and *Orestes*. There is Irishry everywhere in *El envés*, and then, for example, King Arthur's daughter, a Scottish loch which flew away, Pepys and certain English daemons, an anthology of Irish fairies, Hamlet yet again, Marlowe, 'John Howard Bowes-Lyon, Lord Glardy, hijo de Lord Streathmore y tío tatarabuelo de la actual Reina Madre de Inglaterra', Milton, St Brendan, the burial of Yeats, the *Concise Oxford Dictionary*, and the following, a preface to speculation about 'la taberna de Galiana', situated on an imagined 'camino que va por el mar, de Galicia a Bretaña':

> Un profesor inglés [later identified as J. W. Camden] ha escrito un delicioso estudio, que tengo que prestarle a José María Castroviejo, sobre las tabernas y posadas que en sus diversos libros cita Dickens, gran inventor de ellas. El tema me place extraordinariamente, porque yo mismo he sido seducido desde la primera lectura por esas invenciones dickensianas. La literatura inglesa, desde Chaucer a Dickens, pasando por Shakespeare, Pepys, Sterne y James Boswell, está llena de tabernas ... (280)

Rest in peace, Don Alvaro: anything you took from us has been most richly returned.

---

13 *El envés* (Barcelona: Táber, 1969).

G/Z — A Missing Link in the Dis-affiliation of a Post-Romantic Expatriate in Revolt?

PATRICIA McDERMOTT

University of Leeds

Español, he buscado en nuestro suelo mis inspiraciones. Cristiano, he creído que mi religión encierra más poesía que el paganismo. Español, tengo a mengua cantar himnos a Hércules, a Leónidas, a Horacio Cocles y a Julio César, y abandonar en el polvo del olvido al Cid y a don Pedro Ansurez, a Hernán Cortés y García de Paredes. Cristiano, creo que vale más nuestra María llorando, nuestra severa Semana Santa, y las suntuosas ceremonias de nuestros templos, que la impúdica Venus, las nauseabundas fiestas Lupercales y los vergonzosos sacrificios de Baco y de Plutón. Español, hallo cuando menos mezquino y rídiculo buscar héroes en tierras remotas, en menoscabo de los de nuestra patria; y cristiano, tengo por criminal olvidar nuestras creencias por las de otra religión contra cuyos errores protestamos a cada paso.

(José Zorrilla)[1]

En lo que a mí concierne, hace ya bastante tiempo que el apego sentimental a los valores 'patrióticos' me resulta perfectamente extraño: poco, muy poco de cuanto la España oficial encarna significa algo agradable para mí. Mi actitud frente a ella ha sido un largo, continuo proceso de ruptura y desposesión. Si algún impulso de solidaridad siento, no es jamás con la imagen del país que emerge a partir del reinado de los Reyes Católicos, sino con sus víctimas: judíos, musulmanes, cristianos nuevos, luteranos,

1 'A mis amigos don Juan Donoso Cortés y don Nicomedes Pastor Díaz', *Obras completas*, ordenación, prólogo y notas de Narciso Alonso Cortés, (Valladolid: Librería Santarén, 1943), I, 68-69.

enciclopedistas, liberales, anarquistas, marxistas. En los momentos históricos decisivos, el bando que hubiera querido defender fue derrotado siempre. En puridad, ¿puede darse el nombre de patriotismo a la mera reivindicación de posibilidades fallidas, de tentativas aplastadas, de empresas condenadas hasta ahora al fracaso? Llamémosle mejor fraternidad de *outsiders*, parias y marginales — de meteoritos cuya fuerza centrífuga venció el atractivo de nuestra ley nacional de gravedad. La nostalgia de lo que pudo ser y no ha sido ha conducido a algunos de los españoles más lúcidos a enfrentarse con la historia de su propio país y afirmar su propio destino en oposición a aquélla.

(Juan Goytisolo)[2]

In the year after the 'self-banished' Liberal exile José María Blanco White, ex-canon of Seville, died as a Unitarian in Liverpool (1841), José Zorrilla, 'the re-creator *par excellence* of Spanish legend and tradition and the dramatist *par excellence* of patriotism',[3] wrote a one-act play entitled *El puñal del rey godo*, which was performed in the Teatro de la Cruz (Madrid) in January 1843, one hundred years before the Franco Regime would celebrate the millenium of Castile in order to legitimize its own rebellion. That same year (1943) saw the publication in Valladolid of the complete works of Zorrilla as part of an official cultural policy to establish a National-Catholic canon in which the work of the Spanish mystics figured pre-eminently.

Inspired by a random opening of the Jesuit Mariana's *Historia de España* at his account of the battle of Guadalete with its possibility of the defeated Rodrigo's flight into Portugal, the Jesuit-educated Romantic Revivalist composed in one day, according to his memoirs, on the basis of a few historical memories and the legendary fictions of his imagination, a dramatic vindication and rewriting of the fate of the last king of the Goths. Zorrilla's Rodrigo is a tormented conscience in retreat in a hermitage awaiting his pre-ordained end to die by his own dagger at the hands of Julián, the vassal who had opened Spain to Moorish conquest in vengeance for the king's

2 'Presentación crítica', *Obra inglesa de D. José María Blanco White* (Barcelona: Seix Barral, 1972), 96-97. Goytisolo is identified on the frontispiece as the author of *Reivindicación del conde don Julián*.

3 E. Allison Peers, *A History of the Romantic Movement in Spain* (Cambridge: Cambridge U. P., 1940), 270.

violation of his daughter. Teudia, Rodrigo's faithful knight, intervenes in the confrontation between the two arch enemies, killing Julián and releasing the king to sally forth to join Pelayo as an anonymous soldier in the incipient Reconquest. Julián in Zorrilla's revision of the historical legend remains the infamous villain of the piece, making his appearance in the original production wrapped in a yellow cloak (*caperuza*), the colour of betrayal, a figure of Judas and apostasy.[4]

According to Eric Hobsbawm, 'the history which became part of the fund of knowledge or the ideology of nation, state or movement is not what has actually been preserved in popular memory, but what has been selected, written, pictured, popularized and institutionalized by those whose function it is to do so'.[5] Spanish Christian history, which has forged a sense of ethnic identity and community in the chronicles of holy wars against the infidel and the reconquest of territory as moral space, has in the process of collective self-definiton evidenced the dual features of nationalism and racism identified by Benedict Anderson: 'nationalism thinks in terms of historical destinies, while racism dreams of eternal contaminations, transmitted from the origins of time through an endless sequence of loathesome copulations: outside history'.[6] Earlier Anderson points to a different awareness of time in what he calls sacred communities, recalling Walter Benjamin's concept of Messianic time, 'a simultaneity of past and future in an instantaneous present' in the vision of Divine Providence.[7]

In the 1960s the Jesuit-educated Juan Goytisolo, self-banished exile from Franco's Spain, under the influence of

---

4 See 'El puñal del godo', *Recuerdos del tiempo viejo*, J. Zorrilla, *Obras completas*, II, 1768-75; *El puñal del godo*, *ibid.*, 1115-26. In a sequel *La calentura* (1847), after the battle of Covadonga and the failure of Pelayo to recognize his identity, Rodrigo is visited by the shade of Florinda/La Cava who forgives his crime against her, revealing that they were both victims of her mother's treachery. The king exits alone into a storm to seek the peace of the grave.

5 'Introduction: Inventing Traditions', *The Invention of Tradition* (co-editor T. Ranger) (Cambridge: Cambridge U. P., 1983), 13.

6 B. Anderson, *Imagined Communities. Reflections on the Origin and Spread of Nationalism* (London: Verso, 1983), 136.

7 *Ibid.*, 30.

Américo Castro's alternative reading of Spanish history, embarked on a literary challenge to the Nationalist myths of a 'Sacred Spain' of eternal essences, which reached its apogee in *Reivindicación del conde don Julián* (1970). The project is described megalomaniacally in his memoir as:

> esa obra no escrita aún en nuestra lengua, contra ella, a mayor gloria de ella, destrucción y homenaje, profanación y ofrenda, agresión alienada, onírica, esquizofrénica, alianza integral de imaginación y razón, como dice del Gran Sordo Malraux, bajo la apariencia mendaz del delirio. Resoluciones en serie forjadas vertiginosamente a partir de tu huida a la ciudad en donde hoy evocas y fijas por escrito lo sucedido: calar en la historia auténtica del país del que te sentías inexorablemente proscrito; embeberte en el baño lustral de sus clásicos; espulgar la totalidad de su *corpus* literario con la misma frenética minuciosidad con la que rastreabas a diario el caos tangerino; poner el acervo humanístico de la época — lingüística, poética, historiografía — al servicio de dicha empresa; llegar a las raíces de la muerte civil que te ha tocado vivir; sacar a luz demonios y miedos agazapados en lo hondo de tu conciencia. Días, horas, instantes privilegiados, de riqueza y enjundia inigualados después, rumiando tu cólera, agravios, sed de venganza contra esos molinos o gigantes llamados religión-patria-familia-pasado-niñez.[8]

Assuming the literary identity of the Gothic traitor Julián — 'confundido del todo con el felón de la remota leyenda, don Julián *c'est moi*'[9] — Goytisolo creates a counter-discourse to the discourses of power of National-Catholic Spain. An apotheosis of apostasy, his subversive text-in-exile is strategically located in Tangier, identified in an epigraph from his adopted 'patron saint' Jean Genet as 'plutôt repaire de traîtres' (*Journal du voleur*) and represented in the text as a locus of heterodox anarchy and creative chaos in opposition to the monolithic order of the state across the Strait.[10] In an unholy pilgrimage through its market-places, bathhouses and urinals, the narrative consciousness seeks restoration of a repressed other

---

8 *En los reinos de Taifa* (Barcelona: Seix Barral, 1986), 304-05.

9 *Ibid.*, 309.

10 See Linda Gould Levine, *Juan Goytisolo: la destrucción creadora* (México: Joaquín Mortiz, 1976) and Abigail Lee Six, *Juan Goytisolo: The Case for Chaos* (New Haven/London: Yale U. P., 1990).

self through a transvaluation of the prejudices of Eurocentric Orientalism by which the Moorish 'vices' of cruelty and sensuality become positive anti-virtues engaged in the deconstruction of the body politic of the social imaginary of Catholic Imperial Spain.

Reivindicación del conde don Julián corroborates Edward Said's judgement that 'Orientalism responded more to the culture that produced it than to its putative object, which was also produced by the West'.[11] Goytisolo the author, who has subsequently read his Said, is fully aware that in his poetic fiction he does not shed or minimize purely autobiographical, personal sentiment (Said, 157) and that any representation of the Orient which is embedded in the language and culture of the representer is necessarily a misrepresentation (Said, 272).[12] Goytisolo appears to fit Said's bill for his third type of Orientalist consciousness: 'the writer for whom a real or metaphorical trip to the Orient is the fulfilment of some deeply felt and urgent project' (Said, 158), a response to 'certain cultural, professional, national, political and economic requirements of the epoch' and a counter to 'someone else's view of the Orient' (Said, 273): 'En mi novela *Reivindicación del conde don Julián*, me propuse una tarea de sicoanálisis nacional a través de la lectura del discurso colectivo tradicional

---

11 *Orientalism* (Harmondsworth: Penguin Books, 1991), 22. (Subsequent references are bracketed in the text.)

12 See Goytisolo, 'Cara y cruz del moro en nuestra literatura', *Crónicas sarracinas* (Barcelona: Seix Barral, 1989), 8-9: 'Puesto que la objetividad absoluta no existe, la empresa de describir al Otro lleva siempre la marca del lugar de origen. El mayor reproche que podremos hacer a un autor será así su tentativa de disimular éste: pintar o reconstruir el universo ajeno desde un imaginario *no man's land*, en nombre de los valores implícitos de una presunta universalidad'. In 'De "Don Julián" a "Makbara": una posible lección orientalista', *ibid.*, 30-31, Goytisolo draws a distinction between his treatment of contemporary Moroccan issues in his essays and that of the Moor in his novels: 'Ello no obedece tan sólo a la índole específica de la obra literaria: a su esencial ambigüedad, a sus contradicciones inherentes y por tanto insalvables, a la tensión creadora provocada por el choque de dos ideas o emociones opuestas. La literatura no responde tan sólo a un discurso lógico y racional, y la nitidez del ensayo, la simplicidad del panfleto no caben en ningún caso en ella: tiene sus zonas de sombra, sus motivaciones oscuras, sus pulsaciones secretas'.

sobre el Islam en nuestra literatura y en nuestra historia'.[13] In *Reivindicación del conde don Julián* the project of destruction of the Sacred Spain perpetuated by the Nationalist Regime — 'anulando de golpe el orden fingido, revelando la verdad bajo la máscara, catalizando tus fuerzas dispersas y los donjulianescos proyectos de invasión: traición grandiosa, ruina de siglos: ejército cruel de Tariq, destrucción de la España Sagrada'[14] — is complicated by opposition to American capitalist neo-colonialism propagated by mass media pop culture in the global village scenario of the North-South confrontation in contemporary geo-politics.

The film industry's James Bond joins the ranks of cultural contestants within the pages of the book, forming part of what Said calls its strategic formation, that is, 'the relationship between texts and the way in which groups of texts, types of texts, even textual genres, acquire mass, density, and referential power among themselves and thereafter in the culture at large' (Said, 20). Of particular interest to Said and of particular pertinence to Goytisolo's text is the way 'each work on the Orient *affiliates* itself with other works, with audiences, with institutions, with the Orient itself' (*ibid.*). Goytisolo's epigraphs set up his text as a counter-action/communication to the vision of the Orient and Julián's relationship to the invader Tariq as they are presented in the historiographical tradition of the chronicles and ballads — 'genio español del romancero, libro de caballería, auto sacramental' (34) — under the counter-sign of the Marquis de Sade's anti-ideal of criminality, liberation through transgression being identified with the foreigner.[15]

The *Advertencia* appended at the end of *Reivindicación del conde don Julián*, acknowledging the posthumous or unwitting

13 *Crónicas sarracinas*, 32-33.

14 *Reivindicación del conde don Julián* (México: Joaquín Mortiz, 1970), 52. (Subsequent references are bracketed in the text.)

15 'La novela no es fruto de una observación directa y sin anteojeras (la única capaz de abolir los prejuicios de la "alteridad", de la distinción básica entre culturas y hombres): al contrario, la mirada personal del autor en su paseo por las calles de Tánger se diluye en un *corpus* textual de citas, recuerdos, motivos, rimas, ficciones, imágenes acarreados por la tradición española. Se trata, claro, de algo deliberado: su combate es *contra* la tradición, pero actúa *dentro* de ella' ('De "Don Julián" a "Makbara" ', 41).

collaboration in the text of a long list of mainly Spanish-language authors from Alfonso X el Sabio to Luis Vélez de Guevara, contemporaneous in the linguistic community of the book, bears witness to a divided cultural community within the authorial consciousness. The antiphony of literary voices, thrown in the ironical double-voicing of the text as ventriloquist act in parodic play, sets orthodox Classics — 'de Calderón, Tirso o del con razón Vega por lo siempre llano' (36) — against heterodox Modernists, Carlos Fuentes, Julio Cortázar and Guillermo Cabrera Infante — 'amistosa y solidaria colaboración' (242) — inspired throughout by the author's master in ludic literature, Góngora — 'el Poeta'. The canonical texts are contaminated in the Cervantine episode of the Tangerine library, reminiscent of Flaubert's *Bibliothèque des Idées Reçus*, sanctum of the ex-colonial possessing minority, now dispossessed. The Latin-American trinity aids the author to subvert the Academy's domination of the language of power, polluting the linguistic purity of Castilian by infiltrating the street-languages of the former empire into his post-colonial discourse — 'que viene ette gaito con su cuento de limpia, fija y desplendol' (195). The linguistic hegemony of Castilian is further undermined by threat of collapse following the authorial call to rescue the Arabic lexicon from its system, which reveals the consequent vital gaps in the ability of Castilian to express the material necessities of agriculture and commerce, food, civil and military organization, culminating in the loss of its tribal acclamation in the national spectacle of the bullfight — 'no olvides el olé' (199).

The cultural-political intention of this Cervantine parody — 'idioma mirífico del Poeta, vehículo necesario de la traición, hermosa lengua tuya: instrumento indispensable del renegado y del apóstata, esplendoroso y devastador a la vez: arma aguda (insinuante) que conjura (exorcisa) la africana hueste y magnifica (potencia) su denso apetito de destrucción' (70) — is a far cry from the exoticist embroidery of Arabisms in Spanish Romantic Orientalist texts, of which Zorrilla's *Granada* is the supreme example. Published in 1852 but composed around 1848, the year of the revolution whose youthful ideal Zorrilla had betrayed in his public project to win the approval of a disapproving Ultramontane father, the unfinished epic of the reunification of Spain under the Catholic Monarchy stands as a monument to Catholic triumphalism and to the predominantly reactionary nature of the Revival movement in Spanish Romanticism. 'Z' is missing from the alphabetical list of authors to whom Goytisolo's text is affiliated (Espronceda, Larra, Américo Castro) or from whom it is disaffiliated (Menéndez Pelayo, Unamuno, Ortega y Gasset). And yet the shade of the Romantic national poet laureate appears as a ghostly paradigm among the patriarchal authorities that are textually contravened, his name eliminated from the list perhaps, like many others in the literary game of intertextual hide-and-seek, in a voluntary act of cultural amnesia or censorship in retaliation for the fate of the author's own text in Franco's Spain, the punishment for literary revenge being official silence.

Zorrilla had included, as an introduction to his saga of the end of the Nazarite dynasty in the Fall of Granada, a book of the foundation of the dynasty entitled *Leyenda de Muhamad Al-hamar el Nazarita.*[16] It was necessary in Zorrilla's conception of his poetic divine mission to present the founding of Granada and the construction of the Alhambra as part of the Divine Plan for its conquest by the Catholic Monarchs and the eternal triumph of Christianity. The Will of God is revealed to Alhamar in a series of visions by the angel Azael which culminate in his ascension to a celestial Alhambra made of ice, after a magical horse-ride inspired by the Prophet's translation to Paradise on his mount Alborak, and narrated in an *escala métrica* inspired by Espronceda's *Estudiante de Salamanca.* Innoculated with doubt regarding his own faith by the angel, Alhamar in his final vision accepts the Christian Will of God and the future bloodshed of his race in Granada as a baptism of blood that will grant his entry into Eternal Christan Life. Frozen in the limbo of the visionary Alhambra, Alhamar is defrosted shortly before

16 *Obras completas*, I, 1151-97. For a fuller consideration of the complexity of Zorrilla's response to his Hispano-Arabic material, see my 'Romantic Scribe of Another Tribe: The Representation of Spanish Orientalism in Zorrilla's *Granada*', in *José Zorrilla (1893-1993) Centennial Readings*, edited by Richard A. Cardwell and Ricardo Landeira, (Nottingham: Univ. of Nottingham Monographs in the Humanities, 1993), 97-112.

the event to appear dressed in white as a heavenly harbinger of the imminent fall of Granada to the demonized usurper Muley Hasán, who is dressed in Islamic green.

In Alhamar the Romantic poet manipulates the positive stereotype of the noble Moor of Hispano-Arabic romance to subvert the Muslim claim to Divine Providence and to justify the Christian Reconquest. In *Reivindicación del conde don Julián* Goytisolo takes the negative stereotype of the Moor as a sexually-threatening ravening wolf to subvert the Christian myth of ethnic election and national salvation in a Catholic imperial mission and to invert the positional superiority of Christian versus Moor in Western Orientalism. Particularly in his Freudian reworking of the Little Red Riding Hood folk-tale, but throughout the many metamorphoses and disguises of the fictional alter ego as both passive victim (Alvarito) and active executioner (Julián-Tariq), the Moorish avatar always has the upper whip-hand.

The Muslim reinvasion and reoccupation of the holy places and centres of power in Spain, including the Alhambra and the palace of the Emperor Charles V, imagined in Part III, is prepared for by a donation of infectious rabid blood by the narrator and performed under the demonic phallic sign of the serpent — 'dragón vencido, no: maligna vencedora reptante: condensada virtud de ruda vitalidad arábiga' (145). The white-turbaned *harkis* of the renegade's cavalcade metamorphose into a flight of Bond-movie helicopter-pilots as they transform from the air the arid landscape of the mythically spiritual Castile into a lush green natural paradise, likened to the luxuriant body-hair of the archetypal sensual Moor, Tariq. Similarly, they invade the penitential processions of Holy Week transformed into a multi-cultural Afro-Caribbean Bond-movie carnival celebrating the cult of a black Venus. The transformation of the feminine motherland as Isabel la Católica, mother-daughter of Don Álvaro the *perfecto caballero cristiano*, into a Bond-movie mulatto sex symbol in this section, prelude to a guided tour of the Sacred Grotto of her womb and the breaking of linguistic taboos in a litany to her Sacred Cunt, is a sacrilegious antidote to her promotion in Nationalist myth and her symbolic projection in orthodox texts such as Zorrilla's *Granada*. The Isabel of the Romantic Revival is a pure virgin queen, mystically transfigured in the solitude of the chaste nun's cell of her private apartment by the message of her divine mission announced by Azael — 'Un ángel bello, del Señor enviado'.[17] Goytisolo's Isabel in her chamber is turned on by the rhythm of the rock music of the Rolling Stones and performs an auto-erotic masochistic striptease involving black silk pyjamas worn under her nun's habit, a crucifix and a whip, in a profane parody of Teresian mysticism — 'dulce herida de amor, dardo cruel del alma!' (165). Her rape by Julián-Tariq's *harkis*, followed by that of all the virgins of Spain, is further elaborated in Part IV when the Moorish soldiers infiltrate the Spanish national Church, put hashish in the Communion wafers and take advantage of the sexual arousal of the *beatas* in a final orgy which dethrones the esperpentic doll-images of the violated Virgin Mother and Child — 'la caída simultánea de los dos muñecos pone punto final, con sus aullidos, al demente fabuloso happening' (233).

The Holy Family of the National-Catholic social imaginary — authoritarian father (Don Álvaro Peranzules-El Ubícuo [Franco]), virgin mother (Madre de Álvarito-Isabel la Católica-La Muñeca), obedient child (Álvarito-Caperucito Rojo-El Nene) — is systematically and grotesquely destroyed. The mutilated manikin of the authorial child-self, a sodomized suicide Holy Infant, is, however, miraculously resurrected as a Muslim by a Moorish magician accompanied by a host of sorcerer's apprentices — 'vestido con blanca chilaba, ceñido de níveo turbante invoca en árabe puro el nombre de Alá, manifiesta su vivo deseo de ser musulmán: los niños asisten gozosos a tu insólita epifanía' (238). He is borne aloft in a musical mockery of a Holy Week procession led by a snake-charmer's flute from the Calle de Portugal along the Avenida de España — 'en tres ocasiones, por la abrupta cuesta de Grotius, el motivo principal vibrará aún con una distribución cada vez más reducida y débil hasta que el movimiento, y con él toda la sinfonía, se extinguirá suavemente en un melancólico solo de flauta: tal, dulce, suspira la lira que hirió en blando concento del viento la voz, leve, breve son' (239). The dying fall of Espronceda's *escala métrica* in his *Estudiante de Salamanca*, paradoxically part of the modern

17 *Granada, Obras completas*, I, 1282.

canon, is restored to Romantic Revolt, but its lyricism signals the qualitative difference between the satanic individualism of the Romantic rebel who still operates within the Christian world-view, and that of the post-Romantic post-Christian heretic who in his act of transgression substitutes one system, one sacral community for another, that is, the world of Islam. The transformation in the oppositional structures which inform the text reveals, however, the continuing mythic nature of the process of inverted nationalism and racism and the inability of the individual imaginary to free itself from the (de)formative collective historical (mis)understanding: 'la dialéctica España-Islam mantiene su oposición maniquea e irreductible; los valores se truecan en antivalores y viceversa'.[18]

The final act of the children who accompany the triumphal procession of conversion to Islam is to inter the baldy corpse of a mangy cat, interpreted by Linda Gould Levine as a symbol of the rotten body of Sacred Spain, the reiteration of a motif introduced in the opening pages and an indication of the circularity and closed nature of the text.[19] The book ends with an ironic echo of *Gone with the Wind* — 'mañana será otro día, la invasión recomenzará' (240). The final tense is future, the tense proper to hallucination according to Roland Barthes in *S/Z*, where he defines hallucination as 'a scenario in which the object's positions are innumerable ("*every imaginable situation*") but always related, as in voluptuous manipulation, to the subject, who is at the center of the scene ("*he saw, he spoke, beseeched, passed*")'.[20] The subjective centre of Goytisolo's text is a static visionary centre of opposing eternal essences locked in a 'loathesome copulation' of warring twins, outside history in the Messianic time of the world of the book — 'abrazándote a él:

18 'De "Don Julián" a "Makbara" ', 40-41.

19 Note 290 in her edition of the novel (Madrid: Cátedra, 1985), 304.

20 *S/Z*, translated by Richard Miller, (London: Jonathan Cape, 1975), 123: 'When discourse itself speaks of *hallucination* (not to mention subsequently *producing* it), it commits the same act of violence as the mathematician or logician who says; *let us call P the object which* ...; *let us call* P^1 *the image which* ... etc. Readerly discourse is thus shot through with pre-demonstrative nominations which ensure the text's subjection — but which also, perhaps, provoke the nausea brought on by any appropriate violence' (130).

serpiente troglodita, flagelador hircino: en simbiosis fulmínea: impugnando la muerte que os cierne: monstruo no, ni bifronte, ni hermes: tu mismo al fin, único, en el fondo de tu animalidad herida' (230).

Jo Labanyi is right when she identifies the problem of Goytisolo's adoption of transgression as a form of liberation in that it 'inevitably perpetuates the taboos it simultaneously breaks'.[21] But in the declining years of the Francoist dictatorship, the text of *Reivindicación del conde don Julián*, entering the Spanish cultural bloodstream underground like an illegal drug, gave many Spanish dissidents, enduring internal spiritual exile, a fix on their own hallucinatory reality, a heightening of awareness from the expanded vision of the hallucination of external exile; just as Zorrilla's *Granada* was a shot in the arm for Catholic Traditionalists in an age of revolution in Europe. Edgar Allison Peers, in the conclusion to his seminal history of the Romantic Movement in Spain, whose 'failure as a self-conscious movement' he judges to be 'of small importance by comparison with its success as a permeating influence', speculates on the judgement of posterity: 'It may be that centuries to come will see it as nothing more outstanding than a steepening section in the road leading upwards from the low lying eighteenth century and connecting the Golden Age of the sixteenth and seventeenth with another such age of the twentieth or twenty-first, the degree of brilliance of which is as yet undeterminable'.[22] The spirit of Romanticism survived its out-dated rhetoric and continued to link the post-Modernist to a polemical literary past, in the process of textual (dis)affiliation in the brief but brilliant renaissance of prose fiction provoked by reaction to the continuing repression of Franco's Spain in the last decade of the dictatorship. Allison Peers could not foresee how far the spirit of Romantic Revolt would go in the 'shock of the new' administered by *Reivindicación del conde don Julián*, written in response to Menéndez Pidal's challenge to some 'mirada adivinadora de la poesía', to turn its gaze on the legend

21 *Myth and History in the Contemporary Spanish Novel* (Cambridge: Cambridge U. P., 1989), 202.

22 *A History of the Romantic Movement in Spain*, 376 and 374 respectively.

of Julián and the loss of Spain: 'Todavía esperamos al artista fuerte en osadía que quebrante los cerrojos y penetre en el recinto para revelar los viejos misterios imaginativos celados por Hercules'.[23] That long-awaited artist was the dissident Juan Goytisolo.

23 Quoted in 'De "Don Julián" a "Makbara" ', 40.

TABULA IN MEMORIAM

Francisco Aguilar Piñal *Consejo Superior de Investigaciones Científicas, Madrid*
J. M. Alberich *Sevilla*
Adrian R. Allan *University of Liverpool*
Carlos Alvar *Universidad de Alcalá*
Pedro Álvarez de Miranda *Universidad Autónoma de Madrid*
Andrew A. Anderson *University of Michigan*
René Andioc *Université de Perpignan*
Samuel G. Armistead *University of California, Davis*
Juan Bautista de Avalle-Arce *University of California, Santa Barbara*

José María Balcells *Universidad de León*
Edi Bastianelli *Università degli Studi di Firenze*
Vicente Beltrán *Universitat de Barcelona*
Bernard P. E. Bentley *University of St Andrews*
Patrizia Botta *Università di Roma*
Ceri Byrne *University of Glasgow*

Joan F. Cammarata *Manhattan College, New York*
Ysla Campbell *Universidad Autónoma de Ciudad Juárez*
Luis Caparrós Esperante *Universidade da Coruña*
Giovanni Caravaggi *Università di Pavia*
Antonio Carreño *Brown University, Providence, RI*
Clara E. Castro Ponce *Brown University, Providence, RI*
José Cebrián *Universidad de Sevilla*
Joseph F. Chorpenning *St Joseph's University, PA.*
Jesús-Antonio Cid *Universidad Complutense de Madrid*
Universidade da Coruña, Facultade de Humanidades — Biblioteca — Depto. de Filología Española y Latine
Marithelma Costa *Hunter College and Graduate Center, City University of New York*
Manuel da Costa Fontes *Kent State University*
Joanna Courteau *Iowa State University*
D. W. Cruickshank *University College, Dublin*

Mario Damonte *Università di Genova*
Graeme J. Davies *University of Glasgow*
Brian John Dendle *University of Kentucky*
Department of Hispanic Studies, Queen Mary and Westfield College, London

Department of Hispanic Studies, University of Glasgow
Department of Hispanic Studies, University of Liverpool
Department of Spanish, University of St Andrews
Alan Deyermond *Queen Mary and Westfield College, University of London*
José María Díez Borque *Universidad Complutense de Madrid*
Dipartimento di Lingue e Letteratura Romanze, Biblioteca di Spagnolo, Università di Pisa
Victor Dixon *Trinity College, Dublin*
Durham University Library

Gwynne Edwards *University College, Aberystwyth*
Joan Estruch Tobella *I. B. 'Sant Andreu', Barcelona*

Facultad de Filología, Geografía e Historia, Koldo Mitxelena Biblioteca, Spain
Jaime Fernández S.J. *Sophia University, Tokyo*
Hans Flasche† *Universität Hamburg*
Gerard Flynn *University of Wisconsin, Madison*
José Fradejas Lebrero *UNED, Madrid*
Medardo Fraile *University of Strathclyde*
Margit Frenk *Universidad Nacional Autónoma de México*
Rinaldo Froldi *Università di Bologna*

Charles Ganelin *Purdue University*
Regina Geijerstam *Stockholm University*
Glasgow University Library
Nigel Glendinning *Queen Mary and Westfield College, University of London*
José Luis Gotor *Università di Roma*
Sumner M. Greenfield *University of Massachusetts, Amherst*
Patricia Grieve *Columbia University*

Monroe Z. Hafter *University of Michigan*
R. B. Hale *Neath*
Elizabeth Hall *Birkenhead*
L. P. Harvey *King's College, University of London*
The Hispanic Society of America
Richard Hitchcock *University of Exeter*

B. W. Ife *King's College, University of London*
L. E. Ingamells *Queen Mary and Westfield College, University of London*
Instituto Feijoo de Estudios del Siglo XVIII, Universidad de Oviedo
Istituto di Lingue e Letteratura Iberiche, Università degli Studi di Milano
Istituto di Spagnolo, Università degli Studi di Verona

John Rylands Library, University of Manchester
John A. Jones *University of Hull*

John N. Jones *Yale University*

Lloyd A. Kasten *University of Wisconsin, Madison*
R. G. Keightley *Monash University, Australia*
Erna Berndt Kelley *Smith College, Northampton, MA*
Kathleen V. Kish *University of N. Carolina*
Tess Knighton *University of Cambridge*
Edgar C. Knowlton Jr *University of Hawaii at Manoa*

Norman J. Lamb *Llanrhaeadr*
Lia Schwartz Lerner *Dartmouth College, Hanover, NH*
John Lihani *University of Kentucky*
Antonio Linage Conde *Universidad de San Pablo, Madrid*
C. A. Longhurst *University of Exeter*
Audrey Lumsden-Kouvel *University of Illinois at Chicago*

Robert A. MacDonald *University of Richmond, Virginia*
Helder Macedo *King's College, University of London*
Ann L. Mackenzie *University of Glasgow*
Ian Macpherson *Queen Mary and Westfield College, University of London*
Linda S. Materna *Rider College, Lawrenceville, NJ*
I. L. McClelland *University of Glasgow*
Patricia McDermott *University of Leeds*
Robert G. Mead Jr *University of Connecticut*
Edith Metford
J. C. J. Metford *University of Bristol*
Ian Michael *University of Oxford*
Louise Mirrer *Fordham University, New York*
Mª Isabel Montoya Ramírez *Universidad de Granada*
Kenneth Muir† *University of Liverpool*
Martin Murphy *Oxford*

Sandra L. Nielsen *University of Alabama in Huntsville*
José C. Nieto *Juniata College, Huntingdon, PA*

R. J. Oakley *University of Birmingham*
Juan Oleza *Universidad de Valencia*
Julián Olivares Jr *University of Houston*
Marilyn A. Olsen *Mayfield Heights, Ohio*
Germán Orduna *Secrit-Conicet / Universidad de Buenos Aires*
Pedro Ortiz Armengol *Universidad de Madrid*

D. G. Pattison *University of Oxford*
Paul Preston *London School of Economics and Political Science*

Queen Mary and Westfield College Library

Margaret A. Rees *Trinity and All Saints University College, Leeds*
Geoffrey Ribbans *Brown University, Providence, RI*
Francisco Rico *Universidad Autónoma de Barcelona*
Edward C. Riley *University of Edinburgh*
Margaret Roach *Oviedo*
Daniel Rogers *University of Durham*
Romanisches Seminar der Universität Köln
Romanisches Seminar, Heinrich-Heine-Universität, Düsseldorf
Joaquín Roses *Universidad de Córdoba*
Nicholas G. Round *University of Sheffield*
J. M. Ruano de la Haza *University of Ottawa*
Aldo Ruffinatto *Università di Torino*
P. E. Russell *Oxford*

Rubén Sandoval *Universidad de Baja California, México*
Connie L. Scarborough *University of Cincinnati*
Leda Schiavo *University of Illinois at Chicago*
Karl-Ludwig Selig *Columbia University*
Bernard Sesé *Université de Paris X, Nanterre*
Dorothy S. Severin *University of Liverpool*
Harvey L. Sharrer *University of California, Santa Barbara*
Donald L. Shaw *University of Virginia*
Albert Sloman *University of Essex*
Colin Smith† *University of Cambridge*
Joseph T. Snow *Michigan State University*
Luís de Sousa Rebelo *King's College, University of London*
Ana Maria Spitzmesser *Niagara University, Niagara Falls, NY*
Sydney Jones Library, University of Liverpool

Anxo Tarrío-Varela *Universidad de Santiago de Compostela*
Arthur Terry *University of Essex*
Billy Bussell Thompson *Hofstra University, Long Island, NY*
Colin Thompson *University of Oxford*
R. W. Truman *University of Oxford*

Universidad de Sevilla
University of Kentucky Libraries
University of Toronto Library
University of Washington Libraries

John E. Varey *Queen Mary and Westfield College, University of London*

Antonio Bernat Vistarini *Universidad de las Islas Baleares*
Nancy Vogeley *University of San Francisco*

John Walker *Queen's University, Kingston, Canada*
D. Gareth Walters *University of Glasgow*
Bruce Wardropper *Duke University, NC*
Nancy Wardropper *North Carolina Central University*
Christian Wentzlaff-Eggebert *Universität zu Köln*
Margaret Wilson *Hull*

Howard T. Young *Pomona College, Claremont, California*

Patricia Zecevic *University of Glasgow*